To Stella

W

TOWARDS A PHENOMENOLOGY OF REPRESSION – A HUSSERLIAN REPLY TO THE FREUDIAN CHALLENGE

ACTA UNIVERSITATIS STOCKHOLMIENSIS

Stockholm Studies in Philosophy 34

TOWARDS A PHENOMENOLOGY OF REPRESSION – A HUSSERLIAN REPLY TO THE FREUDIAN CHALLENGE

NICHOLAS SMITH

Stockholm University

ISSN 0491-0877
ISBN 978-91-86071-55-4
Printed by US-AB, Stockholm 2010
Distribution by eddy.se ab, Visby SWEDEN

CONTENTS

Acknowledgements

The following work is the result of a long journey and was written in many different places. Long winter storms in a miniscule village in northern Uppland and the blazing heat of the megalopolis Bombay, and perhaps this contrast was also necessary at some stage in order to start to recognize the differences in the continents of thought that are investigated here.

The project was however initiated in Stockholm where it is now completed. During all these years, I had constant discussions on all matters philosophical with my supervisor Hans Ruin, who strongly supported the present choice of subject at a time when I was somewhat reluctantly considering a more traditional theme on Husserl's early philosophy. He has been of invaluable help to me in the completion of this project, both practically and philosophically, from the very beginning to the end.

Amongst colleagues at Stockholm University, I am most grateful to Jim Jakobsson who has been of considerable help, in particular during the last year after having read through a draft of more than eight hundred pages. His critique has been indispensable in focussing and condensing the manuscript.

During its first stage, this work benefited greatly from the seminars and discussions held at the Department of Philosophy at Stockholm University. It was a genuine privilege to be a part of the philosophical culture that emanated from Alexander Orlowski's teaching, who was also my first guide through the landscape of contemporary phenomenology. At that time, our department was led by Dag Prawitz whose open mind created a stimulating atmosphere to work in. I must also mention Per Martin-Löf whose seminars on Husserl I had the great benefit to follow for a number of years, and whose sharp eye forced me back to the texts again and again to try to see what I had missed. Throughout the time that I have been working on this dissertation, I have relied on the kind assistance and unwavering help from Gunnar Svensson.

In the group of young researchers at Stockholm university, I was fortunate enough to encounter Charlotta Weigelt, Johan Eriksson, Anna-Lena Renqvist, Karl Weigelt, Jonna Lappalainen, Christian Nilsson, Anna Petronella Fredlund, Lars-Erik Hjertström, Kate Larson, Fredrik Svenaeus, and Tom Eriksson amongst others.

An important source of inspiration has been my encounter with a great number of students at Södertörn University where I was given the opportunity to teach already in 2000, many of whom have by now become my friends and colleagues. They helped me to discover the meaning of Aristotle's dictum that it is only once you can teach someone else what you think you know, that you actually start knowing it. During the last three years I have really enjoyed teaching at Södertörn again and I realize that I owe many insights to the fruitful discussions that have taken place with my students: thank you all!

I have come to regard the departments cooperating at Södertörn as a constant source of stimulation and delight; the highly creative, professional and friendly atmosphere that has been established there is a very rare thing. My most heartfelt gratitude goes to the Department of Philosophy with staff and in particular to Hans Ruin, Marcia Cavalcante Schuback, Sven-Olov Wallenstein, Fredrika Spindler and Jonna Bornemark.

I also want to thank Rudolf Bernet for clarifying and helpful discussions, as well as for hosting my stay at the Husserl-archives in Leuven. I am indebted to the present and former directors of the Husserl-archives, Ullrich Melle and Rudolf Bernet, for kind permission to quote from Husserl's unpublished manuscripts. I also want to thank Rochus Sowa for his assistance in locating important manuscripts and his generosity in sharing his vast knowledge concerning Husserl's *Nachlass*.

Further, I have benefited greatly from discussions with Françoise Dastur, Sara Heinämaa, Dan Zahavi over the years. For psychoanalytical matters, I have benefited enormously from discussions with notably Lars Härdelin and Gunnar Karlsson.

I have had the pleasure to be able to present my work during all stages at many conferences, and amongst these the annual NOSP meetings have been outstanding for the spirit of discovery and the high level of intellectual stimulation. Amongst the friends I have made there, I especially want to mention Jari Kauppinen, Ulrika Björk, Jonatan Habib

Engqvist, Lisa Folkmarsson-Käll, Joakim Löf, Johanna Oksala, Joel Backström, Martina Reuter and the Lacan-Circle in Helsinki for delightful and delirious discussions.

My father Patrick Smith has helped me in all kinds of ways, also by reading and commenting wisely on numerous manuscripts, I thank you deeply. For his birthday many years ago I gave him *Sein und Zeit* and *Krisis* to read so that he would be prepared for things to come, and now he is explaining Merleau-Ponty and Levinas to me when we talk. I wish everyone writing a dissertation in philosophy could have you as their father.

More than words can express, I owe this work to my family – Martin & Jim, Nils & Henning – and above all to Anna Stina for her wisdom and love. I dedicate this book to my family, both living and dead.

Södermalm, October, 2010

A note on abbreviations and translations

References will be given in a shortened form in the notes and in full in the Bibliography. I have tried to stay as close as possible to the English translations available, but when I have departed from these that will always be indicated.

References to Husserl's works are given primarily to the text-critical edition in *Husserliana* (abbreviated Hua), to *Husserliana Dokumente* (HuDo) and to *Husserliana Materialen* (HuMat), followed by volume number in roman numerals and page number. In order to economize I will often refer to *Husserliana* with only roman numerals and page number, thus skipping "Hua" where possible. I have used the English translations that are available, notably the *Collected Works* (CW). I will always give the reference to the German original first, followed by a slash and the reference to the English translation when necessary. All other translations of Husserl's works are my own.

References to Freud's works are given primarily to the *Penguin Freud Library* (abbreviated PFL) and when necessary to the *Studienausgabe* (SA), followed by volume number and page number. When works are referred to that are not published in these editions, I will refer to the *Standard Edition* (SE) and/or *Gesammelte Werke* (GW).

INTRODUCTION

Jeder Selbstdenker müsste eigentlich nach jedem Jahrzehnt seinen Namen ändern, da er dann zu einem Andern geworden ist. (Husserl)

The big problems are still wholly unresolved. Everything is in flux and dawning, an intellectual hell, with layer upon layer, and in the darkest core glimpses of the contours of Lucifer-Amor (Freud)

1. Phenomenological clarification of Freud's concept of repression: towards a new understanding of the unconscious

The present work investigates the possibility for transcendental phenomenology to clarify Freud's concept of the unconscious, with a focus on the theory of repression. Repression can in a preliminary sense be defined as the unconscious activity of pushing something away from consciousness while ensuring that it remains efficacious, thereby remaining "present" as something hidden and foreign within us. Repression, according to Freud, occurs for instance when a lived experience is deemed too emotionally painful to deal with in the same way that normal experiences are dealt with, by some other aspect or instance of the self. Thus the phenomenon of repression seems to call for a theory of subjectivity that not only allows for but also tries to explain the possibility of self-division, *Ichspaltung*, which is a term that both Freud and Husserl employ frequently although with different implications.[1] At the same time, the division within the self that

[1] For Freud it is most often used in relation to pathological defence processes where two incompatible attitudes to reality are taken up by the same I (see "Splitting of the Ego in the Process of Defence" from 1938, PFL 11 p. 457ff). Husserl on the other hand primarily speaks of the *Ichspaltung* in a methodological sense, as the division that occurs with the onset of the transcendental reduction in relation to the I of the natural attitude (see Hua I, *Cartesianische Meditationen*, § 15 p. 73).

repression brings about means that what is repressed becomes "foreign" to the normal self. This means that the philosophical theory of subjectivity that is called upon to clarify psychoanalytical repression must also be able to account for both self and otherness in various forms, not only otherness *to* the self but also, and more importantly, otherness *within* the self. Such a theory of subjectivity, I argue, is given by Husserl's phenomenology of an extended concept of consciousness, which not only engages with the active strata of the awakened I but also and equally important with the passive layers that precede all conscious activity. It is Husserl's mature theory of passivity that enables a new look at the Freudian unconscious, and that will also lead to a re-evaluation of the positions taken by Ricœur, Merleau-Ponty and Derrida, as we will see later on. These thinkers, although positive to the philosophical resources of Freud's concept of the unconscious, all argued that Husserlian phenomenology was unable to follow Freudian thought as soon as one moves beyond the preconscious and into the dynamic unconscious of repression.[2]

By "phenomenological clarification" is meant the attempt to bring a concept back to its most originary mode of givenness in intuition, something that will put a considerable strain on the phenomenological method when applied to the unconscious.[3] According to Husserl's presentation of "the method of clarification" or *Klärung* in *Ideen I*, it is essential to note that:

> [...] what is given at any particular time is usually surrounded by a halo of undetermined determinability, which has its mode of being brought closer by being "developed" into a separated series of representations; at first one may once more be led into the realm of obscurity, but then anew within the sphere of givenness until what is intended comes into the sharply illuminated circle of perfect givenness (Hua III, § 69 p. 145/CW 2 p. 157; tr. mod.).

If what is given is characterized by an "unbestimmter Bestimmbarkeit", then this suggests that the method of clarification must proceed by means of a stepwise interpretation.[4] In Husserl's later

[2] See § 3 below.

[3] On the method of "clarification", see: Hua III, § 67ff; Hua V, *Ideen III*, Kap. 4; cf. Hua XXV, p. 16f.

[4] See also I, CM § 13 p. 69.

thought, this hermeneutical aspect of the phenomenological method is reinforced by the identification of transcendental phenomenology with the "self-interpretation" of transcendental subjectivity.[5]

In a first step, Freud's concept of the unconscious will accordingly here be led back to its origin in acts of repression, since it is with repression that lived experiences are brought about whose manifestation (as anomalous gaps in the stream of experience) first calls for something like the concept of the unconscious. As Freud states, the unconscious is "derived" from the theory of repression and thereby the theory of repression also becomes the "cornerstone" for the whole structure of psychoanalysis.[6]

The Freudian "unconscious" has become such a worn out concept that its more precise meaning in Freudian metapsychology has become increasingly difficult to locate in the philosophical debate. Although recent attempts from both analytic philosophy and phenomenology have illuminated details and brought about important distinctions where Freud is unclear and even wrong, there is still controversy concerning what the most basic function of the unconscious is in psychoanalytical theory.[7] One particularly persistent view ascribed to Freud is that unconscious phenomena are real parts of consciousness, somewhat like fish swimming at the bottom of a deep lake, but since these cannot be found it is said that there is something fundamentally wrong with the very notion of the unconscious.[8] To put it briefly, the unconscious for Freud is not a "part" of consciousness but something that can only be

---

[5] See XVII, § 104 "Die transzendentale Phänomenologie als die Selbstauslegung der transzendentalen Subjektivität"; cf. I, CM §§ 33, 41, 62. See also XV, Nr. 11.

[6] *The Ego and the Id* (1923), PFL 11, p. 353. "On the History of the Psychoanalytic Movement" (1914), PFL 15, p. 73.

[7] Amongst the most important books on Freud and the unconscious, see for instance Marcia Cavell, *Becoming a Subject. Reflections in Philosophy and Psychoanalysis* (2006); Jonathan Lear, *Freud* (2005); David Livingstone Smith, *Freud's Philosophy of the Unconscious* (1999); Sebastian Gardner, *Irrationality and the Philosophy of Psychoanalysis* (1993); J. Lear, *Love and its Place in Nature: a Philosophical Interpretation of Freudian Psychoanalysis* (1990); Michel Henry, *Généalogie de la psychanalyse. Le commencement perdu* (1985).

[8] See for example Searle's *The Rediscovery of the Mind* (1992), where he argues that the "deep unconscious mental intentional phenomena", i.e. the unconscious in Freud's meaning, simply "do not exist": "Not only is there no evidence for their existence, but the postulation of their existence violates a logical constraint on the notion of intentionality" (p. 173).

introduced from within the clinical situation, which is neither a part of the "natural attitude" in the phenomenological sense, nor of a scientific-psychological examination. In texts from throughout his career, Freud states that the unconscious is a hypothesis; something that is assumed in order to be able to give an account of psychic life without having to accept otherwise inexplicable gaps. At times however, Freud blends this thought of the unconscious as something merely hypothesized, with the thought of the unconscious as something which exists:

> Our right to assume the existence of something mental [*seelisches*] that is unconscious and to employ that assumption for the purposes of scientific work is disputed in many quarters. To this we can reply that our assumption of the unconscious is necessary and legitimate, and that we possess numerous proofs of its existence [*dass wir für die Existenz des Unbewussten mehrfache Beweise besitzen*] ("The Unconscious", PFL 11, p. 167f).[9]

But if the existence of the unconscious has been proven repeatedly, then surely it can no longer be a question of regarding the unconscious as a hypothesis, and by arguing for both of these positions Freud puts himself in an awkward position, as Laplanche & Pontalis (as well as MacIntyre before them) have noticed.[10] The failure to address this movement in modality – from hypothetical existence to reality – lies behind many misconceptions concerning the ontological "realism" of the unconscious. In order to see that it is not just an inconsiderate transgression of borders on Freud's part, the unconscious must be related to the phenomenological theory of intentionality, whereby the psychoanalytical practice comes to be seen as operating a kind of

[9] See also *Introductory Lectures on Psychoanalysis (1916-17)*, PFL 1, p. 319.

[10] Laplanche & Pontalis, *The Language of Psychoanalysis* (1988) p. 326. See also Alasdair MacIntyre, *The Unconscious. A Conceptual Analysis* (1997) p. 71. Of course MacIntyre's claims imply much more than merely an unwarranted shift from one modality to another, but his analysis rests on presuppositions that are highly questionable, the first of which is that what Freud's writings are essentially about is to provide causal explanations for the phenomena analyzed. Although Freud at times adopts a causal terminology and adheres to the general natural-scientific *Weltanschauung*, the radical potential of psychoanalysis is lost when this view is upheld and therefore it has to be abandoned. That is to say, psychoanalysis cannot fulfil the standards of a science employing the hypothetic-deductive model, and to that extent MacIntyre and later critics such as Marc-Wogau (1967) and Grünbaum (1984, 1993) are right. But they fail to address the dimension of meaning and passive intentionality which represents the true break-through of Freud's investigations.

suspension of the world, an epoché of sorts.[11] Husserl argues both in the lectures on phenomenological psychology and in *Krisis* that any practicing psychologist performs such a partial epoché, and although psychoanalysis is not a psychology in any ordinary sense, this also holds for the psychoanalyst. This interpretation emphasizes the fundamental distinction which Freud himself introduced between the psychoanalytical and all the non-psychoanalytical thematizations of subjectivity (which include everyday reflection, philosophy, the sciences of psychology, psychiatry, biology etc.).[12]

From a larger perspective, the work of both Husserl and Freud must be seen in relation to what they both considered to be a genuine crisis in the sciences. Interestingly, they both thought that the roots of this crisis are to be found in psychology, taken in a broad sense. According to Husserl, the crisis of the European sciences is above all a crisis of modern psychology, and the task that psychology faces is thus of the greatest importance for the overcoming of this crisis, or at least for the attempt to lessen the damages. The reason why psychology is singled out is obvious from a transcendental phenomenological point of view: if the crisis consists in the fact that the natural sciences have forgotten their basis in subjective life, and have covered the world in a "garb of ideas" stemming from the Euclidean-Galilean mathematization of the world, then what is called for is a reawakening of their foundations in the life-world, and further still back to the subjective activities wherein the life-world is constituted.[13]

Both Husserl and Freud set about a reform of the very foundations of their disciplines by denying that their subject matter was something that was already determined, prior to their respective investigations. In that sense they both took a part in the fight against what was then the

---

[11] I have discussed this in Nicholas Smith (2003). For further discussions of the phenomenological epoché in psychoanalysis, see Wolfgang Blankenburg (1969, 1979) and Michael Titze (2003).

[12] It should be remembered that although Freud was convinced of the scientific status of psychoanalysis, he insisted that its inclusion within the natural sciences could only become a reality *after* these had undergone a thorough revision, due to the demands that the psychoanalytical thematization of the unconscious poses; this is discussed in for instance "The Claims of Psychoanalysis to Scientific Interest", in PFL 15 (see p. 47 for instance). Critics such as Grünbaum often overlook this.

[13] See *Erfahrung und Urteil*, § 11; and Hua VI, *Krisis*, § 9h) p. 51/Engl. p. 51.

established view, although with different optics. Freud was more naïve in believing that psychoanalytical theory would become a part of the stock of the natural sciences. This faith in the power of rationality never paid off in terms of recognition from the scientific community, and Husserl would have argued that it never could, psychoanalysis and the natural-scientific psychology being devoted to totally different subject matters.

Freud was however trying to expand the limits of science by making it accept the findings of psychoanalysis, but his conception of rationality was finally too narrow, too dependent on scientistic prejudice. He didn't see that the natural scientific conception of rationality that he unquestioningly adhered to could only be maintained by systematically excluding the capital part of his findings, which were focused on subjective lived experience and meaning and not on entities susceptible to strictly causal explanations. Husserl, on the other hand, went to the heart of the matter by seeing that it is rationality itself that first has to be restored. This restoration does not seek out a conception of rationality from a previously existent historical period, but is in his later writings generated by a careful reinterpretation of the history of philosophy. The aim for Husserl is to disclose an alternative conception of rationality that no longer flees from its "irrational" yet evidentially secured sources:

> One would think, after all, that we could attain a scientific concept even of an absolute reason and its accomplishments only after working out a scientific concept of our human reason and of human, or of humanity's, accomplishments – that is, only through a genuine psychology (VI, § 57 p. 206/Engl. p. 202).

And in this process Freud's work plays an important role also for a rationality to come, by contributing in depth knowledge of subjective life that is, as he puts it, "almost inaccessible in any other way".[14]

Although one of the impulses to write this book came from the leading figures in French post-war philosophy, where phenomenology and psychoanalysis were major points of reference, it soon became clear

[14] "Two Encyclopaedia Articles": "Psychoanalysis is the name of a procedure for the investigation of mental processes which are almost inaccessible in any other way [...]" (PFL 15, p. 131).

that for the particular question of the unconscious more was needed. That is to say, in order to give a serious response to the question of whether Husserlian phenomenology must part ways with Freud on the deeper issues going beyond the preconscious (which was the general view), a new look at Husserl's texts was necessary. For it seemed that quite new themes were broached in lectures and manuscripts that were never discussed by interpreters like Derrida, Ricœur and Merleau-Ponty for instance. Notably it was the penetrating investigations in the lectures on "fundamental problems in logic", "transcendental aesthetics" or "transcendental logic" (as they were variously called) that Husserl gave in 1920-21, 1923 and 1925-26 that suggested a completely new possibility.[15]

Husserl's analysis of the passivity of consciousness as that which precedes all active conscious processes opened up a space that had remained unexplored by transcendental philosophy since the German romantics and idealists.[16] The further genetic investigation of the "living present" was a constant theme in the 1920's and became the gravitational centre of the C-manuscripts in the 1930's. These investigations turned out to be also a phenomenology of the "unconscious", in Husserl's sense. What this means and whether or not Husserl's analyses can really be employed to understand the Freudian unconscious is the main theme of this work.

2. Overview of investigation

The present investigation is divided into two parts where Part I presents an overview of central themes in Husserl's genetic phenomenology with a focus on its methodological aspects. The main argument that is developed here is that it is only by means of a clear grasp of the method

---

15 See *Analysen zur passiven Synthesis. Aus Vorlesungs- und Forschungsmanuskripten (1918-1926)*, Hua XI and its companion-volume *Aktive Synthesen: Aus der Vorlesung 'Transzendentale Logik' 1920/21. Ergänzungsband zu 'Analysen zur passiven Synthesis'*, Hua XXXI. Both of these are translated and published together in *Analyses Concerning Passive and Active Synthesis. Lectures on Transcendental Logic*, Collected Works vol. 9.

16 This romantic legacy is also a common root of Husserl's extended phenomenology of consciousness and Freud's metapsychology, that goes beyond the well-known linkage via Brentano's lectures in Vienna (that both Husserl and Freud attended). I have not been able to develop this further here.

of genetic phenomenology (in its cooperation with static analyses), that any progress can be made concerning the unconscious. Therefore, the different "ways" to the reduction that Husserl explores and combines in his later writings are presented, together with an attempt to differentiate the different types of reduction (the "intersubjective", the "radicalized" and the "universal" reduction) that are employed. Husserl's late philosophy is here largely seen as consisting in a perpetually refined reflection upon and development of these various steps involved in what I take to be parts of one, single theory of phenomenological reduction that makes up the core of transcendental phenomenology.

If one considers the standard picture, where the reduction consists in a simple process whereby the transcendental field is directly reached (as in *Ideen I*), then it is clear that Husserl both before and after employed more sophisticated and elaborate versions of it. This standard view of the reduction is however almost universally called upon in critical discussions of phenomenology and the question of the unconscious, but it is particularly ill suited for this purpose. This is because it leads only to an investigation of the correlation between act and object, and not to the streaming process which genetically precedes it. The "unconscious" as it is understood by Husserl in texts from the 1920's and onwards is another name for this streaming process, and thus requires another methodological approach than static investigation of the act-object correlation. The resources of genetic phenomenology have never been fully put to use in previous discussions of Freud and Husserl, and to do so is the task that is chosen for the first part of this investigation.

On the basis of this mainly methodological backdrop, Part II will initiate a series of concrete encounters focussed on the kind of alterity that is specific to Freud's theory of the unconscious. If repression can be seen as the lingering presence of something which is like a hidden "foreign body" within us, then its phenomenological clarification must be based on an ability to account for the constitution of what is foreign. One of the main ideas put forth in Part I is that transcendental phenomenology in its static and genetic complementarity gains its particular force in the tension between the constitution of stable entities (the I, the other and the world) and an openness to otherness. It is argued that it is only due to its inherent ability to account for this otherness that the constitution of being is possible.[17] In a general sense, the in-depth accounts of genetic phenomenology and the themes presented in connection with these, represent an attempt to fill in the gaps left behind by Freud's lack of analysis of what consciousness is. It is symptomatic that Freud wrote a text on consciousness as a part of the projected series of twelve metapsychological papers in 1915 (of which only six remain), but then apparently destroyed it; it has never been found.[18] So what Husserl wrote on consciousness is to meet and in some way join hands with what Freud wrote on the unconscious. The main tools here are Husserl's extended concept of consciousness, extended notably by means of the inclusion of passivity that he worked out in the 1920's and 1930's, as well as an interpretation of Freud's concept of the unconscious that emphasizes its proximity to such an extended concept of consciousness.

At certain intersections (called "direct approaches") in both Part I and II the investigation will turn to passages wherein Husserl himself tentatively discusses psychopathological phenomena (insanity, abnormality, the perseverance of forgotten memories, psychic illness and illusions). These sections (which are specified in the introduction to Chapter One) serve the function of attempting a "direct" clarification of aspects related to Freud's theory of repression, like small speedboats charging ahead of the "indirect", methodical presentation of genetic phenomenology. In this sense, the indirect approach represents by far the larger portion compared to the relatively few attempts at a "direct" clarification of repression, since it is spread out over the major part of both Part I and II. The point of these direct approaches is to investigate the thematic connection between Husserl and Freud, by showing that

[17] Broadly speaking, the various forms of otherness that Husserl investigates can be divided into three major kinds: 1) the otherness of the world and the hyletic material which constitutes it, 2) the otherness of the other person and finally 3) the otherness within me which is notably of a bodily, temporal (retentional-protentional) and imaginative character (I imagine myself being other); see Hua I, CM §§ 12, 41, 48f; Hua IV, § 54. It is the latter two that will be most thoroughly examined here: egological alterity as what can schematically be called the otherness "within me" will be related to intersubjective alterity as the otherness of "the other".

[18] See the editor's introduction to the metapsychological papers in PFL 11, p. 101ff; and some probable references to the lost paper on consciousness on p. 188, 192, 195. For a fuller account, see SA 3, p. 71ff.

Husserl also worked with "psychoanalytical" topics as integrated aspects of transcendental phenomenology.

3. The field of interpretation: overview of previous literature

Although most philosophers who have worked with this issue have been willing to admit that a phenomenological analysis of consciousness can clarify the more superficial aspects of Freud's account (the preconscious), many have denied this when it comes to the unconscious proper.[19] Many of the strongest contemporary philosophers such as Derrida, Merleau-Ponty, Ricœur, Levinas and Henry have therefore come to regard the psychoanalytical unconscious as a "radical alterity" that a transcendental phenomenology of consciousness cannot account for. In a certain sense, these thinkers – despite their many deviations and developments from one another and also from any standard conception of phenomenology – follow the verdict by Husserl in his first book concerning what he calls "the unacceptable hypothesis of unconscious psychical activities".[20]

The assumption of the unconscious would thus merit no further attention, since it represents nothing but an "escape from scientific explanations", as Heidegger put it a few years later.[21] But then how is one to

---

[19] I will not here discuss the pioneering work of those who first saw the potentials of engaging phenomenology with psychoanalysis, such as Max Scheler, Ludwig Binswanger, Paul Schilder, Sartre etc. For although these writers undoubtedly opened the demanding dialogue that has been going on for a century now, they never engaged in an interpretation of Husserl's phenomenology that would have been sufficient for the undertaking attempted here; however I will discuss certain aspects of their work later on. That is not to say that their work would be of little interest for this investigation, to the contrary: they have all developed analyses that would contribute greatly to our themes. To just take one example, Sartre's analysis of the gaze of the other (perhaps more so than his *psychanalyse existentielle*) which shows how the other lives within me prior to my "constituting" her as a worldly being, prior to my seeing her, in my experience of shame before her; see *L'être et le néant*, p. 292ff.

[20] *Philosophie der Arithmetik. Mit ergänzenden Texte (1890-1901)*, Hua XII/Engl. tr. CW 10, p. 215. See also Husserl's *Logische Untersuchungen* where he argues that "obscure, hypothetical events in the soul's unconscious depths" are of no concern to phenomenology (Hua XIX/1, p. 398f/Engl. tr. *Logical Investigations* vol. 2, p. 105).

[21] See the article that Heidegger wrote in 1912 on "Religionspsychologie und Unterbewußtsein": "Und das ist der Grundzug der genannten Unterbewußtseinstheo-

explain the interest in Freud's account of the unconscious that these later phenomenologists have almost unanimously shown in their own work, and often precisely as a means to overcome what was felt to be inner limitations in Husserlian phenomenology? The answer seems to be that although various aspects of Freud's work on the unconscious have been regarded as essential (for notably the French post-war generation of phenomenologists) in order to gain a deeper grasp of subjectivity, these aspects require a break with Husserl's methodology.

The introduction of the unconscious into the hermeneutical, deconstructive or alterological modifications of phenomenology has gone hand in hand with the abandonment of a philosophy based on the "principle of principles".[22] Thus according to Merleau-Ponty, Husserl's intentional analysis is unable to grasp the Freudian unconscious for methodological reasons: "The whole Husserlian analysis is blocked by the framework of acts which the philosophy of consciousness imposes upon it".[23] As for Ricœur, Husserl's phenomenology can only reach the level of the psychoanalytical preconscious, and it is therefore unable to thematize the dynamic unconscious.[24]

Derrida argues in a programmatic text that the "language of presence or absence, i.e. the metaphysical discourse of phenomenology is inadequate" to grasp the "radical alterity" of the Freudian unconscious.[25] In a later text he says more precisely that Freudian repression designates "what, in the eyes of philosophy, perhaps does not let itself be thought or even inspected through a question".[26] And according to Levinas, who is less directly engaged with the concept, it is only the

---

rie, dass sie psychische Phänomene (vor allem anormalen Charakters) für erklärt und begründet hält durch die einfache Annahme eines Unterbewußtseins. Letzten Endes erhalten wir auf diese Weise nur eine platte Umschreibung dessen, was der Lösung harrt. Wir können in diesen Annahmen lediglich eine Flucht vor jeder wissenschaftlichen Erklärung sehen"; Gesamtausgabe Bd. 16, p. 23. (In the following, references to Heidegger's work will be given with the abbreviation GA followed by volume number and page number.)

[22] Hua III, § 24 p. 51/CW 2, p. 44.

[23] Merleau-Ponty, *Le visible et l'invisible*, p. 293/Engl. p. 244 (the note was written in 1960).

[24] Ricœur, *De l'interprétation. Essai sur Freud*, p. 381f. This same point is made by Holenstein, *Phänomenologie der Assoziation. Zu Struktur und Funktion eines Grundprinzips der passiven Genesis bei E. Husserl*, p. 322.

[25] J. Derrida, "La différance", in *Marges de la philosophie*, p. 21f.

[26] *Glas*, p. 215/Engl. p. 191e.

"ethical language" in contrast to that of phenomenology that is capable of explaining the fundamental experience of the givenness of the other. The pre-originary, an-archaic alterity of the other, is lost as soon as phenomenology begins to thematize it, i.e. when we step out of the "absolute passivity", which can only be described with the ethical vocabulary. This originary ethical passivity – which is said to be prior to all conscious phenomenon, and which also precedes the distinction between activity and passivity – is that which constitutes the real meaning of the unconscious.[27]

As for Heidegger, the seemingly unambiguous distantiation towards the unconscious is essentially repeated in the *Zollikoner Seminare*, more than half a century after his initial rejection.[28] Limiting the discussion to Merleau-Ponty, Ricœur and Derrida they all developed positions in works from the 1960's where Freud was used as a kind of lever to take a step beyond Husserl.[29]

So although the issue of the Freudian unconscious may at first sight appear to be marginal if not to say irrelevant for the central aims of transcendental phenomenology, it turns out that it actually plays an important role in the background of one of the major methodological discussions in contemporary philosophy. But in order to better be able to measure the potential gains of these later interpretations, it is necessary to first investigate the possibilities of initiating such a dialogue

[27] E. Levinas, *Autrement qu'être ou au-delà de l'essence*, p. 192ff : "La persécution ramène à une résignation non consentie et, par conséquent, traverse une nuit d'inconscient. C'est le sens de l'inconscient, nuit où se fait le retournement de moi en soi sous le traumatisme de la persécution – passivité plus passive que toute passivité en deçà de l'identité, responsabilité, substitution." (In a first version, the chapter from which this analysis is taken, was published in 1968.)

[28] Cf. M. Heidegger, *Zollikoner Seminare*, p. 260. "Seemingly unambiguous" since what is rejected by Heidegger, as I see it, is more the *concept* of the unconscious than the issue itself. This rejection of the concept of the unconscious has its ground in the obvious relation to the concept of consciousness, and thus to a philosophy of subjectivity: *Dasein* has no unconscious because it is not a "conscious subject". Never the less, much of Heidegger's work covers a similar ground, although in a different register (that of fundamental ontology in *Sein und Zeit* and the lectures leading up to it), such as the analysis of attunement (*Stimmung*) and anxiety (*Angst*).

[29] Although both Merleau-Ponty and Ricœur had dealt with Freud repeatedly in previous works I am here restricting my claims to *Le visible et l'invisible* and *De l'interprétation*. Derrida repeatedly came back to Freud in seminal works; see Nicholas Smith (2001) and (2005).

with psychoanalysis directly from the vantage point of Husserl's transcendental phenomenology. This has become a topic worthy of considerable interest as highly relevant aspects have been made public only quite recently. What I intend to do is to show that there is no reason to part ways with Husserl's transcendental phenomenology on account of its supposed inability to clarify the central aspects of Freud's concept of the unconscious.

Below I will present the most important works that are discussed in this investigation. Some of them more explicitly deal with the relation between transcendental phenomenology and Freudian psychoanalysis (Ricœur, Derrida, Holenstein, Henry, Bernet, Brudzinska) whereas the others are more focussed on the interpretation of Husserl's genetic phenomenology (Held, Landgrebe, Yamaguchi, Lee, Depraz, Zahavi, Bégout) – but there are obviously overlaps. Perhaps needless to say, the works here examined represent merely a culmination of a philosophical investigation at the crossroads between phenomenology and psychoanalysis that has been going on for a century now, starting with Max Scheler's "Die Idole der Selbsterkenntnis" and Moritz Geiger's work on the unconscious.[30]

3.1. Ricœur 1965

Ricœur, in his book *De l'interprétation. Essai sur Freud*, develops a brief yet sustained and highly influential comparative reading of Husserl and Freud, in the course of a complex analysis of the possibilities of present-day hermeneutical discourse.[31] He there suggests the possibility of reaching the Freudian unconscious by way of an interpretation of Husserl's idea of passive genesis.[32] Although this correlation between passive genesis and the unconscious has been the guiding idea behind for instance Binswanger's existential analysis (*Daseinsanalyse*) in many works, Ricœur bases his investigation on a far more detailed

[30] See Scheler, "Die Idole der Selbsterkenntnis" (1911/15); Geiger "Fragment über den Begriff des Unbewußten und die psychische Realität" (1921).

[31] Paul Ricœur, *De l'interprétation. Essai sur Freud*; English tr. *Freud and Philosophy. An Essay on Interpretation*. I will here disregard this larger interpretative framework which by far exceeds the comparison between Husserl and Freud.

[32] "C'est ici qu'intervient l'idée de 'genèse passive' qui, d'une nouvelle façon, 'indique vers' l'inconscient freudien" (*De l'interprétation*, p. 371/Engl. p. 380).

examination of Husserl's phenomenology. The investigation of the resources of Husserl's concept of passive genesis is undertaken in a search for the conditions of possibility for the constitution of the psychoanalytical field.[33] I will come back to the central points in this exposition during the course of my investigation, here I will only point out where I disagree with Ricœur's interpretation, and indicate my reasons briefly. No reflexive philosophy has, according to Ricœur, approached the Freudian unconscious to a degree comparable with that of Husserl's phenomenology and his followers (Ricœur here mentions Merleau-Ponty and De Waelhens), but this attempt he argues is also bound to fail. This failure to capture the specifics of the Freudian unconscious is not due to a misconception of what it is, for there is an *approximation véritable* between the two disciplines, but never the less the phenomenological attempt only manages a partial comprehension:

> It is well to mention at the very start that this attempt is also bound to fail. But this failure does not have the same pattern as the preceding one. It is not a question of a mistake or a misunderstanding, but rather of a true approximation, one that comes very close to the Freudian unconscious but misses it in the end, affording only an approximate understanding of it. In becoming aware of the gap separating the unconscious according to phenomenology from the Freudian unconscious, we will grasp, by a method of approximation and difference, the specificity of the Freudian concepts (*Freud and Philosophy*, p. 367/Fr. p. 376)

This distance between the two is above all due to the phenomenon of repression that is operative in the constitution of the Freudian unconscious, for when we come to understand that the barrier which separates the repressed contents from becoming conscious is a bar between the unconscious and the preconscious, and not one between the preconscious and the conscious, then we have moved from the phenomenological to the psychoanalytical unconscious.[34] This barrier of repression is the true criterion of demarcation for Ricœur, as it distributes the ultimate borders between the phenomenological and the psychoanalytical thematizations of the unconscious:

> The unconscious of phenomenology is the preconscious of psychoanalysis, that is to say, an unconscious that is descriptive and not yet topo-

[33] *Freud and Philosophy*, p. 376- 418/Fr. p. 366-406.
[34] *Freud and Philosophy*, p. 392/Fr. p. 381f.

> graphic. [...] repression is a real exclusion which a phenomenology of the implicit or co-intended can never reach (*Freud and Philosophy*, p. 392/Fr. p. 382)

Thus the point where Husserl's phenomenology must part ways with Freudian psychoanalysis is said by Ricœur to reside in the phenomenon of repression, and no phenomenology of the implicit is able to cross the border into that which is repressed. I will argue against this interpretation that Husserl's genetic phenomenology (and notably the concept of intentional implication) shows that there are no reasons to uphold this view. There are two ways to understand this, the first is that the phenomenologist can never take the place of the psychoanalyst: no amount of philosophical reflection can bring what is repressed into the light of day, which is surely true. But that is not (or not only) the claim that Ricœur is making here. Instead, he argues that phenomenology as an investigation of consciousness is methodologically inapt to reach that which has been repressed, and that is the claim that I contend. Ricœur's interpretation of passivity (which is the key here) is based on the Cartesian way to the reductions which as I will show is simply insufficient. This is in part due to the fact that Ricœur bases his study mainly on *Cartesianische Meditationen* (other relevant material being unavailable at the time), but in part due to questions of interpretation.[35]

3.2. Held 1966

Even though it is nearly half a century old Held's work *Lebendige Gegenwart* still counts as one of the most penetrating interpretations of Husserl's late phenomenology of time.[36] Many of the themes that it investigates are at the heart of the contemporary debate, and Held's analyses are often ahead also of more recent studies.[37] One reason for

---

[35] I refer to the publication of above all the following volumes of Husserliana that have appeared since, and that Ricœur did not have access to: Hua IX, *Analysen zur passiven Synthesis* (1966), Hua XIII-XV, *Zur Phänomenologie der Intersubjektivität I-III* (1973). These volumes, disregarding unpublished manuscripts, contribute in an essential way to the possibility of addressing psychoanalytic thought from a phenomenological point of view.

[36] Klaus Held, *Lebendige Gegenwart. Die Frage nach der Seinsweise des transzendentalen Ich bei Edmund Husserl, entwickelt am Leitfaden der Zeitproblematik.*

[37] See for instance Toine Kortooms, *Phenomenology of Time. Edmund Husserl's Analysis of Time-Consciousness*, where "Part III. Husserl's analysis of time-

this is that Held deals with the problematics of time (mainly in the C-manuscripts) not as an isolated theme but from the outset sees it as an integrated part of egology, intersubjectivity and teleology, and from there on also immediately connected to the basic questions of a phenomenological metaphysics. Held shows convincingly that the question of the temporal self-constitution of transcendental subjectivity *eo ipso* becomes a phenomenology of the unconscious, since the depth dimensions of this process goes far beyond what has been understood by "consciousness" so far in the philosophical tradition.[38]

In Husserl's late philosophy all constitution is led back to the process of temporization (*Zeitigung*), which is the source of all presentification (*Gegenwärtigung*), typically resulting in acts of sensuous perception. The investigation of the "originary passivity" leads to temporization as it unfolds in the living present, and Held argues that the transcendental I at its deepest level must be identified with this temporization.[39] At the heart of Held's analysis is the "enigma" (*Rätsel*) of transcendental life that arises since its pre-temporal present can only be discovered by means of reflection, while at the same time thereby covering the core of this process.[40] Reflection gives the already objectified form of what prior to it was a streaming originary movement, and this means that the enigmatic talk of the pre-present, a pre-temporal giving source whose manifestation we can only know of from the ontified traces it leaves behind, brings phenomenology to the "limits of reflection".[41] The disclosure of this pre-present therefore seems to call for "unphenomenological construction" (later thinkers such as Hart will here speak of downright conjecture), but Held instead convincingly argues that this

consciousness in the C-manuscripts" (p. 227-288) covers the same ground as Held (cf. p. 269ff). The aim (and the strength) of Kortooms work is a different one, it should be said: to give an overview of the "three stages" in the development of Husserl's thinking on inner time-consciousness.

[38] "(Der Begriff 'Bewusstseinsstrom' soll hier ebenso wie der Begriff 'Bewusstsein' nur mit einer gewissen Reserve gebraucht werden, weil 'Bewusstsein' im geläufigen Sinne nur eine, phänomenologisch gesehen, konstitutiv hochstufige Form noetischen Lebens bezeichnet, nicht aber die Ganzheit aller, auch der 'unbewussten' Funktionsweisen)"; see *Lebendige Gegenwart*, p. 48; cf. p. 35, 43, 87.

[39] *Lebendige Gegenwart*, p. 90.

[40] See notably the second part, Ch. D. Die Rätsel der lebendigen Gegenwart (p. 94ff).

[41] *Lebendige Gegenwart*, p. 75.

position is actually a part of the phenomenological project.[42] This means that reflection already "knows" that there is something preceding it, that it "knows" of the originary streaming life which is to say that it knows of itself as something that always and essentially must come after the anonymous, functioning present: phenomenological reflection is *Nachträglichkeit*.[43]

But Held does not investigate this *nachträgliche* dimension of reflection further, instead he pursues the question of what the prereflective sphere is and how we can know of it prior to reflection. The answer according to Held is the notion of self-communalization (*Selbstvergemeinschaftung*) as a prereflective being-together of my anonymous and my reflecting I.[44] Held is careful to present the methodological innovation that permitted this interpretation of the inner self-pluralization of the transcendental I: the "radicalized reduction".[45] Without wishing to criticize Held, what is called for now is that this analysis be continued by means of a clearer grasp of the methodology operative in Husserl's late works: how does the radicalized reduction relate to Husserl's discussion of the different "ways" to the reduction, and what is its relation to the "universal reduction" which is a main theme at the end of *Krisis*?[46]

3.3. Derrida 1966

The work of Jacques Derrida is of particular importance for the present investigation, for several reasons. The first is personal – Derrida was the first philosopher I read, and his work on both Husserl and Freud has been a major source of inspiration. Secondly, Derrida's interpretation (which spans over fifty years) has arguably been the most important

---

[42] *Lebendige Gegenwart*, p. ixf, 118f.

[43] *Lebendige Gegenwart*, p. 122; cf. p. 38, 90, 95f, 119, 131, 172.

[44] *Lebendige Gegenwart*, part 3, Ch. D. Die Selbstvergemeinschaftung im "ich fungiere" p. 164ff.

[45] *Lebendige Gegenwart*, p. 64ff (this Brand never did in *Ich, Welt und Zeit* which Held sees as a major flaw; see p. xii).

[46] Of course many later interpreters have pushed Held's analysis further in various directions – one has only to think of Zahavi's more convincing presentation of prereflective self-awareness in *Self-Awareness and Alterity* (1999) and Taguchi's account of the anonymity of the functioning I in *Das Problem des "Ur-Ich" bei Edmund Husserl* (2006).

ever of Husserl. Building on Heidegger's early reading but also drawing on other resources (notably Levinas and Freud), it has been a driving force behind the renewal of interest in Husserl's thinking that has exploded over the last decades. But despite this attention, the full extent of many of the central aspects of Husserl's philosophy still remains surprisingly unknown.

It is in particular the development of genetic phenomenology that is at stake here, as it plunges ever deeper into "originary constitution" ferreting out the structural relations between inner time-consciousness, bodily affectivity and intersubjectivity, while at the same time never giving up static phenomenology and a certain prioritizing of Cartesian subjectivity. Thus Derrida, who spent his formative first fifteen years (between 1953 and 1967) studying Husserl's *oeuvre*, only turns to Husserl's analysis of the lived body as the sensuous subsoil of reason from *Ideen II* in one of his latest texts – a theme that had been left conspicuously absent in his previous works on Husserl.[47]

But since Derrida's reading of Husserl largely remains within the orbit of Husserl's published texts it will never reach the level of interpretation that is increasingly being called for today, where the deeper genetic layers of subjectivity must be given voice. That being said, it is at the same time clear that many of the themes that are only now becoming visible in Husserl's texts owe much to the patient and inventive interpretative work that Derrida performed, together with that of Merleau-Ponty and Levinas.

Much has been written on Derrida's interpretation of Husserl, and I will come back to it during the course of the present interrogation. But the philosophical importance of psychoanalytical thought in Derrida's early work (after *The Origin of Geometry*) has largely been neglected.[48] In these works Derrida to an important degree began to employ a

---

[47] J. Derrida, *Le toucher, Jean-Luc Nancy* (2000).

[48] To give just one example: in Lawlor's otherwise excellent recent book *Derrida and Husserl: The Basic Problem of Phenomenology* (2002), which is a book that sets out to reconstruct the "formative period from approximately 1954 to 1967" (p. 7), the impact of Freud and psychoanalytical thinking is absent. With the exception of a couple of articles by R. Bernet – notably "Derrida-Husserl-Freud: the Trace of Transference" – I know of few other philosophical works that have sufficiently underlined the necessary role that psychoanalytical thinking plays in Derrida's early work.

psychoanalytical mode of thinking in order to be able to articulate his perspective on the philosophical tradition.[49] In his first published text dealing with psychoanalysis, "Freud and the Scene of Writing" from 1966, Derrida wants to justify a theoretical hesitation in utilizing Freudian concepts otherwise than in quotation marks, for "all these concepts, without exception, belong to the history of metaphysics".[50] But at the same time, Derrida points out that Freudian discourse in its syntax and its labour must not be confused with these traditional concepts, for "it is not exhausted by belonging to them".[51] This is what motivates "the necessity of an immense labour of deconstruction of the metaphysical concepts and phrases that are condensed and sedimented within Freud's precautions".[52] Therefore, a second methodological argument is to open Freudian thought to that which lies unthought within it, to that which is present in Freud's endeavour as a promise, and as a promise that always bears special ties to the other, to the other within me and the other as herself; and thus to politics, to ethics and to justice (themes that although present from the outset gain considerable weight in Derrida's later philosophy).

What is at stake here is nothing less than the fact that philosophy as such is constituted by an *originary act of repression* precisely of writing: "This repression constitutes the origin of philosophy as episteme, and of truth as the unity of logos and phone".[53] It is thus Freud's concept of repression that provides him with the tool required to open a space prior to the Husserlian and Heideggerian horizons of discourse, and to develop a whole new deconstructive conceptuality (*archi-écriture*, *espacement*, *archi-trace* etc). Psychoanalysis can accordingly be seen as a necessary condition of possibility for the deconstructive method. These two trajectories of interpretation – the

---

[49] For programmatic references to Freud, see "Freud and the Scene of Writing", "La différance", *Positions*, "Tympan" and various texts from *L'ecriture et la différence* and *Marges de la philosophie*. See further *De la grammatologie*, *La voix et le phénomène*, *La dissémination*, *Glas*, "Fors", *La carte postale* up until the late texts "Être juste avec Freud: l'histoire de la folie à l'âge de la psychanalyse", *Mal d'archive. Une impression freudienne*, *Résistances - de la psychanalyse* and *États d'âme de la psychanalyse*.

[50] "Freud and the Scene of Writing", in *Writing and Difference*, p. 197.

[51] "Freud and the Scene of Writing", p. 198.

[52] "Freud and the Scene of Writing", p. 198.

[53] "Freud and the Scene of Writing", p. 196.

neglect of Husserl's genetic analyses (of the lived body, originary constitution, the living present etc.) combined with the appropriation of Freud's theory of repression – converge in the "radical alterity" thesis: that phenomenology is inadequate to describe the Freudian unconscious. It is one of the main ambitions of this investigation to problematize this thesis and to show that it does not stand up to scrutiny.

3.4 Holenstein 1972

Holenstein's work from 1972 on *Husserls Phänomenologie der Assoziation. Zu Struktur und Funktion eines Grundprinzips der passiven Genesis bei Edmund Husserl* sprang directly from the impulse that the early French reception of Freud gave rise to. [54] Although it is an important study of both the inner development of the concept of association in Husserl's thought, and a lengthy discussion of its historical background as well as of its relation to thinkers contemporary to Husserl (Scheler, Merleau-Ponty, Gestalt-psychology, Freud and Jung) it only touches briefly upon Husserl's genetic phenomenology.[55] It is in particular the analysis of passivity and Husserl's statements on the unconscious in relation to psychoanalysis that are relevant for my investigation.

In the final chapter, devoted to a discussion of the doctrine of association of psychoanalysis and its relevance for phenomenology, Holenstein makes two claims that will be met with here: 1) in the unpublished work, Husserl when referring to the unconscious, does not regard it as a concept that belongs within phenomenology: whenever it is referred to, Husserl is in fact only "alluding to" (*anspielen*) the psychoanalytical concept. According to Holenstein's view (which has for a long time been the main source for the relation between Husserl's genetic phenomenology and Freud), there is simply no proper phenomenological concept of the unconscious: it belongs to another discipline, and

[54] The impulse came from the "contemporary French phenomenological interpretations of psychoanalytical praxis", which is a reference to Ricœur's *De l'interprétation* (discussed in § 65); see *Phänomenologie der Assoziation. Zu Struktur und Funktion eines Grundprinzips der passiven Genesis bei Edmund Husserl* (1972), p. 2.

[55] See notably §§ 6, 8, 25, 52, 60; and for the attempt to connect Freudian psychoanalysis with Husserl's genetic account of association §§ 65, 68.

whenever mentioned, it is merely an allusion to this other.[56] This is quite obviously a mistake. Holenstein also claims that Husserl's "allusions to the psychoanalytical concept" refer to phenomena that psychoanalysis would relegate to the "level of preconscious", thereby barring from the outset the possibility of any genuine contact between phenomenology and the psychoanalytical unconscious.[57] Holenstein has been repeatedly criticized for neglecting Husserl's analysis of passivity by arguing that the late analysis of the drives is of little or no consequence for transcendental phenomenology.[58] Holenstein also correctly criticizes Ricœur for not investigating Husserl's account of passivity to a sufficient degree in his *De l'interprétation*, and I will come back to both of these points.

3.5 Landgrebe 1974

A pioneering article in the thematization of Husserl's phenomenology of passivity is Landgrebe's short text "Das Problem der passiven Konstitution", which at the time was one of the first in-depth studies of this problem.[59] As Landgrebe points out, the problem of passive

[56] Just to mention one work of recent date that relies on Holenstein's account of the relation between Husserl and Freud, see Bruce Bégout's excellent study *La généalogie de la logique. Husserl, l'antéprédicatif et le catégorial* (2000).

[57] *Husserls Phänomenologie der Assoziation*, p. 322: "In Entwürfen und Vorlesungen und zwar gerade auch im Zusammenhang der Assoziationsthematik verweist Husserl hingegen gelegentlich auf das 'Unbewusste', wobei er eindeutig auf die psychoanalytische Thematisierung des Begriffes anspielt. [...] Es handelt sich dabei [...] um Phänomene, welche die Psychoanalyse als 'vorbewusst' einstuft."

[58] *Husserls Phänomenologie der Assoziation* p. 13 (cf. 323): "In den Forschungsmanuskripten der frühen dreissiger Jahre, insbesondere in C- und E III- Manuskripte, tritt die mögliche Bedeutung von Instinkten und Interessen für die Auslösung von Assoziationen vermehrt in den Blickpunkt. Es handelt sich dabei durchgehend um fragmentarisch gebliebene Aperçus". This view has been criticized by Nam-In Lee, *Edmund Husserls Phänomenologie der Instinkte* (1993), p. 10, 166f; and by Bégout, Depraz, Mavridis & Nagaï in their joint article "Passivité et phénoménologie génétique", in *Alter* 3 (1995), p. 473ff. In a similar vein, Yamaguchi criticizes Holenstein for not integrating the original layer of the associative synthesis, i.e. the "inborn drives", into the systematic outline of the associative synthesis: "Obwohl Holenstein auf die Uraffektion der Triebintentionalität aufmerksam macht, nimmt er diese ursprüngliche Schicht der assoziativen Synthesis nicht in das gesamte System der assoziativen Synthesis hinein"; see his *Passive Synthesis und Intersubjektivität bei Edmund Husserl* (1982) p. 37n1.

[59] Landgrebe, "Das Problem der passiven Konstitution" in *Faktizität und Individuation. Studien zu den Grundfragen der Phänomenologie* (1982), p. 71-87.

constitution is the real dividing line between the transcendental philosophy of Kant and that of Husserl. One thesis that Landgrebe investigates here is that one cannot gain access to the "depth-dimension" of the process of constitution from phenomenological reflection (a main idea already in *Lebendige Gegenwart* which was Held's dissertation written with Landgrebe as supervisor).[60]

But Landgrebe, unlike Held, does not seem to accept the evidence stemming from self-communalization and instead argues that the anonymity of the passive, depth dimension of the functioning I (the living present) cannot be overcome.[61] There are, according to Landgrebe, no signs of the processes of the living present announced in consciousness and thus it becomes "absolute anonymity".[62] This, surprisingly, makes the heart of functioning transcendental subjectivity into something like a "radical alterity" that so many interpreters – and critics! – would have Freud's unconscious be. The absolute anonymity also means that Landgrebe departs from Husserl and instead turns to Heidegger's analysis of *Befindlichkeit* in order to find the philosophical resources necessary to articulate transcendental life prior to reflection.[63] In the following discussion, I will argue against the idea that the depth dimension of the functioning I is an absolute anonymity, partly by showing that a broader conception of evidence than Cartesian reflexivity (as in for instance the psychological way) discloses a prereflexive self-awareness.

3.6 Henry 1985

Michel Henry in his book *Généalogie de la psychanalyse* subjects the psychoanalytical concept of the unconscious to a thorough phenomenological critique, by establishing it as a strict parallel to the traditional Cartesian concept of consciousness.[64] The interpretation presented here

[60] I will disregard the other two theses; see "Das Problem der passiven Konstituiton" p. 75.

[61] "Das Problem der passiven Konstituiton" p. 76f.

[62] "Das Problem der passiven Konstituiton" p. 77.

[63] "Das Problem der passiven Konstituiton" p. 83.

[64] Michel Henry, *Généalogie de la psychanalyse. Le commencement perdu* (1985).

will opt for an alternative to Henry concerning what transcendental phenomenology is and therefore also concerning the philosophical role of Freudian metapsychology. In Descartes Henry also finds the opening to the thought of embodied life, which stands at the centre of the "radical", "material phenomenology" that Henry has pursued in previous works.[65] The true meaning of the "cogito" is therefore not, as we are accustomed to believe, "I think", but actually "life", or that which Descartes called *âme*. The thought of the *ek-stasis*, of the transcendence of the world, of that which seems to be in a structural opposition to original affection and immanence, is taken by Henry to be a part of what he calls a "metaphysics of representation".[66]

Freud's position within this metaphysics of representation, is that of being a late "heir to the whole of western thought", and so it is not primarily Freud and psychoanalytical thought as such that we ought to get rid of, but this whole heritage: the very presuppositions of "classical thought". The criticism advanced in the book is guided by the ambitious aim of throwing light upon the "unthought background" of western philosophy, to the extent that this background "has determined all that preceded Freud, and may still determine all that may come after him".[67]

Besides the well known effort of Cartesian philosophy to ground scientific knowledge through knowledge of the self, Descartes according to Henry also had a "primitive project", "superimposed" upon the more well known: to discern a more profound dimension where life attains itself before the appearance of the world. Due to Descartes' scientific aims, this project disintegrated, and the modern philosophy of consciousness engaged thinking in the "opposite direction" leading to the world, to a transcendental theory of knowledge and science, which in its turn made possible the universe of technology. That which Descartes sought in this primitive project had nothing to do with notions such as perception or representation, with platonic ideas or such, i.e. what Henry labels as pertaining to *ek-stasis* as the transcendence of the world, but all the more to do with their rejection and that which is totally different from the *ek-stasis* (*le tout autre*). With Schopenhauer,

[65] Here I will restrict my comments to *Généalogie de la psychanalyse* and *Phénoménologie materielle* (1990).

[66] *Généalogie de la psychanalyse*, p. 8ff

[67] *Généalogie de la psychanalyse*, p. 6.

this metaphysics of representation is "brutally" overcome, in that categories pertaining to the body, sexuality, the drive and affect are put in to play, and in such a way that the metaphysics of representation is shown to be incapable of exhibiting the condition of real being and of true existence.[68] Schopenhauer thereby touched upon that which Descartes shied away from, after almost having given it conceptual form – what Henry calls *le Commencement.* Nietzsche also approached this Beginning, as did Freud, were it not for his situating the phenomenological essence of life in the unknowable, where affectivity, as "the revelation of Being and as a consubstantiate moment of life", is obfuscated beyond recognition by being pushed into the unconscious.[69]

But "radical phenomenology" as an ontology where affectivity is the revelation of being itself leads to regarding the representative faculties (the eye, memory, thought etc.) not as pertaining to intentional consciousness, but to "life", i.e. the self-affection of immanent subjectivity which underlies reflexive manifestations of the self. [70] This is also the foundation of Henry's reformulation of Husserlian phenomenology, according to which the self-manifestation of life is more originary than the manifestation of the world. Henry in fact even claims that this sphere of pure immanence without intentionality represents the apex of western philosophy. Henry's speculative (and overtly theological) vitalism which celebrates the immanence of pure self-affection, accordingly denies the role of transcendence and the manifestation of otherness in all forms. Although Henry's position is in one respect similar to that of Husserl, where for instance the longitudinal intentionality (*Längsintentionalität*) of inner time-consciousness fulfils a similar function, there are decisive differences. For in Husserl's case, this form of pre-reflexive self-awareness never operates on its own, but is always intimately connected to an intentionality directed towards the world, that is to say to transcendence.[71]

---

[68] The genealogy which Henry presents has four stations: Descartes (Ch. 1-3), Kant (Ch. 4), Schopenhauer (Ch. 5-6) and Nietzsche (Ch. 7-8), before Freud is approached in the final Ch. 9.

[69] *Généalogie de la psychanalyse*, p. 10; 348, 369f.

[70] *Généalogie de la psychanalyse*, p. 8, 12, 15.

[71] This criticism has been pointed out by many: see for instance Rudolf Bernet, *La vie du sujet. Recherches sur l'interprétation de Husserl dans la phénoménologie* (1994) p. 299, 316, 327; Dan Zahavi, *Self-Awareness and Alterity. A Phenomeno-*

Henry's radical immanentist position is then employed in his interpretation of Freud, who is criticized for not being able to live up to the promise that the unconscious holds for philosophy. This promise is that of liberating philosophy from its reliance upon the mediation of representative structures when attempting to disclose the essence of life, which is the central task of Henry's "material phenomenology".[72] The analysis of pure auto-affection of immanent subjective life will disclose the essential and apriori laws that govern the appearance of phenomenality as such, and it is here that Henry finds the condition of possibility for all "representative" notions such as intentionality, the transcendence of the world etc. It is easy to see the potential importance that the Freudian concepts of endogenous excitation, the drive etc. hold in such a project, just like their Schopenhauerian and Nietzschean predecessors (*die Wille, das Es*).[73] Where Freud goes wrong, according to Henry, is when he postulates *representatives* for the drives (*Triebrepräsentanz*), thereby making immanent life once again dependant upon external, mediating factors.

3.7 Yamaguchi 1982

Ichiro Yamaguchi's study *Passive Synthesis und Intersubjektivität bei Edmund Husserl* is an attempt to display bodily pairing (*Paarung*) as the passive foundation of empathy and thus of intersubjectivity.[74] Yamaguchi employs the analysis of passive synthesis (Hua XI) in order to reach sufficiently fundamental levels of passivity to be able to present the genetic basis of *Paarung* in *Cartesianische Meditationen*. This leads him to a preliminary investigation of the role of the drives as

---

logical Investigation (1999), p. 87ff, 110ff; James Hart, "A Phenomenological Theory and Critique of Culture: A Reading of Michel Henry's *La Barbarie*" (1999) and Christian Lotz, "Husserls Genuss. Über den Zusammenhang von Leib, Affektion, Fühlen und Werthaftigkeit" (2002).

[72] The program of material phenomenology is approached on p. 35ff, 391f; see also *Phénoménologie materielle* (1990).

[73] So for instance he writes in *Phénoménologie natérielle*: "C'est avec profondeur que Freud dit que "le moi reste sans défence contre les excitations pulsionnelles". C'est même cette absence de défense de la vie vis-à-vis de soi qui fait, qui est la pulsion" (1990), p. 175.

[74] Ichiro Yamaguchi, *Passive Synthesis und Intersubjektivität bei Edmund Husserl* (1982).

the genetic origin of intentionality in manuscripts from the 1930's, which is one of the earliest attempts to integrate (rather than just mention) the intentionality of drives with transcendental phenomenology.[75]

Yamaguchi criticizes the position often presented in static phenomenology according to which inner time-consciousness is the most fundamental level of constitution from this vantage point, since it does not take into account the previous constitution of temporality as a passive, intersubjective phenomenon. This points to a *Gleichursprünglichkeit* of time, passivity, affection, perceptual structures, bodily kinaesthesia and originary drives, that taken together form an originary structure of consciousness. Yamaguchi speaks of the essential *Verflochtenheit* of these domains for Husserl, arguing from what he takes to be a "Schichtenstruktur der passiven Synthesis" in several layers (although he notes that this intertwinement is at times blurred by Husserl).[76]

This is the most significant thesis advanced by the book, and it is used by Yamaguchi to display the importance of passivity in the analysis of intersubjectivity. There is however a marked tendency to replace transcendental phenomenological insights with the dialogical position of Waldenfels' social philosophy at critical junctions, which brings with it a refusal to see the deeper problem of intersubjectivity that Husserl is working with. Instead of an analysis of the deeply problematic relation between egology and intersubjectivity, Yamaguchi presents the "in-between" of an I-and-you dialogue as the more convincing solution, but this is to confuse what is grounded with the ground itself.[77] For Husserl's investigations of a passive intersubjectivity which

[75] For earlier works that mention the theory of drives, see Alwin Diemer, *Edmund Husserl. Versuch einer systematischen Darstellung seiner Phänomenologie* (1956), p. 118, 122ff; Klaus Held, *Der lebendige Gegenwart* p. 43, 132f, 142; Holenstein, *Husserls Phänomenologie der Assoziation*, p. 323f; Stephan Strasser, "Grundgedanken der Sozialontologie Edmund Husserls" (1975), p. 3-33; Didier Franck, *Chair et corps. Sur la phénoménologie de Husserl* (1981), p. 153.

[76] See *Passive Synthesis und Intersubjektivität bei Edmund Husserl*, p. 37f, 142. Mishara I think mistakenly argues that Yamaguchi places the intentionality of the drives as the sole foundation for transcendental phenomenology; see his *Phenomenology and the Unconscious. The Problem of the Unconscious in the Phenomenological and Existential Traditions: E. Husserl, V. von Weizsaecker and L. Binswanger* (1989) p. 208, 231.

[77] See in particular *Passive Synthesis und Intersubjektivität bei Edmund Husserl*,

is notably articulated in terms of an intentionality of the drives, is situated at a level that is prior to and makes possible the ontic level of social interaction.

3.8 Lee 1993

Nam-In Lee presented the first, systematic investigation of Husserl's theory of instincts in his book *Edmund Husserls Phänomenologie der Instinkte*.[78] He sets out to reconstruct the role of the drives in the "System" of phenomenology that Husserl projected in the 1920's and the early 1930's but never completed, on the basis of Fink's sketch from 1930.[79] This brings Lee to reconsider the very structure of transcendental phenomenology from the bottom upwards: the phenomenology of instincts becomes the *Urstück* of genetic phenomenology.[80] Lee points out that the systematic working out of a phenomenology of instincts, which Husserl began around 1920, brings about a decisive break with Kant's transcendental philosophy. For Kant, the instinct could only be conceived of as a blind capacity of desire, pertaining exclusively to empirical consciousness, whereas Husserl began to work out an interpretation of instincts as a purely transcendental phenomenon.[81] The true nature of the transcendental problem of instincts is wholly concealed

---

p. 1f, 134ff. In a later text (2005) Yamaguchi criticizes Waldenfels interpretation of Husserl for not taking passivity into account to a sufficient degree, something that could be said of Yamaguchis earlier analysis on the issue of intersubjectivity.

[78] Nam-In Lee, *Edmund Husserls Phänomenologie der Instinkte* (1993). Husserl, unlike Freud, uses *Trieb* and *Instinkt* interchangeably and in order to bring out the important connection that the investigation of this theme opens I will in general speak of "drive". "Instinkt" for Freud does not carry the implications for a phenomenology of consciousness that "Trieb" does (see below, Ch. 6, § 1).

[79] This sketch was first published by Iso Kern in the introduction to Hua XV (p. xxxviiff), and is now published with Husserl's comments in Eugen Fink, *VI. Cartesianische Meditation, Teil 2. Ergänzungsband*, in the first part: "I. Assistenzentwürfe zu Husserls systematischem Werk", section "A. Disposition zu "System der phänomenologischen Philosophie" von Edmund Husserl (13. August 1930). Mit Anmerkungen Edmund Husserls" (p. 3-9). It was given to Husserl in August 1930 by Fink whereafter he began to comment on it with the plan to publish a book that was to have been co-authored by Fink and Husserl.

[80] *Husserls Phänomenologie der Instinkte* p. 58; cf. p. 7, 28, 55, 61, 74, 76, 211, 226, 236, 238, 240, 242.

[81] *Husserls Phänomenologie der Instinkte*, p. 52; cf. p. 3, 221. See also J.G. Hart's critical review (1998).

within static phenomenology, and can only be systematically disclosed by genetic phenomenology.

Lee's work is a goldmine for initiated discussions of the problem of the instincts in Husserl's *Nachlass*. He has made clear that the instincts are a central aspect of transcendental phenomenology and has thereby indicated new, lasting paths for the overall interpretation of phenomenology. But some of the main philosophical conclusions that he presents are problematic, above all concerning the foundational role that is ascribed to the self-preservative instincts, which are also understood in a biological sense. Underpinning this argument is a methodological position according to which genesis gradually takes the upper hand over static phenomenology and finally makes it superfluous: "all results of static phenomenology must finally be dissolved into the doctrine of genetic phenomenology" which means that "the very idea of static phenomenology must be dissolved in Husserl's late philosophy".[82] When this position, which is tantamount to giving up the evidential basis of static phenomenology and thus the basic epistemic role of the cogito, is combined with an interpretation of the originary instincts as the most fundamental level of genetic constitution, Husserlian phenomenology comes very close to a transcendental version of biologism.[83]

3.9 Bernet 1994

Rudolf Bernet's work has been of the greatest importance also in the very formation of the philosophical field that is investigated here. In a series of highly influential articles and books, in part devoted to the

---

[82] *Husserls Phänomenologie der Instinkte*, p. 19f: "Nach der bisherigen Darstellung der Idee einer statischen und einer genetischen Phänomenologie würden sich alle Ergebnisse der statischen Phänomenologie schliesslich in die Lehrgehalte der genetischen Phänomenologie auflösen. [...] Danach soll die genetische Phänomenologie die Vollendung der konstitutiven Phänomenologie darstellen, die statische Phänomenologie dagegen die methodische Vorstufe, welche das Sprungbrett zur genetischen Phänomenologie bilden soll. [...] Die notwendige Konsequenz dieser Betrachtung würde danach lauten: Die statische Phänomenologie kann, da sie bloss die Vorstufe der genetischen Phänomenologie darstellt, keine eigenständige Idee der konstitutiven Phänomenologie darstellen. Dementsprechend müsste sich die Idee einer statischen Phänomenologie in der Spätphilosophie Husserls auflösen".

[83] Lee argues throughout his work that the *Selbsterhaltung* of the monad is the final telos of transcendental phenomenology (*Husserls Phänomenologie der Instinkte*, p. 194, 196f, 199f, 211).

phenomenological clarification of the Freudian unconscious, he has attempted to engage phenomenology and psychoanalysis in the double and reciprocal movement of a critical self-examination of their own fundamental presuppositions, in order to thereby open a path for a renewed phenomenological analysis of subjective life.[84] But although a careful and very subtle reading of Husserl stands at the centre of this undertaking, it is the transformation of phenomenology initiated by Heidegger and his critique of subjectivity that brings the impetus to Bernet's interpretations, in particular as this critique was taken up by Derrida whose presence can be felt in many of his texts.[85] The main ambition of Bernet's work can be said to consist in a reinterpretation of Husserl's concept of subjectivity that attempts to liberate it from the most subsistent simplifications.[86] In doing so, he employs the resources of the very phenomenologists who first raised the critique (Heidegger, Sartre, Levinas, Merleau-Ponty, Derrida, Henry), in order to demonstrate how the seeds of their own positions often stem from a Husserl they thought they had already overcome. Thus the image of Husserl has changed, and it is a finite, vulnerable, communicative, embodied and divided subject that Bernet presents, one that has experienced the hurricanes of structuralism, postmodernism and deconstructivism and come out of it not only alive but also actually reinvigorated.

---

[84] Here I will only mention some of the works which have a direct bearing for the present investigation: "Délire et réalité dans la psychose" (1992); "Inconscient et conscience: sur la nature de la pulsion, du désir, de la représentation et de l'affect" (1995) and the nearly identical "The unconscious between representation and drive" (1996b); "Unconscious Consciousness in Husserl and Freud" (2002) with earlier versions in (1996a) and (1997); "Derrida-Husserl-Freud: the Trace of Transference" (2000); "Pulsion, plaisir et déplaisir. Essai d'une fondation philosophique des concepts psychanalytiques" (2001a); "Désirer connaître par intuition" (2001b); "Zur Phänomenologie von Trieb und Lust bei Husserl" (2006). See also in his books: "Une vie intentionelle sans sujet ni objet?" in *La vie du sujet* (1994a) also in (1994b); and "Le sujet traumatisé" in *Conscience et existence* (2004) with an earlier version in (2000b).

[85] The reading of Derrida (notably *La voix et le phénomène* and "Ousia et grammé") already guides his first public interpretations of Husserl from the 1970's onwards. See for instance "Zur Teleologie der Erkenntnis: Eine Antwort an Rudolf Boehm (1978); "Bedeutung und intentionales Bewußtsein. Husserls Begriff des Bedeutungsphänomen" (1979); "Is the Present ever Present? Phenomenology and the Metaphysics of Presence" (1982); Einleitung (1985); "Husserl's Theory of Signs Revisited" (1989).

[86] See the subtitle to *La vie du sujet*, which is his major work so far: "Recherches sur l'interprétation de Husserl dans la phénoménologie".

The basis for Bernet's interpretation of Husserl is his theory of perceptual knowledge in its cooperation with the theory of signs and language (with a focus on *Logische Untersuchungen* and the works surrounding it), inner time-consciousness (in particular with regards to Hua X and the Bernau-texts) and passive genesis. Although the focus on passivity can be found already from the start, it gradually became more explicit.[87] Despite the insistence on the role of language, it is the in-depth analyses of inner time-consciousness that make up the backbone of his work.[88] In the lengthy introduction to the texts on inner time-consciousness, many important themes that were developed at length elsewhere are discussed in relation to Husserl's most basic themes.[89] According to Bernet, a transcendental phenomenology of consciousness faces the task of showing how the manifestation of the unconscious as something absent to consciousness is possible.[90] Bernet's main point is that Freud's unconscious can be clarified by means of Husserl's

---

[87] Thus in one of his earliest texts one reads with presentiment of what was to come after: "That is, a pure noematic description of the process of fulfilment implies a new determination of the teleologically structured cognitive interest, a determination in which this interest can no longer be understood in terms of an egological accomplishment"; from "Perception as a teleological process of cognition" (1979), p. 127. In the 1994 text "Finitude et téléologie de la perception" one finds the corresponding, more explicit passage where the Freudian problematics has moved right into the centre: "L'intérêt de connaissance qui anime le sujet percevant serait donc finalement affaire de forces d'attraction ou même de pulsions anonymes plutôt que l'expression de la volonté d'un ego. Au lieu d'être le résultat d'une action délibérée et d'une construction progressive de la chose, la perception se ferait toute seule au sein d'une vie passive du sujet" (see *La vie du sujet*, p. 135).

[88] Apart from the articles already mentioned on Husserl's theory of language, see the recent *Conscience et existence* (2004), part I Ch. 2 "La vérité des choses dites et la conscience intuitive".

[89] "Einleitung", in E. Husserl, *Texte zur Phänomenologie des inneren Zeitbewusstseins (1893-1917)*, (1985), p. XI-LXVII. See also (1982); "Die ungegenwärtige Gegenwart. Anwesenheit und Abwesenheit in Husserls Analyse des Zeitbewusstseins" (1983); the "Conclusion" to *La vie du sujet*, p. 320ff; and "Unconscious Consciousness in Husserl and Freud" (2002), p. 334ff.

[90] To my knowledge this article, "Unconscious Consciousness in Husserl and Freud" (2002) (and its predecessors in 1996a, 1997) is the one where Bernet most clearly presents the task of a phenomenological clarification of the unconscious, and the methodology required. The title of the German text (1997) clearly suggests that rather than clarification it is actually a question of phenomenological founding: "Husserls Begriff des Phantasiebewußtseins als Fundierung von Freuds Begriff des Unbewußten" (1997). So like a categorial act is founded on a perceptual act, the Freudian unconscious would be founded on Husserlian phantasy, but if "founding" is here understood in the technical sense (6th *Logische Untersuchungen*) this seems perhaps too strong.

analysis of *Vergegenwärtigung*.[91] He claims that understanding the unconscious phenomenologically is impossible without an analysis of this type of inner consciousness.[92] He proceeds by stating that it is Husserl's theory of phantasy alone that "can in fact achieve this apparently impossible task", and adds that the transcendental character of the latter will be sufficiently accounted for by pointing out that phantasy is "grounded" in inner time-consciousness.[93] This became possible only once Husserl had given up his earlier account of phantasy which took consciousness of images (*Bildbewusstsein*) as its model. The new doctrine of phantasy that Bernet employs instead takes memory as its basis, which is interpreted as a positing representification, and phantasy now becomes a non-positing representification.[94] This means that phantasy is a reproductive mode of consciousness which essentially deals with experiences that may, unlike memories, never have occurred. The guiding idea for Husserl here is that phantasy and memory both share the same basic phenomenological characteristic: their distantiated relation to an object that is representified rather than given directly in the flesh.

What I intend to do is to try to give a more concentrated presentation of one particular problem in this field, by developing certain aspects that Bernet mentions but, it seems, has not fully explored in the works considered. Since Bernet aims for the wide project of providing a "phenomenological founding of Freud's concept of the Unconscious in the theory of an originally reproductive consciousness", it seems reasonable to also investigate other aspects of representifying con-

[91] I will translate Husserl's terms *Gegenwärtigung* and *gegenwärtigen* as "presentification" and to "presentify", and accordingly *Vergegenwärtigung* and *vergegenwärtigen* will be translated as "representification" and to "representify". For *Vergegenwärtigung, vergegenwärtigen* Churchill & Ameriks (*Experience and Judgment*) and Carr (*Crisis*) employ "presentification" and "represent", Brough (CW 4) employs "re-presentation", Cairns (CM) uses "non-originary presentations"; though "presentiation" and "representation" are also sometimes used. These alternatives pose great problems when combined with *Vorstellung*, *Repräsentation*, *Gegenwärtigung* etc and their derivatives.

[92] "Unconscious Consciousness in Husserl and Freud", (2002) p. 330; cf. 1996 p. 47.

[93] "Unconscious Consciousness in Husserl and Freud", (2002) p. 329.

[94] This shift in Husserl's theory of phantasy is presented in several articles: apart from 2002 (which contains only minor modifications from 1996 and 1997), see *Conscience et existence*, Ch. 3 and Ch. 4, § 5.

sciousness than phantasy somewhat closer.[95] The emphasis on phantasy in Bernet's analysis means that aspects such as empathy and intersubjectivity are somewhat left out of account. For it is clear already from Freud's most general account of neurosis and hysteria that other people always play a part in their genesis, and thus in the constitution of the unconscious. Further, even though Husserl's analysis of time-consciousness is at the centre of Bernet's account, he does not delve deeper into the question of the temporality of the Freudian unconscious. This means that a central aspect of the relation between the phenomenological concept of consciousness and the Freudian unconscious remains unaccounted for, and if no viable connections can be established here, the whole project risks hanging in midair. Therefore the closer determinations of intersubjectivity and temporality in the context of a clarification of Freud's unconscious are of some concern.

The focus on phantasy is taken a step further in a recent text, where Bernet suggests that reproductive phantasy is the most fundamental form of the experience of alterity.[96] But as long as this suggestion is not investigated in connection with Husserl's analyses of intersubjectivity, and the paradigmatic role of the "double" or "intersubjective reduction", the critique by Levinas and others concerning solipsism threaten to arise once more. In particular, a deeper investigation of Husserl's genetic phenomenology, which analyses the basis of inner time-consciousness in relation to the intentionality of drives, will here find an incipient transcendental account of sexuality that connects with Freud's concept of Eros, thereby indicating the basis of a more comprehensive clarification.

3.9 Depraz 1995

Within a few years in the 1990's, the understanding of the problem of intersubjectivity in Husserl was substantially heightened by means of the publication of four important studies by Georg Römpp, Natalie

[95] "Unconscious Consciousness in Husserl and Freud" (2002), p. 330.

[96] "Nous aurons à préciser la nature de cette altérité qui caractérise le rapport entre le sujet *de* la reproduction imaginaire et le sujet *dans* la reproduction imaginaire et nous aurons à soupeser l'hypothèse selon laquelle la phantasie reproductive représenterai la forme la plus fondamental d'une expérience de l'altérité" (*Conscience et existence*, Ch. 3 p. 113).

Depraz, Dan Zahavi and Daniel Birnbaum.[97] Although earlier works had already approached the issue, these works (together with Yamaguchi) represent some of the first philosophical responses to the publication of the three volumes on intersubjectivity in 1973. Focussing on various aspects in Husserl's late philosophy of intersubjectivity in its relation to the egological starting point of all phenomenology (such as the person, self-alterity, the critique from pragmatism and the openness of the ego respectively), these authors shed new light on the whole field of transcendental phenomenology as it was presented in *Cartesianische Meditationen* above all. One of the most interesting of these works is that of Depraz, whose interpretation of phenomenology as "alterology" also opens up new possibilities for the interpretation of Freudian repression, precisely as something both present and absent-foreign to consciousness. Although she, like Römpp, sets out to reinterpret *Cartesianische Meditationen* from the vantage point of the three volumes on intersubjectivity, her interpretation goes far deeper into the genetic investigation of originary temporisation and spatialisation. I have employed all of these at various stages in working through Husserl's material, in particular Zahavi and Depraz, but as will become apparent in the following it is Depraz' rich analysis that has provided the greatest help.

3.10 Zahavi 1999

In his much acclaimed book *Self-Awareness and Alterity. A Phenomenological Investigation*, Zahavi investigates the relation between intentionality and self-awareness.[98] It is the question of how consciousness is aware of itself that is at stake, and whether our self-manifestation is of a different kind than the manifestation of the world. Already from the outset, this question becomes engaged in a discussion

[97] Georg Römpp, *Husserls Phänomenologie der Intersubjektivität und ihre Bedeutung für eine Theorie intersubjektiver Objektivität und die Konzeption einer phänomenologischer Philosophie* (1992); Natalie Depraz, *Transcendance et incarnation. Le statut de l'intersubjectivité comme altérité à soi chez Husserl* (1995); Dan Zahavi, *Husserl und die transzendentale Intersubjektivität. Eine Antwort auf die sprachpragmatische Kritik* (1996); Daniel Birnbaum, *The Hospitality of Presence: Problems of Otherness in Husserl's Phenomenology* (1998).

[98] Dan Zahavi, *Self-Awareness and Alterity. A Phenomenological Investigation* (1999)

of whether there are unconscious intentional acts, for if it is the case that I am aware of myself in the same fashion as I am aware of things in the world, then this would seem to entail that I am unconscious of myself whenever I am engaged with the world, and vice versa.[99] In order to gain self-awareness I must direct an intentional act back towards my self. As Zahavi discusses the arguments against this reflection theory of self-awareness (presented by the Heidelberg-school and certain analytic philosophers for instance), he also notes that although they are in favour of a prereflective self-awareness as something more basic and presupposed by reflection (which Held also argued), they have never worked out the details.[100] In order to do so, Zahavi turns to Husserl's analyses of inner time-consciousness, the lived body and intersubjectivity which will also provide the resources to address the central question of the book concerning the relation between self-awareness and that which is foreign, be it the world, the other or oneself as other.[101]

The outcome of this investigation is that prereflective self-awareness is shown to be an "immediate, internal, and pervasive feature of our consciousness".[102] It does not address the regional issue of how we manage to become aware of ourselves as distinct from things in the world, but rather the far more fundamental question of "what it means to be conscious" at all. This prereflective self-awareness is a kind of passive self-affection that results not just from some particular type of experience but ultimately from "whatever experience one is undergoing".[103]

As was the case with Bernet and also Depraz, Zahavi reaches his conclusions by means of careful investigations of contemporary phenomenologists and in a similar fashion manages to present a Husserl who has anticipated essential parts of the post-Husserlian discussions (Sartre, Derrida, Levinas). But Zahavi also situates the discussion in the

[99] In fact, Zahavi at one point situates a central part of phenomenology within the unconscious: "The moment phenomenology moves beyond an investigation of object-manifestation and act-intentionality, it enters a realm that has traditionally been called the unconscious" (*Self-Awareness and Alterity*, p. 207).

[100] *Self-Awareness and Alterity*, p. 17ff.

[101] *Self-Awareness and Alterity*, p. 41; cf. p. 195; these themes are developed in Ch. 5-9.

[102] *Self-Awareness and Alterity*, p. 197f.

[103] *Self-Awareness and Alterity*, p. 198.

wider context of contemporary analytic philosophy (Castaneda, Shoemaker, Klawonn) and shows that this dual perspective is beneficial for both sides. Although I differ with him in his analysis of Derrida (and his critique of the latter for allowing a "blind spot" at the core of constituting subjectivity, while Zahavi himself admits that there must be an "unthematic spot" in the same), and also of Freud in the appendix on the unconscious, I draw heavily on his analysis of prereflective self-awareness, and also begin to employ it on Freud's analysis of the unconscious.

3.11 Bégout 2000

Bruce Bégout, *La généalogie de la logique. Husserl, l'antéprédicatif et le catégorial*, has a similar approach compared to Montavont in that his work is essentially a study of the question of passivity in transcendental phenomenology.[104] It is a carefully argued work, both in its over-all structure and detail, examining the role of passivity in logic in Husserl's late published works, based mainly on the lectures on passive synthesis in Hua XI. Unlike Montavont who analyzes the passivity of life, Bégout regards the role of passivity to be strictly confined to the domain of logic and the clarification of predicative thought.

Although the dominating figures in French phenomenology have all been occupied with the question of passivity in Husserl they have, according to Bégout, misunderstood the specific role of passivity. Husserl's concept of passivity has mistakenly been interpreted as forming a countermovement against his classical, rationalist idealism which meant that passivity came to be regarded as an element that could not be assimilated with phenomenology. The central ambition of Bégout's book is therefore to find a way back to the original and proper meaning of the Husserlian conception of passive experience, and

[104] Bruce Bégout, *La généalogie de la logique. Husserl, l'antéprédicatif et le catégorial* (2000). Other works from the "French" Husserl of the late 90's that have been important for my interpretation are: Anne Montavont, who in her book *De la passivité dans la phénoménologie de Husserl* (1999) presents a rich meditation on the concept of transcendental life (*Lebendigkeit*), which came to occupy a central position in Husserl's late philosophy of passivity; and also Emmanuel Housset, who places the notions of the concrete I and the transcendental person at the centre of his work, *La personne et le sujet selon Husserl* (1997).

passivity for Husserl is, according to Bégout, always related to the constitution of logical thought.[105]

One of the greatest achievements of Bégout's work is his careful articulation of the relation between static and genetic phenomenology, which is often presupposed rather than examined in other works. This makes possible one of the best presentations of the relation between pre-predicative, perceptual experience and predicative thought that I have come across.[106] Bégout also offers a brief discussion of Freud and Husserl concerning repression, but since it explicitly relies on Holenstein's account, which I have already argued is insufficient, it does not bring the discussion forward in any substantial way.[107]

3.12 Brudzinska 2006

Finally, I would like to mention a highly promising recent article by Jagna Brudzinska, "Die phänomenologische Erfahrung und die Frage nach dem Unbewussten. Überlegungen im Anschluss an Husserl und Freud".[108] Brudzinska develops the idea presented by Bernet (1997) concerning the foundational role of the consciousness of phantasy for a proper understanding of Freud's unconscious. The article argues that a "phenomenologization" of Freud's concept of the unconscious, and more specifically the notion of "seelische Realität" (which is close to what I in the following have called "psychic reality"), is a necessary requirement in order to secure it from being a speculative hypothesis. But the more ambitious aim of this phenomenologization of the unconscious is to make it possible to include the psychoanalytical investigations within phenomenological reflection. The basis of the attempt is a

[105] *La généalogie de la logique*, p. 8, 11.

[106] See the second part, "L'expérience antéprédicative et la genèse de la logique", p. 233-346.

[107] *La généalogie de la logique*, p. 185ff; see 188n2. Furthermore, in order to get to the heart of Husserl's phenomenology of passivity I would argue that one has to discuss the relations between the different "ways to the transcendental-phenomenological reduction"; Bégout mentions this issue (p. 44f, 247n2) but it is never developed.

[108] Jagda Brudzinska, "Die phänomenologische Erfahrung und die Frage nach dem Unbewussten. Überlegungen im Anschluss an Husserl und Freud" (2006), pp. 54-71. The article is based on an unpublished dissertation: *Assoziation, Imaginäres, Trieb. Phänomenologische Untersuchungen zur Subjektivitätsgenesis bei Husserl und Freud* (Köln, 2005).

strong interpretation of phantasy, which is regarded as of equal constitutive importance as perception, thereby pointing to an "originary bivalence" in the experiential field.[109] This enables a step beyond Bernet's interpretation since phantasy is no longer understood on the basis of the reproductive functions of *Vergegenwärtigung*. The unconscious can instead be understood as the manifestation of "another presencing" (*einer anderen Anwesenheit*), as the "consciousness of an originary otherness".[110]

[109] "Die phänomenologische Erfahrung und die Frage nach dem Unbewussten", p. 58ff.

[110] "Die phänomenologische Erfahrung und die Frage nach dem Unbewussten", p. 62ff.

PART I

Chapter One

REPRESSION AND PERCEPTION: DIFFERING FOUNDATIONS

The physician and the philosopher can only come together if they both recognize that the term "unconscious psychical processes" is the "appropriate and justified expression of a solidly established fact" (Freud)

Um nun in dieser Nacht phänomenologische Lichter aufstrahlen zu lassen, gehen wir von klaren Beispielen aus (Husserl)

1. Introduction

The first Chapter begins with a presentation of the fundamentals of Freud's theory of repression (§ 2) where repression is analyzed in relation to psychic resistance. The repressed, it is shown, strives to break through to consciousness thus making it susceptible for a possible phenomenological retrieval. The resistance which holds the repressed in the unconscious is thereby the source of the peculiar status of being "alien" that Freud ascribes to the repressed.

Next, Husserl's analysis of repression is presented, which takes its starting-point in the perceptual sphere (§ 3). From there it is shown how Husserl employs this model in order to account for the genetic origin of negation, thus expanding the phenomenological analysis of repression from the perceptual sphere to that of judgement. When a given sense content is repressed by another sense content, it is not deleted from consciousness but remains, although it is now in the mode of being other (*Anderssein*) or annulled. As such, it becomes lifeless although it is however still within reach of being brought back to intentional life.

As mentioned previously, a recurring theme in this investigation that will appear here for the first time (§ 4), will be the attempt to show that Freudian repression can be accounted for *directly* from Husserl's texts.

This attempt at a "direct" clarification of repression investigates different texts and manuscripts wherein Husserl himself tentatively approaches psychopathological phenomena related to insanity, the perseverance of forgotten memories and illusions etc. In this section, Husserl's scattered and therefore largely overlooked analyses of psychic illness and abnormality are approached. From Husserl's point of view, these analyses of what are often called "marginal" or "limit" problems are the necessary outcome of the systematic aspect of phenomenology: even that which is in the margin of the "normal" constitution of the world must sooner or later be dealt with. But far from being marginal in the sense of unimportant, it is shown that these analyses shed light on a fundamental aspect: namely the fragility of the constitution of the world. The "direct approach" to the clarification of Freudian repression is then again taken up at the opening of Part II in Chapter Four (§ 2), and then finally in Chapter Five (§§ 5-6).

2. Freudian repression

wo eine neue Erfahrung ist, muss doch auch eine neuartige Wissenschaft erwachsen (Husserl)

The first task here is to present the theme of repression both in its psychoanalytical-experiential context and in the context of Freud's theory. This will mean investigating repression in relation to defence and thereafter also to the unconscious. It is argued that the theory of repression is what enables Freud to criticize psychology for being blind to its own operations. Further, the relation between the repressed and the past is investigated, and the affects are shown to play an important part in bringing repression about. My point of departure in analyzing Freud's theory of repression is, following Ricœur, that it is not a wholesale empirical theory, but one that addresses fundamental questions concerning the conditions of possibility for experience of the world.[1]

[1] On this quasi-transcendental status of the psychoanalytical theory, see Ricœur's important remarks in *Freud and Philosophy* : "In this sense, it [the theory] grounds and at same time limits all the particular concepts appearing in this field. One may, if he so wishes, speak of 'deduction', but in a 'transcendental' and not in a 'formal' sense; deduction is concerned here with what Kant calls the *quaestio juris*; the

In his popular and less theoretical presentations Freud describes repression as comparable to an immediate attempt at flight (*Fluchtversuch*) before a highly distressing situation. It is thereby to be counted as a primary mechanism of defence, and a forerunner to the intellectually more sophisticated response of a condemning judgement.[2] Psychoanalysis can be seen as the long and arduous way towards such judgements, since flight is of little avail when the drive-impulse comes from within.[3] It is the theory of repression that Freud himself highlights as his most important discovery – not the unconscious.[4] But there is no consistent theory of repression in Freud's work, instead several ideas (whose inner relations are not always clear) are presented over time. In some early texts from the 1890's "repression" is used interchangeably with "defence" denoting an active forgetting of either an idea or a feeling which aroused too much distress.[5] In order to be efficient this forgetting must itself be forgotten, so there is a double forgetfulness operative in these cases of mainly hysterical amnesia.[6]

Later on Freud employs "repression" to a far greater extent than "defence", but as the psychoanalytical theory gradually develops it comes to be employed in a wider sense. It refers not only to the unconsciously motivated "forgetting" of something which cannot be endured, but also to several different processes whereby something is kept away from consciousness.[7] Then in *Inhibitions, Symptoms and Anxiety* from 1926, Freud suggests that the term "defence" should be reinstated to

---

concepts of analytic theory are the notions that must be elaborated so that one may order and systematize analytic experience; I will call them the conditions of possibility of a semantics of desire. It is in this sense that they can and should be criticized, perfected, or even rejected, but not as theoretical concepts of an observational science" (p. 375/Fr. p. 366). See further p. 430ff /Fr. p. 418ff.

[2] See for instance *An Autobiographical Study* from 1924, § 3, in PFL 15.

[3] "The Unconscious", PFL 11, p. 187f/SA 3, p. 143.

[4] See *An Autobiographical Study*, PFL 15, p. 213f; and "On the History of the Psychoanalytic Movement" § 1, in PFL 15.

[5] See Breuer and Freud, Preface to the 1st edition of *Studies on Hysteria* in PFL 3, p. 47f.

[6] See "The Neuro-Psychoses of Defence" in SE 3 p. 41-61, and *Studies on Hysteria* in PFL 3.

[7] Peter Madison lists conversion, projection, substitution and isolation amongst these new kinds of repression; see *Freud's Concept of Repression and Defense, Its Theoretical and Observational Language* (1961), p. 18f.

denote the wider term with "repression" as one of its instances.[8] Defence-processes in this wider sense is a "general designation for all the techniques which the ego makes use of in conflicts which may lead to a neurosis", and which more particularly serve the "protection of the I against demands stemming from the drives".[9]

In the following, "repression" will however be employed in the wide sense it is given in for instance the metapsychological papers where it denotes the general effort of pushing something away from consciousness, and its purpose is simply to avoid unpleasure by keeping these now unconscious representations away from consciousness.[10] In these texts, repression is analyzed as being the perhaps most important vicissitude of the drive (*Triebschicksal*).[11]

Furthermore, there is a tension concerning the relation of repression to the unconscious in Freud's texts. In some texts, repression is said to occur only after the distinction between conscious and unconscious has been established, whilst Freud elsewhere states that repression precedes this distinction.[12] However, this inconsistency vanishes once we take

---

[8] See *Inhibitions, Symptoms and Anxiety* , § 11, in PFL 10.

[9] See *Inhibitions, Symptoms and Anxiety* , § 11 p. 324 (tr mod.), in PFL 10. The chief motive for this terminological innovation is the discovery of phenomenological differences in repression: whereas in hysterical repression the experiences were "forgotten and debarred from being reproduced in memory", Freud discovered that in obsessional neurosis the pathogenic experiences which became repressed were not forgotten but "isolated"; see *Inhibitions*, § 11 p. 323 and § 6. Thus the Ratman for instance would isolate the *Vorstellungen* from their emotional contents, thereby making it possible to engage with them as if they caused him no pain; see *Notes upon a Case of Obsessional Neurosis* in PFL 9. We will return to this in Chapter Five (§ 5).

[10] See "Repression", where Freud says that "the essence of repression lies simply in turning something away, and keeping it at a distance, from the conscious" (PFL 11, p. 147). And again in "The Unconscious": "We have learnt from psycho-analysis that the essence of the process of repression lies, not in putting an end to, in annihilating, the idea which represents an instinct, but in preventing it from becoming conscious." (PFL 11, p. 167).

[11] The main *Triebschicksale* that Freud analyzes are: 1) the reversal of a drive into its opposite (*Die Verkehrung ins Gegenteil*), such as when sadism is turned into masochism or scopophilia into exhibitionism; 2) the turning around of the drive against the own person (*Die Wendung gegen die eigene Person*); 3) repression and 4) sublimation (cf. the 1915 essay "Instincts and their Vicissitudes", in PFL 11, p. 123). Only the first two are discussed in that essay, and they are treated together due to their intrinsic closeness. Repression is analyzed separately in the essay entitled "Repression", whereas sublimation is analyzed in for instance the book on Leonardo in PFL 15.

[12] See "Repression", PFL 11, p. 146f; and "A Note on the Unconscious", PFL 11,

the notion of "originary repression" (*Urverdrängung*) into account, which Freud distinguishes from what he calls "repression proper" (*eigentliche Verdrängung* or *Nachdrängung*). The originary repression results in the fixation of a first "representative of the drive" (of which we will speak more in Ch. 6 § 3), which will serve as a first pole of attraction for all secondary, actual instances of repression:

> We have reason to assume that there is a primal repression [*Urverdrängung*], a first phase of repression, which consists in the psychical (representational-) representative of the drive [*der psychischen (Vorstellungs-) Repräsentanz des Triebes*] being denied entrance into the conscious. With this a fixation is established; the representative [*Repräsentanz*] in question persists unaltered from then onwards and the drive remains attached to it ("Repression", PFL 11, p. 147; tr. mod.).

Originary repression is a process which can never be made the object of direct observation, but has to be postulated on the basis of the effects it is supposed to give rise to. The function of originary repression is thus similar to what Husserl calls *Urstiftung*, in that it serves as a first instauration to which later occurrences of repression become attached.[13] Freud is however ambiguous here. On the one hand originary repression is said to occur only once, after which all later instances of actual repression will be drawn in as if to an invisible magnetism. But at other times he speaks of "originary repressions" in plural, suggesting that there can be many such fixations in one and the same psyche.[14] The main point is however clear: it is the repressed which is the key model for Freud when it comes to understanding what the unconscious is:

> Thus we obtain our concept of the unconscious from the theory of repression. The repressed is the prototype of the unconscious for us (*The Ego and the Id*, PFL 10, p. 353)

Combining the two versions we find that originary repression contributes to the opening of an unconscious "space", while that which is

---

p. 55.

[13] In the analysis of the Schreber-case, Freud says that fixation "is the precursor and necessary condition of every 'repression' [*dem Vorläufer und der Bedingung einer jeden 'Verdrängung'*]" (PFL 9, p. 205f/SA 7, p. 190).

[14] "As I have shown elsewhere, most of the repressions with which we have to deal in our therapeutic work are cases of *after*-pressure. They presuppose the operation of earlier, *primal repressions* which exert an attraction on the more recent situation" (*Inhibitions, Symptoms and Anxiety* , PFL 10, p. 245/SA 6, p. 239).

originarily repressed serves as a source of attraction for precisely those representations to which the subject will keep coming back in regression (dreams, neuroses, perversions, psychoses, hysteria etc.). There is accordingly a dual motility operative in repression, both the "repulsion" from the direction of consciousness upon what is to be repressed, but equally important is the "attraction" stemming from the *Urverdrängte* upon everything with which it can establish a connection.[15]

But the barrier of repression not only marks the frontier between the conscious and the unconscious, it also indicates a methodological line of demarcation whereby Freud seeks to distinguish psychoanalysis from other scientific disciplines. Freud speaks of the foundational ambitions of the metapsychology, in particular in relation to the sciences of psychiatry and psychology.[16] When the psychiatrist classifies symptoms in his definitions, he remains, according to Freud, without insight into the origin, the mechanism and the inner relation between these symptoms. How would psychoanalysis claim to found psychiatry? By the leading back (*Zurückführung*) of the symptom to its source, which precedes it in a logical sense.[17] Without this knowledge, psychiatry is blind to the inner meaning of its own operations. Similarly, in the field of psychology there is according to Freud an "evident lack of any common foundation", which is reflected in its inability to explain both dreams and pathological phenomena as consisting in anything else than somatic-physiological malfunctions, devoid of intentionality and meaning.[18] It is above all in order to re-introduce the sphere of meaning

---

[15] "Repression", PFL 11, p. 148.

[16] Two Encyclopaedia Articles, PFL 15, p. 150: "On the contrary, as a depth-psychology, a psychology of those processes in mental life which are withdrawn from consciousness, it is called upon to provide psychiatry with an indispensable groundwork and to free it from its present limitations. *We can foresee that the future will give birth to a scientific psychiatry, to which psychoanalysis has served as an introduction.*"

[17] *Introductory Lectures on Psychoanalysis*, PFL 1, p. 45 (see §§ 1, 16).

[18] "The Question of Lay-Analysis", PFL 15, p. 291ff, 297: "But if you look into the matter more closely you will have to class these great achievements [of psychology] as belonging rather to the physiology of the sense organs. The theory of mental life could not be developed, because it was inhibited by a single essential misunderstanding. [...] There is an evident lack of any common foundation. [...] Psychology had barred its own access to the region of the id [*das Es*] by insisting on a postulate which is plausible enough but untenable: namely, that all mental acts are conscious to

into this domain of so-called marginal problems that Freud appeals to the hypothesis of the unconscious: psychological theories can never reach a unified understanding of subjective life due to the "single essential misunderstanding" that all acts are conscious.[19] Thus he argues from what may at first seem to be an off-hand observation concerning the inability of present day sciences of the psyche to give an account of highly local phenomena (such as neuroses, hysteria, dreams and parapraxes), to the view that these sciences can not achieve a full understanding of subjective life as such, in short, that they are unscientific:

> But it is fair to say that a psychology which cannot explain dreams is also useless for an understanding of normal mental life, that it has no claim to be called a science ("The Question of Lay Analysis", PFL 15, p. 293).

The foundational ambitions of psychoanalysis are never the less restricted: although the unconscious is posited as the most basic hypothesis for the sciences of the soul, psychoanalysis does not claim to provide a complete theory of the psyche. It only sets out to supplement the findings of other already established sciences (such as psychology, psychiatry etc.).[20] The aim is thus to provide a foundation by means of an analysis of the unconscious, and from there to correct the prevalent interpretations notably of abnormal or "pathological" phenomena. But as long as these corrections that psychoanalysis sets out to provide are not integrated with interpretations of normal life, psychoanalysis can have only scant hopes of convincing the world that its status as depth-psychology (*Tiefenpsychologie*) is justified. That which connects the study of the pathological with that of the normal sphere of life is on Freud's view the fact that "normal [thought-]processes and what are described as pathological ones follow the same rules".[21] The prime example of this, as Freud never ceases to remind us, is the dreamprocess for every night the normal and healthy enter the same land as that depicted by the wildest productions of the insane. The aim is to gain

---

us."

[19] *Ibid.* See also the remarkable opening statement of *The Interpretation of Dreams*.

[20] See for instance "The Psychoanalytic Movement", PFL 15, p. 110.

[21] See "The Claims of Psycho-Analysis to Scientific Interest", PFL 15, p. 31.

insight into the essential structures which regulate the constitution of meaning from out of these unconscious processes.[22] For although the dream, as the manifestation of what Freud calls "primary processes", has a meaning, this can only be disclosed by way of its interaction with that conscious, higher level activity which is called "secondary process".

Examining Freud's statements on repression proper, one finds that the general tenor is indeed geared towards visibility and demonstration, despite the fact that we are dealing with this most hidden (and criticized) dimension of subjectivity. So it is really only with cases of repression that totally succeed – which constitute a limit case, the actuality of which we may only surmise from the sheer implausibility that all instances of repression will totally fail – that the notorious problem of the unconscious as an "inaccessible realm of inaccessible entities" can arise at all.[23] The repressed is therefore not absolutely or "radically" inaccessible but only moderately so; and this opens for the possibility of its phenomenological retrieval. Thus it should come as no surprise that the resistance to the treatment does not stem from the unconscious, that is to say the repressed, since there resides in the repressed the constant striving to break through in order to become conscious.[24] This also means that there are constant connections between consciousness and the unconscious also when it comes to repression, since the striving on the part of the repressed must be countered by an even stronger force from consciousness which manages to maintain it in the unconscious:

> The process of repression is not to be regarded as an event which takes place once, the results of which are permanent, as when some living thing has been killed and from that time onward is dead; repression demands a persistent expenditure of force, and if this were to cease the success of the repression would be jeopardized, so that a fresh act of re-

[22] Freud describes the task at hand in the following words: "the [manifest, conscious] dream-content seems like a transcript of the [latent, unconscious] dream-thoughts into another mode of expression, whose characters and syntactic laws [*Fügungsgesetze*] it is our business to discover by comparing the original and the translation" (*The Interpretation of Dreams*, PFL 4, p. 381/SA 2, p. 280).

[23] "Repression", PFL 11, p. 153.

[24] *Beyond the Pleasure Principle*, PFL 11, p. 289.

> pression would be necessary. We may suppose that the repressed exercises a continuous pressure in the direction of the conscious, so that this pressure must be balanced by an unceasing counter-pressure ("Repression", PFL 11, p. 151).[25]

Freud here clearly states the necessary relation – for pushing away is also a form of binding – that consciousness (or the I) upholds with the repressed. So far from propounding mythical constructions of some incommunicable hidden core, Freud is to the best of his abilities performing his version of a phenomenology of extended consciousness.

We must pursue the phenomenon of repression further, and inquire about its relation to time. In his public discourse, Freud often says that his patients live in a repressed past instead of the here and now, that they "suffer from reminiscences" and neglect reality.[26] But if we pay closer attention to Freud's thinking we see that repression is actually governed by a different taxonomy than that of temporal distance between present and past. Instead it is the intra-psychic resistance against presentifying consciousness that matters:

> We may assume that whatever associations, thoughts and memories the patient is unable to communicate to us without internal struggles are in some way connected with the repressed material or are its derivatives ("The Question of Lay Analysis", PFL 15, p. 305).

This means that no particular privilege can be accorded to the distant past when it comes to unravelling the hidden rationality that governs the unconscious in Freud's texts. This resistance is given a concrete form in for instance the negative therapeutical reaction, where the need for

---

[25] See also *Beyond the Pleasure Principle*, PFL 11, p. 289; *The Ego and the Id*, PFL 11, p. 355f; and *Inhibitions, Symptoms and Anxiety* , PFL 10, p. 318ff. In these three passages Freud corrects the idea in "Repression" according to which it is consciousness that exerts the repressing force, and instead finds this in the I. Thus the opposition between the unconscious and consciousness is replaced by that between the repressed and the I. In the case-studies Freud often gives the concrete examples upon which the metapsychological investigations are based, and here it is particularly the various analyses of obsessional neurosis that provide the details. The prime case-study would be the Ratman, *Notes upon a Case of Obsessional Neurosis* . But the fully developed analysis of resistance and anticathexis is only developed in later works; see the "Addenda" to *Inhibitions*..., PFL 10, p. 316ff.

[26] See "Five Lectures on Psychoanalysis", SE 11 p. 16.

illness has taken the upper hand over the desire for recovery.[27] But also in less extreme forms of resistance, it is matters of the heart (feelings, *das Gemüt*) that sets up the distance towards consciousness and keeps the hidden core that governs the visible associative bonds away from daylight.[28] The psychoanalytic "working through" of the resistances that the I opposes to the becoming conscious is an overcoming of repression which may lead to a transformative event. The ethical effects of this were readily acknowledged by Freud, who saw that it implies resuming responsibility over our lives, whereby what was previously experienced as following from an immutable destiny, is now seen to be the result of a particular configuration of life which is closely aligned with our history and tradition as they inform the drives. The lesson of psychoanalysis is that these configurations can be changed.

The repressed should accordingly not be identified with the past, as if the aim of psychoanalysis was the mere reawakening and re-integration of the previously repressed.[29] What the repressed shares with the past is its foremost phenomenological characteristic (its withdrawal from consciousness), but this resemblance covers their differences. Thus the search for a phenomenological model or paradigm for understanding repression gains *some* credibility from the structure of retentional consciousness, but that this is not sufficient should be clear already from the most obvious counter-example: my knowledge of the future

[27] See "The Economic Problem of Masochism"; *Inhibitions, Symptoms and Anxiety* § 5; *New Introductory Lectures* § 32 and *Analysis Terminable and Interminable*, § 6 (where the negative reaction is directly related to the deathdrive).

[28] "We recall the fact that the motive and purpose of repression was nothing else than the avoidance of unpleasure. It follows that the destiny of the *Affektbetrag* belonging to the *Repräsentanz* is far more important than the destiny of the *Vorstellung*, and this fact is decisive for our assessment of the process of repression. If a repression does not succeed in preventing feelings of unpleasure or anxiety from arising, we may say that it has failed, even though it may have achieved its purpose as far as the *Vorstellung* is concerned. Repressions that have failed will of course have more claim on our interest than any that may have been successful; for the latter will for the most part escape our examination" ("Repression", PFL 11, p. 153/ SA 3, p. 114; tr. mod.).

[29] For this reason Ricœur's interpretation of repression seems insufficient: "Mais le facteur décisif de la cure est la réintégration du souvenir traumatique dans le champ de conscience. Là est le cœur de la psychanalyse. [...] Elle guérit par une victoire de la mémoire sur l'inconscient. On ne saurait exagérer l'importance de cette prépétie de la thérapeutique freudienne" (*Le Volontaire et l'involontaire*, p. 360f). The same idea still governs Ricœur's later work *De l'interprétation*: "[c'est] l'unique tâche de devenir-conscient qui définit la finalité même de l'analyse" (p. 474f).

event of my own death, which can surely not be ruled out as a motivating force behind repression.[30]

So far we have dealt with originary and secondary repression, but Freud in the metapsychological papers also discusses a third aspect of repression, namely the return of the repressed.[31] And in fact this is the first aspect that the psychoanalyst encounters, on the basis of which the other two must be reconstructed; this is perhaps also the reason why Freud first elaborated this part before proceeding with the other. The return of the repressed is the symptom, the paralyzed leg although no discernible physical damage is to be found, the illness that finds no plausible cause and therefore no cure.[32] When the first patients came to Freud, who was in those days the last resort, many of them had tried virtually every possible treatment but to no avail. Freud came to regard these bodily symptoms as expressions of a distressed psyche, where repression no longer fulfilled its task of keeping the unbearable away from consciousness. The symptom is therefore the failure of defence, the irruption of the repressed, although it was clear that what "came back" was not the same as that which had once been "repressed". This dynamism whereby for instance an idea or a representation can become disconnected from its affective environment so that the feelings become repressed although the idea remains conscious (but now drained of all its psychic energy), is a key to understanding Freud's theory of repression.[33] That which returns has often undergone far-reaching distortion compared with the

[30] "Fear of death" is a central phenomenon also in applied psychoanalysis, and in his critique of religion Freud sees it as an impetus behind theological beliefs. In phenomenology, Heidegger integrates being-towards-death as an existential together with *Befindlichkeit* in order to account for the central phenomenon of understanding. This dimension of thought is comparatively absent in Husserl's philosophy. As Heidegger says, death is the ultimate certainty, not Descartes' cogito, for the *moribundus* first gives meaning to the *sum* (*Prolegomena zur Geschichte des Zeitbegriffs*, GA 20, p. 438). Cf. SZ, p. 262; GA 27, p. 24.

[31] Although the phenomenon of the return of the repressed occurs already from 1895 onwards (see in particular "The Neuro-Psychoses of Defence" from 1896 in SE 3), and precisely in relation to "innervation", i.e. the formation of hysterical-bodily symptoms, it was only beginning with the Schreber case and then in "Repression" that it became an integrated phase of a three-part theory.

[32] See the case histories in *Studies on Hysteria* by Breuer and Freud, in PFL 3.

[33] See André Green, *The Fabric of Affect in the Psychoanalytic Discourse* (1999), for a thorough investigation of the problem of affect in Freud.

original, and this is why the person has such difficulty in seeing any connection between her suffering and the symptom.

Freud at one place stated that the manifestations of the repressed unconscious can appear to us as an "invasion" or a "sudden intrusion" of alien thoughts, and added that these can be more powerful than those at the command of the I:

> Thoughts emerge suddenly without one's knowing where they come from, nor can one do anything to drive them away. These alien guests even seem to be more powerful than those which are at the ego's command. They resist all the well-proved measures of enforcement used by the will, remain unmoved by logical refutation, and are unaffected by the contradictory assertions of reality. Or else impulses appear which seem like those of a stranger, so that the ego disowns them; yet it has to fear them and take precautions against them. The ego says to itself: 'This is an illness, a foreign invasion.' It increases its vigilance, but cannot understand why it feels so strangely paralysed ("A difficulty in the path of psychoanalysis", SE 17, p. 141f).

Husserl's genetic analyses of consciousness provides rich, structural accounts of the "underground" of active reason, and we must now pose the question of whether these can be employed to explain also this alterity of the repressed? Are there resources in transcendental phenomenology that can negotiate also with these "alien guests"?

3. Repression – phenomenology at the limits

Husserl's analysis of repression, unlike that of Freud, has its source in the perceptual sphere. In the 1904/05 lectures on "Hauptstücke aus der Phänomenologie und Theorie der Erkenntnis" for instance he says that when we focus on a picture on a piece of paper, "[...] the image-apprehension represses the paper apprehension [*die Bildauffassung verdrängt die Papierauffassung*]".[34] This general characterization of repression whereby one mode of consciousness "represses" another, such as perceptual consciousness being repressed by phantasy-consciousness, or presentifying consciousness (*Gegenwärtigung*) being repressed by re-presentifying (*Vergegenwärtigung*), is then in later texts examined further in relation to perceptual judgments. It is above all the

[34] XXIII, Nr. 1 p. 45/CW 11, p. 49 (tr. mod.)

investigation of the phenomenological origin of negation, which is carried out in the lectures on passive synthesis and *Erfahrung und Urteil*, that is of importance here.[35]

When we see a red ball, our expectations of it being uniformly round and red is interrupted when we find out that its backside is green and dented, thereby turning the perception into a disappointment (*Enttäuschung*).[36] What happens here is not the simple eradication of the empty intention (red and ball shaped) but, Husserl says, a "certain duplication" of sense, since the unexpected new and "otherwise" covers the predelineated sense (*Überdeckung*).[37] It covers it by "crossing it out" (*Durchstreichen*), thereby altering the perceptual sense not only in the moment, since the noematic transformation radiates back in a retroactive crossing out in the whole retentional sequence. The earlier sense content is "reinterpreted" so that we have in memory both the original predelineation and superimposed upon it the transformed intentional structure of fulfilment "green and dented".[38] Even though the previous intentional structure is "voided", it is not – and this is essential for Husserl's theory of repression – gone from consciousness but remains there in the mode of being crossed out:

> For we are still conscious of the previous sense, but as "painted over", and where the corresponding moments are concerned, crossed out. Accordingly, here we are studying what the phenomenon of "otherwise", of "annulment", of nullity, or of negation originally looks like. We recognize as basic and essential that the superimposition of a new sense over a sense that is already constituted takes place through repression, just like correlatively in the noetic direction, there is a formation of a second apprehension, a second apperception that is not juxtaposed to a first one, but lies over it and contends with it. [*Wir erkennen, dass grundwesentlich ein in Verdrängung Sich-überlagern eines neuen Sinnes über einen schon konstituierten statthat, wie korrelativ in noetischen Richtung ein Sich-bilden einer zweiten Auffassung, Apperzeption, die nicht neben einer ersten liegt, sondern über ihr liegt und mit ihr streitet*] (XI, § 7 p. 31/CW 9, p. 69f).

---

[35] XI, §§ 6-7; *Erfahrung und Urteil*, § 21 a.

[36] The basis of this analysis is the 6th of the *Logische Untersuchungen*; see XIX/2, §§ 11-12.

[37] XI, § 7 p. 30/CW 9, p. 69.

[38] XI, § 7 p. 31/CW 9, p. 69.

With this characterization we have already reached the basic determination of phenomenological repression that will be employed to meet the Freudian account. Forcing matters to the extreme, it can be said that the remainder of the investigation will consist in an elaboration of this idea. Already at this point, a common critique from psychoanalytical theorizing can be answered. It is said that the phenomenological understanding of repression is from the outset incapable of addressing psychoanalytical repression, since perception plays no (or only a minor) role in it. Here one must note that what Husserl is doing is not to provide an analysis of perception as such, but an investigation of the structure and process of consciousness. If "repression" is the name of a general process occurring in consciousness (which is the hypothesis here), that is to say in both perceptual situations and those investigated by psychoanalysis, then there should be no immediate problem in starting out from the former. Obviously, there are many steps to go from perceptual consciousness to the complexity of psychoanalytical repression, but by following the further genetic investigations we will attempt to show that repression in a wider sense is indeed a necessary aspect of the structure of the living present (the indirect clarification).

The basic property of repression in this passage by Husserl – that what is repressed remains in consciousness – is also a basic characteristic of Freud's theory, once we move beyond his own minimalist definition of consciousness: in fact, the whole theory of psychoanalysis as a practical-clinical endeavour presupposes it. Further, it must also be shown that Husserl's theory can give a satisfactory account of the fact that what is repressed is not "dead", i.e. unable to interact with the rest of intentional life, which is a view one often encounters even amongst specialists.[39] The basis of such a view is often a misunderstanding of

[39] Thus Talia Welsh, in her recent article "The retentional and the repressed: does Freud's concept of the unconscious threaten Husserlian phenomenology?" (2002), argues that since the retentions are said by Husserl to be "lifeless" they are thereby also "non-intentional" (see p. 170, 172). Therefore, phenomenology on her view is unable to explain the psychoanalytical concept of repression: "In conclusion, the conflict comes down to whether or not Husserlian phenomenology and psychology provides an adequate account of the subject. Following Freudian theory, we find a different level of retentions exists. This level could be called a repressed retentional level. The psyche would be composed of near retentions, such as the protentional-retentional structure, far inactive retentions (the Freudian pre-conscious, Husserlian unconscious), and active repressed retentions. This would not only be of importance

intentionality, for it does not take into account that the retentions that have become sedimented and are "lifeless", "dead", can be described so only by means of an artificial abstraction. Concretely understood, the sedimented sphere always interacts with passive associations, although these, as Husserl notes, often go by unnoticed.[40] This means that they are not really "dead" and further that they cannot be regarded as "non-intentional", as for instance Talia Welsh has argued, since they form a necessary part of the very structure of intentional consciousness:

> The constituted object, the identical element, is no longer constitutively vivacious; thus, it is also no longer affectively vivacious, but the sense is still implicitly there in a "dead" shape; it is only without streaming life. [...] How it can become efficacious and even constitutively efficacious in a new shape is the problem of association (XI, § 37 p. 177/CW 9, p. 227).

Husserl even suggests that when something is repressed due to a conflict (as between two intuitions that do not cohere), it becomes suppressed beyond intuition but does not thereby loose its vivacity, for the conflict *itself* increases vivacity.[41] In the analysis of association (as

to psychological studies, but also changes the notion of the subject. It is the contention in this paper that the Freudian unconscious poses a true problem to the Husserlian definition of the unconscious and, subsequently, of the subject. Husserl does not provide sufficient grounds to suppose that the unconscious is inactive (non-intentional), and human behavior gives us ample reason to suppose that, beyond passivity, a type of unconscious activity exists" (p. 181).

[40] See XI, § 26 p. 122. Welsh is surely aware of this, but it seems to me that she doesn't develop the force in Husserl's argumentation, since the Freudian unconscious is – from the outset – said to be beyond reach, thus subscribing to (what I call) the radical alterity thesis: "Thus, a study of consciousness qua conscious, or preconscious, would never reveal the psychoanalytic unconscious to us. The Freudian unconscious differs from the Husserlian account, outlined above, as possessing, for the most part, the opposite set of characteristics Husserl ascribes to it. The Freudian unconscious is not open for investigation; rather, it is barred from entering into conscious life and thus from ever being reconciled with the external world"; (2002), p. 176.

[41] XI, Beilage XIX p. 413/CW 9, p. 514f: "(In this case, a special repression takes place, a repression of elements, which were previously in conflict, into the "unconscious", but not into the integrally cohesive sphere of the distant past; by contrast, in the living conflict, repression takes place as a suppression, as a suppression into non-intuitiveness, but not into non-vivacity – on the contrary, the vivacity gets augmented in the conflict, as analogous to other contrasts.)" Cf. Freud, "Repression": "[Psychoanalysis shows us] that the *Triebrepräsentanz* develops with less interference and more profusely if it is withdrawn by repression from conscious influence" (PFL 11, p. 148).

we will see in Chapter 5), it becomes clear that what is sedimented can also become vivacious in the sense that it can be a source of affection – despite the fact that it is unconscious.

Let us proceed with the question of whether transcendental phenomenology can give an account of the intrusion of "foreignness" that according to Freud is an effect of the return of the repressed. At this point one might ask whether we can go even further and, as some interpreters have suggested, in fact regard Husserl's phenomenology of passivity in general as a "phenomenology of alterity"? This was to a certain extent already Levinas' point of view in his 1959 essay, where he says that "The great contribution of Husserlian phenomenology lies in the idea that intentionality, or the relation with alterity, does not congeal in polarizing as a subject-object relationship".[42] After Levinas, Didier Franck has again suggested this: "Si la phénoménologie devait virer en scepticisme, ne serait-ce pas pour avoir respecté, plus et mieux qu'on ne l'a jamais fait sans doute avant elle, l'altérité? Fût-ce au prix de son projet instaurateur même?"[43]

To examine such an interpretation in detail would clearly lead too far given the limited scope of this investigation.[44] But taking a closer look at some of the central topics involved – such as temporality, the lived body and imagination, which develop and explore what can be seen as various modes of self-alterity – will eventually support the more restricted claim that is being presented here. In short, that claim is that the willingness of genetic phenomenology to engage with and elucidate repression both at the level of perceptual consciousness and its deeper genetic foundations in these domains, opens up a space in which Freudian repression can be given a phenomenological clarification.

In the following, the phenomenological account of repression will be based on this perceptual analysis, but it will also be expanded to designate similar processes such as what Husserl at times calls *Ver-*

[42] Levinas, "Intentionality and metaphysics", in *Discovering existence with Husserl* (1998), p. 123f.

[43] Didier Franck, *Chair et corps*. Sur la Phénoménologie de Husserl (1981), p. 148.

[44] For such an attempt, see Nathalie Depraz, *Transcendance et incarnation* (1995): "La phénoménologie est élucidation exemplaire de la question de l'alterité" (p. 40), which is then developed throughout the book.

deckung (covering over, concealment), *Deckung*, *Unterdrückung*, *Hinuterdrückung* (suppression) and even *Hemmung* (inhibition).[45] In part, this is merely a semantic issue (where they are used synonymously), in part this corresponds to a necessary broadening of the concept from the perceptual sphere to a wider sphere of passive intentionality. This elevation of a relatively minor concept such as *Verdrängung* to cover other, related concepts does some violence not only to Husserl's terminology, but it is deemed necessary in order for this investigation to be possible.

4. Direct approach a) The insane person and the anomalous world

There are at least two trajectories in Husserl's thought that point out the theme that I will develop here, one is a methodological trajectory (which should be sufficient in itself), the other a thematic trajectory which gives a certain directed impetus to the former. For if, following the reduction (methodological trajectory), there can indeed be no philosophical problem that falls outside of the scope of phenomenology; and if Husserl – beginning in the 1910's but developed more fully in the 1920's investigations into the "concrete I" (thematic trajectory) – has embarked on investigations of "factical life", then should not this mean that phenomenology somewhere along the line *must* also encounter the problems of psychic "illness", insanity, neurosis etc., precisely as transcendental problems? It is the crossroads of these two trajectories that will be examined in this and the remaining Chapters. At the very least, the investigations that Husserl undertook in this direction should not be regarded as mere rebounds from stray bullets, which has sometimes been the case. If the hypothesis is correct that Husserl only gradually began to realize the full implications of his theory of the reductions, then this might well explain the uncertainty with which he

[45] In *Glas*, Derrida discusses the relation of the "family" as an instance of concrete intersubjectivity to *le Savoir Absolu* as the telos of nature in Hegel, and he argues that Hegelian *Aufhebung* and Freudian *Verdrängung* are intimately connected. He finds virtually the same concepts in Hegel – *Hemmung*, *Unterdrückung*, *zurückdrängen* etc. – as different forms of *Aufhebung* that I have found in Husserl denoting repression; see *Glas* (1974) p. 214. Instead of investigating psychoanalysis in relation to Hegelian dialectics, which has been standard since Kojève, Hippolyte, de Waehlens, Lacan, Althusser and Zizek, the attempt is here to reopen the path through transcendental genetic phenomenology.

approaches abnormality, insanity etc. in the earlier texts. Clearly the gradual discovery of what genetic phenomenology means and can really bring about plays an important part here, too.

In *Erste Philosophie II* from 1923-24, Husserl for instance speaks of the possibility that the harmonious stream of perceptions is transformed into a meaningless maelstrom of sense data, and goes on to ask: "But what does this mean, other than that a human being, and finally all human beings, can become insane?".[46] Instead of really investigating the consequences this thought has for the idea of the constitution of a common world, Husserl immediately ends this line of questioning.[47] The *Cartesianische Meditationen* can also be said to reflect this position, in that abnormality is there said to be first constituted on the basis of a normality which precedes it.[48] At other times however, this reliance upon what is ultimately a static-phenomenological conception of rationality is questioned, in favour of a more flexible, genetic analysis.

The position in *Krisis* for instance suggests a more radical approach and shows that Husserl now more seriously considers the potential effects that insanity may have for the problem of the constitution of the world. For the normality that precedes abnormality cannot do so in an absolute sense, it also has its genesis of meaning, in the unfiltered being of life prior to its distillation into these two categories.[49] I will come back to the analysis presented in *Krisis* repeatedly in the following Chapters, but first I wish to investigate the background more carefully.

---

[46] VIII, § 34 p. 55. In some earlier texts Husserl also discusses the possibility of madness as a dissolution of the world into a *Gewühl* of sense data, which results in the annihilation of all transcendence; see the references in Kern, *Husserl und Kant* (1964), p. 293ff; and Kaiser, *Das Motiv der Hemmung* (1997), p. 144f.

[47] Also in later texts Husserl at times denies the constitutive contributions from the abnormal sphere (animals and the insane are here often grouped together); see for instance XV, Nr. 11 [C 11/1930-31] p. 165f.

[48] I, § 55 p. 154; see also XV, Nr. 2 [ca. 1925-29] p. 34, 37 for similar statements.

[49] Whereas Marbach in *Das Problem des Ich* (1974) means that Husserl only at a late point thematized normality and abnormality (see p. 332), Steinbock in *Home and Beyond* (1995) shows that Husserl had worked out a consistent theory already by 1920 (p. 126ff). Luft in *"Phänomenologie der Phänomenologie"* (2002) argues that "normality" together with "naturalness" and "naïveté" make up the conceptual structure of the "natural attitude"; and the role of normality here is that it represents the methodological endpoint of the theory of the "natural attitude", thereby enabling its *Aufbruch* and the move into the transcendental attitude (p. 57-72).

Already in 1921 Husserl had asked himself: "How much insanity is compatible with the existence of the world?", and he unambiguously states that the givenness of the insane now belongs within this "extremely important sphere of problems".[50] If there is indeed some sort of shift occurring in Husserl's thinking on this matter, then it seems as if it brings with it a far more humble approach to the philosophical problem of the constitution of the world.[51] Insanity is no longer a possibility that is shown to me by way of the other, but is instead something that is always inherent within me, as my possibility.[52] There is now a continuous movement between normality and abnormality (which includes insanity, the problem of the unconscious), since this difference has been integrated with the possibility of modalization of experience (that I doubt what I see, make mistakes etc.), which is something that always already resides within me.[53]

---

[50] XIV, Beilage XIII p. 124; see also XIV, p. 68f on "die ungeheuren Probleme der Theorie der Anomalitäten"; and XV, Nr. 2, Nr. 11.

[51] Steinbock argues that there is a shift to a genetic account of normality in the early 1920's in comparison to earlier accounts; see *Home and Beyond*, p. 130.

[52] XV, Nr. 2 p. 34: "Ich sehe nun auch die Möglichkeit ein, dass ich selbst verrückt würde und in dieser Verrücktheit keine Welt und keinen Anderen hätte, und sehe dafür auch die reale Möglichkeit in meiner faktischen Konstitution ein unter dem Titel möglicher Erkrankung meiner physischen Leiblichkeit in eins mit psychophysisch zugehöriger psychischer Erkrankung, vielleicht bis zu jener vollständigen Verrücktheit, die mir nicht einmal eine einstimmige Welt beliesse. [...] Ebenso sehe ich ein, dass jeder Andere, der noch nicht verrückt ist, hätte verrückt sein können [...]". Although interesting for its attempt to think through the actuality of insanity for the constitution of the world and its consequences, this text is ultimately unsatisfactory, and on two levels. First, the analysis of insanity remains within the confines of a static analysis and does not question the constitution of normality as such, its genesis. Second, this static perspective also means that the analysis of the other remains insufficient, and still belongs within the orbit of the *Cartesianische Meditationen*, in so far as Husserl ascribes apodicticity only to the ego and merely "hypothetical apodicticity" to intersubjectivity (see title to XV, Nr. 3). In the early 1930's things had begun to change, according to Kern's introduction to Hua XV, and such a division would no longer be possible, since the insight into the streaming communalization (*Vergemeinschaftung*) that genetic phenomenology reveals as underlying the ego-alter ego dichotomy, brings with it that the apdocticity of intersubjectivity is no more hypothetical than that of the I. This will be investigated in Chapter Three. For similar attempts to define normality, cf. XV, Nr. 11 p. 156ff.

[53] Kaiser expresses this in the following way: "Der Unterschied von Normalität und Anomalität betrifft nicht etwa nur Vorfindlichkeiten *in der Welt*, sondern die Welterfahrung als solche und damit die Struktur der *Welt selbst*. [...] Ich als Erfahrender bin prinzipiell (auch) jederzeit verrückt. Das Verhältnis Normalität – Anomalität ist nicht eines, das meine Erfahrung von der anderer trennt, sondern das

But, one may ask, is this shift in Husserl's approach – whereby abnormality approaches a transcendental status for the overarching question of the constitution of the world – isolated from the more "central" issues of Husserlian philosophy? Although the theme of modalization of experience is a central problem in earlier works (cf. *Ideen I*, §§ 103ff), the genetic approach seems to bring with it a reorientation that can be expressed in the following way: whereas modality from the static point of view is considered as a deviation of a perception that is normative, the genetic point of view shows that the possibility of modalization comes first, before the constitution of a "perceptual normality", and is always already at the centre of constitutional life. And if we look at the development of logic and semantics in its most concrete, situation bound context (i.e. occasional expressions), there is a shift there too that seems to be correlated to these reflections.

If we compare Husserl's treatment of occasional expressions in the *Logische Untersuchungen* with that of *Formale und transzendentale Logik* in a very general way, the more successful treatment in the latter can be seen as resulting from the inclusion of the sphere of facticity that was previously excluded.[54] When Husserl in the later work for instance argued that retentional and recollective confusion (*Verworrenheit*) have their own modes of evidence, this means that confusion has become a condition of possibility of scientific knowledge.[55]

Normally, the individual's constitution of the world, i.e. the continuous apperception of things in the unitary stream of consciousness, is only

sich *im Inneren je meiner Erfahrung* findet" (*Das Motiv der Hemmung*, p. 134f). Cf. also Steinbock, *Home and Beyond*, p. 126ff for a similar position, in that what is "normal" or "abnormal", hallucinated or doubted etc. for Husserl from the 1920's onwards is interpreted as *modalizations of experience*, and is not prejudged according to an already established norm as being abnormal.

[54] The theme of facticity in Husserl's phenomenology of meaning has been carefully investigated by Karl Weigelt, *The Signified World. The Problem of Occasionality in Husserl's Phenomenology of Meaning* (2008).

[55] XVII, p. 325f. George Heffernan, who has developed this thesis at length in *Bedeutung und Evidenz* (1983), locates the source of this shift in the inclusion of the *Horizontintentionalität* (see p. 81), and comments on the position in *Formale und transzendentale Logik* in the following way: "Husserl ist jetzt so weit davon entfernt, die Vertreibung der Verworrenheit aus der Wissenschaft zu verlangen, dass er zur Kenntnis genommen hat, dass es bestimmte Arten von Verworrenheit gibt, die als Bedingungen der Möglichkeit der Wissenschaft dienen" (p. 124).

interrupted by sleep; but even the discontinuity of sleep is an occurrence that permits of our re-establishing the order of the world and of ourselves, without further ado.[56] But we can, says Husserl, well imagine a subject that is "strongly abnormal, insane (*verrückt*) and finally so that it no longer brings about a world".[57] In between the two extremes that normality and abnormality represent above, we encounter a manifold ways in which abnormality manifests itself, problematizing the ideal situation of normal perception and life. When the normal lived body becomes abnormal, then abnormal appearances come about: the "original normality" is torn apart (*durchbrochen*), and accordingly the world seems to change.[58]

The world that is constituted in normality, is therefore constituted as containing abnormality within it; so that whereas a normal humanity will experience the world as normal, the abnormal will experience the same world as abnormal. This for Husserl means that every subject must undergo abnormal deviations from the normal experience, although these will be identified precisely as being abnormal either by the subject herself at a later stage, or by her co-subjects.[59] To take a common enough example, the deterioration of eye-sight due to illness or age is analyzed by Husserl as representing modifications of that which is properly mine, that is to say of the *Ureigentliche*.[60] But the lived body is not only the organ of normal and abnormal perceptions, it is also the "expression of a psychic life [*Seelenleben*]", and so there are also "'psychic disturbances', deviations in the psychic types of the norm".[61] We naturally encounter the normal and abnormal functions of the lived body in the everyday sphere of the natural attitude, but as follows from the phenomenological reduction (this becomes particularly clear following the psychological way), this duplicity immediately

---

[56] Cf. for instance the following: IV, p. 253; XI, p. 107; IX, p. 178; XIV, p. 45f; XV, p. 152, 154; XXIX, p. 167, 333ff. The most sustained analysis by Husserl that I have seen of the function of sleep in relation to sedimentation and association for the constitution of the world, is a part of the ms. D 14 entitled *Wachheit, Schlaf, Unbewusstes* (before 1930-1934).

[57] XIII, p. 398.

[58] XIV, p. 69, 121.

[59] XV, p. 155.

[60] XV, p. 157.

[61] XIV, p. 69: "[...] 'seelische Störungen', Abweichungen der Seelischen Typen von der Norm".

manifests itself as a transcendental occurrence, which is also endowed with constitutive power:

> To the biophysical normality and anomality there accordingly corresponds a constitutive normality and anomality, namely for the system of constitutive experiences of the world (XIV, Beilage XII [1921] p. 123).

The investigation of the norm in relation to the abnormal thus comes to serve the function of exhibiting a sphere of otherness in that which is already well-known and familiar. Often Husserl will proceed with this by means of briefly addressing the figures of the child, the insane and the animal as examples of a world constitution that remains in part inexplicable to me in terms of content, even though I can know that it occurs. Marginal in that sense, these examples nevertheless play a central role in that they manifest a sphere of incomprehensibility that is necessarily intertwined with every normal understanding of the world and of the other.

It is also noteworthy that when Fink in August, 1930 handed over a sketch for the final, systematic presentation of phenomenology to Husserl (that the latter had projected and worked on in different periods from the 1920's onwards), he there placed abnormality alongside normality as being of equal importance: that which is pregiven is the difference between them.[62] This view is based on a genetic reconsideration of the status of the "norm" which governs the distinction between normality and abnormality in the personal, surrounding world.[63] When

---

[62] Eugen Fink, "Disposition zu 'System der phänomenologischen Philosophie' von Edmund Husserl (13. August 1930). Mit Anmerkungen Edmund Husserls". This important document is based on a manuscript by Husserl that only exists in an incomplete version (F IV 1/11), and was first published by Kern (Hua XV, p. XXXVff) and then in Fink's *VI. Cartesianische Meditation. Teil 2*; see HuDo 2/2, p. 5 (or equally Hua XV, p. XXXVII): "Vorgegebenheit des Unterschieds von Normalität und Anomalität. Alle Welterfahrung bezogen auf die 'Norm' der bewährenden Erfahrung." On the significance of this document, see Kern's introduction to XV, p. XXXVff; Lee (1993) p. 57ff and Ronald Bruzina (1997), p. 76: "What Fink did was to draw up the only comprehensive and detailed plan for Husserl's phenomenology that we in fact have from that final period of Husserl's life [...] we can gain from it some idea of what *in principle* a systematic and comprehensive treatment of phenomenology might look like."

[63] This is the topic of many texts in Hua XV, see for instance Nr. 12-14 with appendices.

reworking this document, Husserl instead of seeing abnormality as a modification of a normality that is in itself prior (as he had done in his static analyses), suggested to Fink that the very distinction is to be brought back to the concept of "modalization". Thus when revising Fink's text, Husserl suggested that the word "Anomalität" be replaced by the more clarifying "Modalisierbarkeit aller Einzelerfahrungen".[64] That all experiences of the world are susceptible to modalization is an expression of the fact that the concordance (*Einstimmigkeit*) of experiential life as such is always imminently threatened by doubt, inhibition – and perhaps even repression. The facticality of this always-being-open for modal alterations that characterizes experience thus points to a common ground, from which the concepts of normality and abnormality eventually emerge and gain their meaning.[65]

Thus "normality" and "abnormality" are seen as each other's modal differences, rather than the former being the condition of possibility of the latter. Husserl here no longer conceives of the norm from which we judge what is normal and abnormal as a mere given, instead it is something that has become open for questioning and reinterpretation. This genetic position is more in conformity with transcendental phenomenology as a discipline that seriously engages with the fundamental instability of subjectivity and of the world, instead of proclaiming their immutability.[66] But this should not cover the fact that genetic analysis always depends on and presupposes the results of static phenomenology, which make up its necessary starting point: what has been brought up here is merely its complementary temporal-factical deepening.[67]

---

[64] HuDo 2/2, p. 5 note 6.

[65] This is succinctly captured by Ulrich Kaiser, *Das Motiv der Hemmung in Husserls Phänomenologie*, p. 134f.

[66] On this, see Bernet, "Husserl's concept of the world" (1990), p. 16: "As far as the crazy or "insane" are concerned (that is, *Irrsinige*, *Wahnsinnige*, *Verrückte*), Husserl does not deal with these at any great length. Nevertheless, these cases, as with all cases of behaviour related to the unconscious, are particularly interesting. My parapraxes surely contribute to the constitution of my life-world (*Lebenswelt*), even if I do not recognize myself in them. The psychotic delirium, the logic of which remains foreign to me, is however of the same material as my rational apperception of the world and thus contributes to a clarification of the meaning of my world. [...] The proper world of rationality is never an established fact. It is precisely this fragility that lends the world its value."

[67] See for instance XVII, Beilage II (undated but originally published together with FtL in Jahrbuch X, 1929), p. 316: "Während die 'statische' Analyse von der

What is the relevance of this analysis of normality and abnormality for our present concerns? The main point is that Husserl indeed addressed the philosophical issues that Freud's investigations of psychic illness can be seen to pose, and in a non-arbitrary way. Although Husserl's analyses here obviously lack the fine detail of Freud's observations, it is also true that they gain something by becoming an integrated part of the intentional analysis of consciousness. The latter provides a framework that is sufficiently wide to accommodate also Freudian investigations into this field.

Concerning the central question of this investigation, the Husserlian analysis of insanity (and all cases of unconsciously motivated behaviour) is of particular interest in that it throws new light on the meaning of the world which we could not have come by from other sources. By showing that the world is the same for the normal and the abnormal, for the sane and the insane (and that this difference will often pass through one and the same subject at different times), the philosophical analysis forces us to accept the constitutional processes of the demented and insane, precisely as co-constitutional. The world of the insane person can remain essentially incomprehensible to us as normal, but it can also be incomprehensible to the insane himself. This deviation from normality means, speaking in constitutive terms, that the insane cannot be regarded as "my equals" (*meines gleichen*), but this difference in no way implies a break or a rupture: they are "modifications of myself".[68]

The insane person cannot be my equal in this respect, since her contribution to the constitution of the world does not match that of the normal, does not correspond to its history of meaning nor to its projected future as I and other participants of intersubjective normality see

Einheit des vermeinten Gegenstandes geleitet ist und so von der unklaren Gegebenheitsweise, ihrer Verweisung als intentionaler Modifikation folgend, gegen das Klare hinstrebt, ist die genetische Intentionalanalyse auf den ganzen konkreten Zusammenhang gerichtet, in dem jedes Bewusstsein und sein intentionaler Gegenstand als solcher jeweils steht. Es kommen dann alsbald in Frage die anderen intentionalen Verweisungen, die zur *Situation* gehören, in der z.B. der die urteilende Aktivität Übende steht, also mit in Frage die immanente *Einheit der Zeitlichkeit* des Lebens, das in ihr seine '*Geschichte*' hat, derart dass dabei jedes einzelne Bewusstseinserlebnis als zeitlich auftretendes seine eigene 'Geschichte', d.i. seine *zeitliche Genesis* hat."

[68] XV, p. 34, 37, 154, 156f, 169.

it. However, my "insane" acts, my practical life as overdetermined by my neuroses and my unconscious motivations, nevertheless play an important part in the constitution of my world, even though it in part distinguishes itself from the common, "normal" world. The constitutional activities of the insane thus instil a world that in its incomprehensibility remains foreign to my world, and precisely by doing so, they show me that the world is not given once and for all, and that the unity through which it presents itself to me rests on an originary alterity whose dynamic I cannot foresee and even less control.

In other words, the contribution that anomalous experience brings with it is to present us with a fundamental indeterminacy of the world, since a part of the meaning of the world remains unknown to us.[69] Anomalous experience will thus also serve to remind us of the originary withdrawal of the world, which has always been a central aspect of its manifestation in Husserl's analyses, from the early perceptual analyses (*Abschattung*, etc.) onwards. This void in my field of understanding can therefore function as the incitement for further investigation, by propelling the "drive of curiosity" so that a tendency to appropriate also these anomalous modes of constitution is awakened.[70]

Let us try to push this analysis one step further, by taking into account Freud's investigation of more severe forms of psychic ill-being, in order to see whether we can negotiate also with this or whether we must give up here. In a short text from 1924, "The Loss of Reality in Neurosis and Psychosis", Freud states that there are two steps involved in psychosis, "of which the first would drag the ego away [...] from reality (*von der Realität losreisst*), while the second would try to make good the damage done [...], by the creation of a new reality (*Schöpfung einer neuen Realität*) which no longer raises the same objections as the old one that has been given up".[71] Psychosis according to Freud expresses a rebellion against the external world that has its basis in instinctual life; there is an incapacity on the part of the I to adapt to the exigencies of reality. This tendency (as well as the tendency involved in neurosis which is to ignore reality) is, according to Freud, to a certain extent to be found also

[69] XV, Nr. 35 [1933] p. 626f.
[70] This will be discussed in greater detail in Ch. 6.
[71] PFL 10, p. 223f.

in normal or "healthy" behaviour, but in psychosis it is pushed all the way to the limit, where "reality is disavowed" (*verleugnet*).

Here Freud picks up an analysis initiated long before (and also developed elsewhere), which already pointed out the essential direction. In the 1894 paper on "The Neuro-Psychoses of Defence" Freud argued that the defence mechanism operating in psychosis has the function of enabling the I to break away from the representation that is experienced as incompatible.[72] But since the latter is "inseparably connected with a piece of reality", the I, insofar as it manages to detach itself from the representation "has detached itself wholly or in part from reality".[73] The first step involved in psychosis is thus characterized as an experience of the loss of the world, upon which follows a creation of a new reality, one that is incompatible with the original reality.[74]

An exemplary clinical confirmation that phenomenological analysis is a workable and also highly fruitful partner in coming to understand the processes involved here can be found in the works of for instance Ludwig Binswanger.[75] Here we must address the philosophical issues that this analysis is based upon. The world that the psychotic creates, although its heterogeneity may seem to border on the absolute, is as Bernet has argued nevertheless not situated beside my world, nor under or above it, since it is made from out of the same stuff.[76] In text nr. 11 in

---

[72] "The Neuro-Psychoses of Defence", SE 3.

[73] "The Neuro-Psychoses of Defence", SE 3, p. 59.

[74] "The Loss of Reality in Neurosis and Psychosis", PFL 10, p. 224.

[75] Initiator of the *Daseinsanalyse*, which from the 1930's onwards has set out to integrate a phenomenological approach with the psychoanalytical, Binswanger attempted to found the psychoanalytical theory on an extended analysis of the concept of *world*, which became "one of the fundamental concepts, even the very methodological guiding thread". In accordance with this, the treatment of schizophrenia and psychosis is conceived of as aiming at leading the subject "from the distorted transitory world in which he lives and dwells, back to the common world". Binswanger is highly interesting since he studied with and knew both Husserl and Freud, just like Alfred Adler did (this strongly suggests that there must have been discussions going on about Husserl with Freud, and vice versa). See Binswanger's collection of essays in *Analyse existentielle et psychanalyse freudienne* (1970) p. 58, 117f. In later works, such as *Schizophrenie* (1957), *Melancholie und Manie. Phänomenologische Studien* (1960), and *Wahn* (1965), Binswanger develops the phenomenological analysis of insanity and psychosis.

[76] See Bernet, "Délire et réalité dans la psychose" (1992), and also *La vie du sujet*: "Le délire psychotique dont la logique me reste étrangère est pourtant taillé dans la même étoffe que mon aperception rationnelle du monde et il est donc susceptible de m'éclairer sur le sens de mon monde. Il faut se résoudre à admettre qu'il y a des

Hua XV, Husserl speaks of a "correction" that must be undertaken in relation to his many previous analyses of the world, since these (as it is put in text nr. 10) precede from an unquestioned underlying idealization of normality.[77] If all those previous analyses of perception and the world that do proceed from such an idealization have nevertheless taught us something, it is to have shown us with almost infinite patience the structure of the intentionality that lies behind the unity and concordance of the experiences of the world. But this could not have been done without constantly investigating that which is non-functioning, the sphere of error, mistake etc., and the analysis of anomality simply takes these investigations in a new direction. In this text, as in so many others where he approaches similar themes, Husserl seems almost to address Freud face-to-face:

> Within the scope of a unitary personality, of a unitary human life, there are personal anomalies. There is an immense prescientific and scientific experiential material from the past and present that testifies to this. But in these, as they are described and passed on from tradition, only an outer and incomprehensible typicality is expressed. Everyday-interpretations and everyday-psychologies that operate from the outside (and also "modern" psychology) provide no scientific understanding, no reconstruction of anomalies of the soul, no possibility of an inner psychology of anomality. For that purpose a phenomenology that is already highly advanced is required (XV, Nr. 11 p. 159f [C 11/1930-31]).

The possibility to reconstruct *psychische Anomalitäten*, the formation of a psychology that would be able to approach these from the inside, without recourse to psycho-physical concepts and outer intuitions, that is to say, a psychology that operates purely on the level of meaning and interpretation (*Auslegung*) of intentionality and its modifications – that is what Husserl is calling for, and what he has been calling for ever

comportements humains dont je ne peux m'approprier le sens bien qu'ils m'apparaissent comme participant à la constitution du monde humain. L'inconscient et le délire constituent un monde impropre que n'est pourtant ni en dessous, ni derrière, ni à côté du monde propre des sujets rationnels. Ce monde impropre n'en devient pas un monde impropre pour autant, mais il apparaît commme un monde troué par l'étrangeté, comme une demeure hantée, comme un sol miné. Le monde propre de la rationalité n'est jamais un fait acquis. C'est sa fragilité qui lui donne son prix" (p. 110f).

[77] XV, Nr. 11 p. 156f; Nr. 10 p. 141 ("Der normale Mensch im Sinn der Definition ist eine Idealiserung des reifen und dabei in einem anderen Sinn (einem erst zu bestimmenden) normalen Menschen").

since his discovery of Dilthey.[78] And this is what Freudian psychoanalysis – more than any other investigation of the psyche – provides. There is no other psychology that can match Husserl's requirements when it comes to performing this task, which is not to say that psychoanalysis fulfils all of these requirements.

What Freud's analysis of psychosis suggests, is that the psychotic breakdown represents the loss of the intersubjectively constituted world, and the replacement of this common world with one that is strongly coloured by individual phantasies, so that the "psychic reality" (which will be analyzed in Chapter Five, § 5 below) of the psychotic subject becomes strictly speaking fully anomalous compared to the common world. But there are at least two formal aspects of this Freudian sketch that never the less clearly suggest a relation to the world, thus again pointing to the need of a previously performed intentional analysis.

First, the psychotic replacement-world is dependent on the structure of the normal world in order to be able to graft itself on to it: it is only possible as a modification of the world as always already pregiven. Second, since the psychotic subject, although absorbed in a world that is for us totally incomprehensible, according to Freud (and also later psychoanalytical thinkers) all the time keeps one eye open to the normal world.[79] The components of the replacement-world must, in their turn, be associatively connected with each other, and also with the aspects of the world that it overrides, which is what makes possible the long and

[78] Although Dilthey, whom Husserl met with in 1905, is repeatedly hailed by the latter as providing the foremost critique of the naturalizing trend in psychology, he is nevertheless criticized for not being able to account for the generalities, i.e. the apriori, that govern conscious life, since his *Geisteswissenschaft* according to Husserl only deals with singular events in the life-history of the person (see IV, p. 172f; IX, §§ 1-2.). Here, as in many places where Dilthey is discussed by Husserl, it is not difficult to see Freud lurking in the background, barely visible behind the back of the professor in Berlin. That is to say, had Husserl engaged more in a direct discussion of Freudian topics, then he most likely would have directed – at the least – the same kind of criticism against Freud that he did against Dilthey. Be that as it may, the criticism that is directed to Dilthey on this issue is also valid for Freud.

[79] In *An Outline of Psychoanalysis*, Freud said that "one learns from patients after their recovery that at the time in some corner of their mind (as they put it) there was a normal person hidden, who, like a detached spectator, watched the hubbub of illness go past him" (PFL 15, p. 437; cf. PFL 10, p. 195). This view is confirmed by W. R. Bion in *Second thoughts* (1967), who argues on the basis of clinical experience of psychosis that the I is never fully detached from the world (see Ch. 5, § 56).

extremely arduous unravelling of the psychotic world (which Freud at first deemed impossible by means of psychoanalysis).[80]

"What could we learn", Husserl goes on to ask in the same text, from such a highly advanced phenomenology of anomality when it comes to the "task of a phenomenological interpretation of the world as something that is pregiven to us as scientists and philosophers, and in particular concerning the world as collective experience for all?" To which he replies with a stunning formulation:

> As a transcendental ego I thus investigate my own *logos*, which is one with that of the world and those that are my others. [...] It is the concrete universal *eidos* of a possible transcendental subjectivity, the mathesis of transcendental subjectivity and its world: concrete transcendental logic (XV, Nr. 11 p. 160 [C 11/1930-31]).

At the end of section III A of *Krisis*, where Husserl is articulating the passage from the ontological to the psychological way in III B, he in § 55 emphasizes the need not only to get to know the life-world as the foundation of all sciences, but above all the need to get to know the single I as the centre of all constitution. This transcendental version of "know thyself" (*gnothi seauton*), which is really the main task that the psychological way will set before itself, now requires that I systematically inquire back from my worldly being to the transcendental I in its concreteness.[81] The epoché at first shows me myself only as a "mute concreteness" (*stumme Konkretion*), and the task is accordingly to bring this mute I to interpretation, and to express what lies within it in systematic intentional analysis.[82] Once a plurality of co-constituting subjects are taken into consideration, we immediately come to see the correlation between the world and transcendental intersubjectivity, which in an objectified form is called humanity. Here Husserl takes up the question, raised in many previous texts but never before in such a systematic methodological context, of who it is that actually partakes in this humanity:

---

[80] For an interpretation that focuses on the creative aspect of the constitution of the psychotic world, see for instance Piera Castoriadis-Aulagnier *La violence de l'interprétation. Du pictogramme à l'énonçé* (1975), in particular Ch. 7, "En guise de conclusion, les trois épreuves que la pensée délirante remodèle".

[81] See for instance the *Londoner Vorträge* in Hua XXXV, p. 330; the end of CM, I § 64 p. 183/Engl. tr. p. 157.

[82] VI, § 55, p. 190f/Engl. p. 186f.

> But then new questions impose themselves in regard to this mankind: are the insane also objectifications of the subjects being discussed in connection with the accomplishment of world-constitution? And what about children, even those who already have a certain amount of world-consciousness? After all, it is only from the mature and normal human beings who bring them up that they first become acquainted with the world in the full sense of the world-for-all, that is, the world of culture. And what about animals? There arise problems of intentional modifications through which we can and must attribute to all these conscious subjects – those that do not cofunction in respect to the world understood in the hitherto accepted (and always fundamental) sense, that is, the world which has truth through "reason" – their manner of transcendentality, precisely as "analogues" of ourselves (VI, § 55, p. 191/Engl. p. 187).[83]

That the insane, children and also animals must be included in the transcendental problem of the constitution of world as a world of truth and reason – for the simple but equally compelling reason that it is also their world – is a consequence that lies inherent already in the foundational idea of the reduction. They do not co-function in the world of truth and reason since they are anomalous to it in different ways, but they are still my analogues, and we are still bound to the same world. But intriguing as the idea is, it nevertheless poses immediate questions: what is it to be insane, and who can say that they aren't somewhere, sometimes? When do we cease to be children and become members of the transcendental community that constitutes the world of truth and reason? And do we really know what is an animal and what is not? The wish to genuinely approach the world of *empeiría* in a philosophical manner is as haunting as it is difficult, and, being to some extent apostles of the *Krisis*, we come back to the question of where to draw the line of critical reason. Husserl's reply is that, strictly speaking, this transcendental problem is one that finally encompasses "all living beings" (*die schliesslich alle Lebewesen umfassen*) in so far as they have – no matter how indirectly under the condition that it is still verifiable – "something like 'life'" (*so etwas wie "Leben"*) within in them.[84] If the problem of the insane is one of intentional modification of normality, then it must be possible to show this from both directions: that there would always be a bond from insanity to the world of nor-

[83] Cf. XV, Nr. 11 p. 168f for a similar statement.
[84] VI, § 55, p. 191/Engl. p. 187f.

mality, no matter how fragile, and that normality in its concrete, non-idealized configuration is always shot through with insanity.

So where does this leave us? If we take Husserl on his word, then it seems that we are already well on our way towards giving a phenomenological clarification of the central problems raised by Freud:

> And finally, concerning the problem of the "unconscious" that is so much discussed today [*das jetzt so viel verhandelte Problem des "Unbewussten"*] – dreamless sleep, loss of consciousness, and whatever else of the same or similar nature may be included under this title – this is in any case a matter of occurrences in the pregiven world, and they naturally fall under the transcendental problem of constitution [*und so fallen sie selbstverständlich unter die transzendentale Problematik der Konstitution*] (VI, § 55 p. 192/Engl. p. 188; tr. mod.).

The level of generality at which Husserl approaches this means that the question of whether he was thinking of Freud here or not becomes irrelevant. Since the problematics pertaining to the insane and the role of the unconscious are confirmed as being a part of the transcendental problem of the constitution of the world, the whole phenomenological machinery of evidence and verification are brought into play, as the sentence immediately following the previous quotation affirms:

> As something existing in the world common to all, there are manners of verifying the being of this sort of thing, its manners of "self-giving", which are quite particular but which originally create the being-meaning for such particularity. Accordingly, within the absolutely universal epoché, and as concerns beings whose meaningfulness is of this particular kind (as well as for beings of any kind of meaningfulness), the appropriate questions concerning their constitution have to be posed. In accord with all this it is clear that there is no conceivable meaningful problem in previous philosophy, and no conceivable problem of being at all, that transcendental phenomenology must not arrive at, during some point of its ways (VI, § 55, p. 192/Engl. p. 188; tr. mod.).

This is an important confirmation of the major hypothesis of this investigation, and in a certain sense the remainder of this work will consist in an attempt to substantiate the claims made in these passages, which as far as I know have not been examined at any length in the debate. Instead of dismissing it as merely an imprecise and sweeping allusion to marginal issues giving relief to a theoretical 'bad conscience' (the problem of the insane, children, animals, sexuality etc.), this section must be interpreted with the rigour that corresponds to its strategic position in *Krisis* as a whole, at the point where the ontological and the psychological ways to the reduction meet. Husserl is here clearly establishing the need to continue investigating the structure and contents of transcendental subjectivity on both an individual and then an intersubjective level, in order to bring to light how these problems manifest themselves in everyday life. This is something that the way through the life-world simply cannot do, and which therefore necessitates a transition to the psychological way, which is opened in the following section (§ 56). At the heart of this is the difficult methodological question of how the "universal epoché" relates to these two ways.[85] This issue will accordingly be taken up again in Chapter Three, § 6.

[85] The universal reduction has been approached in a preliminary way earlier on in *Krisis*, see VI p. 79, 151ff, 159, 184 before it takes on a central role in the penultimate § 71, p. 247ff.

Chapter Two

DEEPENING OF GENETIC PHENOMENOLOGY. THE "WAYS" TO THE REDUCTION

Es möchte mir scheinen, daß ich, der vermeintliche Reaktionär, weit radikaler bin und weit mehr revolutionär als die sich heutzutage in Worten so radikal Gebärdenden.
(Husserl)

1. Introduction

The themes presented in the first chapter already point out the essentials of this investigation. The attempt was to develop fundamental aspects of both Freud's analysis of repression and Husserl's theory of perception, together with an appraisal of what turned out to be an in fact necessary intertwinement of normality and abnormality in transcendental phenomenology. A central task for the remaining chapters will consist in working out how these themes are to be located and understood in relation to Husserl's theory of reduction. This will inevitably also bring many new, connected themes and concepts into play so that methodological requirements and thematic analyses will go hand in hand. The basic idea behind this is that every step in the genetic process has to be accessed by means of its own proper, corresponding methodological configuration.

In this second chapter, some fundamental aspects of the theory of reduction are presented, as it was worked out in connection with the breakthrough into genetic phenomenology (in the following Chapter Three this sketch will be further developed in relation to Husserl's later theory of reductions). In the second section (§ 2), the idea that a phenomenological account of "otherness" is the key to understand what Freud means by repression is presented in blueprint. It attempts to juxtapose two sets of problems – the phenomenological account of the ego – alter ego relation and the psychoanalytical account of the repressed as the presence within us of what is foreign – in order to shed light on the latter. It is shown that the static analysis of the ego-alter ego relation is insufficient here, and that we will have to bring the genetic analysis into play (something that will occupy us in later chapters).

The third section (§ 3) discusses the "double" or intersubjective reduction as it was first presented in *Grundprobleme*, and argues that although this brings about a major opening for Husserl's theory of reductions (that was only developed later on), it founders on the critical issue of temporality. The two problems of the givenness of the other and time will be discussed extensively in later chapters.

Thereafter, a section (§ 4) is devoted to a presentation of the three different "ways" to the reduction that represent the next, crucial step in the theory of reductions. It is argued that although the Cartesian way is given a foundational role throughout Husserl's career, it is clearly insufficient when considered on its own. The core of Husserl's theory of reductions consists in a measured part assigned to all three ways and it is argued that the key to understand the relation between the "ways" is interplay and not solo-performance.

The following section (§ 5) develops this discussion by showing that Husserl directed severe critique (self-critique) towards the Cartesian way which at times seemed to be presented as if it were the only way. We will investigate this self-critique, and also assess the role that is nevertheless given to the Cartesian way as foundational by showing what it needs from the other ways.

In the final section of this chapter (§ 6), a closer look at the psychological way to the reduction is given, as it was presented in lectures from the 1920's. In the following, the nature of this investigation will lead to a certain favouring of this particular way. It is argued that one of the more frequent interpretations of the psychological way leads to a possibly close interaction between everyday life in the natural attitude and the transcendental attitude. This interpretation will be employed on a general level in the investigation in order to establish a kind of isomorphism between psychoanalytical investigations and everyday life. This will in turn enable the possibility of an easy come and go between the experiences of psychoanalysis and these experiences as transcendental "facts".

2. The otherness of the other as a way to understand the possibility of repression

As the investigation proceeds we will eventually be led into the massive root system of Husserl's late, published texts such as *Formale und transzendentale Logik*, *Méditations Cartésiennes* and *Die Krisis*.[1] Amongst all the issues presented therein, it is in particular certain aspects pertaining to the discussion of intersubjectivity that are of interest. This topic has its well known focal point in the 5th *Cartesianische Meditationen*, where it is treated as the relation between my ego and that of the other, that is to say, the problem of how I can come to experience a "foreign" I (*Fremderfahrung*). As is well known, this has been the subject of major controversy and has yielded sharp

[1] Husserl wrote *Formale und transzendentale Logik* in the winter of 1928-29, and it was first published in Husserl's *Jahrbuch*, vol. 10, in July 1929, and then as Hua XVII. The other two works have a more tortuous background. After the so called "Paris lectures" at the Sorbonne in February, 1929, Husserl immediately began to elaborate them into book form. By May he sent the document to his former student Levinas for the French translation (which Levinas undertook together with Gabrielle Peiffer under the supervision of Alexandre Koyré), and the French volume *Méditations Cartésiennes* appeared in 1931 (Paris: Colin). As soon as Husserl had finished this, he set about writing a somewhat revised version for a forthcoming German edition. Work on this continued until the middle of 1930 (see Hua XV, Nr. 1-5), when it was interrupted and then taken up again a year later (see Hua XV, Nr. 13-18); but the German edition was never completed, and the *Cartesianische Meditationen* was first published as Hua I in 1950. Husserl began work on *Krisis* in August 1934, lectured in Vienna in May 1935 (see VI, the third *Abhandlung*), and in Prague in November 1935 which was Husserl's final public lecture (see XXIX, Nr. 10). In January, 1936 Husserl sent the manuscript for "Die Krisis der europäischen Wissenschaften und die transzendentale Phänomenologie. Eine Einleitung in die phänomenologische Philosophie" to be published in Liebert's new journal *Philosophia*, where it appeared the same year in vol. 1 (Belgrad, p. 77-176). This corresponds to Part I-II of the work that was published as Hua VI. Husserl regarded Part III, the final and by far the longest part, as unfinished and it never existed in the form of a ready-to-print manuscript (Smid, Einleitung to Hua XXIX). There is also a sketch by Fink indicating that additional Parts IV-V were planned to be included, dealing with a theory of science (notably biology and anthropology as empirical counterparts to transcendental philosophy) and selfresponsibility (VI, Beilage XXIX). So the book we know as *Krisis* is really an unfinished torso of a much larger work that no one has seen.

criticism both from within the phenomenological movement (Sartre, Merleau-Ponty, Levinas) and outside of it.[2] However, this early critique (as signalled in the Introduction, § 3) is now being re-evaluated in works undertaken after the publication of notably the three volumes on Husserl's phenomenology of intersubjectivity (Hua XIII-XV) in 1973. In the following, I have tried to take these developments into account.

One of the main, philosophical points made in *Cartesianische Meditationen*, is to establish the essential and insurmountable difference between the ego and the alter ego. It is therefore in this work that – despite appearances – we find Husserl at his perhaps closest to Levinas, at least the Levinas of before *Autrement qu'être*, for whom the alterity of the other is precisely such that she can never be my symmetrical equal and is characterized by a "height" that I can never attain.[3] That is to say, being a subject (or a person, an I, etc.) for Husserl means to live one's life in an unassailable difference from all other subjects that can never be overcome. For sure, Husserl does not deny (in other texts) that there are limit-experiences (friendship, being in love, the love for a child, sexual intercourse, the being with God), wherein my fundamental solitude (which is not primarily existential but structural) may perhaps even momentarily be experienced as being overcome.

But these limit situations in no way alter the basic situation: that I can only live my life and not that of the other, that I can experience only what is given to me and never that which is given to the other, and so the inaccessibility and elusiveness of the other becomes an adequate manifestation of the otherness of the other.[4] In order to show this fundamental philosophical point, Husserl confronts the question of solipsism from the outset and even isolates a "sphere of ownness"

---

[2] The critique of Husserl for not being able to avoid solipsism despite the attempt to introduce intersubjectivity in the 5th CM has been presented from virtually all directions of commentary, and apart from those just mentioned, also from sociological, hermeneutical and analytical perspectives in the works of for instance Alfred Schütz, Jürgen Habermas and Daniel Bell.

[3] See Levinas, *Totalité et infini. Essai sur l'extériorité* (1990), p. 23, 73ff, 236f.

[4] I, CM, § 50, p. 139/Engl. p. 109: "if what belongs to the other's own essence were directly accessible, it would be merely a moment of my own essence, and ultimately he himself and I myself would be the same." Breathing new life into the analysis of the indicative sign in LU, Husserl often makes this point by saying that the mode of appearance of the other is that of *Indikation*; see IX, Beilage XXVII p. 488; I, *Pariser Vorträge*, p. 35; VIII, p. 180f.

where all the constitutive contributions of the other are disregarded. This move has been the subject of much controversy and has led many to erroneously ascribe the solipsism that Husserl investigates to his own position. A fuller account of the deeper, genetic mode of analysis would no doubt have made it even clearer that the sphere of ownness as pertaining to my ego is only possible on the basis of static phenomenology, thus revealing an intersubjective sphere of ownness at its genetic foundation. However, this deeper level is not really developed in that work, and in order to get a grasp of how alterity is accounted for by Husserl we must approach some other texts.[5]

With this fuller account in hand, we will try to account for Freudian repression as an instance of otherness in our psychic flesh that lives on passively, that is to say beyond the control of the I, while yet playing an active part in our lives. For the two problems that we are left with are not unrelated: the central problem for Husserl's philosophy of intersubjectivity is how to connect the idea of the transcendental field as being constituted by the singular ego cogito, with that of the transcendental field as already from the outset being intersubjectively constituted.[6] Similarly, the problem concerning the presence of the unconscious as the return of the repressed, is (as we have seen) interpreted by Freud himself as the problem of the presence of what is foreign, of a certain

[5] Many commentators have pointed out the fact that the analyses in CM remain almost exclusively at the level of static approach (see also Husserl's own statements to this effect on p. 136, 150), even though the necessity of genetic phenomenology is duly noted at several places (CM, §§ 37f).

[6] The tension that arises between the first four meditations with their egological-apodictical emphasis, and the fifth which instead attempts to proceed from non-apodictic intersubjectivity, led also Kern to the conclusion that CM is a "mistaken and ambiguous" work (XV, Einl., p. xxxiif). This harsh judgement is difficult to reconcile with Husserl's selfinterpretation, for instance when he told Dorion Cairns that the CM must be read as a "mathematical work" (*Conversations with EH*, 1931-08-13, p. 10), and I think there are good reasons to question the view of CM as being a work of failure on these grounds. An important hint as to how to solve the paradoxical character of the inner relation between the meditations is provided by Husserl in his letters (see for instance *Briefe an Roman Ingarden*, p. 82), where he says that the transcendental idealism is only understood *after* the 5th CM. This is the propedeutical method of "Emporleitung" (cf. VIII, p. 313; XVII, p. 340), of gradually bringing the reader to a higher level that Husserl practiced already in the *Logische Untersuchungen*, as I have argued in Nicholas Smith (1996).

non-digested otherness stemming from the other, within my egological life-world. Here is how Freud presents the two issues:

> The assumption of an unconscious is, moreover, a perfectly legitimate one, inasmuch as in postulating it we are not departing a single step from our customary and generally accepted mode of thinking [...] that other people, too, possess a consciousness is an inference which we draw by analogy from their observable utterances and actions, in order to make this behaviour of theirs intelligible to us [...] Psycho-analysis demands nothing more than that we should apply this process of inference to ourselves also [...] If we do this, we must say: all the acts and manifestations which I notice in myself and do not know how to link up with the rest of my mental life must be judged as if they belonged to someone else: they are to be explained by a mental life ascribed to this other person ("The Unconscious", PFL 11 p. 170f).

By thus juxtaposing these two themes, where the former problem admittedly belongs to a more "formal" dimension and the latter more to a dimension of "experience", the aim is to try to make one kind of otherness intelligible by means of another, not to add vagueness to mystery.

3. Elaborating the reduction: the double (intersubjective) reduction and the question of time

It is well known that Husserl attached great importance to the revision of the reduction as it was first presented, since it was there restricted to a single consciousness.[7] By contrast, the reduction in *Grundprobleme* (hereby making it into one of the most important methodological developments in Husserl's thought) showed that it leads to consciousness in plural, thereby overcoming the haunting problem of "transcendental solipsism".[8] Husserl's plan for the publication of the second book

[7] The first public presentation of the phenomenological reduction is in the lectures from 1906-07 in XXIV, § 35d; and then in *Die Idee der Phänomenologie* from 1907 (Hua II) which serves as an introduction to the 1907 lectures on *Ding und Raum* where it is presupposed throughout (see XVI, p. 3ff).

[8] This is how Husserl expresses it in *Formale und transzendentale Logik*: "The chief points for the solution of the problem of intersubjectivity and for the overcoming of transcendental solipsism were already developed in lectures that I gave at Göttingen during the winter semester of 1910-11. But the actual carrying-out required further difficult single investigations, which did not reach their conclusion until much later. A short exposition of the theory itself will be presented soon in my *Cartesianische Meditationen*. I hope that, within the next year, I shall be able to

of *Ideas* was to correct the "Fundamentalbetrachtung" of *Ideen I* on this point, but he never published that book (nor does the material presented in *Ideen II* contain such a correction), and the first book of *Ideen* is therefore by Husserl often referred to as a "torso" (*Bruchstück*).[9] The use that Husserl makes of the phenomenological reduction as a "double reduction" in *Grundprobleme* is extraordinary, and it should not be seen as just another step sideways that enables the phenomenologist to address the regional ontology of the other through empathy.[10] Nor is it an attempt to solve the specific problem of the givenness of the other, for it was only a couple of years later that Husserl began to develop an investigation of *Fremderfahrung*, of the experience of the other.[11]

Instead, the philosophical import of the "double" or "intersubjective reduction" (as it is called when applied to empathic acts) in *Grundprobleme* is mainly of a methodological character. As Kern has suggested, it represents a move that sets the whole enterprise on a new footing: "die ganze Idee der Phänomenologie erscheint in dieser Vorlesung von 1910/11 durch ihre Ausdehnung auf die Intersubjektivität in neuer Gestalt".[12] In lectures and texts from the early 1920's Husserl once more investigates the phenomenological reduction in terms of an "intersubjective reduction", and from there on it remains a fundamental part of the phenomenological methodology in many texts.[13] We will

---

publish the pertinent explicit investigations." (XVII, § 96 p. 243n/Engl. p. 215n). These "schwierige Einzeluntersuchungen" were never published by Husserl, and now make up a central part of Hua XIII-XV. For other discussions of *Grundprobleme*, see for instance XIII, p. 234, 448 and also Beilagen XXVIIf; XIV, Nr 1; VIII, p. 174n2, 433f; V, p. 150n2; *Briefe an Ingarden*, p. 31, 36. As Iso Kern points out in the introduction to Hua XIII (p. XXXIII), Husserl in his *Nachlass* refers to no other lectures as often as to *Grundprobleme*.

[9] See "Nachwort zu meinen *Ideen*" [1930], Hua V p. 150n2. The letter to Hicks, 15th of March, 1930 (*Briefwechsel*, Bd. 6, p. 180f) is clear on this; see also XXXIV, Beilage VII, [1929], p. 123f.

[10] The first presentation of the "double" or intersubjective reduction occurs in preparatory notes to the 1910-11 lectures from October, 1910 (see Hua XIII, Nr. 5 p. 85f). The public presentation is now in XIII, Nr. 6 §§ 34, 39; see also Beilage XXX.

[11] See texts Nr. 8-13 in Hua XIII.

[12] Kern, Hua XIII, p. XXXVI.

[13] It plays a prominent role for instance in the 1922-23 lectures *Einleitung in die Philosophie*

(Hua XXXV, §§ 22, 24), the 1923-24 lectures on *Erste Philosophie* (Hua VIII, §§ 47, 53; Beilage XIX), the lectureseries *Einführung in die Phänomenologie* WS 1926/27 (see Kern's introduction to XIV, p. XXVIIIff). See also Hua XXXIV, Nr. 4

come back this theme in the discussion of the "radicalized reduction" from the C-manuscripts (see Ch. 3, § 3). This extension of the reduction surprisingly did not make its way into Husserl's major published investigation on intersubjectivity, the 5th *Cartesianische Meditationen*, which is something that Kern for instance has pointed out as a major weakness in that work.[14]

There are two notable things that lie behind this extension of the reduction in *Grundprobleme*. The first is that Husserl here investigates the possibility of developing a phenomenology that proceeds without eidetics.[15] The reason for this is that he wants to avoid predetermining "the phenomenological stream of consciousness": if the eidetic reduction is applied without further ado to the material provided by the epoché, then there is always a risk that it will never be known for what it really is.[16] This is of particular importance here since Husserl is not (unlike say in *Ideen I*) immediately engaged in the project of establishing "phenomenology itself as an *eidetic* science, as the theory of the essence of transcendentally purified consciousness".[17] The eidetic reduction, as is well known, is a separate methodological operation that can be applied to the field of pure phenomena that the epoché has provided. The epoché is therefore said by Husserl to be the "first reduction" which makes possible the disclosure of the phenomenologi-

---

§ 4; Hua XIV, Nr. 21; HuMat 8, Nr. 94; Hua XV, Nr. 4f, Nr. 33f and *Krisis*, §§ 71f.

[14] See Kern, XV, p. XXf. In a letter to Ingarden from 1925 Husserl says that the "extension of the phenomenological reduction to intersubjectivity for a long time remained completely unused"; *Briefe an Ingarden*, p. 36.

[15] "'Phenomenology' is here from the outset not regarded as a theory concerned with *essence* but rather the attempt is made to consider whether an experiential phenomenology is possible, which is not a theory concerned with essence" (XIII, p. 111n1/CW 12, p. 1n1); cf. pp. 156n, 162n6.

[16] XIII, p. 177. See Costa, "Transcendental Aesthetic and the Problem of Transcendentality" (1998) p. 13; and Depraz, *Transcendance et incarnation*, p. 199ff.

[17] III, § 60, p. 128/CW 2, p. 137; cf. p. 6/xx; § 75. Cf. Housset, who regards the eidetic reduction as the consummation of Husserl's whole methodology, and sees the epoché as a mere preliminary step to attain the *eide*; see *Husserl et l'énigme du monde* (2000), p. 101ff. But there is no real discrepancy here: the task in *Grundprobleme* (which will be taken up again in many texts, notably in relation to the genetic problem of *Urkonstitution* and the life-world) is independent research into the basic structure of transcendental subjectivity, the results of which will become a part of the foundation of all sciences.

cal field as such, whereas the eidetic reduction is a "secondary" reduction which presupposes the first.[18]

The second noteworthy feature is that Husserl here extends the sphere of givens beyond that which is absolutely given (i.e. given by way of immanent reflection).[19] This step beyond the presentation of the reduction in *Die Idee der Phänomenologie* (1907) means that not only actual but also inactual lived experiences are reduced.[20] The vehicle for this is the second or "double" reduction, which takes place within the already reduced experience.[21] Say that I perform the reduction on a memory I have of seeing Nike of Samothrace at the Louvre for the first time. This will give me the memory as a pure lived experience in the sense that it is present for me not as a worldly happening but as an intentional structure of consciousness in the form of an act with its correlate. Now Husserl argues that it is possible to perform a further reduction on this already reduced structure, which would take the memory as its starting point.

This would primarily enable the disclosure of the horizons surrounding the memory, which were previously unattended to, such as the café at the other end of the hall.[22] These two reductions are not on a par strictly speaking, since the second doesn't lead to the same radical break with the natural attitude that the first epoché brings about: instead, it follows in the traces of the first reduction, drawing on its already

[18] III, § 60, p. 129f/CW 2, p. 138f.

[19] See XIII, Nr. 6 p. 159ff/CW 12, p. 53ff: Ch. 4 "Phenomenology's move beyond the realm of the absolute given".

[20] See XIII, Nr. 6 § 33 p. 176f/CW 12, p. 72 (tr. mod.): "[...] it becomes really evident that phenomenological experience does not depend on isolated *cogitationes* that are presentifications [*Gegenwärtigkeiten*] noticed now, but, rather, phenomenological experience extends over the whole stream of consciousness, as a unique temporal context which, however, in its total breadth and length does not fall under the light of intuition". By way of contrast, cf. II, p. 29f, 45f, 61f. On the basis of the new approach in 1910, Husser in *Ideen I* assigned an intentional status to the consciousness of background and "inactualities" (III/1, § 35 p. 72f; § 84 p. 189).

[21] XIII, Nr. 6 § 34 p. 178.

[22] "That is, just as in recollecting 'afterwards [*"nachträglich"*] we can attend to the remembered object's background, which in the original perception was unnoticed perceptual background, so we can *in* the recollection exercise a phenomenological reduction on the foreground and background, which was not achieved in the original perception and which, therefore, is not a recollection of an earlier reduction" (XIII, Nr. 6 § 34 p. 178/CW 12 p. 74).

achieved position so that it becomes a sort of "reflection *within* the memory".[23] In this sense, the double reduction is best described as a deepening of the epoché that will be of great importance for the coming genetic analyses.

In order to avoid prejudging the sphere to be obtained by means of this double reduction as being limited to the "apodictic", Husserl suggested that we place ourselves from the outset in the natural attitude.[24] There we encounter not only the absolutely given but instead "all individual being".[25] This is how Husserl expresses it:

> But somehow interwoven with it [the absolutely given] are other modes of givenness (always within the phenomenological attitude) whose absolute character is not defensible in the same way (namely as indubitability). In this regard, we will have to expand [*erweitern*] the concept of phenomenological viewing so that it runs parallel to empirical experience; so that it becomes, as it were, phenomenological experience: phenomenological presentification and representification [*phänomenologische Gegenwärtigung und Vergegenwärtigung*] (XIII, Nr. 6 § 23 p. 159/CW 12 p. 53; tr. mod.)

Accordingly, Husserl here includes phenomena such as "retentions, memories, expectations" in a first step before moving on to investigate also acts of empathy as phenomenological givens, in a controlled progression of increased otherness.[26] The reduction as previously outlined only operated thanks to an "artificial limitation", *a künstlichen Einschränkung*, which, he says now, can be overcome only by means of extending the reduction to the other.[27] Thus in chapter 6, entitled "The

[23] XIII, Nr. 6 § 34 p. 178/CW 12, p. 74 (tr. mod.).

[24] See XIII, Nr. 6 p. 111n1/CW 12, p. 1n1; the first chapter "The Natural Attitude and the 'Natural Concept of the World'" and § 34 p. 178/CW 12, p. 73: "Let us take the stream of consciousness as it is [*wie er ist*] , i.e. let us, from within the natural attitude, in which after all we find ourselves, cast a glance at the I-experiences and perform on them and in them the phenomenological reduction".

[25] XIII, Nr. 6 § 32 p. 174/CW 12, p. 70.

[26] See XIII, Nr. 6 § 34 p. 178/CW 12, p. 73; cf. §§ 36ff.

[27] XIII, Nr. 6 § 34, p. 177f/CW 12, p. 73. Françoise Dastur, in her article "Réduction et intersubjectivité", also underlines the intimate relation between these two themes: "la problématique de la réduction et celle de l'intersubjectivité, loin d'être inconciliables, forment au contraire une seule et même problématique" (1989), p. 61. For a different view, however, see John Drummond who in the article "Husserl on the Three Ways to the Performance of the Reduction", *Man and World* (1975), argues that Husserl's inclusion of intersubjectivity is something that can only be had

uncovering of the phenomenological multiplicity of monads" (*Die Gewinnung der phänomenologischen Monadenvielheit*) Husserl applies the idea of a second reduction to acts of empathy.[28] The extraordinary force of the double reduction that is characteristic of the psychological way, therefore comes out most clearly in relation to acts of empathy. For when I direct myself towards another person with the intention of empathically understanding her, the endpoint of that second reduction is not a dead thing, but precisely another I, someone alive with her own motivational systems and intentional powers, who will always respond to my approach and to my being in ways that I can never fully foresee.[29]

It lies within the horizon of my act of empathy directed to another person, that she is also an empathizing consciousness who has the possibility to "live-herself-into-me". As Nathalie Depraz has lucidly pointed out, the double reduction in *Grundprobleme* is thus not merely a reduction *to* intersubjectivity, but the discovery of an intersubjectivity *within myself* in the form of a co-existence of two I's (the one empathising, the other being empathised with).[30] Of course, the experience may fail and end with only my empathic act emptily directed toward the other. But Husserl's point here is that the possibility of this mutual transfer of meaning whereby I empathise with you as empathising with me and vice versa, is what makes up the essence of this type of experience and which distinguishes it from other experiences.

It is a great merit of Husserl's theory of the reductions to have opened itself also for this kind of phenomenon, that has become so important for contemporary thought in the wake of Husserl (Sartre, Schütz, Merleau-Ponty, Levinas and others); especially since many amongst them have regarded Husserl's most well known attempt in the fifth *Cartesianische Meditationen* as being severely flawed. Here the

---

prior to the "completely effected" reduction (p. 60); intersubjectivity is merely regarded as one amongst many "constituted objectivities" (p. 62) which have their source in the transcendental ego. Thus, intersubjectivity cannot be transcendental in any important sense according to Drummond.

[28] XIII, Nr. 6 § 39 p. 188f/CW 12, p. 84f.

[29] See for instance IX, p. 507: "ich erfahre ihn, er erfährt mich und ich erfahre mich auch als den, der erfährt – in verschiedenen subjektiven Modis natürlich, die Personen in verschiedener personaler 'Orientierung'". Cf. also VIII, § 54, p. 185; FtL, XVII, § 96 p. 244f; CM, § 56, p. 158.

[30] Depraz, *Transcendance et incarnation* p. 201ff.

later extension of genetic phenomenology to cover all possible intentional implications is already clearly suggested: not only as concerns that which is beyond my attention in the sense of my horizontal field of consciousness, but also – and this is decisive – the whole sphere of *Vergegenwärtigung* (memory, expectations, phantasy, the other).

However, the investigation of this theme in the *Grundprobleme* (and all the related texts in Hua XIII) breaks off on the difficult question of the temporality involved. For how are we to think of temporality now that we are suddenly confronted with the puzzling notion of not only one subject but two? That is to say, how does it affect the idea of "inner time-consciousness" that it now suddenly has to be considered to be *my* inner time-consciousness, and not that of a subject in general? How are we to distinguish between my temporal stream and that of the other? Does the intersubjective reduction bring about an alteration of what my inner consciousness is, so that its borders are expanded, or does it leave everything as it was before the intersubjective reduction was performed? For given that my temporal stream indeed does admit of a certain division, since it harbours both the empathising I and the I that is empathised with (as I intend her), does this division bring with it that the temporal stream of the other can also be included within my stream, and vice versa that my stream becomes a part of her? These questions suggest that the fundamental issue of the individualization of the stream of consciousness, was something that only became a problem for Husserl after he had discovered the intersubjective reduction.

There is as Husserl puts it "no channel" leading from my stream to that of the other, but never the less there seem to be good grounds for stating that both my consciousness and that of the other belong to the same time.[31] By acknowledging on the one hand the unsurpassable principle of the unity of the I and its stream of consciousness, such that there can be no question of my stream opening up to becoming incorporated into that of another stream of consciousness, and on the other hand the likewise seemingly unsurpassable idea that time is indeed what unites my entire stream of consciousness with that of the other, Husserl

[31] See *Grundprobleme*, XIII, Nr. 6 § 39 p. 189 and the later alterations to the text in Beilage XXVII, as well as Beilagen XXVI and XXX.

was caught in an unsolvable or at least extremely difficult aporia. This is the background to the "antinomy" that according to Iso Kern still dominates Husserl's philosophy of intersubjectivity in for instance the 1929-30 manuscripts on a projected German edition of the *Méditations Cartésiennes*.[32]

4. The interplay of the three ways to the reduction and concrete subjectivity

In order to grasp the foundations of what has somewhat misleadingly been called the "esoteric" side of Husserl's late works, we must take a closer look at the dynamics of perspective that is inaugurated by the different "ways" to the reduction.[33] Now it must be said at the outset that Husserl generally proceeds directly to the subject matter at hand that he is investigating, without specifying by what way the reduction is reached.[34] The texts that discuss the various ways to the reduction are therefore, as we will see, usually texts that deal explicitly with this kind of methodological (or meta-methodological) issue. The basic idea behind the motility of the different ways to the reduction, is that for instance the transcendental experience of the other is not one, homogenous experience but something that not only admits of but moreover demands a multitude of different modes of access.

What the three ways that are most commonly referred to indicate, are thus three different conceptions of intersubjectivity: the Cartesian way is a manifestation of the other as an alter ego, the ontological way manifests the community of the life-world and the psychological way how a prolonged genetic self-reflection reveals an alterity that is shared

[32] See Kern, Einleitung, XV, p. LXIf.

[33] Spiegelberg makes the distinction in Husserl's late philosophy between "exoteric" contents (in the published works), and "esoteric" contents, hidden in manuscripts and mainly devoted to the theme of "originary constitution" and the necessary "reconstruction" of its most passive aspects; see *The Phenomenological Movement*, p. 138. It is inappropriate in so far as "esoteric" suggests a hidden, higher level truth whereas in Husserl's case, all that is contained in the latter is already to be found in the former.

[34] Typical in this respect is the following: "Der Begriff lebendige, urtümliche Gegenwart ist hier schon vorausgesetzt und nicht etwa der Weg aufgewiesen, wie, durch welche Reduktion, lebendige Gegenwart thematisch wird und erschlossen wird" (HuMat 8, Nr. 67 p. 300n2).

by both me and the other. Clearly, the Cartesian way, with its emphasis on the opposition between me and the other captures (more so than the other ways) an essential aspect of the phenomenal appearance of the other, but this is not to say that it must lead to solipsism, dualism or even objectification. The bodily experience of the other, which is at the heart of Husserl's Cartesian account, prevents that by showing how pairing constitutes both me and the other as both external body (*Körper*) and lived body (*Leib*). But as soon static phenomenology with its focus on the correlation between act and object gives way to genetic phenomenology, the abundantly rich, passive ways in which the other is "implicated" within my intentionality come to the fore, both via the ontological and the psychological ways.[35]

What is at stake here is no longer the transcendental examination of the actual encounter with the other, but (in particular through the psychological way) instead how my own self is already impermeated with the alterity of the other. Although Husserl never gave anything like an extended, systematic overview of the different ways, the repeated thematic discussions clearly show that it is an issue of major importance for the understanding of his philosophy at large. For by its initial turn away from the world, the Cartesian way in its hunger for certainty also turns away from the soil of philosophical thought, from the "facticity" or "concreteness" of life, and this is clearly a very difficult position for a philosophy that strives to be nothing less than universal.[36]

But as soon as one takes a closer look, virtually all of Husserl's works – whether published or lectures – reveal an emphasis on one or the other of the three main ways. Even in the seemingly most one-sided texts, such as the Cartesianism of *Ideen I* and the 1907 lectures *Die Idee*

[35] The analysis that emphasizes the interaction between the three ways most clearly that I have found is by Depraz, *Transcendance et incarnation*. It is a central issue in her work, the main point being that the three ways cooperate in order to broaden the perspective from a narrow "subjectivism" connected to the Cartesian way, in order to be able to give an account of alterity as the central problem of phenomenology.

[36] This *hubris* of transcendental phenomenology – which is so problematic because it is actually methodologically well founded – is clearly stated in a letter from Husserl to Dilthey, written on the 5th/6th of July, 1911, in *Husserl. Shorter Works*, p. 207 (this idea is often repeated, cf. CM p. 102f; VI, p. 191f for later statements). See also D 17 in Farber (ed.), *Philosophical Essays in Memory of Edmund Husserl*, p. 324.

der Phänomenologie, there is an interplay with the non-Cartesian ways going on. In this and also following chapters, the analysis will focus on the psychological way to the reduction as a necessary complement to the Cartesian and the ontological ways, since it is this way which – more than the other ways – explores otherness as the middle ground between egology and intersubjectivity.[37] Whereas the ontological way proceeds from the givenness of the world with its objective validity in order to investigate how this is constituted by a manifold of subjects, the Cartesian way investigates the constitutive function of the one, single constituting subject. The full constitution of the world can never be accounted for by the sole means of the Cartesian way, just as the ontological way can never account for the necessary starting point of transcendental idealism: the first person perspective.[38]

[37] There is thus a certain bias in favour of the Cartesian and the psychological ways in this investigation, although a fuller analysis of the constitution of the world would have to correct this by paying closer attention to the ontological way or way through the life-world to the reduction (see for instance the interpretation of the different ways in CM by John Tryssesoone (2006)). The third way to the reduction, which proceeds via the life-world, focusses on the ultimately *unclarified* status of the basic concepts of the positive sciences. Its point of departure is thus not the idea of apodictic knowledge and the reduction to the *ego cogito*, but instead that which precedes all the sciences, i.e. the world as a pre-given fact. By following the pre-given world as the guiding thread, this way has also become known as "the ontological way" to the reductions. The benefits of this way lie wholly in the possibility of relating the world back to the constituting subjectivity, which in its full scope means constituting intersubjectivity (VIII, Beilage XX). Thus the disclosure of the correlation between the world and intersubjectivity forms the end-point of the ontological way. This means that the psychological way in a sense can be seen as the more deep-probing continuation of the ontological way, in that it proceeds deeper into the subjective dimension of this correlation (this can also be seen from the structure of the *Krisis*: in the part A the ontological way is presented, then in part B it is followed by the psychological way). Although the ontological way has obvious merits of its own, that cannot be taken into account here, I believe that the psychological way for Husserl is still ultimately the most important when it comes to investigating originary constitution.

[38] See III, p. 179/CW 2, p. 191. This tension has led recent commentators to posit an unsurpassable rift in Husserl's late philosophy. Thus Sebastian Luft, by downplaying the importance of the psychological way, argues that Husserl was "unable to systematically unify these two strands" and that he has therefore ultimately "failed to combine" the Cartesian and the ontological ways; see "Husserl's Theory of the Phenomenological Reduction" (2004), p. 198, 227.

When Husserl first introduces the "way of psychology" in the lectures on *Erste Philosophie II*, he says that the reason for doing so is that the transcendental subject would otherwise remain "an empty word". Husserl speaks here of the "need" to better get to know the "singular configurations or types of configuration" of "transcendental life".[39] The attempt to fill out an I which according to *Ideen I* was "totally empty" and without any kind of explicable content, led Husserl to a more concrete conception of the I in the years immediately following *Ideen I*.[40] Here we encounter a further theme that is decisive for our investigation (and that will be developed at length in the following): the notion of "concrete subjectivity" or the "concrete I". This notion, which grew out of an unsatisfactoriness of the "pure I", is also part and parcel of the genetic breakthrough and already originates from the 1912-manuscripts for *Ideen II*.[41] But the concrete I came to fruition only with the thematization of the psychological way; in fact, stretching historical truth a bit, one could say that the discovery of the concrete I is what motivated the discovery of the psychological way as the proper methodological means for its disclosure.[42]

Neither substance as in the Cartesian tradition nor a merely formal principle as in the Kantian, Husserl has however not yet come to terms with the problems of how to relate the notion of a pure I as a "source" for intentional life, with my factical I as an embodied and temporally situated I. To this extent, Heidegger's criticism that the Husserl of *Ideen I* remains a prisoner of the traditional distinction between a transcenden-

[39] VIII, p. 126.

[40] In fact, this critique of the Cartesian way was raised by Husserl himself in *Ideen I*: "...ins Schrankenlose können wir Transzendenzen nicht ausschalten, [...] da sonst ein reines Bewusstsein, aber kein Möglichkeit für eine Wissenschaft vom reinen Bewusstsein übrig bliebe" (III/1, p. 126). Raising the issue again, in the lectures on passive synthesis, Husserl formulates the same criticism that later appears in the *Krisis*: "Zunächst sehen wir wesensmässig ein, dass immanent konstituiertes Sein in seiner lebendigen Gegenwart nicht nur selbstgegeben ist als seiend, sondern dass dieses Sein undurchstreichbar ist. Sowie wir den Ansatz machen, es sei nicht, was wir immer können, sehen wir, dass apodiktisch dieser Ansatz sich am Gegebenen aufhebt. Hier ist die unzweifelhafte, unaufhebbare Gültigkeit klar. Aber was nützt sie, da sie nur eine momentane ist?" (XI, § 24 p. 109f; cf. VI, p. 158).

[41] See Sakakibara, "Das Problem des Ich und der Ursprung der genetischen Phänomenologie bei Husserl" (1997).

[42] The psychological way (although it is not mentioned explicitly) and the concrete I are thematized together in for instance Hua XIV, Beilage II-III, XXXI, XLV, Nr. 13, 21; Hua IX, p. 294, 342, 469; Hua XXXIV, Nr. 13-14.

tal and an empirical I is valid. But Husserl was at this time already well on his way to a more genuine comprehension of the factical dimension of the I, although it was not until the phenomenological method had developed into taking the genetic dimension into account, that he would have the proper resources to articulate the relation between the transcendental and the factical I in a satisfactory way. Although the notion of "facticity" is not one of the central concepts of transcendental phenomenology, its repeated appearance in connection with themes such as the analysis of language and truth, temporality, the life-world, the body, intersubjectivity and history, in short, themes related to genetic phenomenology, has warranted its right as a source for separate investigations.[43] Despite appearances, it is also clear that Husserl's preoccupancy with themes that he himself gathered under the heading of a *Faktizität des menschlichen Lebens, das faktische Leben, die faktische Subjektivität*, etc., does not stem from the influence of Heidegger's hermeneutics of facticity.[44]

In the light of the attempts on Husserl's part to disclose the concrete horizon of the pure I, Heidegger's criticism could strictly speaking only be valid of Husserl's position in *Ideen I*.[45] But as long as the underlying

[43] See above all the essays in Ludwig Landgrebe's *Faktizität und Individuation: Studien zu den Grundlagen der Phänomenologie* (1982). See also for instance Karl-Heinz Lembeck, *Gegenstand Geschichte: Geschichtswissenschaftstheorie in Husserls Phänomenologie* (1988); Nathalie Depraz & Dan Zahavi (eds.) *Alterity and Facticity* (1998); and Friederike Kuster, *Wege der Verantwortung. Husserls Phänomenologie als Gang durch die Faktizität* (1996).

[44] Landgrebe mistakenly assumes this to be the case, see *Faktizität und Individuation*, p. 109. For some of Husserl's early positive analyses of "Faktizität" and its role for the development of genetic phenomenology, see XIV, Nr. 14 p. 305f; and the letter to Cassirer from 1925 in *Briefwechsel*, Bd. 2 p. 5. See also Steinbock's introduction to CW IX.

[45] See the famous letter from Heidegger to Husserl, 22nd of October, 1927, printed in Husserl CW 7, p. 138f (in German in Hua IX, p. 601f, also in *Husserl. Briefwechsel*, vol. IV, p. 146ff). This criticism on Heidegger's part, which rightly points out the inadequacy of appealing to the pure I to account for the constitution of the world, was however already prepared long before, for Heidegger (together with Julius Ebbinghaus and Gerda Walther) criticized his conception of the pure I already in June 1919, at one of the regularly held "Saturday-discussions" in Husserl's home. See Husserl's letter to Gerda Walther of the 20th of June, 1919; in HuDo 1 p. 235. Such a criticism can only be advanced by disregarding the in-depth analyses into the concrete I that Husserl had undertaken outside of *Ideen I*, which was the only publication apart from the essay "Philosophie als strenge Wissenschaft" (1911) to appear after *Logische Untersuchungen*. But then again, and as Heidegger himself

unity of the factical I and the pure I has not been brought out, it nevertheless remains true that that which Husserl himself had diagnosed as one of Kant's central problems – namely the radical separation between the empirical and the transcendental I – is not yet fully overcome. No doubt there are important similarities between Kant and Husserl concerning the pure I, and Husserl's conception of it in *Ideen I* is just about as formal and empty as that of Kant. This, however, was not to be Husserl's final word and he therefore concluded that the presentation of the I in *Ideen I* was only preliminary: "the interrogation of what specifically characterizes the I was not yet broached in the first volume of the *Ideas*".[46]

With the richer and more concrete conception of the pure I that Husserl envisaged, wherein the idea of individualization began to be urgent, a new determination of the I was called for. To this end, Husserl in the 1920's began to speak of "the concrete I" (*das konkrete Ich*), thereby indicating that the pure I, as the accomplisher of all acts, was addressed in its full, authentic situation, rather than in a merely abstract, theoretical sense.[47] The deeper Husserl probed into the concreteness of subjectivity, the more he became convinced that these determinations, won through the analysis of what had seemed purely contingent, were in fact what made the pure I possible in its abstract function as accomplisher of acts.[48] As a result of this, the I became "not empty", but the

---

repeatedly notes, he was not up to date on Husserl's development (see *Prolegomena zur Geschichte des Zeitbegriffs*, GA 20, p. 167); although as Heidegger notes, he was familiar with *Ideen II* already prior to the writing of *Sein und Zeit* (see *Sein und Zeit*, p. 47 n. 1).

[46] V, p. 159.

[47] For important references from the early 1920's to the "concrete I", see Hua XIV appendices II, III, XLV; Hua VII, p. 281f; see also CM §§ 33, 37f, 46f, 56.

[48] See XXVII, p. 176 [1931]: "Jedenfalls klar ist, was wir zu tun haben, um sie in eine Verständlichkeit zu verwandeln und um so zu einer wirklich konkreten und radikal begründeten Welterkenntnis zu kommen. Wir müssen in ein systematisches Studium der konkreten transzendentalen Subjektivität eintreten, und zwar in der Frage, wie sie in sich objektive Welt zu Sinn und Geltung bringt." See also the letter to Misch from November 16, 1930: "For with the 'transcendental reduction' I was won over to my conviction of ultimate and concrete subjectivity in the whole fullness of its being and life, not the mere theoretically accomplishing life in it but universal accomplishing life: absolute subjectivity in its historicity" (*Briefwechsel*, Bd. VI p. 282f; here from Sandmeyer (2009), p. 129).

living centre, a pole of action and affection, and this pole was through and through determined by these as well as by its habitualities.[49]

Much of this is to be found already in *Ideen II* (even though there is no talk of psychological or any other "ways" to the reduction there), and this fact can be taken to imply that Husserl *de facto* employed the psychological way already at that time. However, in one of the appendices, where Husserl begins to revise the theory of habitualities as presented in the main text, he mentions the "way through the *Geisteswissenschaften*" as "the best" point of entry, and states that it is even better than the way from psychology.[50] This points to a fact that is often overlooked, namely that the way through psychology is not at all of a later date compared to the Cartesian way: it was actually Husserl's first "way" into philosophy:

> So it seems that within psychology itself we encounter phenomenology and that eidetic phenomenology has to be inserted into eidetic psychology as a part of it. Doubtlessly, there is an element of truth expressed here (but certainly not the pure truth), and connected with this is the fact that descriptive psychology offers a genuine and natural point of departure for the working out of the idea of phenomenology. This was in fact the way which led me to phenomenology (IV, Beilage IV [1913] p. 313/CW 3, p. 326f).

The psychological way, from its first anticipation in *Grundprobleme* until its final presentation in *Krisis*, examines the critical givenness of alterity in its many forms, first in relation to my past and future self as being in some sense foreign to my present self, then, typically, in

---

[49] See for instance XIV, p. 29, 275f; IX, p. 209; I, p. 100. This is discussed by Bergmann & Hoffmann, (1984) p. 281. Marbach in his book *Das Problem des Ich in der Phänomenologie Husserls* (1972), only approaches Husserl's thoughts on the concrete, factically and historically situated I in a marginal way towards the end. Here Kern's account in *Husserl und Kant* (1964) is actually more promising since Husserl's critique of Kant for neglecting to take passivity and concrete subjectivity into account is one of the main points developed by Kern; see p. 67ff, 107, 160f, 362. For a more recent investigation of this which focusses on the concrete I, see Emmanuel Housset, *Personne et sujet selon Husserl* (1997). With the notion of concrete subjectivity one finds important similarities between Husserl and Levinas: "La philosophie ne tranche pas sur la vie, dans un instant privilégié, mais coïncide avec elle, elle est l'événement essentiel de la vie, mais de la vie concrète, de la vie qui n'enjambe pas ses limites"; *En découvrant l'existance*, p. 97.

[50] IV, p. 314, Beilage IV [1913].

relation to acts of phantasy, after which Husserl ventures the step to other persons as being foreign to me.[51] This movement from my own self-alterity, which has its basis in the temporal structure of consciousness, to the analysis of how a "radicalized", "double" reduction can lead to the discovery of how other subjects come to presence within the transcendental field, is investigated time and again in Husserl's writings.[52] At the heart of these analyses we find two different methodological approaches to time, and ultimately two different modes of manifestation of temporality that correspond, roughly speaking, to static and genetic phenomenology. The basis for these themes is the extension of the transcendental field that the intersubjective reduction opens onto, but the incorporation of this into the general theory of the phenomenological reductions was not something that came easily:

> For myself, as I readily admit, the first knowledge of the phenomenological reduction was a restricted one [...]. For many years I saw no possibility to formulate it as an intersubjective reduction. But finally a way was opened that is of decisive importance for the enabling of a full transcendental phenomenology and – at a higher level – a transcendental philosophy (VIII, p. 174n2 [1923-24]).[53]

The further investigation of the intersubjective reduction as it was developed in texts from the 1930's will be taken up again in Chapter Three.

---

[51] For the so important analogy between the givenness of my own past and the givenness of the other, see XIII Nr. 2, Nr. 6, Nr. 8-13, Nr. 16; XIV, p. 527f; VII, p. 175ff; I, § 52; VI § 54b; XV, p. 96, 192, 416, 447, 487ff, 586ff, 598, 641; and finally see Held (1966), p. 151-156 for an interpretation of this analogy in the C-ms.

[52] For presentations of the double or intersubjective reduction, see XIII, § 39; XXXV, §§ 22ff; VIII, §§ 47, 53b; XXXIV, Nr. 4, § 4; XV, Nr. 5, Nr. 33, p. 587. In *Krisis*, the central movement of the final paragraphs (§§ 69-72) is to present the insufficiency of the "first" reduction of the individual's lived experiences, and to argue for the necessary expansion of this to what he there calls the "universal reduction" which is also a reduction to intersubjectivity. See also Depraz (1995), Ch. 4 "La réduction intersubjective" (p. 198-238).

[53] This reflection was later deleted by Husserl and is replaced in the text of § 53. This revolutionary insight from 1910-11 seems to have been so foreign to Husserl's ordinary conception of the reduction that he simply forgot about it at times. For instance, reflecting on the lectures from the summer semester of 1915, he made the following comment: "Here I have forgotten the whole doctrine of intersubjectivity, in the whole lectureseries. Was it war psychosis?" (quoted in Kern, Hua XIII, Einleitung, p. XLIII; see also *Briefe an Ingarden*, p. 117).

5. The critique of the "Cartesian way" and its retained validity

The self-criticism that Husserl repeatedly raised against the Cartesian way to the reduction is directed at the presentation in *Ideen I*, and consists mainly of two points: that the evidence that we obtain from the cogito is only punctual and instantaneous, and that it leads to solipsism.[54] All later statements from Husserl on this issue go back to the groundbreaking lectures on *Grundprobleme* which, remarkably enough, in this respect comes out as a thorough and carefully argued critique of the Cartesian way even prior to its first major public manifestation in *Ideen I*.[55]

Before we proceed with the discussion of the Cartesian way, let me first digress on its background and the necessity to go beyond a philosophy based on reflection on acts of consciousness. This will also bring up a point that has frozen a lot of the debate concerning Husserl and Freud and that was first brought up by Paul Ricœur. What Husserl had come to discover was that the method of reflection is insufficient in order to disclose the functioning I at its most fundamental level. At this point it becomes clear that even Husserl himself cannot bring about an articulation of concrete life without appealing to what may at first sight seem to be "un-phenomenological" methods, i.e. without stretching a too literal interpretation of the "principle of principles". The principle states that the "originarily giving intuition" is the "source" of all knowledge, and if this source is understood to be the reflection upon the immanent contents of consciousness, as seems to be the case in *Ideen I* (§ 24), then Husserl was indeed led to disavow it. With the discovery of

[54] For Husserl's critique of the Cartesian way, see XIII, p. 181ff, 234f, 449; VIII, p. 84f, 169, 174f, 410f, 433f; XI, p. 109f, 366; I, p. 66f, 69f; VI, p. 157f; XXIX, p. 425f, XXXIV, Nr. 27-29.

[55] In *Grundprobleme* there is a blend of ontological (mostly in Ch. 1-3) and psychological ways that taken together make up a marked non-Cartesian approach. In Ch. 4 the title announces the necessity to "transgress" that which is absolutely given, i.e. to go beyond reflection, and then the idea that lies inherent in the non-eidetic phenomenology is developed: that the whole domain of the natural attitude can be turned into phenomenological givens. Thereafter, Ch. 5 investigates how to gain access to the *whole* stream of consciousness, and that must include also *Vergegenwärtigungen* (the past and the future). Then in Ch. 6, which is the peak of the lecture, the reduction, when performed in a sufficiently radical way, is extended so as to include also the other.

passivity as founding all activity of consciousness, and the need to phenomenologically clarify the essential structures of passive consciousness, which by necessity withdraw from the field of that which is immanently given, the method of reflection upon acts of consciousness is in urgent need of more finely calibrated tools.

That Husserl soon came to see this and took the necessary steps to accommodate the novel findings of passivity into his method went largely unnoticed by many influential critics. So for instance Merleau-Ponty as late as the 1960's, criticized Husserl for remaining within a phenomenology of "acts" of consciousness through which he would never be able to correctly understand and interpret the functioning intentionality of passive life.[56] Although it had been known to Husserl all along that there is a prereflexive self-presence that precedes and founds that which reflection is able to present, its further investigation became a primary object of research only in the 1920's and -30's. For now, the main point is to establish the need for a genetic phenomenology to further investigate such depth-levels of constituting subjectivity, and to show that the method commonly assumed to be the only one operative in transcendental phenomenology – reflection – must be complemented with methods suitable to disclose these hidden sources of rationality. For thereby, the criticism against Freud according to which he neglects displaying an intuitive basis for some of his findings, i.e., what Ricœur calls his *anti-phénoménologie*, can also be disarmed and loses much of its edge.[57]

What Ricœur means by Freud's "anti-phenomenology" is the "reconstruction" of the subject-object relation (the natural starting point of descriptive, empirical psychology in the wake of Brentano), from out of dynamic-topic-economic processes in terms of the basic concept of drives and their "vicissitudes" (*Triebschicksale*). So that instead of consciousness being the Archimedean point, being conscious is one possible outcome amongst many, and one that ultimately depends on unconscious processes.[58] Had Ricœur investigated Husserl's phenomenology further than what is presented in *Cartesianische Meditationen*,

[56] See Merleau-Ponty, *Le visible et l'invisible*, p. 297f.

[57] See Ricœur, *De l'interprétation*, p. 122ff, 126, 137, 412/Engl. p. 117ff, 122, 133, 423.

[58] *De l'interprétation*, II. Analytique, Ch. 3, § 1 (p. 122-137).

he would have found that Husserl was engaged in a similar attempt to reconstruct the subject-object relationship genetically from out of processes of the drives.[59] It is thus not a question of two bad deeds cancelling each other out here, but of coming to accept that other methodological approaches than immanent reflection are simply necessary if we want to understand the deeper lying intricacies of intentional life.[60] Freud found his way to that vineyard seemingly on autopilot (and immediately started to work on its conceptualization and systematization), whereas Husserl laboriously charted the terrain, methodical step by methodical step, starting from the conscious reflection on the cogito. What we can know about ourselves as anonymously functioning subjectivity by means of reflection, is thus always a mediated, later objectivation of processes that occurred before. Husserl's whole account of self-consciousness is based on this dual process of an objectification after the event and a pre-reflective self-awareness that is contemporary with its event.

Let me now come back to Husserl's self-critique of the Cartesian way to the reduction (which will be continued in the following section). The Cartesian way only admits that which is apodictically given ("I am thinking – now!", "I am making a wish – now!", etc.), and Husserl therefore states that the apodictic evidence that the cogito provides can "only be the beginning and not the end".[61] In one of the most harsh statements, where static phenomenology seems almost pitted against genetic (with its emphasis on the I as streaming, etc.) Husserl writes:

> If I repeat the statement ['I am thinking'], I have a new statement that I could only verify by recourse to the remembering that is unfortunately of no use. For this reason I may not speak of my unending stream of life, of my life spanning an endless past and extending into an endless future; I may no longer speak of phenomenological time as an actual form of actual life, etc. Thus, I am arrested, so it seems, at the absulutely sterile "I am": I perceive – now while I perceive, I think, namely, while I think now, I feel, and only while I am feeling, etc. During all of this, I

[59] *De l'interprétation*, III. Dialectique, Ch. 1, § 3 "Approche phénoménologiques du champ psychanalytique" (p. 366-379/Engl. p. 375-390).

[60] On this, see Zahavi, *Self-Awareness and Alterity*.

[61] VIII, p. 169.

> can by reflecting make observations and can make completely useless assertions, none of which have even the slightest tinge of enduring truth; they only gave the barren, fleeting relevance bearing on the fleeting life of the present. Yes, actually barren, for fecundity is precisely something of abiding value and not something merely existing in a moment of growth (XI, Beilage VIII [1922-23] p. 366).

If the evidence of the cogito is "only a beginning", then how should we understand the relation between Husserl's Cartesianism and the transcendental field as opened by the non-Cartesian ways to the reduction? What comes after this beginning? This has been the subject of some controversy amongst the commentators, starting with Husserl's own assistants: Landgrebe in a highly influential article argued that Husserl in his later thinking "abandons" the earlier Cartesianism wholesale.[62] Before that, Boehm had already claimed, somewhat regrettably, that Husserl by the time of *Krisis* no longer made use of the Cartesian way.[63] Both of these standpoints are exaggerated. In all lectures and texts from Husserl's later thinking where alternative ways are presented, the apodictic evidence of the cogito is safeguarded as providing foundational knowledge, even if the "foundationalism" that is at stake here, as James Dodd put it, "has a demand for renewal, or re-founding built into its very structure".[64] The evidence obtained by the Cartesian way is apodictic yet unfertile, and accordingly has to be supplemented by other types of non-apodictic evidence.[65]

So even if Husserl in *Krisis* directs severe criticism against the Cartesian way, and if the insistence on the role of the life-world (in section A of the final part three) and on intersubjectivity (in section B of part three) may seem to propel the analysis in what are fundamentally non-

---

[62] Landgrebe, "Husserls Abschied vom Cartesianismus" (1978).

[63] Boehm, Einleitung, Hua VIII, p. XXXVII. By abandoning the Cartesian way, Boehm correctly notes, Husserl would have forfeited all possibilities to fulfil the project of transcendental phenomenology as a first philosophy. Boehm therefore sees Husserl's prodigious attempt at opening a "second way" to the reduction in *Erste Philosophie II* as leading to the "dissolution" of transcendental phenomenology as such (p. IXLf).

[64] James Dodd, *Crisis and Reflection. An Essay on Husserl's* Crisis of the European Sciences (2004) p. 6.

[65] See Dodd, *Crisis and Reflection* p. 216f. Much the same point is made by Lacan in "La science et la vérité", *Écrits* (1966) p. 858, when he speaks of the knowing implied in the cogito as being "ponctuel et évanouissant".

apodictic directions, there can be no question as to the foundational function of egology:

> Only by starting from the ego and the system of its transcendental functions and accomplishments can we methodically exhibit transcendental intersubjectivity and its transcendental communalization, through which, in the functioning system of ego-poles, the "world for all", and for each subject as world for all, is constituted. Only in this way, in an essential system of forward steps, can we gain an ultimate comprehension of the fact that each transcendental "I" within intersubjectivity (as coconstituting the world in the way indicated) must necessarily be constituted in the world as a human being [...]. At all events, however, we must – for the most profound philosophical reasons, which we cannot go into further, and which are not only methodical in character – do justice to the absolute singularity of the ego and its central position in all constitution (VI, § 54b, p. 189f/Engl. p. 185f).[66]

This passage states clearly that the only way to come to understand intersubjectivity as constitutive, is via an investigation of the singular I.[67] A preliminary key to understand how these two lines of thought interact, is to see the Cartesian egology as an epistemological and the constitutive intersubjectivity as an ontological order.[68] The methodological requirements of a philosophy that operates in a rigorously scientific way, state that my first person perspective must never be abandoned in questions concerning the foundations of knowledge. This enables me to understand how an open intersubjectivity has always

---

[66] See also I, CM § 12, p. 66f; § 13 p. 69f.

[67] This important methodological statement occurs at the very transition in Part III from the section on the way through the life-world (III. A) to that of the psychological way (III. B). That Husserl regarded the investigation into the life-world here as a preliminary step towards the psychological way, which ends the *Krisis*, is further suggested by the title of Part III – "The clarification of the transcendental problem and the related function of psychology" – which thus extends over *both* the ontological and the psychological ways. The Cartesian way here actually functions as a kind of bridge between the two ways, reminding us that we must proceed with a deeper intentional analysis of the function of this egological subjectivity, which calls for section B and the psychological way to the reduction.

[68] This distinction rests on the Aristotelian between what is "first for me" and what is "first by nature" (that has been touched upon previously), common in all scholastic philosophy as that between *ordo cognoscendi* and *ordo essendi*. It entered contemporary philosophy (if not by other means) by Bolzano in the *Wissenschaftslehre*, one of the most important works for Husserl's early philosophy.

already preceded my own constitutive powers, and that ontologically speaking, I necessarily depend on their world-constitutive powers in order to orient myself in this world. But I can only come to know this with the certainty that is required, by an investigation that proceeds from my own, i.e. egological, point of view.

6. The psychological way in Erste Philosophie II

The "second way to the reduction" that is opened in *Erste Philosophie II* picks up on this critique of the Cartesian way, and is based on a different understanding of temporality.[69] Whereas the Cartesian way emphasizes the I as the pole of unity in the Heraclitean flux of lived experiences, this second way instead emphasizes the flow itself. This change of focus (which is based on the Bernau-texts on the individuation of the temporal stream as well as the investigations of the concrete I), enables the bringing to light of the whole series of what is intentionally implicated within a lived experience. That is to say, once the emphasis is on the stream as my stream rather than on the ego-pole, the whole chain of intentional implications and associations become available as temporal givens.

It is therefore with the development of the concept of intentional implication (and its temporal foundations) that *Erste Philosophie* brings the critique of the Cartesian way to a higher level than in the *Grundprobleme*.[70] Further, we can also see how the results from Husserl's previous analysis of the "concrete I" have become operative, since one here finds that the philosophical I which has now become rich with life, can no longer hide itself within the confinements of the mere present now. Instead, it draws on its depth-dimensions and discovers a whole

---

[69] See Hua VIII, the third section entitled "Zur Phänomenologie der phänomenologischen Reduktion. Eröffnung eines zweiten Weges zur transzendentalen Reduktion".

[70] See VIII, § 47 "Intentionale Implikationen und Iterationen", and p. 115, 123f, 131, 141ff, 149ff, 173ff. However, the idea of intentional implication was clearly presented already in *Grundprobleme*, as when Husserl speaks of the *Vergegenwärtigungs*-phenomena in general: "Hier kommen sie in Betracht um einer bestimmten, höchst wunderbaren Leistung willen, die sie ermöglichen: nämlich der allumfassenden Wendung aller natürlichen Erfahrung nicht nur nach dem, was in ihr cogitatio ist, sondern auch nach dem, *was in ihr intentional liegt*" (XIII, p. 178f). See also IV, p. 267f; IX, p. 36ff, 45f; I, p. 144, 154; VI, p. 248, 259, 262; XV, p. 383f, 595f, 608.

chain of lived experiences and associations implicated within itself, sedimented as its personal history and thus also helping to shape its future course and projects – all as parts of the transcendental field.

If, as Husserl says, it has been the "principal error" of all previous presentations of the reduction that it has been restricted to the singular I, and that the extension to "monadic intersubjectivity" that lies inherent within it has been accordingly restrained, then the charge of phenomenology as a "new kind of solipsism" seems to be inevitable.[71] Husserl's remedy in these 1923-24 lectures consists in displaying that the reduction to the stream of consciousness is not only – as one might on good grounds have imagined – a reduction to the "actual" stream with its ego pole, but that its scope in fact extends to the "infinite manifold of possible experience" which is "rooted" in the momentary lived experience as its "horizon" in the form of intentional implications.[72] The solution that gradually dawned upon Husserl, and which is one of the central points that *Erste Philosophie II* establishes, is that intersubjectivity can be shown to be operative from the very outset already within the Cartesian reduction, and that it is only a matter of explicating more thoroughly that which is implicated within it:

> In my streaming present my past and future are implicated – primordially –, in my primordiality (and thereby already in my living present) a foreign present, a foreign primordiality is "implicated". All secrets lie in the clarification of implication and explication, horizon, index etc (VIII, Beilage XX, p. 436n).

But this solution – although clearly pointing out insufficiencies of most of his earlier presentations of the reduction – merely points the way, and does not after all tell us much, concretely speaking, about how a plurality of transcendental subjects are actually there for me as "intentionally implicated" within my stream. So long as this problem is not confronted in a more substantial way – something that neither the philosophical resources of the *Grundprobleme* nor *Erste Philosophie II* seem able to do – Husserl can not really hope for anything more than a

[71] VIII, p. 433f.
[72] VIII, p. 433f.

sympathetic nod from his readers for wanting to avoid the charge of solipsism.

For now, however, we must investigate what more Husserl is able to do with this "second way", which from the outset is conceived of as a "modification" of the Cartesian way (and not, it must be underlined, its replacement).[73] There is some controversy about this however, and the general idea amongst some of the first generation of interpreters who have paid specific attention to it, is that the psychological way is a mere stepping stone from the Cartesian to the ontological way.[74] Unlike these, Rudolf Boehm sees the psychological way as one which "unites the motives of all the other non-Cartesian ways", and as an important aspect in all of Husserl's major later works, to the point of smothering the Cartesian way.[75] Amongst recent interpreters, Nam In Lee and Nathalie Depraz have both (setting all other differences apart) provided extended interpretations of the psychological way that uncover its extraordinary fertility for deepening the egology of static phenomenology into the intersubjectivity of genetic phenomenology.[76] But if we disregard the evaluation of its merits, and focus on the central aspects of

[73] VIII, p. 316.

[74] Thus both Iso Kern & Ludwig Landgrebe argue that the psychological way is an unnecessary "abstraction" and a mere forerunner to the major, ontological, way; see Kern "Die drei Wege zur transzendental-phänomenologischen Reduktion in der Philosophie E. Husserls" (1962), and *Husserl und Kant* (1964), p. 213ff; Landgrebe "Husserls Abschied vom Cartesianismus" (1963). Kern, speaking of the lectures in 1926/27 where Husserl instead of the Cartesian way begins with the ontological and then moves on to the psychological way (just as he was to do in *Krisis*), argues that such an attempt is incompatible with Husserl's major works: "Diese Linie repräsentiert einen ganz 'besonderen Husserl', der sich kaum mit dem 'Cartesianischen Husserl' etwa der *Ideen I* oder der *Meditationen* in eine harmoinsche Einheit bringen lässt" (XIV, p. XXXI). Although he discerned the three most important ways to the reduction, Kern did not always recognize their inner relation. More recently, Sebastian Luft also neglects the importance of the psychological way in his "Husserl's Theory of the Phenomenological Reduction: Between Life-World and Cartesianism" (2004), p. 211 ff.

[75] Boehm (1959), Einleitung, VIII, p. IXLf.

[76] Lee (1993) sees the psychological way as "nothing less than the general method of genetic phenomenology", and even argues that it is "the only possible method" that is able to disclose the phenomena pertaining to the deepest, anonymously functioning of subjective life, i.e. the drives (p. 74, 155f). Although Depraz (1995) in a similar fashion regards the psychological way as the singularly most important at the level of genetic phenomenology, she argues strongly for regarding the three ways as complementary (see p. 24f, 203f).

what this arguably first non-Cartesian way actually consists in, we see that there are three major lines for interpreting the psychological way: 1) it is the method for the "transformation" (*Umschlag*) of "pure psychological" or even of "worldly" experience into transcendental givens.[77] 2) It is the method that through the discovery of the "intentional implications" in consciousness opens the possibility for genetic inquiry to move unrestricted along the temporal lines forward and backward in horizontal consciousness, thus unfolding the psychological givens in the past and future of consciousness.[78] 3) It is the method that enables the deep-investigation of transcendental subjectivity (beyond the cogito) by means of the *Ichspaltung* between the "non-participating" or "uninterested" transcendental onlooker and the person-in-the-world.[79] These three characteristics all portray parts that taken together give a picture of the psychological way.

Let us take a brief look at some of these issues that are of particular interest, beginning with the psychological way as "transformation" (*Umschlag*, *Wendung*). Husserl's waxing concerns about bringing out the "concreteness" of transcendental subjectivity is closely related to this, and it has its basis in the methodological expansion of the field of transcendental phenomenology that genetic phenomenology initiated. Although to be precise, speaking of "expansion" as if it were a question

[77] The thematical and textual support for this interpretation is the closeness, siblingship or even "identity" between pure psychology and transcendental phenomenology that Husserl presents in for instance the Amsterdam-lectures, the Encyclopaedia Britannica-article, the 1925 lectures on phenomenological psychology, the *Nachwort* to *Ideen I*, and the *Krisis*; as well as several texts in Hua XXIX and XXXIV. It can be traced back to *Grundprobleme*, and also *Ideen I* (as can be seen from the notes and marginal comments that K. Schuhmann presented in Hua III/2, and from the 1929 so-called "Gibson convolute", drafts for a revised edition of *Ideen I* that are now published in Hua XXXIV, Nr. 6), although Husserl clearly wanted to hold this similarity back in order to avoid any accusations of having lapsed back into psychologism. This *Umschlag*-interpretation is championed by Kern (1962) and (1964), Bernet, Kern and Marbach (1989) and Lee (1993).

[78] The main textual support in favour of this interpretation is *Erste Philosophie II*, Hua IX and *Krisis*. This interpretation is championed by Boehm (1959), Bernet, Kern and Marbach (1989) and Depraz (1995).

[79] The textual basis here is rich (since the distinction is *in nuce* present from the very beginning of phenomenology in *Logische Untersuchungen*, *Ideen I*) although as a concept it was introduced in Hua VIII, then in for instance Hua XI, CM, *Krisis* and Hua XXXIV; this is championed by Fink in his 6th *Cartesianische Meditationen*, Kern (1962) and (1964), Depraz (1995) and Luft (2004).

of a quantitative step (whether temporal, spatial or even hermeneutical) can be misleading; it is not the conquering of previously uncharted terrain that is at stake, but exposing a richness that is already inherent in experiential life (which is clearly reflected in the guiding concept of "implication").

The notion of the "concrete I", as it is developed in the monadology, receives its whole impetus from this expansion (for want of a better word), and the psychological way enables the incorporation of phenomena from the "psychological" sphere, rich with concrete experience, into the transcendental sphere. This process has all the apparent simplicity of a magic trick, which by the same token makes it vulnerable to the criticism of being psychologistic, but if we look at it carefully we see that there is no reason for alarm. Again, the simplicity of the operation stems from the originary closeness between the world of the natural attitude and the same world as reduced. The process permits of the possible conversion of all phenomena occurring at the "empirical" level, or that of life in the natural attitude, into the transcendental sphere.[80] The basis for this methodological expansion, which in principle knows of no limitations, is the identity in difference that holds between the transcendental I and the I of the natural attitude: my transcendental I is, according to Husserl, not a second I, existing besides the empirical I:

> It is just the field of transcendental self-experience (conceived in full concreteness) which can in every case, through mere alteration of attitude, be changed into psychological self-experience. [...] Manifestly, this parallelism spells nothing less than theoretical equivalence [*theoretischer Gleichwertigkeit*] (IX, p. 294/CW 6, p. 173).

This relation of identity in difference has as its immediate corollary that all experiences from the natural attitude can be converted into transcendental experiences:

> Every single pure psychic experience [...] produces a transcendental experience that is identical as regards content but that is freed of its "psychic" (that is, worldly, real) sense. In precisely this way the psychic ego is transformed into the transcendental ego, which, in each of its self-

[80] See VIII, p. 166; IX, p. 294; V, p. 146f; XV, p. 193.

> disclosing reflections (transcendental reflections), always rediscovers itself in its own transcendental peculiarities (IX, p. 275/ CW 6, p. 132).[81]

Now that the investigation moves on to the second and third characteristics of the psychological way, which will be treated together, it sets out to gain a clearer understanding of the complex and in so many respects difficult relation between the I and the others who participate – in the most various ways – in my life-world. By showing how Husserl gradually began to realize the more profound ways through which the static analyses conjoin with the genetic, we can show how the naïve supposition of an I that is externally distinct from all other I's harbours what in *Krisis* (and other texts from the 1920's onwards) is called a "communalization" (*Vergemeinschaftung*), according to which I and the other are mutually implicated one within the other.

If we follow the genetic path sufficiently far, we eventually come to see the other not as an alter ego that is externally opposite to me, but instead as someone whom I already from the outset am inextricably bound to. But in order to shed light on this communalization, I must first come to acknowledge the ways in which I am other to myself. The extent to which I am able to acknowledge this self-alterity determines the extent to which I will be able to acknowledge the other in her necessary being-other from me. This investigation (which draws on material from *Krisis*, the C-manuscripts and Hua XV, although prefigured in earlier texts such as the *Grundprobleme*, *Erste Philosophie II* and the 1925 lectures on *Phänomenologische Psychologie*) will be taken to show how a self-alterity such as that described by Freud when he speaks of repression, is merely a so to speak ontic particularization of structures of consciousness and subjectivity that have a much wider bearing.

When Husserl in *Erste Philosophie II* describes how the reduction of the Cartesian way has to be "extended", this extension will not merely

[81] See also from Hua IX, pp. 276, 294, 340ff, 344, 457f, 461f, 468ff, 470ff, 616. We will come back to the relation between psychology and transcendental phenomenology as presented in *Krisis* later on (Chapter Three, § 6).

encompass a wider domain but more to the point, it will "so to speak absorb everything psychological":

> Then by following this way not only do I, the I that is the subject of this phenomenological reducing, gain myself as transcendental I – by including also the foreign subjectivity in the method, I gain the transcendental intersubjectivity (VIII, § 46, p. 129; cf. p. 316).

It must be kept in mind that the investigation does not set out to "find" the other as if she were somewhere inside me, hidden under the scattered debris of my own innermost being. What is at stake is to show how I can come to experience something like an alter ego at all.[82] It is indisputable that my own transcendental I and my own life has the priority of being a first, original given, in that I only have direct access to myself and my memories, expectations etc. The other, who has access to herself in a similar way, is for me only given in a mediate fashion: her life is present for me by means of indication (*Anzeige*), and I have to representify her self-experience in an interpretative way in order to experience her as another person proper, and not as a dead thing.[83] Thus we are here dealing with an "intentionality of a second level, one that is mediate".[84]

So far the distribution of concepts delimiting what is mine and what pertains to the other is clear, and in accordance with the most traditional metaphysical schemes: apodictic immediacy and presence against the blurred knowledge of interpretation, indication, mediated intentionality and representification. But things get more interesting once we are led to acknowledge, as Husserl does in the decisive § 53 ("Das Problem der Intersubjektivität") of *Erste Philosophie II*, that transcendental subjectivity itself contains levels of both immediacy and mediacy. The analysis of intentional implication is an important part in opening for this step, since it connects the present with just about everything non-present, whether from the past, future or imagination, as long as

[82] Hua I, CM, § 42 "Exposition des Problems der Fremderfahrung in Gegenstellung gegen den Einwand des Solipsismus" (p. 121f).

[83] For the analysis of indication as my access to understanding the other, see Hua IV, p. 166, 411; VIII, p. 134f, 175. Husserl also describes the step from perceiving the other as physical body to someone in full possession of a lived body (*Leib*) in terms of interpretation: what is outer appearance to me, is interpreted as being lived body to her; see XIII, p. 250f, 267; XIV, p. 477, 484f, 527.

[84] VIII, § 53, p. 175.

intentional bonds can be established.[85] This means effectively that even in the "presence of my own life [*Lebensgegenwart*] where I am given to myself in a completely immediate way", even in this "sphere of presence" or correlatively, this "pure self-perception", there are intentionalities operative that are mediate.[86]

The whole movement of these paragraphs is to introduce self-alterity into the heart of my own being, in order to prepare for the arrival of the other – who will then be shown to always already have lived so to speak within me. The introduction of alterity already within my own self-perception, at the core of the cogito (given that the *Urimpression* cannot be conceived of without retention and protention), will thus serve to show that I am always already shot through with alterity, and that the alterity of the other is a question of more or less in relation to my own self-alterity.

What gives added credibility to Husserl's analyses of intersubjectivity here, is no doubt the possibility to found them in the investigations of inner time-consciousness. The methodological shift initiated in *Erste Philosophie II* brings with it that the philosophical interest is no longer directed towards the I as a pole (characteristic of the Cartesian way), but is instead aimed at "the life of the present", i.e. the "endless horizon of memory and expectation" which when properly disclosed, reveals itself as "an endless transcendental lifestream in both dimensions".[87] It is therefore no surprise to see that the very "opening" of the psychological way should begin with an investigation of the horizons of the "living streaming present", as these have been made available by the double reduction.[88] What can we expect to find when we investigate these horizons?

---

[85] VIII, § 53, p. 175.

[86] "Sehen wir näher zu, so ist aber auch die Gegenwartssphäre von einer ähnlichen Struktur, die intentional Unmittelbares und Mittelbares scheiden lässt. Wir kommen auf den fliessenden Grenzpunkt des reinen Jetzt, oder korrelativ der reinen Selbstwahrnehmung dieses momentanen urlebendigen Jetzt, und auf eine Strecke der ursprünglichen Retention und einer ursprünglichen Protention, deren Intentionalität eine mittelbare ist." (VIII, § 53, p. 175)

[87] VIII, § 39, p. 86.

[88] See *Erste Philosophie II*, 4th section, Ch. 2 "Die Eröffnung des Reiches transzendentaler Erfahrung auf dem zweiten Wege", § 49 "Die Horizonte der lebendig strömenden Gegenwart" (p. 146-152).

In *Erste Philosophie II* Husserl takes a decisive methodological step beyond the restrictions of the instantaneous Cartesian reduction, when he shows that the horizon of consciousness consists of and is held together by a network of "intentional implications" that are founded on retentional and protential structures.[89] These implications extend far beyond the simple case of a separate memory or act of phantasy, since what we encounter in the full concreteness of transcendental life are "multiplications" of these at various levels. There are for instance possibilities of iterations not only within each act-type (memory of memory, etc.), but also across different types of acts (phantasies of memories, etc.). One decisive consequence of this is that the reduction can no longer be conceived of as a single step (like the Cartesian reduction in *Ideen I*), but must instead be performed in a series of steps, based on the first reduction, depending on where the intentional analysis is headed. We will come back to this point in the next Chapter, and also to the double reduction later on in relation to the intentionality of drives.

[89] VIII, § 49, p. 149f.

Chapter Three

INDIRECT CLARIFICATION OF REPRESSION BY MEANS OF THE LIVING PRESENT AND THE LATE THEORY OF REDUCTIONS

The empty generality of the epoché does not of itself clarify anything; it is only the gate of entry through which one must pass in order to be able to discover the new world of pure subjectivity. The actual discovery is a matter of concrete, extremely subtle and differentiated work. (Husserl)

1. Introduction

In this chapter we will return again to the most fundamental methodological operation of transcendental phenomenology, in an attempt to outline the later theory of reductions in its rich diversity.[1] More precisely, the relations between some of the more prominent denominations of the reduction in the 1930's will be presented. This will be done with a view to the developments of Husserl's theory of inner time-consciousness in the C-manuscripts, which is the most complete genetic presentation of temporality we have.[2]

In the second section (§ 2) the "archaeology" of transcendental subjectivity will be presented, as a propaedeutic point of entry to the later genetic investigations. New features of the reduction (notably the

[1] For an indication of what is at stake, see XXXV [1922/23], § 23 "Neubestimmung des Begriffs der transzendentalen Reduktion in Abgrenzung zu dem der apodiktischen Reduktion" p. 98f: "Wir werden in der Tat den Begriff der Reduktion vervielfältigen müssen. Zunächst aber scheiden wir 1. transzendentale Reduktion schlechthin als Reduktion auf die transzendentale Subjektivität überhaupt; 2. die apodiktische Reduktion, d.i. die Reduktion auf die transzendentale Subjektivität, aber unter Einschränkung auf festgestellte Apodiktizität".

[2] The genetic approach is already sketched out in the Bernau-texts – in fact, that is where it occurs for the first time – but is not yet worked out in a systematic fashion; see XXXIII, Nr. 14f and how these texts further the analyses of sedimentation, habituality and the historicity of the I from *Ideen II* (cf. IV, §§ 29, 32f, 49, 56).

"radicalized" and the "universal" reduction) pertaining to Husserl's late genetic phenomenology will gradually be brought into play. These will show more clearly the interplay between the different ways to the reduction *in actu* in the attempt to bring concrete subjectivity into unconcealment. This attempt also requires a partly new conceptuality (*Abbau*, *Rückfrage*, *Rekonstruktion*) which underscores the innovative character of Husserl's attempt (§ 3).

The central theme of this chapter is however the notion of the "living present" (*lebendige Gegenwart*), and the investigation will proceed from this as a centre for Husserl's late philosophy (§ 4). This also means that this chapter plays a pivotal role for the remainder of the investigation which (in Part II) will continue the "indirect" attempt at a clarification of Freudian repression that is presented here. All of Husserl's phenomenological investigations of passivity and the unconscious, it will be argued, must be led back to the concept of the living present. Here the egological attempt will be brought to its genetically deepest level by means of a new, "radicalized" aspect of the reduction which discloses the "originary I". It will be shown that this *Ur-Ich* is no stable self-enclosed substance, but consists primarily in a constant process of self-alteration.

The relation between egology and intersubjectivity will be investigated in three steps, first in relation to the radicalized reduction (§§ 4-5), then in relation to monadology and the intersubjective reduction (§ 6) and finally in relation to the universal reduction (§ 7). The analysis of the *Ur-Ich* is continued in the following section (§ 5), and it is shown that when the reduction is performed to a sufficiently deep genetic level, the living present reveals in itself processes of alterity of a manifold kind (temporal, imaginative and in relation to the other).

These are, in a sense, that by virtue of which there is subjective unity, but it can only be had by means of a constant inner differentiation: the unity of subjective life is accordingly for Husserl the constant achievement of holding together that which strives to dissipate itself. These processes indicate that the experience of the other, which in Levinas' sense is the experience of a "radical alterity", has a prehistory in my own subjective life. It will be argued that these constitutive processes represent the basic structure that Freudian theory works within and presupposes, when it finds that what is repressed is encountered as something foreign within us.

After thus following the egological attempt as far as Husserl goes in terms of genetic analysis, the next section (§ 6) explores monadology as a theory that encompasses both egology and intersubjectivity. Focus here is on the genetic deepening of monadology that is brought about by the new methodological aspects that Husserl develops. The radicalized reduction that led from the I to the streaming living present, also shows that this streaming is ultimately not restricted to my own being but leads to the acknowledgement of a streaming intersubjectivity. The relation between the single monad and this streaming intersubjectivity is analyzed in terms of the relation between what is "first for me" and what is "first by nature". Husserl's analysis, which follows both the egological-epistemological way (what is first for me) and the genetically founding way (what is first by nature), thus avoids being pinned down to the alternative of either the-other-is-prior-to-me or I-am-prior-to-the-other. This means that intersubjectivity is genetically foundational in relation to egology from the perspective of being; however, in terms of evidence it is still the egological-epistemological perspective which remains basic: I can only come to know of this intersubjective streaming being if I proceed from its manifestation for me. An important lesson from this is that no ontological conclusions can be drawn from Husserl's epistemological analyses: thus for instance, the egological starting point does not mean that he conceives of the world in a solipsistic manner.

The final section (§ 7) proceeds by investigating the "universal reduction" as it is presented at the end of *Krisis*. Here (and in the following sections) we will take a step beyond Held's investigation, which situated the living present as the core from which to think transcendental subjectivity but which only took up the radicalized reduction. What the universal reduction brings to this discussion is twofold: it brings the focus back to the transcendental problem of the constitution of the world as a world for all, and it shows how this thought must interact with the deepest genetic investigations of temporising self-constitution which leads to streaming intersubjective being. Thus genetic phenomenology in full power, so to speak, engages both processes of alteration and those of unification (in relation to the self and to others). This very process of self-alteration (in its double form of temporal and personal de-presentification), via the mediation of originary temporisation which leads to the *Monadenall*, then partakes in the universal constitution of the world. This is the final step taken in *Krisis* and also represents the point at which the psychologist parts way with the philosopher, thereby indicating that the closeness between them at this point reveals itself to be immeasurable distance.

The differentiation of these types of reduction is often difficult and obviously no claim is being made that it is final or complete.[3] The radicalized reduction is at first quite easily distinguished from the latter two in that it seems to lead clearly to the genetic foundation of the individual noema-noesis correlation that the first, static reduction opened up.[4] The difference between the "double" and the "intersubjective" or "universal" reductions is more straightforward. For it seems clear, as we have seen, that the "double" reduction refers mainly to the basic idea in *Grundprobleme* of performing the reduction twice, and after Husserl had discovered that this led to a disclosure of the other by way of empathy it is more often referred to as the "intersubjective reduction".[5]

The relation between the intersubjective and universal reductions poses more difficulty since they both lead to intersubjectivity and are even referred to together by Husserl.[6] However in certain texts Husserl

---

[3] As Luft points out in his recent article "Husserl's Theory of the Phenomenological Reduction: Between Life-World and Cartesianism" (2004), the reduction has been at the centre of attention for the past 60 years. There is even a renewed interest, notably amongst French-speaking philosophers such as Jean-Luc Marion, *Réduction et donation* (1989); Bernet, *La vie du sujet* and Depraz, *Transcendance et incarnation*; see also Donn Welton, *The Other Husserl* (2000). Despite this, the different types of reduction in genetic phenomenology and their relation to the different ways to the reduction has to my knowledge never been investigated in more than partial attempts.

[4] However the radicalized reduction seems to cooperate with an intersubjective reduction in certain texts (such as C3 for instance) – although this of course is not announced by Husserl but is something that must be reconstructed – since we are led into "originary streaming intersubjectivity", i.e. no longer the originary streaming of the invidual or the *Ur-Ich*.

[5] See for instance the decisive presentations of the intersubjective reduction in XXXV, § 24; VIII, § 53b; Beilage XIX.

[6] See the reference to the 1910-11 lectures *Grundprobleme* as "Vorlesung über phänomenologische Reduktion als universale intersubjektive Reduktion" (in Kern

distinguishes between two steps within the intersubjective reduction, such that there is, after the bracketing of the world (which establishes the intersubjective universe), a "second step": a further reduction to the "communalization of everything that is egological".[7] It is this final step, so I argue, that in later texts is called "universal reduction".[8]

The presentation of the living present plays an important part in the overall argument. Since this is a central theme, I will say some words in advance that can only later become subjected to the evidence of argumentation. Based on this first display of the *lebendige Gegenwart* as the core of Husserl's theory of passivity, later chapters will show that its basic, concrete meaning-structure consists of preforms of bodily kinaesthesia, feelings and drives in a constantly ongoing process where repression occurs as a necessary part in all constitution. Most of what becomes repressed in this process has no inner motivation to become conscious at a later stage and remains in a state of zero affectivity: these contents are simply surplus building blocks.

But certain contents will not come to rest even though they have been pushed away from the path leading towards manifestation: they persevere and exercise influence over other contents of consciousness, thereby affecting the further constitution of self, other and world. It is here that Freudian repression can be situated, and its clarification thus takes place by showing how it presupposes a broad conception of consciousness such as that presented by Husserl's genetic phenomenology. Certainly, even if it is granted that this picture would help in showing what Freudian repression is all about, it would only be a small step in the right direction. Understanding the further details from the phenomenological side would require much additional work, not to mention the benefits coming from the other direction: how the Freudian analysis would teach us what has to be developed in phenomenology and perhaps thought through in a different fashion. My aim here is more modest: merely to outline a basic approach where the structure of the

---

XIII, p. XXXV).

7 XV, Nr 4 [1930] p. 69.

8 The universal reduction is intimately connected with genetic phenomenology, but it occurs with two different meanings: there is a first phase (genetic but not depth-genetic) in for instance XXXV, § 25 p. 113; see also VIII, Beilage II p. 316. Then there is a second phase (depthgenetic) in VI, § 71 p. 257ff where the level of communalization (*Vergemeinschaftung*) is reached.

living present, made accessible by means of a systematic and controlled methodology of reductions, can be shown to accommodate a general process where repression plays a central part and which Freud implicitly makes use of in his theory of repression.

2. A phenomenological archaeology of constitutive subjectivity

In a letter from 1920 to Gerda Walther (who had studied with both Husserl and Pfänder and who received her Ph.D. in the following year), Husserl explains that static descriptions are ultimately deficient since one never knows what is really meaningful in them in terms of constitution. He goes on to say that when it comes to really understanding what is given phenomenologically, he tries to adopt the same attitude as the archaeologist doing excavations: "the correct piecing together of the dispersed parts is important, however the real work does not reside in the description, but in the reconstruction".[9] At times, Husserl expressed regret over the fact that the concept of archaeology had already been claimed by a positive science.[10] But even though phenomenology could only borrow its signification, Husserl repeatedly identified the investigation of genetic constitution with archaeology:

> Phenomenological archaeology, the digging up of the hidden constitutive constructions [that are already to be found] in the building-blocks, of the apperceptive meaning-operations in the constructions that lie before us as a ready world of experience. The questioning backwards and then the laying bare of the separate operations that create a being-meaning, all the way to the last, the *archai* [...]. As in ordinary archaeology: reconstruction, an understanding in "zig-zag" (HuMat 8, Nr. 80 p. 356f [C 16/1932]).[11]

---

[9] *Briefwechsel II*, p. 260: "Ich pflege mich gegen phänomenologische Gegebenheiten so zu verhalten wie der Archäologe bei der Ausgrabung: sie werden sauber zusammengestellt, aber die eigentliche Arbeit ist nicht ihre Beschreibung, sondern die Rekonstruktion." Walther's dissertation, *Zur Ontologie der sozialen Gemeinschaften*, was published in the *Jahrbuch*, vol. VI (1923).

[10] See Fink, "Das Problem der Phänomenologie Edmund Husserls", p. 199. For an elaboration of "*archéology*" as a project in common for phenomenology and psychoanalysis, see Stephan Günzel, "Zick-Zack. Edmund Husserls phänomenologische Archäologie" (2004).

[11] Cf. VIII, § 31 p. 29f.

But where does this archaeology of constitutive layers lead? Does it end with a complete retrieval of the series of first *Stiftungen*? Is the aim of this kind of genetic questioning backwards (*Rückfrage*) to be able to present a systematic and merely quantitative overview of the genetic *archai* as consisting of my "first perception of trees", "first perception of blue", etc.? This type of question points to something problematic with Husserl's choice of metaphors, for his talk of "archaeology" and *archai* inevitably suggests that the search is on for a series of actual proto-experiences, "konstitutiven Bauten", ready to be excavated intact, underneath layers consisting of lived experiences and habitus.[12] What, then, are the originary constituents that Husserl here discusses, what are these *archai*?

At least two alternatives that are investigated by Husserl suggest themselves here, the first of which has to do with the ontology of the lifeworld as providing the *archai* for the postive sciences.[13] Secondly, as a closer determination of that, he speaks of archaeology as a *Rückfrage* towards the concrete I.[14] Here I will focus on two options in relation to this: either the *arché* is "latent being" in a local sense as the domain of forgotten experience which can be made "patent"; or it is

---

[12] See HuMat 8, Nr. 80 p. 356f. This question could also be extended to Heidegger in *Sein und Zeit*, who asks for the "ursprüngliche Erfahrungen" that would precede the traditional determination of being; also here we find the archaeological conceptuality at work in the calling for an "Auflockerung der verhärteten Tradition" (§ 6, p. 22). For a discussion of Husserlian archaeology in relation to Foucault's *archéologie du savoir*, see Hyder (2003). For a historical overview of "archaeology" in philosophy, see *Die Aktualität des Archäologischen. Wissenschaft, Medien, Künste*, Hrsg. Ebeling & Altekamp (2004).

[13] See for instance XXIX, Nr. 11 p. 154: "Alles 'Logische' entspringt eben aus einer vorlogischen Sphäre, die ihre eigene Vernunft hat, ihre eigene, alles tragenden Wahrheit. Sie hat, wie sehr sie 'vorlogisch' ist, ihre Wesensallgemeinheiten, ihre Normen, welche als die *archai* aller logischen, aller idealisiert-weltwissenschaftlichen Wahrheit (der der 'objektiven', 'positiven' Wissenschaften) nicht die geringwertigsten, sondern die ehrwürdigsten sind, als die den gesamten, auf hypothetischen Substruktionen beruhenden Erkenntnisbau tragenden." This determination of the *archai* is also expressed in several other texts.

[14] HuMat 8, Nr. 80 p. 356n2: "Mai 1932. Wichtig. Phänomenologische Archäologie. Rückfrage auf das Ich und das subjektive in der Originalität. Uroriginalität und Erinnerungen – Vergegenwärtigungen. Ich in meiner Eigenheit. Das Ich in seiner ichlichen Habitualität (Entschiedenheiten). Das verharrende Subjekt (Person) für sein Universum von 'Seienden'. Ich als Person für Andere, Mitfunktion der Einfühlungen. Objektive Zeitigung gegenüber meiner Selbstzeitigung."

related to my childhood as the beginning of constitution on a general level.[15] We will come back to the analysis of childhood in the final chapter (Ch. 6, § 6). Let us here first address the issue of latent being or "the unconscious", of what happens with the sedimented experiences that approximate the degree zero of affectivity.[16] In the lectures on transcendental logic Husserl, speaking of background lived experiences, says that these undergo a transformation when they undergo the shift from latent to patent being:

> It is not like shoving things in a room away from the window into dark corners, where the things themselves remain unchanged. The moment a background lived-experience becomes present, that is, the moment the ego becomes an ego carrying out acts through it, it has, as lived-experience, become completely and essentially transformed (XVII, p. 365/CW 9, p. 21 [1921]).

The potential *archai* in this sense then are clearly not conceived of as once and for all finished material to be excavated.[17] This already suggests that the idea of a phenomenological archaeology should not be taken too literally and that it operates according to different principles, based on intentional life. Moving on towards more complex genetic issues, we also encounter the unconscious as "consciousness of an indeterminate, undifferentiated, completely obscure past as a whole".[18] Whereas "patent being" is related to the constitution of the active and awakened I, latent being is not given by means of reflection on immanent contents of consciousness.

[15] Not always clearly distinguished, "childhood" is sometimes said to be "latent being" in the sense that it is not accessible and thus concealed from me (see XV, p. 608f), but latent being is also investigated as a mere structural component in the build-up of constitution. On "latent", "latency" in relation to what is "patent", see IV, p. 248; XXXVIII, p. 401; XVII, p. 365f/CW 9 p. 21ff; XX/2, Nr. 14; XI, p. 52f, 55, 64, 74; HuMat 8, Nr. 7 p. 22; Nr. 62 p. 269; Nr. 67; VI, p. 122. On "childhood" in this sense, see I, CM §§ 38, 50, 61.

[16] See HuMat 8, Nr. 67 p. 300n2: "Fundamentalanalyse der lebendigen Gegenwart nach der Aktstruktur; das Wache (Patente) und Latente (Unbewusste) [...]"; cf. p. 307n1. See also XV, Beilage XLVI p. 608.

[17] Steinbock argues for the opposite: "Phenomenological archaeology, [Husserl] writes, 'digs up' piecemeal the concealed constitutive structures that lie there ready-made for us as the world of experience"; *Home and Beyond*, p. 89.

[18] XI, Beilage XIII [1920-1926] p. 388. For a discussion of latent being in relation to reconstruction, see for instance XV, Beilage XLVI "Monadologie" p. 608ff.

Other modes of givenness are here called for (this will be examined further in the following section), that Husserl often calls "reconstruction". This reconstruction takes its cue from patent being and latent being is therefore construed of as an "intentional modification" of the former.[19] It is important to note that this reconstructed sphere of being does not exist as something covered that merely awaits the veils being pulled off.[20] It is not "pure being" that is covered over, disguised and which could be revealed as such, but essentially something that has to be reconstructed starting from my present life:

> But strictly speaking that means that there is precisely no "originary" being, no unmodified being, no being that is constituted in an originary mode, it is unthinkable as that, it is what it is as an intentional modification and only that (XV, Beilage XLVI p. 608).

This means that we can provisionally at least conclude that the *archai* Husserl is looking for cannot be conceived of as ready-made building-blocks: that would be an ill-concealed phenomenological version of logical atomism which runs counter to the experiential basis of phenomenology.

By way of concluding this introductory section I would like to present a hypothesis that will be developed in the following chapters, namely that the extended archaeology of subjectivity that Husserl opens up on at least these two levels (genetic constitution and reconstruction of childhood) does not stand in opposition to the more official program of the foundation of the sciences, as Kern for instance seems to suggest in a recent article.[21] Instead, the more urgent the situation around him

---

[19] XV, p. 608. As Bégout lucidly points out, Husserl's archaeological method means that he is forced to deduce the anterior from the posterior, while at the same time showing that it is the posterior which flows from the anterior; see *La généalogie de la logique*, p. 108f.

[20] This also touches upon Derrida's earliest critique of Husserl in *Le problème de la genèse*. According to Derrida, Husserl's philosophy cannot live up to its promise, since neither the *arché* nor the *telos* that frame transcendental phenomenology (understood as both archaeology and teleology) are given in intuition. (This is still a major theme in the transitional text "Genèse et structure"; see Lawlor, *Derrida and Husserl*, p. 34; cf. p. 11, 47, 82.) But Derrida's criticism also here can be overruled by a more thorough genetic grasp of what "*arché*" and "telos" is.

[21] "Je mehr von seinem Nachlass in der Husserliana veröffentlicht wird, umso deutlicher stellt sich heraus, dass Husserls philosophisches Hauptproblem weniger das einer apodiktischen Begründung der Wissenschaften ("cartesianisches Motiv"), sondern weit mehr das einer gegenüber der Naturwissenschaft eigenständigen

became in a both philosophical and political sense (as many letters from this period show), the more important it became to secure scientific rationality in as broad a grasp of subjectivity as possible. The phenomenological archaeology is the excavation of "originary constitution" in its most concrete possible sense, and this can only be a remedy for the crisis of the sciences – which is also immediately a politico-ethical crisis – if it aims to grasp the whole of subjective life, even though this is an infinite task. It is this comprehensive ambition that brings with it the renewed interest in the theory of reduction, which first escalated in the 1920's and then again in the 1930's.[22]

3. New methodological concepts in the genetic method: Rückfrage*,* Abbau *and reconstruction.*

In this section the new conceptuality brought into play with genetic analyses is introduced by means of three central examples: *Rückfrage*, *Abbau* and *Rekonstruktion*. After this, the investigation will proceed with a discussion of the latter two (since *Rückfrage* has already been discussed repeatedly), but now the focus will be set on the question of evidence as well as some of the objections that have been raised.

As soon as the idea of sedimentation and the historicity of the soul is introduced (*Ideen II*), the need for some methodological procedure to separate and see through the gradually increasing layers of subjective life is called for. Indeed, there could be no idea of "sedimentation" if there was not a "method" of some sort that would first enable us to see this structure precisely as different layers, in an open series of past and coming experience. It is this temporal structure of the correlation between the I and the world, first thematized by genetic phenomenology, that stands at the centre of both *Abbau*, *Rückfrage* and *Rekonstruktion*.[23] I believe Husserl has pointed to the appropriate level of gener-

Wissenschaft und Philosophie des Bewusstseins, der Subjektivität, der Personalität, des Geistes war" (Iso Kern, 2003, p. 169). See *Briefe an Ingarden*, 1930-12-21, p. 62ff.

[22] For a general survey of Husserl's late philosophy of the reductions (which will be specified as the investigation proceeds), see the selection of texts mainly from the B-group of manuscripts in Hua XXXIV, *Zur phänomenologischen Reduktion. Texte aus dem Nachlass (1926-1935)*; in particular texts Nr. 11, 22. See also for instance Hua XV, Nr. 4f, 22, 33; cf. also Cairns, *Conversations with Husserl and Fink* p. 11ff.

[23] These themes are discussed together in HuMat 8, Nr 52 [Dez. 1930] p. 223f.

ality for these analyses when he stated that: "Alle [...] Urintentionalität wird erst durch Abbau und Rekonstruktion ausgelegt".[24]

Closely connected to this is the insight that the epoché of *Ideas 1* is insufficient since it does not by itself lead to an already present transcendental field. Instead, further reductive steps are required and these can be more easily distinguished when they are given names. Although it is difficult to differentiate between these concepts in a clear and unambiguous way, the following can be said by way of a general characterization. *Abbau* is the dismantling of sedimented structures that cover the world, for instance our historical scientific-rational tradition which has thrown a garb of idealizations over it (EU, §§ 10f).[25] *Rückfrage* is the regressive inquiry that accompanies the dismantling and which is directed back to the constitutive sources of meaning that have preceded the sedimentation. It is therefore always a questioning that is directed back towards transcendental subjectivity:

> It is necessary to dismantle [*Abbau*] everything which already pre-exists in the sedimentations of sense in the world of our present experience, to interrogate [*Zurückfragen*] these sedimentations relative to the subjective sources out of which they have developed and, consequently, relative to an effective subjectivity. This is not the subjectivity of psychological reflection (*Erfahrung und Urteil*, § 11 p. 47/ Engl. p. 48).[26]

Abbau, unlike *Rückfrage*, is often said to be a kind of reduction, but it is clear that the latter is only a concept that is available from within the already performed reduction: it is not there in the natural attitude.[27] *Rekonstruktion*, finally, is the general name for the procedure Husserl employs when going beyond immanent reflection on acts of consciousness in order to articulate the constitutive steps that must have preceded

---

[24] HuMat 8, Nr. 96 p. 437. This is also suggested by Hans-Rainer Sepp (1997) when he says (p. 16): "Die transzendentalphänomenologische Analyse entwirft nicht ein neues Sein des Lebens, sie will das Leben in seinem Sein aufdecken: *Sie rekonstruiert*. Die Freilegung des transzendentalen Sinnes des Weltlebens durch die transzendentale Phänomenologie fasst Husserl selbst als Rekonstruktion."

[25] On *Abbau*, see also for instance HuMat 8, Nr. 13, Nr. 23, Nr. 90. Discussions of Rekonstruktion

[26] But *Abbau* is also used in dismantling the living present; see HuMat 8, Nr. 23 p. 107n.

[27] On *Abbau-reduktion*, see HuMat 8, Nr. 23 p. 109 and Nr. 90 p. 394; on *Rückfrage* and the reduction, see VI, § 59 p. 212f/209.

these acts and their objects.[28] This "deeper constitution" which lies behind that which memory is able to provide, can only be given by means of reconstruction.[29] This means, as has already been suggested repeatedly, that the primary mode of givenness of the whole sphere of latent being, of my own childhood and of the unconscious is that of reconstruction.[30]

Husserl's analysis of evidence allows us to connect the strong evidence that reflection upon our immanent contents of consciousness provides, with the weaker, more elusive evidence of experiences that are written in the prose of that deep, inner world that can only be gained by means of reconstruction and dismantling. An important step in this direction was taken with the 1922-23 lectures on *Einleitung in die Philosophie*, where Husserl argues for a radical extension of philosophy by means of universalizing the phenomenological critique of evidence. The basis for this move lies in the insight that genuine, scientific phenomenology cannot limit itself to an analysis of acts, but must begin to find its sources in the richness of life.[31]

---

[28] See further XV, Beilage XLVI, Nr. 34; HuMat 8, Nr. 52, 97; XXXIX, Nr. 26, 43. According to Kern, Husserl develops Natorps' reconstructive method (as presented in *Allgemeine Psychologie* from 1912) in his account of *Urkonstitution*; see *Husserl und Kant*, p. 109f, 367ff, 371. Kern also points out that Husserl spoke of a "transcendental reconstruction" as early as in 1919-20 (A I 36/163ab): "Die Probleme der *transzendentalen Rekonstruktion* der notwendigen Konstituentien des phänomenalen Gegenstandes und der methodischen Voraussetzungen seiner Objektivierung – auf Grund der Forderung, dass von ihm objektive Wissenschaft möglich sei, dass er Objekt einer Natur als definiter Mannigfaltigkeit sein kann"; cit. Kern (1964), p. 372.

[29] XV, Beilage IL p. 632 [1933].

[30] See XV, Beilage XLVI p. 608; XXIX, Nr. 28 p. 332f.

[31] The concept of life is rarely made the object of an explicit thematization by Husserl, which is probably why it has received so little attention. It is however, as Anne Montavont has carefully argued in *De la passivité dans la phénoménologie de Husserl*, a keyword that escapes conceptual and categorical fixation, since there is not "life" in the singular but many forms of life in Husserl's thought (see in particular her Ch. 1). Montavont argues that "life" as it functions in Husserl's text is a "shadow-zone" which is left partly unexamined since it precedes all conceptuality. The aim of her analysis is not to make this "shadow" disappear, but to show that it is that which brings phenomenology into movement: "que l'ombre produite est en même temps l'élan producteur, ce qui met l'analyse en mouvement. Il s'agira de montrer que la notion de vie est peut-être ce qui oblige Husserl à déplacer la frontière traditionnelle qui sépare la passivité de l'activité, que les analyses de la passivité préparent une vie qui n'est plus l'actualisme pur" (p. 17).

The *Wissenschaftslehre* must according to Husserl now be complemented with a "much more universal […] *Lebenslehre*", both considered under the aegis of reason.[32] What Husserl here calls a "total doctrine of reason" is one that goes beyond its present "naïve state", and which strives towards "absolute responsibility" as the basis of a "truly humane culture".[33] In order to become possible however, such a theory of reason must universalize its evidential critique, such that if there was previously a demand for a radical critique of subjectivity in the field of knowledge, this must now be extended to the evidence obtaining in all fields of "social activity":

> Thus what is required is the universal study of subjectivity in full [*das universale Studium der vollen und ganzen Subjektivität*], in so far as it somehow stands under possible norms of reason. […] Thereby we would accordingly have a far more extensive philosophy (XXXV, p. 42f).

It is of course this exceptionally broad analysis of conscious life that Husserl presents which makes the general hypothesis concerning the phenomenological clarification of psychoanalytical repression possible, and the underlying thesis is simply that everything which somehow, be it directly or indirectly, manifests itself for consciousness, thereby becomes a subject for phenomenological clarification. Once it is there in natural or personal life, this lived experience is immediately and *eo ipso* available for transcendental life following the psychological way to the reduction.[34]

By pointing out the necessity to go beyond the confinements of the reflective method, the investigation wishes to disarm in advance all half-baked criticism that regards Husserl's analyses of dismantling and reconstruction as late, *ad hoc* solutions to problems he would have avoided had he stuck to some supposedly more "originary" notion of phenomenology. The standard objection that comes up as soon as the issue of a reconstructive phenomenology is raised, is that the evidential claims that are normally associated with phenomenology as a "rigorous science" no longer apply, and that what is reconstructively "given" (i.e.,

---

[32] XXXV, p. 40f.
[33] XXXV, p. 42.
[34] See for instance V, p. 146/CW 3, p. 413.

therefore not given but precisely posited, conjectured) should therefore be ruled out. Another insufficient position is to claim that the field that is reached by means of these analyses is no longer that of transcendental phenomenology, but instead reflects Husserl's supposedly growing interest in anthropology, considered as a straightforward investigation of natural experience.

What these objections fail to recognize is that Husserl during the 1920's and -30's had to adapt the method of the transcendental reduction so that it does not impeach but precisely enables manifestation.[35] This is why Husserl went to such lengths to differentiate the concept of evidence around this time, for even though that which is reconstructed does not have the same high degree of evidence as that which is given for immanent reflection, it can still be relevant in the uncovering of concrete subjectivity precisely as additional, secondary evidence.

It is important to see the degree to which these analyses of dismantling and reconstruction are a continuation of the genetic analyses of association, which will be analyzed in Chapter Five. To give a preliminary name to this mode of investigation we may call it "depth phenomenology".[36] Arriving here did not come easily for Husserl: one only needs to recall his initial rejection of all investigations into "hypothetically assumed processes in the unconscious depths of the soul" in *Logische Untersuchungen*.[37] By the 1920's Husserl had gained a clearer picture of what such an investigation must amount to. Behind the constitution of nature and the world as pregiven, which includes both the active and passive participation of intersubjectivity, there is, he says in a text from 1925, the "hidden subjectivity of hidden intentionality and its syn-

[35] Cf. the appendix 4 in *Ideen II*, where Husserl speaks – in general terms – of this as a "a matter of life and death" for phenomenology (IV, p. 312/CW 3, p. 326). The core of this methodological ideal is expressed already in LU, where Husserl says that the choice of descriptive expressions has to comply with the concrete examples (XIX/1, p. 410), which is only another way of expressing the phenomenological slogan *zu den Sachen selbst*.

[36] This accords with general positive statements from Husserl on the necessity of investigating the "hidden depths of transcendental subjectivity" (VIII, p. 168) and the "hidden apriori of deeper constitution" (IX, p. 505); cf. also *Erfahrung und Urteil*, § 11 for instance.

[37] XIX/1, p. 398f.

theses".[38] This Husserl tentatively relates to "the streaming intentional life" in which all pregiven is constituted, but it carries a yet further dimension within itself (rather than making up a separate constitutive layer), which was to serve as the starting point of many of Husserl's later investigations in the C-manuscripts for instance:

> ... but "behind" this there is the deeper subjective which discloses the constitution of immanent time, and so everywhere. The task of bringing this deeper layer forth and clarifying the motivational way that leads to it, was something that I came to see late (IX, Beilage XXVII [1925] p. 507).

This represents a further step along the lines initiated by some of the Bernau-texts, notably those where Husserl began to relate the analyses of temporality to those of concrete subjectivity, for these early genetic analyses are a good starting point for the further investigation of the subjective *Tiefenschichten* that lie "behind" the constitution of the pregiven in streaming intentional life.[39] In a yet later text, Husserl connects this depth-phenomenology with the investigation of the "prebeing" (*das Vorseiende*):

> Compare the differentiation between the first phenomenology as disentanglement of the constitution of the world as pregiven being, wherein the prebeing does not appear, and the deeper layer of phenomenology which concerns the (not-active) constitution of prebeing (XV, Nr. 35 p. 613n [1933]).

The full move beyond the realm of reflection is taken once it is granted that there are constitutive processes operative even though they are presently not available for reflection. This problem was encountered by Husserl in connection with the passive syntheses operating in preconstitution, and it is only with these new aspects of the genetic methodology that he is in a position to really explain how this is possible.[40] In this sense, the methodological position of the lectures on

---

[38] IX, Beilage XXVII p. 505n.

[39] XXXIII, Nr. 14-15.

[40] On "Vorkonstitution", see for instance Hua XXXI, §§ 1, 4, 10ff; Beilage VIII/CW 9, §§ 49, 52, 58ff; appendix 36. See also Hua XI *passim*; *Erfahrung und Urteil*, §§ 23a, 36, 50, 61, 81. The relation between what is passively preconstituted and its cooperation with the active constitution of the I is the main theme in Bégout, *La généalogie de la logique*.

passive synthesis in Hua XI is not on a par with its concrete analyses. The method of dismantling allows the investigator to infer constitutive processes that can only be brought to light after the event (*nachträglich*). What matters here above all, is that the necessary step beyond reflection occurs since the dismantling of a present experience in the direction of its prehistory, will encounter a limit where the constitutive steps can only be "given" through a reconstruction of what must have occurred. Although there is general agreement that this originary passive sphere of genetic constitution is not available by means of immediate egological reflection, it is quite common to regard the anonymity of the deepest genetic functioning I as an absolute anonymity.[41]

This led for instance Landgrebe to part ways with Husserl's phenomenology and, here following Gadamer, to opt for a Heideggerian hermeneutical approach.[42] Held, and following him Lee, instead argued that due to this absolute anonymity, the originary passivity must first be analyzed as it manifests itself in the other, and that I can only thereafter apply this to my own sphere of anonymity.[43] But there is a problem with this that neither Held nor Lee seems to acknowledge: why would the anonymity of the other be more clearly given to me than my own anonymity? In a sense, both Gadamer and Landgrebe were correct when they saw that the way out of this aporia resides in adopting hermeneutics, and although choosing to do so by means of Heidegger is as good

[41] See for instance Held (1966), p. 94ff, Landgrebe (1982), p. 77 and Lee (1993), p. 114ff. Also Kortooms comes close to this since it is argued that the notion of a passive intentionality is given up by Husserl in the C-manuscripts in favour of a "completely passive" fusion with no links to the I (see *Phenomenology of Time*, p. xviiif, 258ff, 288).

[42] See Gadamer's analysis in *Wahrheit und Methode*, p. 250ff, 258ff. On Landgrebe's equally influential interpretation, Husserl's concept of passive consciousness paradoxically becomes very similar to Freud's concept of the unconscious, for the heart of functioning transcendental subjectivity thereby becomes just such a "radical alterity" that philosophers have criticized Freud for; see "Das Problem der passiven Konstitution" (1982), p. 75ff.

[43] See Held (1966), p. 151-163; Lee (1993), p. 156ff. Lee connects this task with the psychological way: "Den einzigen Zugang zu dieser urpassiven Sphäre der genetischen Konstitution bietet der Weg zur Reduktion über die intentionale Psychologie [...]. Meine Bewusstseinsgestalten im urpassiven Zeitstrom sind mir in ihrer rein psychologischen Struktur nicht völlig verschlossen, sondern sie sind mir prinzipiell zugänglich auf dem Umweg über die Mitsubjekte, denen ich in der Lebenswelt begegne" (p. 115).

an option as any, an alternative reading of Husserl's account of passivity will show that the anonymity of the functioning I can be accounted for in a way that they never considered.

The dismantling of experiences-already-had proceeds via the web of intentional implication, which accounts for its relation to intuition and the reverberation of the *Urstiftung* of the experience. But besides accounting for a view of the build-up of meaning in subjective life, Husserl also employs *Abbau* for larger historico-cultural projects, such as the dismantling of the scientific "idealizations" that cover over the life-world.[44] This process however leads back to subjectivity, since the only way to really come to grips with this "covering over" is, ideally speaking, to go through the whole history from Galileo onwards and so to speak interiorize the determining points, in order to subject them to the phenomenological critique of evidence: this each one has to do for himself in order to achieve the necessary evidence.[45] Thereby one will accomplish the "breakthrough to the concealed foundation of [...] sense" of these idealizations in the "most original experience".[46] In this way, intentional implications will connect this "original" experience – which is a limit-concept that states more the striving not to acquiesce in the scientistic prejudgement than a positive experience in its own right – of the life-world, with the end result of the idealizations which is the full covering-over of it:

> The revealing of these intentional implications and with them the history of the world itself, in which the subject of psychology already finds himself as in one ready-made, also means, therefore, a retrogression to what is subjective since it is through the intentional activity of the subject that the world has obtained this form; but it is a retrogression to a hidden subjectivity – hidden because it is not capable of being exhibited as present in reflection in its intentional activity but can only be indicated by the sedimentations left by this activity in the pregiven world (*Erfahrung und Urteil*, § 11 p. 47/Engl. p. 48).

But while it is important to emphasize this connection between *Abbau* and experience, it must not be overvalued, as if the dismantling

[44] *Erfahrung und Urteil*, § 11. This is also the theme of *Krisis*, § 9f; see also VI, p. 498 .
[45] *Erfahrung und Urteil*, § 11, p. 47f/Engl. p. 49.
[46] *Erfahrung und Urteil*, § 11, p. 46/Engl. p. 47.

could never go wrong. On the contrary, there is little to go by, restricting ourselves here to subjective life, since the richness of life tends to cover the sedimentations just as efficiently as the naturalistic worldview covers the life-world. Therefore Husserl already from the outset found it necessary to impose constraints in the form of negative restrictions:

> We can in a certain way [...] systematically dismantle our complete experience, we can consider for ourselves how the perception must be construed according to its horizons, when we exclude certain experiences from the genesis, that is when we assume that certain groups of experiences were never possible (XIV, Nr. 6 p. 115 [1921]).

Given this framework, the main point for introducing the concept of dismantling is that transcendental phenomenology needs a method that enables it to go beyond the description of the present, in the direction of its meaning-history, which is to say that it is a concept that seems to be immediately called for as soon as the genetic move has been thoroughly established. However, dismantling comes into play notably when it comes to investigating the "hidden" dimensions of life that are out of reach for reflection. This could be taken to imply the actuality of a random temporal limit, but it is something else that is at stake, of a structural order:

> The "chaos" of "impressions" organizes itself – the impressions are not yet objects, they are elements of reduction, genetical originary elements to which the dismantling of intentionality and its genesis leads back (XI, Beilage XIX "Zur Phänomenologie der Assoziation" p. 413 [1926]).

Dismantling thus engages with elements in life that for essential reasons must remain inaccessible.[47] This *eo ipso* means that transcendental phenomenology becomes a hermeneutical project to a greater extent, which again stands in some contrast to Husserl's earlier approach.[48] It is only at this level that it becomes possible to seriously

[47] See Vincenzo Costa (1998), p. 22f.

[48] On this, see Christian Lotz, "Das Ereignis des Unverständlichen. Husserls Hermeneutik und der Ursprung der genetischen Phänomenologie" (2004), who argues that the basic methodological idea of hemeneutics (in Gadamer's sense) is to be found *in nuce* in Husserl's phenomenology, and more precisely in the motivation to go from static to genetic phenomenology.

maintain that "genuine analysis of consciousness is so to speak a hermeneutics of conscious life".[49]

4. The "living present" as the source of the "unconscious" and its disclosure by means of the radicalized reduction

In Husserl's rich lectures on passive syntheses there is a short passage that brings the analysis opened there to a limit, which will only be surpassed in his *Nachlass*. The theme discussed there is not developed any further in the text, but it contains the core of what will be pursued in the following sections:

> Only a radical theory that does justice in the same way to the concrete structure of the living present and to the structure of the particular concretions themselves arising from constitutive elements, can solve the enigma of association, and with this all enigmas of the "unconscious" and of varying modes of "becoming conscious" (XI, § 34 p. 165/CW 9, p. 214).

Although just as reluctant to accept "hypothetically assumed" unconscious processes as he was in *Logische Untersuchungen*, Husserl has by now found a method to account for them that is intuitive, based on experience within the reduced field. Like Freud, he has come to regard the key to understanding these processes in associative consciousness. In the lectures on passive syntheses, Husserl does not proceed much further in the direction hinted at here, but in many other later texts the program indicated is richly developed.

From these texts the structures and processes in conscious life that Freudian repression presents us with can ultimately begin to be clarified. In order to show this, the living present and its fundamental structure must be outlined on the basis of the investigations into

[49] "Phänomenologie und Anthropologie" [1931], in Hua XXVII, p. 177/CW 6, p. 497: "Genuine analysis of consciousness is, so to say, the hermeneutic of conscious life". The distance between the investigation and its theme is thus no longer accidental, something that could be overcome by means of a more refined method, another reduction or greater concreteness of the phenomena, and in this sense there is a genuine rapprochement to Heidegger's position in *Sein und Zeit*. Phenomenology, he there states at the opening, is to investigate "solches, was sich zunächst und zumeist gerade nicht zeigt, was gegenüber dem, was sich zunächst und zumeist zeigt, verborgen ist" (SZ, p. 35); cf. the *Seminare* (1973) for a further discussion of such a "Phänomenologie des Unscheinbaren", p. 399.

passivity in our previous discussion. This will first be attempted by means of the standard method of the reduction that Husserl employs in the lectures on passive synthesis to account for association, which explores the psychological way to some degree.[50] But the more precise outline of the structure of the "unconscious" and the living present necessitate a different methodological approach, since it becomes clear to Husserl that they function at a level that genetically precedes the noetic-noematic correlation that the reduction thematizes.

The "unconscious" for Husserl has its basic structure in the retentional processes that have lost their own affective force and will only be awakened by means of an association. This "universal substratum" of consciousness is in a sense the centre towards which all genetic *Rückfrage* will aim, since it is here that all our sedimented experiential life with all of its unlimited intentional connections resides. Although unavailable for the active I, in the sense that we cannot at will reach into this sphere that lacks affective prominence, it is still "given" as a horizon that is present for every living present:

> Continuous retentional modification proceeds up to an essentially necessary limit. That is to say: with this intentional modification there goes hand in hand a gradual diminution of prominence; and precisely this has its limit, at which the formerly prominent subsides into the universal substratum – the so called "unconscious", which, far from being a phenomenological nothing, is itself a limit-mode of consciousness. The whole intentional genesis relates back to this substratum of sedimented prominences, which, as a horizon, accompanies every living present and shows its own continuously changing sense when it becomes "awakened" [*Auf diesen Hintergrund der sedimentierten Abgehobenheiten, der als Horizont alle lebendige Gegenwart begleitet und seinen kontinuierliche wechselnden Sinn in der "Weckung" zeigt, bezieht sich die ganze intentionale Genesis zurück*] (XVII, Beilage II, p. 318f/*Formal and Transcendental Logic*, p. 319).

Even though the sedimented activity has lost its direct power to affect us consciously (just as an ordinary meal eaten long ago by now lacks all distinctive features), it never the less co-functions in (ideally)

[50] XI, § 26 p. 118f/CW 9, p. 163f. The psychological way is, as is often the case, not explicitly mentioned here, but the *Umschlag*-thematics is abundantly present: it is what makes the transcendental phenomenological analysis of association possible, it is thus what makes possible the determination of association as the most fundamental principle of passive genesis.

all associative awakenings. Thus it also informs our secondary passivity, our habituality which while expressing a "core" of our personal style, is also in ceaseless self-alteration:

> To put it simply, the sedimented activity and its constant co-functioning in the awakenings, in the constant association, is unconscious in the utmost sense; and intimately connected to this is the constant habituality, which constantly changes itself (B II 3/4b [1934]).[51]

So what is "unconscious" will in part determine our habituality, which co-determines our being in the surrounding world.[52] More than so, it is one's entire world as experienced that is affected by these habitualities, in so far as these determine one's "individuality as the total style and habitus" which pervades "all one's modes of behaviour, all one's activities and passivities, and to which the entire psychic basis constantly contributes".[53]

If the "unconscious" in Husserl's sense is only accessible by way of the long and seemingly abstract detour of inner time-consciousness, as was suggested at the beginning of this section, then how are we from there to proceed to a philosophical understanding of the living richness of perversion, neurosis and other features of repressed life? The hypothesis presented here (and developed throughout the remainder of this chapter) is that it is only with the "radicalized reduction to the streaming living present" (as it is called in manuscript C 3), and closely connected to this

---

[51] B II 3/4b: "Schlechthin, im äussersten Sinn unbewusst ist die sedimentierte Aktivität und ihr ständiges Mit-fungieren in den Weckungen, in der ständigen Assoziation; und damit innig zusammengehörig die ständige und ständig sich wandelnde Habitualität." See also HuMat 8, Nr. 97 [1931], p. 446: "Das erste Unbewusste also in der Sphäre der Primordialität als schlafende Assoziation; die Assoziation mit Anderen, die explizite Assoziation der Einfühlung, Assoziation also ausserordentlich erweitert, auch Assoziation der Akte, der Stellunghaben als Habitualitäten, Assoziation durch Einfühlung etc. immer assoziativ Geltungsassoziationen implizierend, Notwendigkeit der Mitgeltung, Notwendigkeit des In-Widerspruch-Kommens, der Modalisierung, die Restitution der Einstimmigkeit."

[52] Bergmann & Hoffmann in their joint article "Habitualität als Potentialität: Zur Konkretisierung des Ich bei Husserl" investigate the role of intentional modification in relation to the constitution of unconscious habitualities: "Husserl geht soweit zu sagen dass zwar, bevor ein jeweiliger Akt sich konkret vollzieht, eine Mannigfaltigkeit von möglichen Akten denkbar, anschaulich ist, dass aber letztlich – in Bezug auf seinen bewussten und unbewussten Voraussetzungen (Habitualitäten) – nur ein Akt möglich ist" (1984, p. 290).

[53] IV, p. 277.

the method of *Rückfrage* (both it seems first thematized around 1930), that the deepest level of subjective functioning can begin to be disclosed. This phenomenological investigation will then provide a sketch of the basic outline of passive consciousness that is both sufficiently subtle and broad to account for the possibility of the Freudian ideas of repression, association and the drives as central yet only loosely connected features.

One of the main features of the C-manuscripts in comparison to the 1905 and the 1917-18 texts on inner time-consciousness is that the predominantly formal aspects of the latter gives way to a decisively more "concrete" analysis, which stems from the investigation of transcendental life that was undertaken in the meantime. This is clearly reflected in the central concept of *lebendige Gegenwart*, which is analyzed from various angles in virtually all the C-manuscripts. When Husserl refers to the expression *lebendige Gegenwart* in earlier texts, it does not yet have the particular connotations that were first developed in connection precisely with the "radicalized reduction" in March, 1930.[54] So for instance in the Bernau texts, the expression occurs in relation to the analysis of the individualization of the stream, and it is treated as equivalent with the "subjective present" as the living, i.e. "movable" present that belongs to my stream of experience.[55] This enables Husserl to investigate the constitution of time as pertaining to the I more thoroughly in later texts and from this self-transcending source as a living streaming presence, to further account for all the layers of constitution ending with communally constituted objective time.[56]

---

[54] The "radicalized reduction" is first presented in XXXIV, Nr. 11 after which the manuscript (C 3) is continued in HuMat 8, Nr. 8-20. Curiously, the expression itself only seems to appear in a quotation by Held: "Die Reduktion auf die lebendige Gegenwart ist die radikalisierte Reduktion auf diejenige Subjektivität, in der alles mir-Gelten ursprünglich sich vollzieht, in der aller Seinssinn für mich Sinn ist als mir erlebnismässig bewusster, geltender Sinn" (C 3 I, S. 3 [1930]) (*Lebendige Gegenwart*, p. 66); this fragment is not part of the printed text in Hua XXXIV. In the latter it is referred to as "radical reduction" and even "the most radical": "Die Reduktion auf die lebendige Gegenwart ist die radikalste Reduktion auf diejenige Subjektivität, in der alles Mir-Gelten sich ursprünglich vollzieht" (XXXIV, Nr. 11 p. 187).

[55] XXXIII, Nr. 14, p. 274f; cf. also p. 140, 150.

[56] The notion of "Selbsttranszendenz" is developed in for instance C7; see HuMat 8, Nr. 32 p. 130ff.

If Husserl has now discovered that the reduction must lead us to a constitutive layer that precedes the noesis-noema structure, then how does this relate to the "absolute" consciousness for which we "lack names" that was reached already in the early lectures on time-consciousness? Fundamentally they are the same, and Held was right when he said that these names that are "lacking" must eventually be given through the phenomenological *Rückfrage* that is attempted again and again in these texts.[57] The "absolute" is now shown to be "absolute temporisation", the very "temporisation of reason".[58] The *Rückfrage* into the genetic sources of our world-apperception thus gains a new focus by revealing yet another prejudgement that clouds our self-understanding:

> The reduction to the living present is the most radicalized reduction to the subjectivity in which the process of all becoming-valid-for-me is originarily completed, in which all being-meaning is meaning for me and experientially given for me as consciously valid meaning. It is the reduction to the sphere of originary temporisation [*Urzeitigung*], in which the first and original-source-like meaning of time appears – time precisely as living streaming present (XXXIV, Nr. 11 p. 187 [C 3/1930]).

After this new, radicalized reduction is performed that which has been the basis of our previous investigation – namely, the view of consciousness as a stream of experiences – is no longer valid and is shown to be a naïve presupposition. What does this leave us with? With this new reduction, we are asked to give up a notion of ourselves that has not only been reached by demanding philosophical labour, but which is also deeply rooted in our everyday self-understanding. For once I parenthesize the validity of regarding myself in terms of my own life process, as my own sequential flow in which one experience is linked with another, we are left only with the very functioning "there" which gives these experiences.

---

[57] Held (1966), p. 94: "Doch diese Bemerkung ist im sinne Husserls so zu ergänzen, dass diese Namen sich prinzipiell durch aufweisende phänomenologische Rückfragen finden lassen müssen."

[58] XV, Nr. 38 "Zeitigung – Monade" [1934/C 1], p. 669. "Das Absolute ist nichts anderes als absolute Zeitigung, und schon ihre Auslegung als das Absolute, das ich direkt als meine stehend-strömende Urtümlichkeit vorfinde, ist Zeitigung, dieses zum Urseienden" (p. 670).

Like the absolute consciousness of the early lectures, this functioning centre is not itself in time and has no location on a temporal scale, since the radicalized reduction has bracketed the representation of time as a stream consisting of one now after the other.[59] This "pre-temporal" present does not come and go but is the constant source of my world-presentifying life, the presentifying present I that in this sense must be understood as being my "living" source, my "living" present. By virtue of all the passively pre-constituted and higher level constituted temporal objects that affect the living present when we consider it in its full concretion, it can appear to itself as "costreaming" with these noetic-noematic structures.[60] Likewise, this "streaming" character of the living present must not be understood in a spatial sense in any worldly way, nor as the coexistence that the normal epoché would disclose. The streaming character of the living present is not distinct from its enduring aspect, and it designates an originary spacing that is neither external *Aussereinandersein* nor internal *Ineinandersein*, but which produces these.[61] But there is more to it than this, since the radicalized reduction brings into view – for the first time – that deeply hidden source which is at the same time that which is closest to us and, precisely because of this the most foreign, most inaccessible aspect of our functioning lives.[62] Husserl tries to capture this paradoxical egoic aspect of the streaming living present with the term *Ur-Ich* or *Ur-Ego*:

> The transcendental I is already a constituted image and as such something that must be parenthesized. That is to say, through this reduction we finally come upon a transcendental *Ur-Ich* and a transcendental originary life in which every concrete I [...] becomes temporized, and gains being in an immanent transcendental temporality.

---

[59] See XXXIV, Nr. 11 p. 187. Cf. also HuMat 8, Nr. 27 p. 117 [C 6/1932]: "Aber im Grunde ist die Urzeit noch nicht ernstlich Zeit, sondern nur Vorstufe der Zeit als Koexistenzform".

[60] Cf. HuMat 8, Nr. 95 p. 430.

[61] See XXXIV, Nr. 11 p. 187: "Die strömende lebendige Gegenwart ist 'kontinuierlich' strömendes Sein und doch nicht in einem Aussereinandersein, nicht in raumzeitlicher (welträumlicher), nicht in 'immanent zeitlicher' Extension Sein (also in keinem Außereinander, das Nacheinander heißt, Nacheinander in dem Sinne eines Stellen-auseinander in einer eigentlich so zu nennenden Zeit)."

[62] See HuMat 8, Nr. 27 p. 115: "Die transzendentale Reduktion als Reduktion auf mein transzendentales Ego in seiner unausgelegten 'stummen' Konkretion – die erste Wesensschau und Deskription, die der allgemeinsten ständige Formstruktur des transzendentalen Ego, ist die des ständigen Strömens."

> [...] On the one hand we have the temporal stream of consciousness and related to this temporality the transcendental I with its acts, its capabilities, its acquired habitualities which has constituted a spatio-temporal world and still does so. On the other hand, as the originary ground of this temporisation [*Urgrund dieser Zeitigung*] and of everything that stands against this immanent "transcendent" temporisation we have the *Ur-Ich*, concretely grasped as the I of this all-temporising life. In a certain sense one can say that all time springs forth from temporisation, and all temporisation springs forth from an originary temporisation [*Urzeitigung*] (XXXIV, Nr. 20 p. 300 [C2/1931]).

The problematics of the *Ur-Ich*, which in Husserl's published works most notably surfaces in *Krisis*, is only thematized once intersubjectivity has been properly presented.[63] As Taguchi has pointed out, the problem of the *Ur-Ich* comes to the fore as soon as the seeming discrepancy between the intersubjective and the radically egological conceptions of phenomenology demands a solution.[64] This means that the level of the streaming living present, as the standing-moving source of all intentional life, can be seen as one at which the distinction between "I" and "we" is invalid.[65] It is in this sense that Husserl speaks of the epoché, i.e. the radicalized reduction, as creating "a unique sort of philosophical solitude which is the fundamental methodical requirement for a truly radical philosophy".[66] Thus the "I" that is reached in the epoché is not an I, properly speaking, and can only be called "I" "by equivocation". With the reduction to the level of the *Ur-Ich*, we instead encounter an utmost alert mode of consciousness that is at once deeply embedded in this "self-forgetfulness" that Husserl speaks of, while at the same time participating in the unfolding of this *Selbstvergessenheit* into unconcealedness by means of the self-interpretation.[67]

---

[63] VI, § 54b [title:] "As primal ego [*Ur-Ich*], I constitute my horizon of transcendental others as cosubjects [*Mitsubjekte*] within the transcendental intersubjectivity which constitutes the world" (pp. 187-190/Engl. tr. pp. 184-186). This section follows on the rich presentation of the intersubjective life-world in §§ 28ff.

[64] Shigeru Taguchi, *Das Problem des ,Ur-Ich' bei Edmund Husserl. Die Frage nach der selbstverständlichen ,Nähe' des Selbst* (2006), p. 112.

[65] "All of mankind, and the whole distinction and ordering of the personal pronouns, has become a phenomenon within my epoché; and so has the privilege of I-the-man among other men" (VI, § 54 b p. 188/Engl. p. 184).

[66] VI, § 54 b, p. 188/ Engl. p. 184.

[67] VI, § 54 b, p. 188/ Engl. p. 184. On this, see Taguchi (2006), p. 112f.

Natural, everyday life covers over the processes of the *Ur-Ich* to such a degree that they appear completely foreign, "unheard of" for the I when they eventually become disclosed by means of the radicalized reduction.[68] This deepest functioning source of time and also space, conjoined by the originary hyletic that affects our living flesh and thus triggers temporisation, is almost fully concealed from our everyday life.[69] These processes that are simply taken for granted are still what is in a sense closest to us since they are our functioning intentionality, that which gives us the world. The functioning life of transcendental constitution is first "by nature" but not first "for me"; it represents the hidden philosophical foundation of our naïve, worldly life which, in turn, necessarily must precede philosophical reflection.

What we encounter here is a deepening of the "splitting of the I" (*Ichspaltung*) that has been an integral part of phenomenology from its conception (approached in *Logische Untersuchungen* already as the distinction between the subject in the world and the phenomenologist reflecting upon her worldly self). The position accorded to the phenomenological (which became the transcendental) I is now shown to be an

[68] Taguchi analyses the *Ur-Ich* precisely by means of this movement between what is closest and therefore farthest away. See also Lee (1993), p. 212, 214-217 who also emphasizes that the *Ur-Ich*, in distinction to the *Vor-Ich*, is in immediate closeness to the "brightness" of selfconsciousness.

[69] I introduce the concept of "flesh", "living flesh" at this level to designate a distance or shift of meaning from "lived body" that I have used previously to translate *Leib*. I have found no concept such as *Ur-Leib* or *Leibigung* to designate this in the C-ms., but it is clear that the concept of *Leib* also undergoes a change of meaning with the radicalized reduction that would, so I argue, correspond to *Ur-Zeit* and *Zeitigung*. In earlier texts Husserl however speaks of an *Urleib* in order to distinguish my own, one and only originary lived body from the body that appears in mirror-images (XIII, Nr. 12 p. 327f; cf. p. 55ff; see also IX, p. 107). It is also clear that the radically reduced *Leib* as it appears in the C-ms. was prepared for in many earlier texts and drafts: see XXXIII, Nr. 17 p. 300; see also the rich analyses of the lived body in relation to the constitution of space in Hua XIV (p. 540f for instance); a theme that was investigated at length in the D-ms. In D 17 from 1934 for instance Husserl speaks of my *Urleib* as corresponding to the function of the earth [*Erde*] as the *Ur-Arche* of the world; see Farber (ed.), *Philosophical Essays in Memory of Edmund Husserl*, p. 323. For a discussion of the body as *Urleib* at the level of the radicalized reduction, see the analysis by Depraz, *Transcendance et incarnation* p. 269ff. For an interpretation of the Freudian unconscious along the lines of the lived body/flesh, see Birgit Frostholm, *Leib und Unbewußtes. Freuds Begriff des Unbewußten interpretiert durch den Leib-Begriff Merleau-Pontys* (1978); see also Ricœur's remark in *De l'interprétation*, p. 372.

intermediary between the worldly I and the *Ur-Ich*, which is to say that the transcendental position has been given a new grounding.[70] Husserl's *Ichspaltung* thus shows how selfhood and otherness in their deepest functioning source are inseparably intertwined, and that consciousness is essentially subjected to a necessary fissure, as long as it wants to understand its own processes.[71]

The method of questioning backwards seeks out the ultimate genetic basis which makes experience possible, and this has led to the living present as the heart of functioning transcendental life. In this sense the living present is the absolute I in its most originary form, and is therefore the *letztfungierende* I. It is therefore clear that genetically early configurations of both the I and time are called for, in order to conceptualize this process:

> The *Rückfrage* must here make everything clear. The stream is to be temporalized apriori from the I. This temporalization is in itself streaming; the streaming is always there in advance. But also the I is there in advance, it is as awakened I (transcendental-phenomenological awakened) always the I of consciousness (XXXIV, Nr. 10 p. 181 [C 17/1932]).

The living present is therefore not only a major phenomenon in itself, it is that which makes up "the concrete originary reality of phenomenology, towards which all transcendental self-understanding must come back, in its endlessly progressive work of interpretation".[72] This analysis enables Husserl to show that all constitution resides on two presuppositions that are located at the level of the streaming living present. A closer look will also reveal that the *Ur-Ich* and the process of

---

[70] XXXIV, Nr. 20 p. 299f [C2/1931]: "Wir können sagen, *ich muss die phänomenologische Reduktion nicht abschliessen damit, dass ich die Welt einklammere* und darin mein raumzeitlich reales Menschsein in der Welt (und erst recht das anderer Menschen) einklammere, sondern auf mich als transzendentales Ich und transzendentales Leisten, also transzendentales Leben zurückgeworfen, muss ich *an diesem selbst transzendentale Reduktion* üben, nämlich alle mir naiv auferlegten Apperzeptionen einklammern, die selbst schon fundierte Leistungen sind." And in a footnote Husserl adds: "Das naiv gewonnene transzendentale Ich muss selbst wieder einer transzendentalen Reduktion unterworfen werden."

[71] See HuMat 8 Nr. 1 p. 2 [C 2/August 1931].

[72] See B III 9/10 [1931], where the living present is described as "die konkrete Urwirklichkeit der Phänomenologie, auf die alle transzendentale Selbstverständigung in ihrer unendlich aufsteigenden Auslegungsarbeit zurückgehen muss" (quoted in Held 1966, p. 68).

temporisation that I have treated together so far, must in fact be distinguished as parts within this whole:

> Constitution of being [...] has two originary presuppositions, two originary sources that temporally speaking [...] always "lie at its foundation": 1) my primal I as functioning, as *Ur-Ich* in its affections and actions, with all the essential configurations that belong to it; 2) my primal not-I as originary stream of temporisation and even as originary form of temporisation, constituting a temporal field, that of the originary materiality. But both originary grounds are united, inseparable, and thus when each is considered for itself it is abstract (HuMat 8, Nr. 49 p. 199 [C 10/Sept. 1931]).

Here Husserl posits the division of the I more clearly within the very structure of the streaming living present, thus disclosing the presence of the *Ichspaltung* also at the genetically deepest functioning level. At the very heart of what is most intimately my "own" there is a fissure, a fundamental difference between what pertains to the *Ur-Ich* and to the *Nicht-Ich*. Although in the vicinity of both Heidegger's and Derrida's thought here (*Riß*, *différance*), Husserl does not (unlike Derrida) emphasize the difference itself as originary, as "productive" of the two themes brought together. But that does not mean that we remain safely on the shores of foundational metaphysics, for the "absolute has in itself its ground and in its groundless being its absolute necessity".[73] It is true that the absolute is "groundless being" precisely because it is its own ground, but this ground is itself (so I will argue) openness to otherness.

5. The self-constitution of the Ur-Ich*:* Ent-Fremdung *and* Ent-Gegenwärtigung

Having presented the preliminary outline of the streaming living present in relation to the *Ur-Ich* and the not-I as a self-transcending temporising and spatialising unity, we can now proceed to investigate its structure closer. Husserl devoted many important manuscripts to the closer determination of the structure of the streaming living present in the early 1930's and as Dorion Cairns reports, he felt this to be "the ultimate problem of phenomenology".[74] It is immediately clear that we

---

[73] "Das Absolute hat in sich selbst seinen Grund und in seinem grundlosen Sein seine absolute Notwendigkeit [...]" (XV, Nr. 22 p. 385f [E III 9/1931]). Cf. VI, § 53.

[74] Cairns, *Conversations with Husserl and Fink*, June 1932, p. 91f. See for in-

are not dealing with anything like a solipsistic substance closed upon itself, as if Husserl's late philosophy was based on the foundation of a solid subjectual core. What we do find is prerequisites that enable the ceaselessly ongoing self-transcending movement in relation both to myself, the world and the other, kept at bay and in relative yet fragile stability due to the uninterrupted passive syntheses at work.

The gradual unfolding of the structure of the living present indeed poses problems as long as one refuses to go along with the genetic deepening of the static ego-alter ego position that remains Husserl's answer in for instance *Cartesianische Meditationen*.[75] There are however clear indications that suggest further investigations along the lines attempted here.[76] But in order to get a clearer grasp of how alterity is at work at the core of the egological approach, we must push the examination further and see how alterity comes to expression in the sphere of primordiality. Here the analyses of the C-manuscripts – where the reduction to the sphere of primordiality is approached in virtually all the texts – make up a bridge between the *Cartesianische Meditationen* and *Krisis*, where the primordial sphere reappears.[77]

---

stance (restricting ourselves to the C-ms.) HuMat 8 Nr. 10 "Grundstrukturen der konkreten Subjektivität", Nr. 11-13; Hua XXXIV Nr. 9 "Rückgang auf das Ich in der urlebendigen Gegenwart. Zur Strukturlehre der lebendigen Gegenwart: von der Weltepoché rückfragend. Methodische Schwierigkeiten der naiven phänomenologischen Selbstbesinnung"; HuMat 8 Nr. 22, Nr. 23 "Vorstoss zu einer Methode des Abbaus, des radikalen Abbaus der vorgegebenen Welt im Rückgang zur strömenden Gegenwart und systematischer Abbau dieser Gegenwart. <Aufdeckung von Kernstrukturen in der immanenten Zeit und der Konstitution der Natur>", Nr. 24, Nr. 25 "Notiz: Formstruktur der lebendigen Gegenwart", Nr. 26; Hua XV Nr. 11 "<Apodiktische Struktur der transzendentalen Subjektivität.> Problem der transzendentalen Konstitution der Welt von der Normalität aus"; HuMat 8 Nr. 67-87, 95.

[75] For such an interpretation see Tryssesoone 2006 (p. 16f), which although clarifying in many aspects fails to take temporality into account to a sufficient degree.

[76] Most notably in CM, §§ 55-58 where the genetic perspective is approached but just as soon brought back to the level of static analysis, which although it remains determinative in that text all the time cooperates with genetic monadology.

[77] See VI, §§ 54b, 72. Before 1930 Husserl apparently did not distinguish between the reduction to *Eigenheitssphäre* (see CM, §§ 44ff) and the reduction to that which is primordial (such as the *Ur-Ich* for instance). Later he came to realize that the *eigene* is a product of static inquiry (the exclusion of all intentionalities related to the other), whereas the primordial is reached by a genetic analysis (the radicalized reduction), and includes the other as my intentional positing.

Amongst Husserl's publications it is only towards the very end of *Krisis* that we find a sustained account of this problem. The intersubjectivity that is discussed there must not however be construed as a social community "given in the life-world", for this would indefinitely postpone the whole problematic of how to think intersubjectivity as a *reductive* and not a natural intersubjectivity.[78] This, as has often been pointed out, was Alfred Schütz' solution to what he considered to be an insolvable problem in Husserl's transcendental phenomenology.[79] In a certain sense, this example highlights a potential weakness with the ontological way, for if not properly understood, it will easily settle with a reference to the intersubjective world as if that were the ultimate fact, and will thus not lead forth to the deeper reductive attitude. This is why Husserl at the transition of the ontological way and the psychological way in *Krisis* introduces the theme of "self-forgetfulness" of the I, so as to recall that the "we" which has been the centre of the life-world, by necessity must now become an "I".[80] This shift which opens the final section III B of *Krisis* is required in order to correct a methodological "naivety" of the ontological way, for it has now become clear that I have to initiate a reductive reflection upon *myself* as the philosopher that is actually performing the reduction.[81]

Having established the necessity to open up the level of *Ur-Ich* in § 54b as a bridge between the ontological and the psychological ways by means of a (non-explicit) radicalized reduction, Husserl brings the previous investigation of life-worldly intersubjectivity to a halt. But the communitarian aspect is not abandoned, for the aim of the analysis of the "originary I" is also to further investigate the genetically-transcendental status of the communalization (*Vergemeinschaftung*) and temporisation (*Zeitigung*) that were reached in a preliminary fashion in §§ 47, 50. It is therefore in a sense the very process by which the life-

[78] See Depraz, *Transcendance et incarnation*, p. 228ff.

[79] A. Schütz, "The Problem of Transcendental Intersubjectivity in Husserl" (1970), pp. 51-84.

[80] See VI, § 54a, p. 186/ Engl. p. 182 for the need to shift from the ontological to the psychological way: "These are problems that did not announce themselves on the pathway we allowed ourselves to be drawn into, along which we allowed ourselves to be propelled."

[81] VI, § 54b.

world must come to understand itself that is at stake, and for this it can only rely on its singular participants.

From the position of extreme "philosophical solitude" that the radicalized reduction disclosed – which is not the mere "unnaturalness" that the first epoché disclosed but its genetic deepening – Husserl begins the complex movement that will in a first step lead to a radical decentring of the ego.[82] But this should not be conceived of as the abandonment of egology nor a questioning of its validity: the egological starting point remains just as ever our sole access to transcendental phenomenological inquiry. This very inquiry however also brings us to the experience of its limits, and the experience that there in the order of constitution is a genetically deeper layer that is not egological and that in this sense precedes the I. The whole differentiation and ordering of the personal pronouns is at this stage rendered invalid – there is no "you", no "we" etc. – since all of mankind has become a phenomenon in my epoché. Yet the *Ur-Ich* is something that can never lose its "uniqueness and personal indeclinability":

> It is only an apparent contradiction to this that the ego [...] makes itself declinable, for itself, transcendentally; that, starting from itself and in itself, it constitutes transcendental intersubjectivity, to which it then adds itself as a merely privileged member, namely, as "I" among the transcendental others. This is what philosophical self-exposition [*Selbstauslegung*] in the epoché actually teaches us (VI, § 54b p. 188f/Engl. p. 184).

In order to show that the contradiction is indeed only "apparent", Husserl brings into play the two-sided process of "de-presentification" (*Ent-Gegenwärtigung*) and "self-alienation" (*Ent-Fremdung*). This process brings out the fundamental self-alterity that inhabits the I at the deepest genetic level of investigation. It does so first by showing that there is within me a ceaseless and constitutive movement away from presence into the past and the future as a de-presentification. Secondly, there is also a movement away in the form of a self-alienation, which is a modification of this de-presentification by means of empathy. Husserl captures this double movement in a high-density formulation:

[82] VI § 54b p. 188; cf. XV, Nr. 33 p. 586; HuMat 8, Nr. 13 p. 53ff.

> The self-temporisation through de-presentification, so to speak (through recollection), has its analogue in my self-alienation (empathy as a de-presentification of a higher level – de-presentification of my primal presence into a merely representified primal presence) [*Die Selbstzeitigung sozusagen durch Ent-Gegenwärtigung (durch Wiedererinnerung) hat ihre Analogie in meiner Ent-Fremdung (Einfühlung als eine Ent-Gegenwärtigung höherer Stufe – die meiner Urpräsenz in eine bloss vergegenwärtigte Urpräsenz)*]. Thus, in me, "another I" achieves validity of being as compresent [*als kompräsent*] with his own ways of being self-evidently verified, which are obviously quite different from those of a "sense"-perception (VI, § 54b, p. 188f/Engl. p. 184f; tr. mod.).

The problem of the individualization of the "intersubjective streaming being" that characterizes the monadic totality here finds a preliminary solution (to be examined in the following section), by means of a ceaselessly ongoing and self-altering duplicity which accounts for my pre-identity at the deepest genetic level. The self-presence that characterizes the transcendental I at the level of streaming living present thus ultimately consists of two different modes of self-alteration, which by their very movement bring about this "self".[83] It is thus not a question of a fixed and stable unit that is stirred to life from out of its eternal slumber in passivity, but a "self" that is constituted through these "unconscious" movements away from it. It manifests itself as a dual movement away from "itself", the "self" gaining contour only by the traces that these two motions leave behind as constantly shifting sedimentation, with the arrival of ever new hyletic material that by means of temporisation provides material for the pre-constitution, and from which eventually lived experiences are constituted.[84]

---

[83] See Depraz, *Transcendance et incarnation*, p. 250: "À un niveau originaire de la constitution, l'ego s'auto-temporalise, se défaisant par là même de son présent, se 'dé-présentant', et s'aperçoit ainsi de façon auto-constitutive comme autre dans la temporalisation de soi."

[84] Bruzina develops this Finkian theme (*Entgegenwärtigung*) at length in *Edmund Husserl and Eugen Fink: Beginnings and Ends in Phenomenology, 1928-1938* (2004); see in particular pp. 146f, 227-257. He argues that Fink's interpretation emphasizes the horizonal character of temporality to a larger degree than Husserl, and that this is what lies behind Fink's "step beyond Husserl", according to which "it is *depresencing* [i.e. Entgegenwärtigung] that, not itself in time, makes temporal process both temporal and a process and, accordingly, gives to the living present its temporal character as *living*" (p. 236).

Ent-Gegenwärtigung here accounts for our temporal projects, and although Husserl only mentions the past (to explicate the analogy between the givenness of my past and the other), its scope must be extended to the future also. Unlike retention, the emphasis is now more on the self-transcending movement than on the living-on of temporal objects. It's task is not to assure that the objects are not lost as soon as the now has brought another phase of the object into presence, but to account for the deepest pre-egological structuration. This means that the aspect of non-presence that retentional and protentional intentionality brought with them is now reinforced, bringing out the foreignness that inheres in memories and expectations, and confronting them with their own limits: complete oblivion and death.

Ent-Fremdung on the other hand is more immediately foreign since it involves not my own self-alterity but the alterity of the other. Beneath empathy, and making it possible for the I at higher levels of constitution to intend the other empathically, there is a constant process wherein the *Ur-Ich* (which is prior to all differences between "I" and "we") by moving away from itself in the direction of the other, thereby produces itself.

To speak of "self-alienation" as Carr does, is therefore incorrect to the extent that it encourages one to hold on to the illusory notion of a "self" that only afterwards and almost by accident encounters alienating tendencies, for in *Ent-Fremdung* there is no self heard, only movement away and foreignness. In between these two intimately connected movements (*Ent-Gegenwärtigung* and *-Fremdung*), an "in-between" that is produced by them, a zone for possible centering occurs. The *Ichzentrierung* that comes about together with these two processes is thus not due to some subjective gravitational force, but is a field of tension that is not located in any specific part within the structure of the living present, but is in a sense "everywhere", atopic.[85] On my under-

[85] "Subjekt ist dabei nur ein anderes Wort für die Zentrierung, die alles Leben als Ich-Leben, und somit lebend etwas zu erleben, etwas bewusst zu haben, hat" (HuMat 8, Nr. 10 p. 35 [1931]). The texts Nr. 10-13 all deal with this issue; cf. also the following: "Das Ichzentrum ist in schwer zu beschreibender Weise überall in der lebendigen Gegenwart und überall ist Aktivität in verschiedenen Modis" (HuMat 8, Nr. 67 p. 306 [1931]). "Natürlich ist die Rede vom Ich letztlich bestimmt von der 'Polarisierung' der Ichakte. In der genetischen Rückfrage konstruieren wir als Anfang das noch weltlose Vorfeld und Vor-Ich, das schon Zentrum ist, aber noch

standing, Husserl means that this constitutive self-altering duplicity is a constant process which always underlies our passive intentional life as well as our entire experiential act-life, and not something that occurs just at one time. If we didn't continue this passive and dual self-alteration, there would be no self, no egoic centre that could reflectively-narcissistically reach out to itself in apodictic evidence. The constitution of the I is a ceaseless process that knows of no pauses.

If the living present at its core harbours the dual movement of standing (the *nunc stans*) and streaming (as the C-manuscripts indicated), then one can here see even more concretely how these two aspects of what is one and the same process cooperate. For it is only as streaming movement away that it can bring about a continuous renewal of the self-constitution (what Held calls *Selbstvergemeinschaftung*), which occurs by means of the also passive tendencies towards unification of this sequence of streaming I-projects.[86] The functioning I is always gliding away, since the pre-temporal, temporising original present de-presentifies itself, and thereby it undergoes a self-pluralization. In connection with this, Held therefore speaks of the originary structure of the I as one that is "dilapidated" (*hinfällig*), picking up an idea developed by Merleau-Ponty, who spoke of a *faiblesse intérieur* of the *letztfungierende Ich*.[87] This inner dilapidation brings to light that the *Ur-Ich* cannot uphold itself but constantly loses itself in the streaming, which is also its source of renewal.

As Held points out, this inner dilapidation of the originary I is the basis for the inability of the reflecting I to grasp itself as absolutely transparent, it is the reason why the intentional having of itself is always also an experience of elusion. There is therefore no presentification without de-presentification, no *Gegenwärtigung* without *Ent-Gegenwärtigung*, and similarly, no pure *nunc stans* in absolute immanence and without intentional implications, but always only a function-

nicht 'Person', geschweige denn Person im gewöhnlichen Sinn von menschlicher Person" (HuMat 8, Nr. 79 p. 352 [1931]).

[86] Held, *Lebendige Gegenwart*, p. 171f; cf. p. XI, 164f, 168f.

[87] Held, *Lebendige Gegenwart*, p. 171f; Merleau-Ponty, *Phénoménologie de la perception*, p. vii, 489.

ing present, which is always directed over and beyond itself to something transcendent.[88]

The singularity of the *Ur-Ich* is therefore something that is first gained from a pre-reflective plurality of I's, when one considers this from the perspective of the order of being. The process of communalization therefore brings to light both the visibility of the I (as open potential for reflection) and its invisibility (as that which constantly withdraws from reflection). When the static conception gives way to the process of self-temporisation that founds it, there can be no other ego that is opposed to my ego, and the otherness of the other must be reinterpreted, no longer the-other-within-me but something else: compresence (*Kompräsenz*).[89] This shift signals that the radicalized reduction has been brought into play, displaying the self-temporisation whereby the *Ur-Ich* frees itself from its present and similarly frees itself from the other as alter ego, bringing to light this dual process as an integral part of its self-constitution. This is alterity in process, not as something externally encountered.

6. Monadology and the problem of individuation. The intersubjective reduction

Moving upwards from the depth of genetic self-constitution, the analysis must now confront the higher order concept of the monad, for the analysis of the *Ur-Ich* also had repercussions for Husserl's conception of transcendental phenomenology as a monadology. After introducing monadology in this context, the discussion will proceed with a presentation of the intersubjective reduction. The "monad", it will be recalled, is a concept that Husserl in the 1920's employs to denote not merely the "concrete I" as historical being with its habitualities, but in

---

[88] Held, *Lebendige Gegenwart*, p. 172. See also the analysis by Derrida in *Of Grammatology*: "In the originary temporalization and the movement of relationship with the outside, as Husserl actually describes them, nonpresentation or depresentation is as 'originary' as presentation. *That is why a thought of the trace can no more break with a transcendental* phenomenology *than be reduced to* it. Here as elsewhere, to pose the problem in terms of choice, to oblige or to believe oneself obliged to answer it by a *yes* or no, to conceive of appurtenance as an allegiance or non-appurtenance as plain speaking, is to confuse very different levels, paths, and styles. In the deconstruction of the *arché*, one does not make a choice" (p. 61f).

[89] VI, § 54 b p. 188f/ Engl. p. 184f.

the more encompassing sense of including also the flowing multiformity of all intentional life.[90]

Although at first essentially correlated with the Cartesian perspective of static phenomenology, Husserl already at a crucial junction in his lectures on *Grundprobleme* began to explore a more dynamic approach to monadology in relation to the "double reduction".[91] Developing this theme in the early 1920's in several texts in Hua XIV notably in relation to empathy, the concept of the monad underwent substantial revision in the direction of genetic phenomenology, where it became an important tool for stressing the self-transcending character of consciousness as a source of constant "development".[92] The monad, according to this non-Cartesian interpretation, is now a living unit of both awakened and concealed life, whose hidden and thus "unconscious" dimensions must be examined "in its own particular ways".[93] It is only in texts from 1930 onwards that the real genetic sense of the monadology starts to take on a more concrete form, and in a text from 1933 Husserl says that "the community of monads is implicated in the absolute concrete I".[94] But thereby the question of individuation becomes acute: how are we to understand the position of the singular monad in this community?

As we recall, Husserl broke off his early investigation of the double reduction in 1910-11 precisely due to the difficulties he encountered concerning the question of how to understand temporality in relation to

---

[90] I, CM § 33 p. 102f/ Engl. p. 68: "Since the monadically concrete ego includes also the whole of actual and potential conscious life, it is clear that the problem of explicating this monadic ego phenomenologically (the problem of his constitution for himself) must include all constitutional problems without exception. Consequently the phenomenology of this self-constitution coincides with phenomenology as a whole."

[91] See XIII, Beilage III "Monadologie" [1908], and then XIII, Nr. 6 (*Grundprobleme*), § 39.

[92] See XXV, "Natur und Geist" p. 322 [1919]; XIV, Beilage I p. 34ff [1921]; Beilage II p. 43f [1921]; Beilage XIII p. 128 [1921]; Nr. 13 p. 267ff [1922].

[93] "Die Monade ist eine lebendige Einheit, die ein Ich als Pol des Wirkens und Leidens [und als Pol personaler Charaktere] in sich trägt, und eine Einheit des wachen und des verborgenen Lebens, eine Einheit von Vermögen, von 'Dispositionen', und das Verborgene, 'Unbewusste' ist ein eigener Modus für monadische Beschlossenheiten, dessen notwendiger Sinn man in eigenen Weisen ursprünglich schöpfen muss." (XIV, Beilage I p. 34 [1921])

[94] "Hier gewinne ich doch in der intentionalen Verflochtenheit der Primordialitätetn mit ihren Ich die Gemeinschaft der Monaden – im absolut konkreten Ich" (XV, Nr. 33 p. 587 [1933]).

a manifold of subjects. This remained a vexing question for him, as can be seen from many texts from the early 1920's, where he again reflects on the (as he puts it in one place) "problem of the possibility of connection and separation of the streams of consciousness and that of unification and pluralisation".[95] He rejects the thesis according to which there is an originary fusion between the monads, and in this sense the whole analysis of individuation of the stream of consciousness which spans over the larger part of Husserl's career (Hua XIII-XV, the Bernauer-texts, the C-ms., Hua XXXIV, Hua VI) can be seen as a prolonged phenomenological grounding of Leibniz' principle of individuation.[96]

Once the monad is reinterpreted in terms of the later theory of reduction, it becomes an expression of this "intersubjective streaming being" as the *Monadenall*, i.e. non-egological transcendental community.[97] This reinterpretation is closely connected to the theory of intentional implications which enables Husserl to finally see that the plurality of monads is *implicated* in my monad.[98]

This interpretation of monadology shows that there remains a core-level of differentiation even in the deepest intersubjective streaming temporality, otherwise there would be no possibility of implication.[99] The monadology at this founding genetic level does not manifest any egological differentiation, which also implies that the inseparability of the monads in the stream will not appear as such at higher levels of constitution, but there is still sufficient pre-egoic material to maintain a kind of pre-identity of the monads.[100] One way to express this is to say

---

[95] XIV, Beilage XLI p. 300 [1922].

[96] See XIV, p. 300.

[97] XV, Nr. 38 p. 668.

[98] Thus in the title of a text from 1922, Husserl wrote: "Substanz und Monade. Sehr wichtig. Implikation der Monaden noch nicht gesehen" (XIV, Beilage XLI p. 292). See XV, Nr. 36 p. 636f for this implication of the monads.

[99] Depraz speaks of this originary unity in difference as one which always remains "transie d'altération première, fluante et non fusionnante, de sorte que subsiste dans le flux lui-même ce minimum essentiel d'écart à soi qui laisse être ce par quoi toutes les différenciations ultérieures pourront apparaître"; see *Transcendance et incarnation*, p. 328.

[100] Zahavi however seems to reject this idea in *Husserl und die transzendentale Intersubjektivität* p. 67f: "Es ist zwar so, daß die transzendentale Subjektivität schlechthin die transzendentale Intersubjektivität ist, in daß sie und sie allein das konstitutive Korrelat der Welt ist. In ihr ist aber eine notwendige Ich-Zentrierung vogezeichnet als das Ich, das Wir-Bewußtsein hat (XV:426). Das heißt durchaus nicht, daß eine vor-individuierte Intersubjektivität (was genau besehen eine *contra-*

that what is in common is the formal and apodictic structure of originary temporising, whereas what is "pre-individual" is the pre-having of what at higher levels of constitution appear as our concrete temporal projects related to the past and the future, the precise determination of which remains non-apodictic, although they have their mode of evidence.[101]

Having spelt out some of the consequences of the radicalized reduction for Husserl's analysis of egological subjectivity, we must now proceed with the investigation of how this affects his analysis of intersubjectivity. The first outline of the double or intersubjective reduction, as we have seen, offered a revolutionizing possibility to present the transcendental field as being "extended" by means of my ability to so to speak "live myself into the other" in empathic acts.[102] But it is not until the analysis of the reduction in *Grundprobleme* could be founded in intersubjective, flowing time in manuscripts from the early 1930's, that the true significance of this early investigation could be laid bare.

With this new, temporal foundation for the analyses of intersubjectivity (obtained through genetic dismantling following notably the psychological way to the reduction), a radical decentering of the I takes place. For Husserl it is never a question of giving up the egological perspective by dissolving it into some higher unity of undifferentiated being, as if this were the end towards which all egoic life was striving. Instead, what the analyses of intersubjectivity show is that there is a

---

dictio in adjecto wäre) sich nachträglich 'zentriert', sondern die transzendentale Intersubjektivität faßt in sich die transzendentale Subjektivität (XV:75) als den Ort ihrer Entfaltung". But against this one can argue that such a rejection is only possible as long as one does not take temporality into account, for as I have shown by bringing the analyses in Hua XV and the C-ms. together, time as originary temporisation is precisely what makes it necessary to speak of a pre-individuated intersubjectivity (if this is not taken in a strong sense). In the later work *Self-Awareness and Alterity* (p. 153), Zahavi however emphasizes that the rejection of "preindividuation" is only to be upheld if taken in a strong sense: "The term 'preegological' [...] means that the ego is not participating or contributing to the (self-)constitution of the process in any active or attentive way", not that the ego is wholly missing, above all not as though it were question of an absolutely preindividuated ground.

[101] See HuMat 8, Nr. 9 p. 30; Nr. 27 p. 117. For a contrary view however, see XXXIV, Nr. 10 p. 183f (the additions from 1932).

[102] On this *Erweiterung* from me to the other in the texts surrounding the *Cartesianische Meditationen*, see for instance I, *Pariser Vorträge*, p. 35, 38; XV, Nr 7 p. 109.

genetic deepening of egology in that it can be shown to stem from more originary constitutive processes, so that the constitution of the I is always also a process of constitution of the not-I, that which is foreign, other etc.

The basic idea of Husserl's early insights into empathy and intersubjectivity was in a first step more clearly expounded in texts from the 1920's by appealing to the notion of intentional implication.[103] But all along these analyses, there was never any question of presenting the otherness of the other in ways that would move beyond her givenness for me as retraceable from out of my present intentional situation. That is to say, the other was always an alter ego that I could account for by means of my own intentional life, both active and passive, but never beyond what a genetic questioning would be able to come up with as belonging within my retrievable horizon.

The question now is whether or not the radicalized reduction, which brings forth a hitherto concealed genetically primal level of constitution, may disclose an intersubjective dimension that precedes this. For sure, there are plenty of texts from Husserl's late philosophy that merely follow the direction that was pointed out in the *Grundprobleme*, and that analyze the relation between the I and the other in terms of static copresence.[104] But there is also a whole group of texts from 1931 onwards that attempt to work out this relation by means of a somewhat different approach, where the static position of an ego standing over against an other ego is further geneticized.[105]

Kern at one place speaks of a "transformation" occurring in Husserl's theory of intersubjectivity in 1931, so that whereas the streaming living present prior to this was conceived of in egological terms, he establishes

[103] See the remarkable analyses in *Erste Philosophie II*, Hua VIII.

[104] See for instance XV, Nr. 5 "Zum Problem der Intersubjektivität in den *Cartesianischen Meditationen*" [wohl 1930]; and in particular "b) Besonders ad Fünfte Meditation. Der Gang von der phänomenologischen Reduktion" (p. 73f). Cf. Depraz (1995), p. 252.

[105] See HuMat 8, Nr. 13 "Reduktion" [C 3/März 1931]; XV, Nr. 12 p. 189: "Ad fünfte *Meditation*: Konstitution von Realien in der Primordialität als 'Gebilde' des 'ego' und Konstitution von Anderen, nicht als egologischen Gebilden, sondern allen solchen Gebilden transzendent und mit meinem Ego koexistierend" [1931 oder später]; VI, § 71 "The danger of misunderstanding the 'universality' of the phenomenological-psychological epoché. The decisive significance of the correct understanding."

in one text (from March 1931) that the other as streaming co-presence is inseparable from the streaming present of the ego.[106] To put it bluntly, instead of the other being "appresented" by me as an alter ego, we have reached its genetic foundation which discloses itself as *urströmend seienden Intersubjektivität.*[107] The genetization of the I which led to the *Ur-Ich*, is now extended to the other and reaches something that could (at the limit) be called the "primal us" or the *Ur-Wir*. The investigation of the givenness of the other here encounters a greater freedom of manifestation than is to be found in static analysis. Let us investigate this closer as it will also shed light on the actually quite complex position reached in *Krisis*, where Husserl relates the egological analysis of the *Ur-Ich* to transcendental intersubjectivity (communalization) in the final paragraphs. The analysis of the relation between egology and intersubjectivity in *Krisis* thus seems to be based on the investigations of the C-manuscripts that are analyzed here.

In the "concrete living present" understood from the radicalized reduction as presented in C 3 we also, Husserl says, find every other ego that is transcendentally streaming present being, constituted in me as streaming copresent (*mitgegenwärtig*) subjectivity, which itself is concrete, streaming living present: "the other is copresent in me".[108] This analysis of *Mitgegenwart* will be used to stretch the Cartesian dualism that still stands in the way of a more genuine grasp of intersubjectivity.[109] This means that the analogy between recollection and the

[106] Kern XV, p. XLVIII (the passage he refers to, C 3/44a-45b, is now published in HuMat 8, Nr. 13 p. 55ff).

[107] HuMat 8, Nr. 13 p. 57.

[108] "Da ist auch jeder Andere, jedes andere Ego Transzendental-strömendes-Gegenwart-Sein, in mir konstituiert als strömend mit-gegenwärtige Subjektivität, die konkret selbst ist, strömende lebendig konkrete Gegenwart, sowie in mir konstituiert ist strömend meine eigene Zeitlichkeit des Seins als vergangenes Sein, als konkrete strömende Gegenwart, und so für jede Vergangenheit. [...] Der Andere ist in mir mitgegenwärtig" (HuMat 8, Nr. 13 p. 56). Cf. XV, Nr.13 p. 192 [1931] for a similar analysis of copresence, headed towards the genetic foundation of the Cartesian duality of my *Urpräsenz* and the thereupon founded *Kompräsenz* of the other. The analysis of *Mitgegenwart* in CM remains within the static dimension of "appresentation" (cf. § 50 p. 139; see also XIV, Nr. 1 p. 7 [1921]). Inbetween these two positions (C 3 vs. *Cartesianische Meditationen*) there are many texts that seem to hover: now exploring genetic foundations, now resting on the *terra firma* of the static ego/alter ego duality (see Hua XV, Nr. 4f, 7f, 12ff).

[109] It is not so much a conceptual difference (*Mitgegenwart* or *Kompräsenz* etc.)

other undergoes a shift in meaning, in that the "copresent-being" of the other in the originary empathy is now described as a "co-recollection" (*Miterinnerung*), that is to say a "self-recollection of the other" (*ein Selbsterinnern der Anderen*).[110]

At the opening of this analysis, Husserl is once more careful to stress that the identity of the self is reassured by means of reflection, stating that the I as ego-pole is abstract as long as the contents of the streaming living present are not taken into account: this alone makes it "concrete".[111] This identity will be subjected to quite severe pressure during the following pages of this manuscript, now that the "I" has been rethought in terms of the living streaming present. The full force of the streaming as pre-egoic will here be shown to include also the other, so that the transcendental field will be shown to be intersubjective. The being of the other as an other living present is related to me, in that her co-being is inseparable from me in *my* living present, and this co-presence of the other is a founding presupposition for the objectivity of the world. This means that now the ontological way to the reductions is also brought in to play (apart from the Cartesian, which granted the identity of the I by means of the possibility of reflection).

But for the move which is to establish "transcendental intersubjectivity as the 'absolute ground for all my validities'" as Kern puts it, the intersubjective reduction (which has been the hallmark of the psychological way ever since *Grundprobleme*) and the radicalized reduction must be brought to interact. That is to say, it is only once the analysis has reached the deepest genetic level by means of the radicalized reduction that the full scope of the givenness of the other can begin to be unearthed. Only then does it make sense to say, as Kern does in his presentation of this text (thereby beforehand assuring the future integration of C3 with the analyses of Hua XV), that "phenomenology from the moment it is established as transcendental in the regression from the world to the constituting streaming living present is placed on

as the level of genetic analysis reached that is decisive: "Mitgegenwart" for instance is used both in static and depth-genetic contexts. Also "Appräsentation" is employed in both contexts, but in the latter it is so to speak geneticized.

110 HuMat 8, Nr. 13 "Reduktion" p. 57 [C 3/March 1931].

111 HuMat 8, Nr. 13 p. 53f.

an intersubjective ground: that of 'originarily streaming intersubjectivity'".[112] Here is Husserl's text:

> In transcendental reduction: [...] I am in relation to the others, which I have in persistent validity or as open potentialities for persistent validities to come, and that I have in this way as co-constituting etc. so that my constituted having under the title "world" is a communal having of the streaming being intersubjectivity, therein included the persisting being for me and for us as past, future, as being in time – constituted as persistent having in the originarily streaming intersubjective being (HuMat 8, Nr. 13 p. 57 [C 3/March, 1931]).

The step that Husserl takes here (which Kern described as a transformation) is the starting point of many analyses in Hua XV, the C-ms. and other texts from 1931 onwards that investigate the deepening of static egology in the direction of a genetic constitutive intersubjectivity that is originarily streaming being.[113] Obviously many interpreters have raised objections to this step, claiming that it is "unphenomenological", but as this represents the outcome of Husserl's transcendental genetic *Rückfrage* it cannot be dismissed without proper argumentation.[114]

How can we find a way to combine these two perspectives, the egological as essentially first for every transcendental knowledge, and the intersubjective as essentially first in some other sense? One way to understand this seeming paradox lies in the differentiation that Husserl so often falls back upon between an "order of knowledge" and an "order of being".[115] The former corresponds to the methodological solipsism

[112] Kern, Einleitung, XV, p. XLVIII.

[113] Depraz singles out texts Nr. 12-14 in XV as belonging to a "third group" of texts related to the "creusement de l'égologie et de la mise en œuvre consécutive de la réduction intersubjective" (*Transcendance et incarnation*, p. 225). See also XXXIV, No. 35; and most notably *Krisis*, § 71.

[114] Landgrebe (1982) argues that since Husserl relies solely upon the method of reflection he has no way to determine whether it is the "diffuse flow" itself which constitutes individuation, or whether individualization is merely "projected into" the anonymous originary stream (p. 105f). See also Zahavi (1996), p. 69n7, 60f for an interpretation of the position in C3 as being ultimately "unphenomenological"; in a later work, Zahavi however seems to be less critical (see *Self-Awareness and Alterity*, Ch. 5).

[115] See for instance XI, § 26 p. 120; see also XVIII, p. 255; III/1, § 50; XIV, p. 39; XXIX, p. 157. See also Kern, *Husserl und Kant*, p. 91n, 237; Bégout, *La généalogie de la logique*, p. 105ff. This distinction (see *Met.* 1029 b3ff; *Phys.* 184 a16ff) was frequently employed by Bolzano in his *Wissenschaftslehre*; cf. also Heidegger's commentary in *Der Satz vom Grund*, p. 112 ff.

characteristic of the Cartesian way, which holds that it is "only by starting from the I" that transcendental intersubjectivity (and thus communalization) can be methodically exhibited as that which constitutes the genuine sense of the world as a world for all.[116] The latter claims that it is transcendental intersubjectivity, as the world-constituting source, that is the first being in itself.[117] But ultimately it is a distinction between two different ways of manifestation, where I have to start with that which shows itself for me in order to get to know what can show itself only later.

In a late text (which Kern refers to as a kind of "testament" where an all-encompassing presentation of the stakes of transcendental phenomenology is given), Husserl describes the relation between the egological-epistemological level and that of intersubjectivity in these terms. First we have intersubjectivity in the form of (non-egological) monadic totality, which we know from so many other texts to represent the absolute, i.e. the "order of being", the *ordo essendi* (or *proteron te physei*):

> We must also speak of the one, standing primal livingness (the originary present that is no modality of time) as that of the monadic totality. The absolute itself is this universal primal present, in it "lies" all time and world in every sense (XV, Nr. 38 p. 668 [C 1/1934]).

But the passage continues by pointing out that this can only be known and made explicit from an egological point of view, which therefore becomes the *ordo cognoscendi* (or *proteron pros hemas*):

> But this [the universal primal present of the monad-all] can only be gained from out of my primal present (which itself is a given from *Rückfrage*) by way of a *Rückfrage* that spans over the world-temporality and monadic temporality, so that it is only explicit being in this

[116] VI, § 54b p. 189f/Engl. p. 185. For further references to the epistemological primacy of the I (*ordo cognoscendi*), see also I, CM § 64 p. 181 (but they abound).

[117] "Das an sich erste Sein, das jeder weltlichen Objektivität vorangehende und sie tragende, ist die transzendentale Intersubjektivität, das in verschiedenen Formen sich vergemeinschaftende All der Monaden." (I, *Pariser Vorträge*, p. 38f). For further references to the primacy of the intersubjective being of the world (*ordo essendi*), see XXXV, § 25 p. 111; I, CM p. 182/Engl. p. 156; XV, Nr. 22 p. 380. The importance of this distinction in Husserl's phenomenology was first suggested to me by my first and foremost teacher in philosophy at Stockholm University, the late assistant professor Alexander Orlowski, during a seminar in 1993.

> phenomenological operation [*Leistung*] – which however is also a temporisation (XV, p. 668).

Thus it is only by bringing out the temporal foundation as presented in the C-ms. that Husserl's many investigations of constitutive intersubjectivity in Hua XV can ultimately be clarified. The *Rückfrage* leads to the experience of a community of streams that are not located in my ego but precisely in a manifold of streaming living presents, united by means of an "intersubjective association".[118] This deepening of the egology that served as the starting point of *Cartesianische Meditationen*, leads to a level of investigation where the "I" is no longer statically opposed to its other in terms of an alter ego.[119] It is only by this radical intersubjective reduction which brings into unconcealment the deepest functioning source of both my life and that of the others, that the experience of the other as co-presence is enabled. From this originary streaming intersubjectivity a progressive analysis can proceed in displaying the founded static level of ego – alter ego, and from there on also the social relations at a worldly level. It is the temporal flow itself that makes up this originary community of a plurality of living streaming presents, and this co-presence is to be found at a level where the opposition between different egological streams no longer makes sense.

7. The universal reduction: communalization and world-consciousness

As the final step in this sketch of Husserl's late theory of reductions the analysis now approaches the relation between the radicalized, the intersubjective and the universal reduction. This will pick up the trail of the previous investigation concerning the relation between egology and intersubjectivity. If focus so far has been set mainly upon the psychological way and how this way enabled the analysis to probe into the most fundamental structures of subjective life (while maintaining the validity of the Cartesian way), this last step will establish a connection with the ontological way again, thus bringing to the fore the necessary interplay between these ways. Although the universal reduction is of an

---

[118] XV, Nr. 12 p. 191 [1931].

[119] See XV, Nr. 33 p. 586; Beilage XLI p. 589f; and *Krisis* VI, § 54b p. 188.

earlier date than the radicalized reduction, it connects with the latter by also taking the level of the streaming living present into account when it reappears in the final paragraphs of *Krisis*.[120] But when Husserl first introduced it in the 1920's, the universal reduction was a means to disclose the idea of a common world and thus primarily connected to the ontological way.[121]

It will be argued that the universal reduction represents the final step in the reductive methodology in the sense that it combines the outcome of the radicalized and intersubjective reductions, thereby enabling the manifestation of intersubjectivity in its deepest genetic configuration.[122] To that extent that the universal reduction makes manifest the depth-genetic configuration of intersubjectivity as foundational in the *ordo essendi*, it will also help elucidating the Aristotelian distinction between the two orders (what is first for me versus what is first by nature). The new and decisive phenomenon that the universal reduction brings into view is that of communalization (*Vergemeinschaftung*), which is the genetic basis for all world-experiencing life.

Ultimately it would be a misconception – false is what Husserl actually says (already in 1922-23) – to conceive of the transcendental reduction as if it led only to my own inner being and life, to my own transcendental subjectivity. One way to start to understand this is to recall that a guiding motif in the development from static to genetic phenomenology was the thematization of life. If it is lived life that the reduction strives

[120] The core of this discussion is the relation between egology and intersubjectivity, and *Krisis* should therefore, despite its unfinished status, be seen as Husserl's final outline of the philosophical issues that guided the *Cartesianische Meditationen* which centred around the vexing problem of alterity and *Fremderfahrung* in its culminating 5th meditation. I argue that there are strong inner connections between these two major works that have largely been overlooked, but that surface once they are approached from the point of view of the C-manuscripts on time and the late reflections on intersubjectivity.

[121] See XXXV, *Einleitung in die Phänomenologie 1922-23*, §§ 23-25. Cf. Depraz, *Transcendance et incarnation*, p. 222: "Voie de la psychologie et voie de l'ontologie sont donc conjuguées pour faire droit à une réduction intersubjective conçue comme le telos même de la voie cartésienne."

[122] This final reductive step that reaches communalization however presupposes the results from the radicalized reduction. This means that it is references to the universal reduction from March, 1931 and onwards that are of particular interest here.

to disclose in its meandering intentionalities, then it would immediately find that we are not primarily directed to the self-certainty of the cogito etc. but towards other people, those in our "homeworld". Thus, as Husserl put it in this early presentation of the universal reduction, the epoché reduces me to my inner experience where it discovers foreign subjectivity, this or that person or even a multitude of alter egos: it brings forth a "multiheaded transcendental subjectivity", although of course they are not as originarily given as my own I is.[123]

Even though this is an early text, it is capital to realize that the givenness of the other is not restricted to those actually in my mind; on the contrary, since the basis here is horizontal consciousness (just as in *Grundprobleme*) understood from the intentional implications it harbours, this horizon is potentially open-ended. And at the radicalized level that is proper to genetic phenomenology, the focus will instead be on the processes that constitute this presence of others within me. But if Husserl (as has been argued in previous sections) has situated a ceaseless process of self-alteration at the heart of the streaming living present, how does this connect with the guiding idea of the universal reduction, which is to present the world as a world for all? This manifestation of the world, it must be recalled, cannot be reached by means of any worldly, transcendentally naïve method (such as relying on sociological facts), but has to be the outcome of a truly reductive procedure. How is one to combine constitutive self-transcendence and self-alteration with the likewise constitutive idea of the unity of the world? Do they not point in different directions?

As was the case with the radicalized reduction, the universal reduction demands of us that we give up a notion that is central to our everyday self-understanding. Ordinarily we think that just as my body is separate from your body, so my "psychic interior" or "individual soul" is separate from your "psychic interior" or "individual soul", but that is not so says Husserl.[124] Here at the end of *Krisis* Husserl makes clear that the universal reduction must not be understood, as he had suggested earlier on (for propaedeutical reasons), as a universality of a series of individual reductions which would lead to a multiplicity of separated

[123] XXXV, § 25 p. 111.
[124] VI, § 71 p. 249f/Engl. p. 246f.

souls.[125] Instead, disclosing the "genuine sense of the epoché" means that we conceive of the universal reduction as bringing into view:

> a sole psychic framework, a total framework of all souls, which are united not externally but internally, namely, through the intentional interpenetration which is the communalization of their lives (VI, § 71 p. 258/Engl. p. 255).[126]

The universal reduction in *Krisis* (and other late texts) goes one step further than the intersubjective reduction in previous texts by reaching the level of streaming intentionality (which in C 3 is called the "originarily streaming intersubjectivity").[127] But unlike the radicalized reduction it does not stop there, but instead goes on to show how this leads to a consciousness of the world (*Weltbewusstsein*) as a communal having of the world.[128]

This discussion of communalization and world consciousness at the end of *Krisis* occurs in the context of a discussion concerning the much discussed relation between psychology and transcendental phenomenology, which have previously been said to be "parallel" or even "identical" (see Chapter 2, § 5).[129] However, failure to distinguish them – "one of those seemingly trivial nuances" – ultimately "makes a genuine

[125] VI, § 71 p. 254/Engl. p. 250f.

[126] VI, § 71 p. 258/Engl. p. 255: "[...] so gibt es nur einen einzigen seelischen Zusammenhang, einen allheitlichen Zusammenhang aller Seelen, alle nicht äusserlich sondern innerlich, nämlich durch das intentionale Ineinander der Vergemeinschaftung ihres Lebens, einig".

[127] See VI, § 71 p. 259/Engl. p. 255f: "Das sagt aber zugleich, dass in der lebendig strömenden Intentionalität, in der das Leben eines Ichsubjektes besteht, in der Weise der Einfühlung und des Einfühlungshorizontes jedes andere Ich im voraus schon intentional impliziert ist." Cf. p. 260/257: "Alle Seele bilden eine einzige durch die Phänomenologie systematisch zu entfaltende Einheit der Intentionalität in wechselseitiger Implikation der Lebensströme der einzelnen Subjekte". See also XXXIV, Nr. 33 p. 460 [1931]; VI, § 71, p. 257f/254.

[128] "Weltbewusstsein" is correlated to the universal reduction from the start (XXXV, § 25 p. 112f) but attains its depth-genetic level in HuMat 8, Nr. 32 p. 127; Nr. 82 p. 368; and VI, § 71. See also XXXIV, Nr. 7 p. 132f; Nr. 22 p. 323; Nr. 33 p. 460.

[129] "Thus psychology in itself is identical with transcendental philosophy as the science of transcendental subjectivity. This is unassailable" (VI, § 72 p. 261/Engl. p. 258). Kern is skeptical here (1977, p. 136): "But let us stress that this extremely doubtful identification by Husserl was not always defended, and can be explained simply by the incomplete character of that work, which issued from the mind of someone who was almost eighty years old."

philosophy impossible".[130] Now the key to overcoming the threat of transcendental psychologism is to present the difference between the full transcendental reduction and the merely partial reduction as performed by all psychologists, in an unequivocal manner.[131]

It is a matter of staying as close as possible to the rich sources of evidence available within the psychological sphere – this is done to the point of identity – while keeping the final, methodological step outside of this relation such that it enables the transcendental distinction between the constituted and the constituting to maintain all its original force. By doing so, we may enter the transcendental field with all the psychological evidence safely harboured, but without the unthought reliance upon the world as constituted that in the final analysis remains unassailable for psychology. The psychologist cannot fully leave the *Boden* of the world, cannot see the soul in any other way than as that of the individual, and in this sense there is an irrepressible realist remnant in the position of the psychologist. But as soon as he realizes that the difference between the world as it appears to him and the world in itself is a difference posited by *himself*, as soon as this distinction is uplated, then he has reached the transcendental sphere. This is clearly stated in *Krisis* where the solution to the problem is the guiding thread to the concluding part III B, and the first step is the insight into communalization of souls whereafter the world can no longer be seen from the dual perspective of "my" world versus "the" world:

> Within the universal epoché which actually understands itself, it becomes evident that there is no separation of mutual externality at all for souls in their own essential nature. What is a mutual externality for the natural-mundane attitude of world-life prior to the epoché, because of the localization of souls in living bodies, is transformed in the epoché into a pure, intentional, mutual internality. With this the world [...] is transformed into the all-communal phenomenon "world", "world for all actual and possible subjects", none of whom can escape the intentional implication according to which he belongs in advance within the horizon of every other subject (VI, § 71 p. 259/ Engl. p. 255f).[132]

---

[130] I, CM § 14, p. 70f.

[131] At "this decisive point", Husserl says, "everything hinges on whether one keeps in view with unerring seriousness the thematic meaning of the transcendental mode of inquiry" (IX, p. 335/CW 6, p. 242).

[132] For similar statements, see VIII, p. 427; IX, p. 274; XXIX, p. 128.

The universal reduction is accordingly the ultimate methodological step that the psychologist cannot, but eventually must come to see in order for psychology to finally be able to thematize its own proper subject-matter.[133]

Finally, there are certain misunderstandings that must be dispelled. The universal reduction does not warrant the conclusion that we have come across an isolated, ultimate foundation of transcendental phenomenology, nor that its reductive movement leads to a homogeneous sameness (communalization, the world). More precisely, the interpretation given connects the communalization that is the result of the universal reduction, with the dual process of self-alteration in terms of *Ent-Fremdung* and *Ent-Gegenwärtigung*, and this means that such a Levinasian type of critique loses much of its force. The universal reduction brings into light aspects that first became visible with the intersubjective and the radicalized reduction (but that were held back), by showing that the temporisation is ultimately not restricted to the individual.[134] At its deepest level temporisation shows how the streaming living present is actually structured: it is communalization. This means that at the most basic level that genetic transcendental phenomenology can reach, temporisation is not individual but intersubjective. Furthermore, the genetic level reached by the universal reduction only gains validity in its dependence upon and cooperation with the static phenomenology of the cogito.

It is not the question of genetic phenomenology or the psychological way replacing static phenomenology and the Cartesian way, or of static phenomenology being dissolved into genetic (as for instance Lee has suggested).[135] The *Vergemeinschaftung* that is the result of the universal

[133] "Psychology failed, however, because, even in its primal establishment as a new kind of psychology alongside the new natural science, it failed to inquire after what was essentially the only genuine sense of its task as the universal science of psychic being [*Universalwissenschaft vom psychischen Sein*]. Rather, it let its task and method be set according to the model of natural science [...]. Thus the history of psychology is actually only a history of crises [*Darum ist die Geschichte der Psychologie eigentlich nur eine Geschichte der Krisen*]." (VI, § 57 p. 207/ Engl. p. 202f). Cf. VI, Beilage XXIX, "Finks Entwurf zur Fortsetzung der *Krisis*" p. 514f/Engl. p. 397f.

[134] XV, Nr. 36 p. 636.

[135] See Lee, *Husserls Phänomenologie der Instinkte*, p. 19f.

reduction is an extension of the self-transcendence of the *Ur-Ich*: there is communalization *since* there is movement of transcendence in immanence, *because* the *Ur-Ich* is originary self-alterity as past self in de-presentifiction and more importantly as foreign self in de-alienation.

This basic idea is fully explored in *Krisis*, although now with the in-depth clarifications of the originary structure of the living present ready at hand. The previous analysis of the radicalized reduction showed that the manifestation of its central object was to some extent held back at the last minute, and that the givenness of the streaming intersubjective being could not be fully grasped. The radicalized reduction thus led us to the doorway, but it could not lead us into the field it opens onto. Similarly, the universal reduction cannot on its own accord bring into view the full genetic structure of the living present, although it can display the true universality of communal subjectivity.[136]

The process of communalization (*Vergemeinschaftung*) that is indicated here also means that the pre-reflective self-awareness that has been discussed repeatedly previously again comes to the centre of attention. In the final part of *Krisis* communalization signifies a pre-reflective originary being-together both of me to myself and of me to the not-I's, to the others. The anonymity of the other, her being always beyond my potential grasp, is structurally similar to my own self-anonymity, but this originary being-together reveals itself as a pre-objectivated relation that is given in the anonymously streaming living present. The pre-reflective self-awareness of the functioning I, when approached from the deepest genetic level of temporisation, shows itself to rest in a temporisation that is communal, that of the monadic totality:

---

[136] In a text from the 1920's Husserl indicates German romanticism as the philosophical source for this idea of communalization; see XIV, Nr. 21 "Die phänomenologische Reduktion am alter ego und an der Intersubjektivität. Die soziale und instinktive Verbundenheit der Subjekte als rein subjektive Einheit in der rein psychologischen Erfahrung" [1927], p. 404 (= IX p. 513). On the relation between romantic philosophy and Husserl's early theory of intersubjectivity, see Ravalli's historical analysis (2003). For other discussions of this "communal spirit", see also XXV, p. 47; IV, p. 196ff, 208; but more importantly XIV, Nr. 9 "Gemeingeist I. – Person, personale Ganze, personale Wirkungsgemeinschaften. Gemeinschaft – Gesellschaft" [1921] (p. 165-183); Nr. 10. "Gemeingeist II. – Personale Einheiten höherer Ordnung und ihre Wirkungskorrelate [1918 or 1921] (p. 192-204); and VI, Abhandlung III, Wiener Vortrag [1935], part 2.

> Temporisation of the temporisations, a temporisation of the originary temporising primal beings, that is an inner communalization of these [...] In this sense we can also speak of the one, standing primal livingness (the originary present, which is not a modality of time) as that of the totality of monads. The absolute itself is this universal primal present, in it "lies" all time and world in every sense of the words [...] But this can only be gained from out of my primal present (which itself is a given from the *Rückfrage*) by way of a *Rückfrage* of the temporality of the world and monadic temporality, that is to say that it is only an explicit being in this phenomenological activity – which however is also a temporisation (XV, Nr. 38 p. 668 [C1/1934]).

This talk of communalized subjectivity must not be mistaken for undifferentiated fusion. The radicalized reduction has shown that there is a constant process of self-alteration operative at the heart of the living present. The position that is developed in relation to the universal reduction in the late texts therefore manages to bring these two high-tension ideas – originary communalization and primal self-alteration – into relation with one another without either of them giving up their uniqueness.[137]

[137] On this, see Held *Lebendige Gegenwart*, p. 168f: "Es [the anonymously functioning I at the level of self-temporisation] darf dann sowenig als gegenständliche Einheit und so wenig überhaupt primär als Einheit gedacht werden, dass der Gedanke innerer ichlicher Pluralität für das ursprünglichste Verständnis des einzigen *nunc stans* dem Gedanken der Einheit zumindest gleichwesentlich ist".

PART II

Chapter Four

THE TEMPORALITY OF THE UNCONSCIOUS

Die Frage, was bin ich, was ist der Mensch, die Menschheit, beantwortet die Transzendentalphilosophie durch ihre tiefste Auslegung der Subjektivität als sich selbst und Welt konstituierender (Husserl)

1. Introduction

Based on the interpretation of the methodological foundations of genetic phenomenology in the first part, Part II now proceeds to a more direct encounter between Husserl and Freud. After having introduced the main themes in Chapter One, such as perception and repression, the attempt was made to proceed directly to Husserl's analysis of madness. However, it became clear that although promising material surfaced, its haphazard character called for a more rigorous order, which was to be found only in a clearer grasp of the theory of reductions. Thus the following Chapters Two and Three first presented the motility of the three, main ways to the reduction and thereafter showed how notably the psychological way permitted decisive new insights into the functioning of transcendental subjectivity as the living present. On the basis of these primarily methodological insights, the investigations in Part II will attempt to engage both disciplines in concrete, thematic encounters around three central areas: the temporality of the unconscious, association and the drives (Chapters Four, Five and Six respectively). I will shortly come back to Chapter Four, but first let me announce what is discussed in the final two chapters.

As became increasingly clear to Husserl, time-consciousness alone is unable to clarify "originary constitution" since it only provides the "formal" framework: it is temporalization in its necessary cooperation with sensuous affectivity that makes this abstract structure more concrete, by also bringing the "contents" into play.[1] This will be the theme of Chapter Five where the fundamentals of Husserl's theory of association are outlined. This means that association is intimately connected to both inner time-consciousness and originary affection, in that it brings unity to the living present. Husserl's transcendental analysis of association in the ordinary sense (where it occurs between already constituted objects) is argued to provide a clarification of Freud's theory of "free association", which is the "basic rule" (*Grundregel*) of psychoanalysis. Interspersed with these analyses are two renewed, "direct approaches" where the problem of affection stemming from the repressed and the return of the repressed are examined from the vantage point of transcendental phenomenology. In both these cases, association plays a decisive role.

In the final Chapter Six, the "indirect" approach that was first presented in relation to the structure of the living present (in Chapter Three) will be taken up again. Now a new feature of the living present, namely the drives or instincts, will be analyzed and it will be shown that for Husserl the drive is a genetic preliminary stage of intentionality. On Freud's theory, the drive is a basic concept which mediates between body and soul, and in his late theory of drives we encounter two kinds of drives that together make up the foundation of psychic life: the lifedrives and the deathdrives. The latter represent the will to destruction and ultimately to bring an end to life, and this has posed some trouble for the overall interpretation: it seems that here we encounter the point of no return for psychoanalysis, and no immediate theoretical resources in Husserl's phenomenology are to be found that can account for the deathdrives.

This is true to a certain extent, which is something that puts strain on the argument. We are forced to fall back on everything that the "indirect" approach has provided so far, in order not to be swept away from the field by the force of the deathdrives. Although appeal to the self-constitution of the living present as being partly based on dispersive movements away (into the past, the future and the other) to some degree mitigates the problem, the indirect way is insufficient. Instead, we take

[1] See *Erfahrung und Urteil*, § 16; Hua XI, § 27.

a step back and turn to Husserl's analysis of the crisis of the sciences. The techno-scientific culture that prevails around us has a double aspect: one liberating (that Husserl perhaps did not pay sufficient attention to in his writings), and one devastating. It is argued that the latter aspect represents an interpretation of our contemporary culture on Husserl's part that from early on is conceived of as mortal to genuine life of the spirit.

But now let me introduce the theme of this chapter. Chapter Four opens with a look at the two brief texts from 1934 where Husserl mentions Freud by name (§ 2). The discussions by Husserl here represent what I have called the "direct" and "indirect" approaches respectively, and although Husserl himself in one of the texts seems to suggest the possibility of accounting for the fundamentals of the Freudian method by means of a direct approach, it is argued that this suggestion is ultimately unwarranted.

The next section (§ 3) presents Husserl's analysis of perceptual conflict and tries to demonstrate that, already from its inception, the phenomenological theory of knowledge paid careful attention to gaps or breaches in experiential life. Similarly, gaps in the course of experience are also the preferred mode of manifestation of the Freudian unconscious. It became clearer to Husserl with genetic analysis that passive syntheses of inner time-consciousness are always at work underneath these breaches in experience, and this is used as an argument against all conceptions of the unconscious that do not give a sufficient account of the unity of consciousness.

Next (§ 4) the investigation examines a notorious problem in Freud's analysis of the unconscious, namely its supposed "timelessness". It is argued that this is not only an impossibility for philosophical reasons, but also that Freud himself provides convincing arguments against it. A key to unravel this problem is given with an interpretation of Freud's concept of *Nachträglichkeit* (which for reasons presented later on I will not translate). Although it may be argued, and not without cause, that Freud's talk of the contents of the unconscious as being "without relation to time" is of a more metaphorical character, it becomes a serious problem for any theory of consciousness (in a wide sense) that does not give a convincing account of the temporal connections between the unconscious and consciousness. And so metaphorical or not, the relation has to be investigated.

In the final section (§ 5) we will examine *Nachträglichkeit* from a phenomenological point of view and try to show that at least some central aspects of Freud's theory can be accounted for. This section also serves to bring home the results from the preceding sections: Husserl's brief texts on Freud (§ 2) come to an end with the question of how the repressed (or "covered") contents can still be operative. Likewise, the analysis of conflict (§ 3) shows that time-consciousness is always called for, also to account for gaps in consciousness. Finally, Freud's discussion of the atemporality of the unconscious also leads to the need to integrate the unconscious with inner time-consciousness.

2. Repression: the direct and indirect approaches revisited. Genetic phenomenology as a Vordeutung *of psychoanalysis*

Now we approach the question concerning the possibility of accounting for psychoanalytic repression in relation to sexuality. As will be shown later (Ch. 6, § 2f), the sexual drive-intention in the originary mode (*Urmodus*) is uninhibitedly directed towards the other, and this drive is, at best, met with a corresponding drive from the other. There is also the possibility of inhibition when this originary mode is transformed into a one-sided or possibly two-sided counter-will, and we shall now take a closer look at this phenomenon. For as Husserl notes, the repeated experience that fulfilment of a drive is inhibited (for whatever reason) may eventually become a habituality, a second nature, so that the whole consisting of drive, kinaesthesia and feeling gets "jammed up" (*eingeklemmt*) and its protentional strive forwards is hindered to varying degrees.

One place where he discusses this is in a brief but for my purposes important unpublished text written in 1934, which is a part of the manuscript E III 10.[2] The passage is just over a page long, with the title

[2] The theme and also the tone of Husserl's voice in this manuscript suggests that he is here attempting a translation of sorts from a vocabulary that is not entirely his own: it could be a commentary to something he was reading or so. But even if this is not a "true" expression of his own thought, the link to what has been investigated

"Eingeklemmte Affekte – Askese" and I will quote and analyze it following its order of composition. The text opens with Husserl acutely noting that lack of fulfilment does not mean that the drive-determined, jammed up affect is obliterated, which is an idea we recognize from the previous discussions of perseverance:

> Jammed up affects, passionate desires, that remain unfulfilled, that are subjected to an epoché – but they are not crossed out! They remain in validity (E III 10/3a [1934]).[3]

The refraining "epoché" (which is here, Husserl says, more a "kind of negation", a "crossing out of the consequences") is in some cases brought about by means of an active willing. Here it is not merely a question of refraining from giving in to the desires should the opportunities of active fulfilment arise.[4] Even more, it is a refraining in the form of an active abstaining from the drive-fulfilment under *all* circumstances – *eine Enthaltung, die unter allem Umständen innegehalten werden soll* – in order to avoid being ostracized by society:

> The main events are obvious: it is generally considered to be indecent for a gentleman, I would bring about a boycott from society. Or it is against the religious prescriptions (E III 10/3a [1934]).[5]

Although this is a solution of sorts – it is what Freud describes as the basic clash between the demands of the individual and those of society, analyzed at length in *Civilization and its Discontents* – it does not mean that the desire itself has been cancelled. In connection with this, Husserl

---

here under the rubric of "direct approach" is strong enough to examine its contents closer. As concerns connections to Husserl's public or meant-to-be public texts, this manuscript expands on the division of labour suggested in *Ideen II* and also on the discussion of "depth-psychology" in *Krisis*, § 69.

[3] "Eingeklemmte Affekte, leidenschaftliche Begehrungen, die unerfüllt bleiben, die einer Epoché unterworfen werden – aber nicht durchstrichen! Sie gelten fort." (E III 10/3a)

[4] "Nicht nur Enthaltung davon, ihnen Folge zu leisten, obschon ev. Möglichkeiten der aktiven Erfüllung beständen, etwa gar solche Möglichkeiten herzustellen versuchen." (E III 10/3a)

[5] "Hauptfälle offenbar: es gilt allgemein als unanständig für eine Gentleman, ich setze mich gesellschaftlichem Boykott aus. Oder es ist wider die religiösen Vorschriften." (E III 10/3a)

notes the possible relation between such a covering-over of the desire and the emergence of psychic illness:

> The problem of "jammed up affects" as "illness" of the soul; a habitual dissatisfaction, which isn't reduced to nothing even though one may not think about it. [...] The intensity of desire increases when one turns towards what is desired, and in particular if it is intuitively present, although that isn't necessary. Looking away and wanting to look away. But thereby the affect is only "covered over", pressed down. Images of illness! (E III 10/3a [1934]).[6]

Husserl continues the analysis of this *kranken Seele*, whose desire has to be reined in and pressed down, and finds that the drive has hit upon alternative venues, which of course means new possibilities of giving-in etc. , and so the wheel of desire can keep spinning, drawing us along in its aftermath. As soon as we realize that we have been taken for a ride once more, we react harshly against ourselves:

> Compensation – dissatisfied one seeks for satisfaction in other spheres. And often one falls deeply into the compensating activity (drinking, the sexual drive), and then one reacts with a violent bracketing. (E III 10/3a [1934]).[7]

But Husserl wouldn't be Husserl if this was a truly vicious circle and there was no way out. There is a cure, but here it isn't doing more transcendental philosophy; instead, it is the help of the doctor that is required, at least for the particular case of affect-goal-complexes (action determined by drives) that are in some sense or other perilous or foolish, in a way that we can't really pin down by ourselves. Such affects can be reawakened with the help of the doctor so that we can begin to see things clearer, and here Husserl has moved into the vicinity of the transference neurosis:

---

[6] "Problem des 'eingeklemmten Affektes' als 'Krankheit' der Seele; eine habituelle Unbefriedigung, die nicht ein Nichts ist, auch wenn nicht daran gedacht wird. [...] Steigerung der Intensität des Begehrens in der Hinwendung auf das Begehrte, und insbesondere anschaulich, obschon das nicht notwendig ist. Wegsehen und Wegsehen-wollen. Aber damit ist der Affekt nur 'verdeckt', heruntergedrückt. Krankheitsbilder!" (E III 10/3a) Freud proposes a similar approach in for instance the analysis of repetition and compulsory behaviour; see *Notes upon a Case of Obsessional Neurosis*.

[7] "Kompensation – unbefriedigt sucht man nach Befriedigung anderer Sphäre. Dazu gehört wohl auch, gelegentlich fällt man herein (Trinken, Geschlechtstrieb) und reagiert erst recht mit gewaltsamen Einklammern." (E III 10/3a)

> The cure from such affects. The case that is of the most comprehensible kind: in the generality of the concept of jammed up affect (following our description) there also belongs an affect, also directed at goals, but the stupidity of which one cannot see due to lack of circumspection. At a later stage this may be easier, since the wholly jammed up affect can be reawakened with the help of the doctor [...]: completely clear representation of the satisfaction but also of the mistake, insofar as the satisfaction will transform itself into the utmost dissatisfaction – which may eventually lead to a crossing out of the desire itself [...] (E III 10/3a [1934]).[8]

In a footnote Husserl has added another possibility of the reawakening of the affect with the doctor, besides the completely immobilized affect: "Or: reawakening of the strenuously forgotten affect and (if possible) providing it with a normal 'progression'". This idea comes very close to Freud's mature views on the hopes that can reasonably be tied to a psychoanalytical process. For whereas he in earlier works spoke with perhaps exaggerated confidence of the "permanent release" from the claims posed by a malicious drive, along the lines of the optimistic formula of "making conscious what was previously unconscious", he now more realistically speaks of "bending" the drive so that its claims can become integrated with the I.[9]

---

[8] "Heilung von solchen Affekten. Fall verständlichster Art: in die Allgemeinheit des Begriffs eingeklemmter Affekt (nach unserer Beschreibung) gehört auch ein Affekt, gerichtet auf Ziele, deren Torheit man nicht sieht, weil man nicht weit genug die Zusammenhänge verfolgt. Späterhin mag das leichter sein, die Wiedererweckung des völlig eingeklemmten Affektes mit hilfe des Arztes [*Footnote:* Oder: Wiedererweckung des kramphaft vergessenen Affektes und (nach Möglichkeit) ihm eine normale 'Auswirkung' verschaffen]: völlig klare Vorstellung der Befriedigung aber auch der Täuschung, sofern die Befriedigung zur äussersten Unbefriedigung sich wandeln würde – führt zu einer Durchstreichung des Begehrens selbst [...]." (E III 10/3b)

[9] This is how this idea is expressed in *Die endliche und die unendliche Analyse*: "'Is it possible by means of analytic therapy to dispose of a conflict between a drive and the I, or of a pathogenic demand upon the I from the drives, permanently and definitively?' To avoid misunderstanding it is not unnecessary, perhaps, to explain more exactly what is meant by 'permanently disposing of demand from the drive'. Certainly not 'causing the demand to disappear so that nothing more is ever heard from it again'. This is in general impossible, nor is it at all to be desired. No, we mean something else, something which may be roughly described as a 'taming' of the drive [*"Bändigung" des Triebes*]. That is to say, the drive is brought completely into the harmony of the I, becomes accessible to all the influences of the other trends in the I and no longer seeks to go its independent way to satisfaction." (SE 23, p. 224f/SA Ergänzungsband, p. 365; tr. mod.).

But just how far is it possible to pursue this business of a bracketing of the instinctual affects? Can a drive be crossed out? Can we immobilize an originary drive for good, such as the sexual drive or the drive of self-preservation? These limit questions are approached at the end of this brief manuscript:

> But how would this relate to the more difficult bracketing of the sexual sphere etc.? Here we would strike upon the problem of askesis. How is that possible, how can an originary drive be crossed out? One here also thinks of the problem of suicide (E III 10/3b [1934]).[10]

Thereafter a typical succinct evaluation, followed by an additional reflection that concludes the brief meditation by tying the analysis to Freud. It is important to note that the main philosophical problem that repression poses – how can it be operative while being kept away from consciousness? – is also here said to be "presupposed" by Freud, and thus still in need of clarification:

> The question arises as to what extent these reflections can be of any use at all – perhaps to some degree though. Addition: Everything that has been covered over, each validity that has been covered over co-functions in an associative and apperceptive manner, which the Freudian method makes possible and presupposes (E III 10/3b [1934]).[11]

This whole discussion, despite the slight unfamiliarity that Husserl as a neophyte displays with this way of thinking, nevertheless suggests several important things for the final discussion. First of all it confirms the idea of a division of labour, and even shows Husserl trying on a doctor's white coat, taking full advantage of the earlier analyses of the closeness between psychology and phenomenology, of the partial epoché of the psychologist and confirming the perseverance of the sedimented sexual drives. But it also clearly shows a plasticity of the drives in relation to concrete lived experience that is surprising, and that

---

[10] "[…] aber wie stünde es mit den schwierigeren Einklammerungen der Sphäre der Geschlechtlichkeit u.dgl. Hier käme das Problem der Askese. Wie ist sie möglich, wie kann ein Urtrieb durchstrichen werden. Man wird hier auch an das Problem des Selbstmordes denken." (E III 10/3b)

[11] "Es fragt sich, wie weit das hier Überlegte überhaupt brauchbar ist – in etwa vielleicht doch. Zusatz: Alles Verdeckte, jede verdeckte Geltung fungiert mit assoziativ und apperzeptiv, was die Freudsche Methode ermöglicht und voraussetzt." (E III 10/3b)

confirms the basic assumption of Freud's theory of *Triebschicksale*. And most importantly, it confirms the actuality of repression of sexual affect-life on the basis of Husserl's extended theory of drives.

Let me focus on the last point. If we recall Freud's analysis of repression, we saw there that he recognized three stages, from the originary repression (whose status as a real, empirical event was unclear) to secondary repression or repression proper, which remained the basis for his interpretation, and then the possible return of the repressed, as the outbreak of pathological phenomena.[12] Repression proper – something which may easily be forgotten – according to Freud emanates from the conscious ego, and is an "essentially active process", just as the abstaining of which Husserl speaks. These two processes – repression proper and abstention – could nevertheless be said to make up two essentially different processes: the former an act with the express purpose of pushing a desire or a drive-complex away from consciousness and holding it there, the latter an act whose main purpose is to see to it that the fulfilment of the drive does not occur under any circumstances. But on closer examination, we see that what we have is actually two descriptions of one and the same process, with different aspects emphasized.

As Husserl says, the fact that a drive-complex is actively hindered in reaching fulfilment, does not mean that it loses its affective force, that it is annihilated: it retains its validity. But where then does it go? What happens to the drive with its horizon of kinaesthesia and feeling, when there is no outlet in action? Although Husserl, as far as I know, never systematically worked out the possible relations between the drives – one thinks here of Freud's clarifying phenomenological distinctions between the source, aim, object and pressure of the drive, combined with the analysis of the various *Triebschicksale* – we see here that he at least reckons with the possibility of drives alternating for each other, so

[12] See for instance *Notes on a Case of Paranoia*: "The second phase of repression is that of repression proper [...]. It emanates from the more highly developed systems of the ego – systems which are capable of being conscious – and may in fact be described as "after-pressure". It gives an impression of being an essentially active process [...]. The third phase, and the most important as regards pathological phenomena, is that of failure of repression, of irruption, of return of the repressed"; PFL 9, p. 205f.

that the sought after fulfilment pertaining to one drive-complex is transferred onto another drive.

And this is why there can be talk of "compensation" here, when dissatisfaction in one sphere can lead to "satisfaction from another sphere". For if it were not a question of drive-complexes and their affective meaning being somehow linked with one another, then how could the one function as a "compensation" for another? How could drinking compensate for say an obstructed sexual desire (staying within the boundaries of Husserl's examples), if it were not that it is a proxy for the latter? In order for this to be at all possible, there must be an exchange of sorts from the one drive-complex to the other, as in the processes which Freud described as *Triebschicksale*; of course, such an exchange of hostages will never be completely successful, for ultimately all transferences of drive-fulfilments will leave intact a core of desire that knows no articulation and which therefore will always elude mediate or immediate satisfaction: "It is no accident that human beings never obtain peace of mind".[13] After a specific drive-complex has been put to a halt by an active manifestation of will, it will sink down along the retentional structure, and become sedimented in the I. If a transference of meaning through the positing of a new goal has not occurred, then the drive due to the repetitive structure of the originary drives will shortly thereafter be awakened again, forcing the I to take position, and to engage with the world (if only in the mode of an active refraining). But if it has managed to transfer the meaning attached to it's previous goal to another drive, with another goal, which has taken over also the force with which it affects the I, then the drive with its horizon will sink down into the unconscious, where it of course remains alive.

There seem to be only two references to Freud by name in the whole corpus of Husserl's texts, both of them are in manuscripts written during the summer break in Kappel (June, 1934): the one just quoted from E III 10, p. 3 and the other in B II 3, p. 16b.[14] The latter manu-

---

[13] XV, Beilage XXIII p. 404.

[14] Holenstein gives one reference (E III 10) in *Husserls Phänomenologie der Assoziation*, p. 323; and Karl Schuhmann's unpublished *Index Nominum* at the Husserl-archives in Leuven gives the second (B II 3). There is however a third reference in a marginal note to Husserl's private copy of Max Scheler's book *Die*

script does not focus on the repression of drives to the same extent as E III 10/3, and is thus not as psychoanalytically interesting.[15] But by instead connecting the phenomenological analysis of drives explicitly to Freud, and suggesting that the former in all its concreteness (drives together with feelings and moods in relation to acting and life) makes up a "preliminary interpretation of Freudian psychoanalysis", it is actually even more interesting. Roughly speaking, the two texts correspond to what I have referred to as "direct" and "indirect" approaches to the clarification of repression.

In the opening of the text, Husserl raises the question if there could not be drive-processes that awaken and continue all the way to fulfilment without the participation of the I, and as an example of this suggests the drive to cure sickness.[16] The central part of this text is a reinterpretation of life from the perspective of drives, "healthy life" as consisting of the many-dimensional cycle of drives reaching fulfilment, but not in isolation, all the partial drives (*Sondertriebe*, *Partialtriebe*) are united in the total drive (*Totaltrieb*) with a corresponding total feeling or total mood (*Gesamtgefühl*, *Gesamtstimmung*).[17] Here one would often find that some partial drives would remain in a state of inhibition, thereby creating an obstacle in the movement of life, whereas

Stellung des Menschen im Kosmos (1928) which is in Husserl's *Privatbibliothek* in Leuven. It carries the note "durchgelesen 20/4/31" on the title page. On p. 66, Husserl has written the following in the margin: "Ragout: Husserl (Induktion, phänomenologische Reduktion). Dilthey, Widerstand, Freud (Triebverdrängung)"; see Kaiser, *Das Problem der Hemmung*, p. 59 for this reference.

[15] B II 3/14-19, comprising some six pages with the title: "Trieb – Instinktleben – Aktleben – Askese – Epoché". This is from the unpublished continuation of Hua XXXIV, No. 35, entitled "Trieb – Trieb-Instinktleben. Aktleben – Askese, Epoché" (p. 470-480, corresponding to B II 3/2a-13b. The published text is also from the 16th of June, 1934, in Kappel.

[16] B II 3/14a.

[17] B II 3/14b. See also B II 3/15a: "The feelings are always moments of a complete lifefeeling. They are not data (like colour data) that blend and separate, there is a law-likeness here according to which the partial drives in their modes of fulfilment and inhibition (that is non-fulfilment) have their feelings, and how these then influence the total feeling." [*Die Gefühle sind dabei immer Momente eines gesamten Lebensgefühls. Sie sind nicht Daten (wie etwa Farbendaten) die sich mischen und entmischend trennen, aber es ist ene Wesensmässigkeit da, wonach Sondertriebe in ihrer Weise der Erfüllung und Hemmung (also Nicht-Erfüllung) ihre Gefühle haben und wie diese das Gesamtgefühl beeinflussen.*]

other parts of the total drive flow on uninhibited.[18] And now the reference to Freud:

> A drive in the mode of saturation in the positivity of fulfilment, that is the opposite of complete inhibition. But when saturation enters life it does so in a totally different manner, as "liberation", with an element of well-being that remains active in the background of life throughout the transformation of the comportment (which here means a passivity, that is to say the "sedimentation"), while the drive which remains unfulfilled in the sense of being totally inhibited endures in subjectivity, as a pushing actuality in each living present, and so to speak constantly cries out for liberation. This is of course a preliminary interpretation of Freudian psychoanalysis with its jammed up affects, its "repressions" etc. For here we obviously find what is radical for the clarification of what is really subjective fact in these psychoanalytical matters (B II 3/15a-16a [1934]).[19]

It seems clear (also from the published part of this manuscript in Hua XXXIV, Nr. 35 which immediately precedes this part) that Husserl is here talking so to say in his own voice, unlike in E III 10. This suggests something that is of no small consequence for our undertaking, namely that he himself saw the possibility – if not the actuality – for genetic phenomenology to give a clarification of the psychoanalytical conceptuality. The present investigation is an attempt to sketch out a part of this.

---

[18] B II 3/14b: "Ein Partialtrieb – im Totaltrieb – kann in der Erfüllungsweise so sein, dass er stockt, dass er als rein gehemmter Trieb ist, nämlich aktuelle Verlaufsform hat." Freud takes this phenomenological possibility one step further, by arguing that such an inhibition means that the drive can remain tied to its infantile surrounding world: "One instinct or instinctual component fails to accompany the rest along the anticipated normal path of development, and, in consequence of this inhibition in its development, it is left behind at a more infantile stage. The libidinal current in question then behaves in relation to later psychological structures like one belonging to the system of the unconscious, like one that is repressed" (*Notes on a Case of Paranoia* [1910], PFL 9, p. 205).

[19] B II 3/15a-16a: "Trieb im Modus der Sättigung in der Positivität der Erfüllung, das ist das Gegenstück der vollen Hemmung. Aber ganz anders geht Sättigung ins Leben ein, als 'Erledigung', mit der ein Element des Wohlgefühls in der Verwandlung des Behaltens (das hier eine Passivität besagt, also der 'Sedimentierung') im Lebensuntergrund fortfungiert, während das ganze unerfüllt-bleiben eines Triebs als absolut gehemmt sein fortdauernd in der Subjektivität, in jeder lebendigen Gegenwart treibende Aktualität ist, sozusagen ständig nach Erledigung schreit. Natürlich ist das eine Vordeutung auf die Freudsche Psycho-Analyse, mit ihren eingeklammerten Affekten, ihren 'Verdrängungen', usw. Denn hier liegt offenbar das Radikale für die Aufklärung dessen, was an diesen psychoanalytischen Dingen wirklich subjektive Tatsache ist."

3. Consciousness of conflict

A potentially rewarding way into the complex issue of temporality and the unconscious is Husserl's analysis of conflict (*Widerstreit*) as it manifests itself in the perceptual field. For that which motivates Freud to speak of the unconscious, as has been argued, is that something inexplicable manifests itself for consciousness, that there appears a conflict or a breach in experiential life. If it can be shown that the passive syntheses of time-consciousness also operate so to speak "beneath" the phenomena of conflict, that is to say, if the I before the conflict can be shown to be temporally connected with the I after the conflict, then this result might prove to be useful in coming to terms with Freud's analysis. In particular, it might be used to question the notion that the psychoanalytical unconscious is "timeless".

As we have seen, the investigations into passive pre-constitution disclosed a continuously ongoing conflict in affective force between hyletic matter that, as Husserl put it, knocks on the door of consciousness. At a higher level of constitution, we encounter other phenomena of conflict (*Widerstreit*); that is to say, phenomena that bring about a break in experience, that bring with them rupture so that the concordance (*Einstimmigkeit*) of our experiential life is shattered, notably in relation to the analyses of perceptual (pre-predicative) and predicative disappointment (*Enttäuschung*). Husserl was far from ignorant of such matters, and the attentive reader will even find that the theme of conflict runs through Husserl's *œuvre* from the very start, together with its specific mode of consciousness, which Husserl in *Logische Untersuchungen* calls *Widerstreitsbewusstsein.*[20]

Later on Husserl for instance appeals to the peculiar situation whereby a noema previously adhered to "explodes" due to its no longer being confirmed by the course of experience. And the recurring theme of the instability of perception (is it a wax doll I see at the museum or is it a real person?) likewise testifies to the attention given by Husserl to

[20] Already in *Logische Untersuchungen* Husserl speaks of the synthesis of knowledge as a consciousness of a certain *Übereinstimmung*, and notes that to this there always corresponds the possibility of *Nicht-Übereinstimmung*, i.e. of *Widerstreit* (XIX/2, §§ 11f, 32-35). See also III/1:103; IV:220; XIV:155. For later in-depth treatments, see XX/1 § 57; VIII, lectures 33-34; XI, p. 29ff; and I, § 7.

this problem.[21] These phenomenological investigations into perceptual conflict will for Husserl later on serve in the highly important context of prepredicative experience understood as the origin of negation.[22] Now, the first response in situations where we encounter perceptual conflict, or an abnormality in our surrounding world, is to relegate it to the world of hallucination and mistake, to simply dismiss it as being irrelevant. This tendency is a very strong motivational force in the constitution of our world of experience.[23] However, this will not always do the trick, and we are therefore often left with the brute fact of shattered belief.

But instead of simply dismissing this unpleasant (but often in the end beneficial) experience whereby one aspect of the world has to be abandoned in favour of a more sustained and coherent view, Husserl argues that this can strictly speaking only happen in the case of singular experiences, so that the overall unity of the world is never threatened.[24]

---

[21] See the fifth of the *Logische Untersuchungen*, § 27; XXIII [1904-5] p. 40f, 48f; *Erfahrung und Urteil*, p. 99ff, 372; XI, p. 33f, 42, 59.

[22] *Erfahrung und Urteil* § 21a, "The origin of negation". The textual basis for this analysis in *Erfahrung und Urteil* is in Hua XI, p. 29-33; although the same movement from perceptual conflict to the sphere of predication and judgmental conflict is present in the fifth *Investigation*, §§ 27ff. Freud, as is now well known, presented a similar genealogical account of the origin of judgment in "Negation" from 1925: "The study of judgement affords us, perhaps for the first time, an insight into the origin of an intellectual function from the interplay of the primary drive-impulses. Judging is a continuation, along the lines of expediency, of the original process by which the ego took things into itself or expelled them from itself, according to the pleasure principle. The polarity of judgement appears to correspond to the opposition of the two groups of drives which we have supposed to exist. Affirmation – as a substitute for uniting – belongs to Eros; negation – the successor to expulsion – belongs to the drive of destruction" (PFL 11, p. 441).

[23] On this, see Paolo Volontés analysis in *Edmund Husserls Phänomenologie der Imagination. Zur Funktion der Phantasie bei der Konstitution von Erkenntnis* (1997), p. 183: "Wo immer wir einen Wiederstreit, eine Inkonsequenz in unserer Umwelt wahrnehmen, sind wir dazu getrieben, den störenden Bestandteil dadurch aufzuheben, dass wir ihn in die Täuschungs- und Halluzinationswelt versetzen. Dieses Konsequenzprinzip ist eine äusserst starke Motivation in der Konstitution unserer Erfahrungswelt".

[24] See for instance IX, p. 106f [1926]: "occasionally discordances do also occur. We speak of illusions, experiential belief being ruptured, passing over into doubt; but in the progression of experience, which never undergoes breaks in each and every respect, a thoroughgoing concordance [*durchgehende Einstimmigkeit*] is indeeed restored [...]; that is, running through our consciousness is a sustained unity of world-certainty that is produced again and again over against the disturbances. 'The' one world is constantly there, only it is determined more closely and occasionally determined somewhat differently [*'die' eine Welt ist beständig da, sich nur immer näher und gelegentlich etwas anders bestimmend*]".

In fact, drawing on our previous investigations into the passive field of pre-constitution, one may even go so far as to state that conflict and breach in experience is constitutive for the experience of the unity of the world. For to every constitutive experience that makes it over the threshold of consciousness, there is a number of possible ways that the flow of experience could have taken, had the affective incitement been sufficiently strong. Similarly, when seen from the perspective of higher levels of constitution, we find that without these experiences of shattered belief and rupture, there would be no experience of the world as one world, since this world is never given in a finished form once and for all, but is the result of continuously ongoing constitutive processes in the form of trial and error.

Coming back to the question concerning the role of inner time-consciousness in these processes, one must now ask whether or not temporality so conceived underlies also these experiences of conflict. From the brief analysis of Husserl's theory of inner time-consciousness above, I think it is clear that this is indeed the case. For if temporality was not always already at work, synthesizing the I before the conflict with the I after it, there would simply be no point in speaking of the same I undergoing an experience of conflict.

And this argument obviously also holds in Freud's case: if the unconscious indeed shatters our normal flow of experience when an association occurs that carries us so to speak into another world; if sexuality amongst other things means that we at times leave our normal self-perception and through the other (or others), become immersed in bodily and psychical experiences that transcend everyday life and that may even border on insanity; and if the deathdrive can manifest itself in that kind of continuous self-torture that Freud calls "moral masochism", i.e. a not wanting to give up suffering and neuroses, then this is only possible if inner time-consciousness continuously and passively synthesizes these limit-experiences with the remainder of conscious life so that the unity of the I can be maintained in at least some sense.

Husserl was led to introduce the notion of the pure I in *Grundprobleme* because of the threatening dissolution of the I, once the reduction was shown to lead also to a plurality of constituting subjects.[25] It is important to see that it is not simply a question of "gluing" fleeting or odd experiences to the rest of intentional life, but of something much more fundamental, which underlies life as such in all its manifestations. A critique of Husserl according to which he would sidestep what today is conceived of as a more "contemporary", often psychoanalytically inspired focus on the instability of the world, on the whole issue of a reason shot through with undecidability, hiatus and errancy, misses the point. It does not take into consideration the dynamics of experience in Husserl's thinking, i.e. the interplay between successful and failed intentional experiences. It is precisely *because* the world is given as an unstable entity, always open to renewed correction, that Husserl is so attentive to the phenomena of concordance (*Einstimmigkeit*), of the unity of the world and of the I.[26]

With this examination of the consciousness of conflict, which has shown that inner time-consciousness runs through all the phases of such experiences, it has been argued that the Freudian unconscious in its most radical manifestations does not imply a break with intentionality, but that in fact it even presupposes the passive syntheses of inner time-consciousness. How can these insights into inner time-consciousness be employed to make sense of the supposed atemporality of the unconscious? For we have just seen that Husserl presents strong arguments that deny this claim, or at least that demand much stronger evidence if such a view is to be upheld.

4. The temporality of the unconscious and Nachträglichkeit

Here we will investigate whether or not the analysis of inner time-consciousness could also provide a key to unlock more specific prob-

[25] See XIII, Nr. 6 § 19, p. 155.

[26] See for instance XV, Nr. 14 p. 214: "The being of the world has only an appearance of stability, in truth it is merely the stability of a normal picture. But from there, insofar as this mode of instability is discovered or at least something that can be felt, emerges the highest questions pertaining to the world, the world becoming philosophically questionable in its totality, and understood radically, so that all horizons become aired and are drawn into the question". See also Bernet (1979a): "The basic fact from which Husserl proceeds is the possibility of error, and the tension between the desire for absolute cognition and the necessary frustration of this desire" (p. 119).

lems in Freud's conception of the repressed unconscious. In particular, this might prove to be valuable in coming to terms with Freud's idea that the unconscious is "timeless" (*zeitlos*). What this means, according to Freud, is that the processes of the unconscious are not ordered temporally, that they are not in any way altered or affected by the passage of time, in fact, that they have no reference to time at all, since reference to time is bound up with the work of consciousness.[27] Since Freud never worked out anything resembling an analysis of time-consciousness that could make this claim valid, it is difficult to see what meaning one can attach to it, as long as the interpretation remains at the level of explicit statements. Freud's determination of the unconscious as timeless has received some attention in the literature but virtually nothing that goes beyond its status as being enigmatic.[28]

In all fairness, it must be stated that Freud relies on a conception of temporality that stems from what Husserl would call the natural attitude, and his denial of a relation between time and the unconscious is better understood as a first step towards discovering more originary modes of temporality pertaining to conscious life. Derrida, speaking of Freud's concept of *Nachträglichkeit*, has pointed the way for my interpretation:

> That [i.e. Freud's analysis of *Nachträglichkeit*] should lead, if not to the solution, at least to a new way of posing the formidable problem of the temporalization and the so-called "timelessness" of the unconscious.

---

[27] See above all "The unconscious", SA 3, p. 145f/PFL 11, p. 191. The first printed statement where Freud speaks of the unconscious as *zeitlos* is probably in the 1907 addition to *Psychopathology of everyday life*, PFL 5, p. 339; although the idea was clearly presented already in texts from the late 1890's. See also *Beyond the Pleasure Principle* (1920), PFL 11, p. 299f; and *New Introductory Lectures* (1933) PFL 2, p. 106ff.

[28] Ricœur for instance develops an interpretation of Freud's concept of the unconscious which emphasizes its status as being "outside of time" (*hors le temps*); but since he does not engage in a discussion of what such a position "outside" of the temporal order should be taken to mean, it is difficult to see where it would lead (cf. *De l'interprétation*, p. 111, 113, 428ff; neither is Freud discussed in *Temps et Récit*). See also Hans-Dieter Gondek, *Angst, Einbildungskraft, Sprache* (2002), p. 91; Paul-Laurent Assoun, *Freud, la philosophie et les philosophes* (1995), p. 211f; Julia Kristeva, *La révolte intime. Pouvoirs et limites de la psychanalyse 2* (2000) p. 40-67; and David L. Smith, *Freud's Philosophy of the Unconscious* (1999) p. 97, 221f, for further attempts that tend to bypass the complexity of the issue, rather than to take hold of the problem presented.

> The timelessness of the unconscious is no doubt determined only in opposition to a common concept of time, a traditional concept, the metaphysical concept: the time of mechanics or the time of consciousness. We ought perhaps to read Freud the way Heidegger read Kant: like the cogito, the unconscious is no doubt timeless only from the standpoint of a certain vulgar conception of time ("Freud and the Scene of Writing", in *Writing and Difference*, p. 215/Fr. p. 318).

Derrida does not develop this suggestive remark any further in relation to Freud, but I think that there are at least two important trends of thought in Freud's texts that would support the kind of reading envisaged.[29] For instance in the brief text called "Zur Einleitung der Behandlung", Freud seems to argue against his own convictions, since he there states that the long duration of the cure corresponds to "the 'timelessness' of our unconscious processes [*die "Zeitlosigkeit" unserer unbewussten Vorgänge*]", which implies the obvious, namely that there after all is a temporal correspondence between conscious processes in the cure and the unconscious.[30] This is what makes the cure possible, for as Freud states elsewhere: "psychoanalytic treatment is based upon an influencing of the Ucs. from the direction of the Cs., and at any rate [it] shows that this, though a laborious task, is not impossible".[31]

Secondly, there are repeated attempts on Freud's part to initiate a reflection on precisely the origin of our conception of time, in order to gain further clarity on the "temporality" that seems to be proper to the unconscious. On Freud's view, it falls upon the preconscious to make

[29] See also the analyses in *Of Grammatology*, p. 66f and *La voix et le phénomène*, p. 70f from roughly the same time. In "Freud and the scene", Derrida highlights *Nachträglichkeit* as "Freud's discovery", the "guiding concept" which "determines all his other concepts" and it is said to be the "only one" of Freud's concepts that is neither exhausted by metaphysics nor science (p. 203, 212/Fr. p. 303, 314). In the work of Lacan *Nachträglichkeit* is given a fundamental role and is generalized into a theory of subjectivity going beyond Freud's more restricted usage; see Boothby's excellent account in *Freud as Philosopher. Metapsychology after Lacan* (2001).

[30] This text from 1913 is in SA *Ergänzungs Band*, p. 190/SE 12, p. 130. Likewise, in *Beyond the Pleasure Principle*, Freud after having enumerated the negative characteristics of the timelessness of unconscious processes – that they are *not* ordered temporally, that time does *not* change them in any way and that the idea of time *cannot* be applied to them – states that these characteristics "can only be clearly understood if a comparison is made with conscious mental processes" (PFL 11, p. 299f). In a similar vein, cf. "The Unconscious": "The full significance of the characteristics of the system Ucs. [...] could only be appreciated by us if we were to contrast and compare them with those of the system Pcs." (PFL 11, p. 192).

[31] "The Unconscious", PFL 11, p. 199.

communication possible between its contents and those of the unconscious, and thereby the unconscious processes are given "an order in time [*zeitliche Anordnung*]".[32] But the preconscious does not have this insight into the inner workings of the temporal order from itself, instead it must rely on its vicinity to the system Cs., for strictly speaking, "reference to time is bound up, once again, with the work of the system Cs.".[33] Not only is temporality bound to consciousness, such that it is only through conscious life (including the "preconscious" in Freud's sense) that the other systems of the psychical apparatus are able to connect with one another and socialize, as it were (*Verkehr* is the expression Freud uses); our representation of time according to Freud has its very source in a self-reflection upon consciousness:

> … our abstract representation of time [*abstrakte Zeitvorstellung*] seems to be wholly derived from the mode of working of the system Pcpt.-Cs. and to correspond to a self-perception [*Selbstwahrnehmung*] of that mode of working" (*Beyond the Pleasure Principle*, PFL 11, p. 300/SA 3, p. 238; tr. mod.).[34]

Therefore, it seems correct to say that it is after all temporality that makes the "communication" between the unconscious and the preconscious-conscious systems possible.[35] The preconscious upholds a number of other crucial relations to the unconscious, not the least of which is "co-operation". This takes place primarily through the derivatives (*Abkömmlingen*) of the unconscious, which are a sort of continuation (*Fortsetzung*) of the unconscious into the preconscious. Through these, the unconscious is always susceptible to the ongoings and effects of life, and stands in a reciprocal relation of influence to the preconscious.[36] Amongst these derivatives of the unconscious, which continuously

---

[32] "The Unconscious", PFL 11, p. 193.

[33] "The Unconscious", PFL 11, p. 191.

[34] For a different interpretation, see Assoun, *Freud, la philosophie et les philosophes*, p. 211f.

[35] The title of the penultimate section of "The Unconscious": "Communication between the two systems". See also "Repression", PFL 11, p. 149.

[36] "In brief, it must be said that the Ucs. is continued into what are known as derivatives, that it is accessible to the impressions of life, that it constantly influences the Pcs., and is even, for its part, subjected to influences from the Pcs" ("The Unconscious", PFL 11, p. 194).

transgress the border between these two dimensions within subjective life, are phantasies, associations, dreams and bodily symptoms. These phenomena thus represent the primary modes of a "communication" (*Verkehr*) between the unconscious and consciousness that is essentially reciprocal, in that movements in both directions occur. The distinction between the two systems is therefore shown to be one that is relative and not absolute: "Study of the derivatives of the Ucs. will completely disappoint our expectations of a schematically clear-cut distinction between the two psychical systems".[37] Having established in a preliminary fashion that temporal interaction between consciousness and the unconscious occurs, the analysis must now proceed to investigate whether this "temporality" of the unconscious can be further determined.

The hypothesis presented here is that the most central idea that Freud put forth for the philosophy of time is that of *Nachträglichkeit*, which stands in a direct relation to the unconscious, repression, sexuality and memory and is furthermore a constant in Freud's work.[38] Freud never gave a definition of it nor presented a theory of *Nachträglichkeit*, and its present day interest to a large degree stems from the French reception.[39] For Freud, it denotes instances where the understanding of an event is postponed to a later time, so that it comes to be understood from a different point of view. It refers notably to events that have been impossible to incorporate into a meaningful structure, and here the sexual traumatization of children (which is frequently discussed by Freud in the early texts) is paradigmatic. The memory of the trauma cannot come to rest, and in this sense, says Freud, "acts like a foreign

---

[37] "The Unconscious", PFL 11, p. 194.

[38] Freud employs *nachträglich* and *Nachträglichkeit* from early on (see the letters to Fliess; *Studies on Hysteria* in PFL 3; *Project for a Scientific Psychology* in SE 1; "Further Remarks on the Neuro-Psychoses of Defence" in SE 3; "Sexuality in the Aetiology of the Neurosis" in SE 3. See also for instance *The Interpretation of Dreams* in PFL 4, *Little Hans* in PFL 8; *The Wolfman* in PFL 9; "Female sexuality" in PFL 7 and *Moses and Monotheism* in PFL 13.

[39] It was Lacan who reopened the discussion of *Nachträglichkeit* in his commentary to the Wolfman in 1953-54; see "Fonction et champ de la parole et du langage" in *Écrits*, p. 256 and *Le séminaire I (1953-54)*, p. 215. Derrida was probably the first philosopher to integrate this aspect into his thought, and Freud's concepts of repression and *Nachträglichkeit* are crucial for the concepts of trace, *différance* and for deconstruction in general in its classical phase.

body which long after its entry must be continued to be regarded as an agent that is still at work".[40]

In the 1895 *Project* and surrounding texts Freud presents some essential characteristics of *Nachträglichkeit*, and the basis here is the discovery that certain past events undergo "revision" when they are brought back to memory.[41] This revision brings new meaning upon the previous events, a meaning that they did not have at the time of their occurring, and, the revision is often strong enough to bring about pathological alterations in the person. This is what lies behind the choice of words of the English translators, when they render *Nachträglichkeit* as "deferred action": the action which is triggered by the experience, only comes into being after the event.[42]

Although thus stressing the performative nature of recollection, this translation (as has often been pointed out) misses an important aspect for what is at stake is certainly more than the postponement of an action from time A to time B. Besides the delay between an experience and its later understanding (which implies a temporal movement from the past to the present), there is also a movement backwards (from the present to the past) involved in all cases of *Nachträglichkeit*.[43] The previous event

---

[40] *Studies on Hysteria*, SE 2, p. 6.

[41] As this was formulated briefly thereafter in the letter to Fliess, 6th Dec. 1896: "I am working on the assumption that our psychic mechanism has come into being by a process of stratification [*durch Aufeinanderschichtung entstanden ist*]: the material present in the form of memory traces being subjected from time to time to a *rearrangement* in accordance with fresh circumstances – to a *retranscription* [*eine* Umordnung *nach neuen Beziehungen, eine* Umschrift *erfährt*]. Das wesentlich neue an meiner Theorie ist also die Behauptung, dass das Gedächtnis nicht einfach, sondern mehrfach vorhanden ist, in verschiedenen Arten von Zeichen niedergelegt" (*Aus den Anfängen der Psychoanalyse*, p. 185/*The Complete Letters of Freud to Fliess 1887-1904*, p. 207). Cf. *From the History of an Infantile Neurosis* (herafter referred to as: the Wolfman), PFL 9, p. 269f/SA 8, p. 157f.

[42] Strachey also employs a wide variety of other terms, besides "deferred action", in the translation of *nachträglich* and *Nachträglichkeit*, such as: "subsequently", "in a deferred fashion", "aftereffect", "deferred effect", "later" etc. This makes it near impossible to follow Freud's train of thought. More recently, Thomä and Cheshire have argued that "retrospective attribution" should be employed, but for reasons developed in the text, I do not think this suggestion represents a step forward; see their "Freud's *Nachträglichkeit* and Strachey's "Deferred Action": Trauma, Construction and the Direction of Causality" (1991). Laplanche suggests the rather inelegant "afterwardsness" for *Nachträglichkeit* in many texts; see for instance *Essays on otherness*, p. 260ff.

[43] Here I disregard instances where Freud speaks of *nachträglich* in an ordinary

is thus always reinterpreted from the standpoint of the present. A clear example of this is to be found in *The Interpretation of Dreams*, where an adult situates himself in a position he had as an infant but with intentions that stem from later on, thereby projecting a new meaning into the previous event.[44]

What then is the structure of this phenomenon according to Freud? In his early accounts of *Nachträglichkeit* in relation to trauma (which will be my chosen example), Freud refers to a threefold series of events that together make up a process of retroactive understanding that involves temporal movements both forwards and backwards.[45] We must remember the clinical starting point here, where the analytical project – in part, for it is always also and in fact primarily directed to the future – consists in a mutual attempt to gain insight into the genesis of the various "symptoms" (neurotic, phobic etc.) displayed.[46] So we typically have an adult who by means of the technique of free association, gradually gains access to past complexes of experience. The whole complex of experiences may span over decades, and it can only be given as reconstructed from out of a successful psychoanalysis. The full phenomenon of *Nachträglichkeit* is thus manifested by looking back on a completed process where an understanding of its component events has been achieved. Now let us go back in time to the chronologically first part in this process.

The first event is one that cannot be incorporated into the stream of experience due to an excess of meaning, it is inexplicable to the subject at that time and so it becomes "present" for her only in the form of a passive enigma: it undergoes repression. In Freud's most well-known

---

sense where there is no repression involved.

[44] "Love and hunger, I reflected, meet at a woman's breast. A young man who was a great admirer of feminine beauty was talking once – so the story went – of the good-looking wet-nurse who had suckled him when he was a baby: 'I'm sorry,' he remarked, 'that I didn't make a better use of my opportunity.' I was in the habit of quoting this anecdote to explain the factor of 'deferred action' [*Nachträglichkeit*] in the mechanism of the psychoneuroses" (PFL 4, p. 295). Further examples abound in the case-stories. See also the account in the Wolfman where the motility of the I is emphasized: "[Er] setzt sich dann mit Recht über die drei Zeitphasen hinweg und setzt sein gegenwärtiges Ich in die längstvergangene Situation ein" (SA 8, p. 163fn).

[45] See notably the case of Emma (*Aus den Anfängen der Pscychoanalyse*, p. 432ff/SE 1, p. 353ff); and the Wolfman (PFL 9/ SA 8).

[46] The formation of symptoms is by and large identified with the return of the repressed; see "Repression", PFL 11, p. 154.

examples of traumatization (Emma, the Wolfman etc.) the first event is an act of a sexual nature, but which occurred at a time when they were too young to realize the sexual significance of the act.

Secondly, there is the constitution of the trauma proper, which occurs at a later time (in Freud's examples often years later). This event is similar to the first repressed event, which permits the formation of an unconscious, associative bond between them. Here an interpretation of the first event occurs, based on a transformation having occurred in the interval; typically Freud here points to the oncome of puberty which involves the development of *both* bodily and psychic functions.[47] It is important to underline this fact, since it shows that *Nachträglichkeit* was never a simple determinist conception for Freud (according to which the past determines the future).[48]

The fact that a "re-arrangement" (*Umordnung*, *Umschrift*) of the memory occurs from a new situation in life brings out a hermeneutical aspect inherent in *Nachträglichkeit*: it involves not only a temporal dynamics but also an interpretation of the past and thus a new outline of the future. The new situation in the case of Emma and the Wolfman is that they have now become sexually mature, and are thus able to recognize the previously hidden significance of the first event.[49] It is remarkable that it is this second event which is responsible for so to speak filling the previous event with a trauma-constitutive force, something that it did not have by itself: "... a memory is repressed which has become a trauma only after the event [*nur nachträglich*]".[50]

---

[47] "Here we have the case of a memory arousing an affect which it did not arouse as an experience, because in the meantime the change of puberty had made possible a different understanding [*ein anderes Verständnis*] of what was remembered. Now this case is typical of repression in hysteria" (*Project for a scientific psychology*, SE 1, p. 356/*Aus den Anfängen der Psychoanalyse*, p. 435; tr. mod.).

[48] Here I disagree with Laplanche, who claims that Freud "always chooses" the "determinist conception that proceeds from the past to the future", and that there is a "consistent rejection" on Freud's part of the "hermeneutic conception that proceeds from the present to the past" (*Essays on otherness,* p. 261f).

[49] While Freud in 1895 thought that it was the oncoming of puberty that was decisive, by 1915 he argued that sufficient maturation had been brought about by the Wolfman when he had reached 4-5 years. The discovery of infantile sexuality (see the *Three essays on sexuality*) during the interval obviously a played a role in this change.

[50] See "Entwurf", in *Aus den Anfängen der Psychoanalyse*, p. 435/SE 1, p. 356.

However, the real significance of Freud's theory is only obtained once we move on to the third event, that of understanding. This often takes place many years after also the second event, which has clearly been a factor for Freud in the determination of the unconscious as *zeitlos*.[51] Understanding the event thus brings about a "dissolution" of the symptom, as the early Freud somewhat exaltedly puts it.[52] This *Verständlichmachung* is the distant aim of the analysis of repression that Freud initiates here at the opening of part 2 (on "Psychopathology") of the *Project*, and it corresponds to an experience of what we may call psychoanalytical truth.

To sum this up, we have three events that follow chronological time: 1) the sexual attack (not understood as such) in childhood becomes repressed; then 2) a similar event (in later childhood or puberty) which unconsciously connects with the first, the partial understanding of which leads to traumatization and the constitution of symptoms (the return of the repressed); and 3) the decision to initiate a psychoanalysis (in adulthood) in order to avoid the oppression of the symptom. But there is also temporality in the opposite direction, since what is first given is only 3) and from there on eventually a relation back to 2). The discovery of the connection between the symptom at 3) and the event at 2) gradually leads to the further discovery (or "remembering") of 1). Speaking of the understanding that becomes available to the Wolfman as an adult in analysis, Freud says: "This is simply a second instance of *Nachträglichkeit* [*Es ist dies einfach ein zweiter Fall von Nachträglichkeit*]".[53] And in an attempt to explain the difference between the first

[51] Consider *Nachträglichkeit* in the Wolfman case where the first event (or the phantasy of it) occurred when he was one year old: "We must not forget the actual situation which lies behind the abbreviated description given in the text: the patient under analysis, at an age of over twenty-five years, was putting the impressions and impulses of his fourth year into words which he would never have found at that time [*nach 25 Jahren Eindrücken und Regungen [...] Worte verleiht, die er damals nicht gefunden hätte*]" (PFL 9, p. 278n/SA 8, p. 163n).

[52] "Now our analyses show that a hysterical compulsion is resolved immediately it is explained (made intelligible) [*dass der hysterische Zwang sofort gelöst ist, wenn er aufgeklärt (verständlich gemacht) ist*]. Thus these two characteristics are in essence one" (SE 1, p. 348/*Aus den Anfängen der Psychoanalyse*, p. 428).

[53] The English translation has: "This is simply another instance of deferred action" (PFL 9, p. 278n); but that obliterates Freud's major point: it is precisely a *second* instance, one that occurs after the trauma has been constituted (which represents the

and the second instance of *Nachträglichkeit*, Freud immediately goes on to say:

> At the age of one and a half the child receives an impression to which he is unable to react adequately; he is only able to understand it and to be moved by it when the impression is revived in him at the age of four; and only twenty years later, during the analysis, is he able to grasp with his conscious activity of thought what was then going on in him. The patient justifiably disregards the three periods of time, and puts his present I into the situation which is as long past (PFL 9, p. 278n; tr. mod.).

The postponed understanding can (in the cases considered here) only come about through a deferral that is structural, i.e., inherent in the very being of these experiences themselves, and so does not depend on psychological factors in any ordinary sense. Here everything seems finally clear: a lived experience that was previously hidden and furthermore inarticulate is now brought to words. As Freud eventually came to acknowledge, the first event may never have occurred – it may equally well have been a phantasy – but that is beside the point.[54] The reconstruction of the series of events thus points to something undecidable as its very source, the bringing into being of an event that perhaps – and how could we ever know? – did not exist prior to its articulation, but which yet, and this is the interesting complication, plays a determinative role.[55]

Having presented the broad outlines of Freud's theory of *Nachträglichkeit*, we must now see what can be gained from this in the attempt of coming to terms with the timelessness of the unconscious. Speaking of the despairingly slow progress made by the Wolfman during the first years of analysis, Freud says that it would under normal circumstances have been given up as hopeless. However, this turned out to be Freud's longest analysis ever, which made it possible for him to descend into what he calls "the deepest and most primitive layers of mental devel-

---

first instance), and now with the "full" understanding.

[54] PFL 9, p. 294.

[55] "Every adolescent person has memory-traces which can only be understood with the emergence of sexual feelings of his own; and accordingly *everyone must carry the germ of hysteria within oneself*" (SE 1, p. 356/*Aus den Anfängen der Psychoanalyse*, p. 435; tr. mod., my italics).

opment".[56] The timelessness of the unconscious that was encountered there, could only be overcome (*Überwindung*) by means of so to speak becoming timeless oneself:

> From the doctor's point of view I can only declare that in a case of this kind he must behave as "timelessly" as the unconscious itself [*ebenso "zeitlos" verhalten muss wie das Unbewusste selbst*], if he wishes to learn anything or to achieve anything. And in the end he will succeed in doing so, if he has the strength to renounce any short-sighted therapeutic ambition. [...] But the analyst has the right to feel that the results which he has attained from such lengthy work in one case will help substantially to reduce the length of the treatment in a subsequent case of equal severity, and that by submitting on a single occasion to the timelessness of the unconscious he will be brought nearer to vanquishing it in the end [*so die Zeitlosigkeit des Unbewussten fortschreitend zu überwinden, nachdem man sich ihr ein erstes Mal unterworfen hat*]" (PFL 9, p. 237; tr. mod./SA 8, p. 132).

In Freud's hermeneutics of life, "understanding the event" is a task that is potentially open-ended, since we are constantly engaged in re-evaluating ourselves and in reinterpreting our past in relation to our present and our future projects.[57] The modification of the concepts of experience and of memory that the notion of *Nachträglichkeit* brings about, is based on an understanding of temporality that takes the sexual aspects of the facticity of subjectivity into account in a new way.

5. Attempt at a phenomenological clarification of Nachträglichkeit

Let us now approach the question of whether there are resources in Husserl's philosophy to account for, or at least to approach, the idea of *Nachträglichkeit* in the more specific sense that Freud assigned to it. The first step which immediately announces itself is simply to say that Husserl's theory of consciousness as it was presented already in

[56] "Only in such cases do we succeed in descending into the deepest and most primitive strata of mental developent, and in hauling from there solutions for the problems of the later formations [*in die tiefsten und primitivsten Schichten der seelischen Entwicklung herabzusteigen und von dort die Lösungen für die Probleme der späteren Gestaltungen zu holen*]. And we feel afterwards that, strictly speaking, only an analysis which has penetrated so far deserves the name" (*From the History of an Infantile Neurosis*, PFL 9, p. 236f; tr. mod./SA 8, p. 131).

[57] This is the topic of above all "Die endliche und die unendliche Analyse" (1937), SA Ergänzungsband.

Logische Untersuchungen is sufficient to account for at least the basic component of Freudian *Nachträglichkeit*, namely the reinterpretation of the event. In the fifth investigation Husserl distinguishes between two fundamental aspects of the act: the "quality of the act" and the "matter of the act". The act-quality, it will be recalled, is that which determines whether the phenomenological content is present as wished, asked, regretted etc., whereas the act-matter is that aspect of the intentional act which first gives it a reference to an object. It is the act-matter that is of particular interest here, or more specifically the notion of interpretative sense (*Auffassungssinn*), which is presented as that which "not only determines *that* it grasps the object but also *as what* it grasps it".[58]

Whenever we perceive or reflect upon something, it is always perceived *as* something, and in genetic phenomenology Husserl expands the possibilities so that this interpretative sense is conceived of in the larger framework of sedimentation and habitus.[59] This is what really opens the possibility to approach Freudian *Nachträglichkeit*. What is at stake in Freud's account when the subject reinterprets her own past events, can accordingly be said to consist in that she is ascribing a new interpretative sense to them. Let us investigate this possibility briefly.

The object (or event) is never given as an isolated thing, but is always an object within its horizon of anticipation and precognition. Now this horizon itself is "constantly in motion" which means that as soon as new determinations are encountered the horizon also alters, and equally so whenever we lose sight of the object or aspects of it.[60] In the normal course of experience, every object progressively sinks away by means of the retentional structure of time-consciousness and finally submerges into the empty past, the unconscious.

The lived experience may itself become completely forgotten, but that does not mean that it disappears without a trace, it is still "there" but in passivity; it is always ready to become awakened again by means of an association.[61] Whenever the object is brought back to life, it

[58] XIX/1, § 20 p. 430/*Logical Investigations* vol. 2, p. 121. Cf. XIX/2, §§ 26f, 49ff.

[59] See notably *Erfahrung und Urteil*, § 25.

[60] *Erfahrung und Urteil*, § 25 p. 136f/Engl. p. 122.

[61] *Erfahrung und Urteil*, § 25 p. 137/Engl. p. 122.

appears with the previously acquired determinations of meaning as a part of its manifestation, since the subjective activities that have been accomplished remain attached to the object as its habitus. This means that also when one returns to the object after an interruption it will be given as having these acquired determinations, and therefore the new encounter with the event will have "a content of sense essentially other than the preceding perceptions".[62]

The event that is recalled is given by means of this new interpretative sense, which has incorporated the sedimentation of previous determinations. The basis of this analysis could, if suitably complemented with resources from other texts, well be employed for the clarification of reinterpretation over time that is an essential aspect of Freud's theory of *Nachträglichkeit*. Developing this line of thought, one could show that such a new interpretative sense, developed over time, could lead from a non-sexual to a sexual understanding of the event. This would reach fairly deep into Freud's account.

Promising as it may seem, the continued analysis of this theme will however be interrupted here. The reason for this is that it bypasses a question, more fundamental, which will be addressed in the remainder of this section. Given that the phenomenological analysis of consciousness and theory of meaning can explain the processes involved in the attribution of new meaning, also to events that are deeply sedimented in the unconscious, we still face the question of where this new interpretative sense comes from. What is the motivation that lies behind it? It may seem as if the reference to biological-sexual maturation, or even the suggested interpretations from the analyst when in a psychoanalytical situation are sufficient here.

What I would like to suggest as a means for further investigation is that there are important aspects related to Husserl's concept of horizon that merit our attention here. The general idea is Husserl's notion of a thematization of that which is in the perceptual background of a lived experience, in its horizon, but which was not attended to at the time of its occurrence. This aspect of the horizon can be brought to actualization, and here we may find experiential traces of something that was

[62] *Erfahrung und Urteil*, § 25 p. 138/Engl. p. 122.

only vaguely apperceived at the time (if at all). This vague apperception can function as a presentiment later to be explored, or it could be the source of an unconscious interpretation only later to be announced.

Here I will come back to the idea of a "double reduction" from *Grundprobleme*, discussed above (Ch. 2, § 3). Husserl's analysis, we recall, proceeds stepwise, first by insisting that the Cartesian reduction to immanence must be extended and complemented by a new reduction: "we discover the noteworthy fact that each lived experience permits of a double reduction".[63] Such a renewed reduction would permit us to also reach in to the horizons that surround that which is apodictically given in *Gegenwärtigung*, i.e. to include also the sphere of *Vergegenwärtigungen*. This, again recapitulating, means that we reduce not only the punctual ego cogito, but also the sphere of its "retentions, rememberings, expectations".[64]

When for instance the reduction is applied to a memory, then we also reduce and thus make available for transcendental inquiry that which was given in the background of that which was then at the centre of attention, so that its whole horizon also becomes a possible theme. This paying attention to that which at the time was not given any attention, i.e. to the background, can only occur *nachträglich* Husserl says. So that with this new, double reduction, all that which is in one way or another intentionally connected to the first thing or event, becomes available in the transcendental field for a possible retrieval (this was worked out in greater detail with the notion of intentional implication, in *Erste Philosophie II*):

> The most remarkable thing turned out to be that every experience admits a doubled phenomenological reduction: on the one hand, the reduction that renders the experience itself to pure immanent seeing; and on the other hand, the reduction that is exercised on the experience's intentional content and object. Thus there is a phenomenological reduction that is exercised on the intentional content and object of recollection. That is, just as in recollecting "afterwards" [*"nachträglich"*] we can attend to the remembered object's background, which in the original perception was unnoticed perceptual background, so we can *in* the recollection exercise a phenomenological reduction on the foreground and

[63] XIII, Nr. 6 § 34 p. 178/CW 12, p. 74 (tr. mod.).
[64] XIII, Nr. 6 § 34 p. 178/CW 12, p. 73 (tr. mod.).

> background, which was not achieved in the original perception and which, therefore, is not a recollection of an earlier reduction (XIII, Nr. 6 § 34 p. 178f/CW 12, p. 74).

Then in a further step (that will be examined later on) Husserl shows how this also holds in the case of the other, so that we can reduce not only my empathising with the other, that is to say, my living-myself-into-her-life, but also her as empathising with me, i.e. her living-herself-into-my-life.[65] But what role is actually ascribed to the concept of *"Nachträglichkeit"* – carefully placed in brackets – here? That is to say, could it be replaced at will by another concept merely emphasizing that it belongs to the past, or does its appearance signify something else? It is clear that some concept or other that is able to account for the phenomenon of bringing a whole segment of previously lived experience back to experiential life must be employed.

If *nachträglich* means only this however, then it could indeed be replaced, it seems. But if we consider the specific context, namely the bringing back of the horizon of an object that was previously perceived, that is to say, the background which was precisely not attended to at the time (and thus not perceived), then, it seems to me, things begin to look different. For what is at stake is the "bringing back" of a background that was not perceived at the time, and which thus has to be constituted after the event, for the first time. The hyletic material would be there as a potentiality to constitution, dormant in the sedimented sphere, but only as the source of a later and non-apodictical project of what was there, one that is always open for confusion and unclarity.

Thus it seems to me that it is clearly not the question of a mere revival of a previously lived experience, but something closer to what Derrida said concerning *Nachträglichkeit*: that "it produces the present past".[66] This "production" of the past must not be misunderstood, it is

---

[65] XIII, Nr. 6 § 39/CW 12, § 39: "The uncovering of other phenomenological I's through a doubled phenomenological reduction".

[66] "This impression has left behind a laborious trace which has never been perceived, whose meaning has never beeen lived in the present, i.e., has never been lived consciously. The postscript which constitutes the past present as such is not satisfied, as Plato, Hegel, and Proust perhaps thought, with reawakening or revealing the present past in its truth. It produces the present past. Is sexual deferral the best example or the essence of this movement?" ("Freud and the Scene of Writing", in *Writing and Difference*, p. 215)

not the question of random fabrication, it is of course guided by the object as remembered and other constitutive signals. The much discussed analogy between the givenness of my own past and the givenness of the other – which is given its paradigmatic presentation in *Grundprobleme* – to me testify what is at stake: given the problematic character of the phenomena at hand, i.e. my past and the other, Husserl insists that we must make do with this. The constitution that is at stake occurs in a kind of inevitable grey zone: not private phantasy, nor objective reality, but a reconstruction of a "reality" that was supposed to have occurred.

Its evidential validity is of necessity weaker than the object that is at the centre of attention, for as far as the latter is concerned, there is always a possibility of comparison with how it is at first remembered, and how it can be presented through an active act of recollection, where our searchlight is set upon the recalling of details that we want to fill out. This is why Husserl always insisted that the Cartesian way to the reduction has evidential priority over and above the non-Cartesian ways, which supplement it. The tentative outcome of this is that *Nachträglichkeit* in the more radical Freudian sense is indeed, to at least some extent, operative in a fundamental way in Husserl's first analysis of the extended reduction to intersubjectivity through an intentional analysis of *Vergegenwärtigung*.

Later on, the development of genetic phenomenology led Husserl to again consider the possibility of unconscious contents becoming conscious at a later point. For as he says in a text from 1926, it is possible that there are affective tendencies going out from that which is repressed in the "unconscious", whilst our attention is directed to other matters:

> The one winning out does not annihilate the other ones, but suppresses them. [...] Perseverance. There can accordingly be affections progressing from the "unconscious", but suppressed. [...] In the movable present something new appears that is advantageous to something that is suppressed and awakens it." (XI, Beilage XIX "Zur Phänomenologie der Assoziation" p. 416/CW 9, p. 518f; tr. mod. [1926]).

And in a yet later text Husserl also approaches the aspect of *Nachträglichkeit* that Freud calls the "revision" of a former event through a present recollection. At the time I only had eyes for this and that, Husserl says, but I could have seen it in a different light, since the recollection shows now that it is different than I thought it was; and he goes on:

> But precisely this constant possibility to let my present powers of interest play a part in the representified past, and from now onwards not only bring to words how that past concretely was, but also to bring to words *nachträglich* that which "lies" within it, is nevertheless important also from a constitutive perspective (D 14/21 [1931-32]).[67]

Here, unlike the previously discussed passage from the lectures on inner time-consciousness, Husserl actually seems to discuss something like the general possibility of *Nachträglichkeit*, understood in its Freudian sense, were it not for the lack of references to sexual life. The question must therefore be suspended until later, for it is only in Chapter 6, § 3 that the investigation will have reached the role of sexuality in transcendental phenomenology. At the least, the analysis undertaken so far permits one to question the position reached by Derrida, when he states that phenomenology and psychoanalysis must go separate ways precisely when confronted with the phenomenon of *Nachträglichkeit*:

> It is the problem of the deferred effect (*Nachträglichkeit*) of which Freud speaks. The temporality to which he refers cannot be that which lends itself to a phenomenology of consciousness or of presence and one may indeed wonder by what right all that is in question here should still be called time, now, anterior present, delay, etc. (*Of Grammatology* p. 67/Fr. p. 97f).
>
> It is no accident that *The Phenomenology of Internal Time-Consciousness* both confirms the dominance of the present and rejects the "after-event" of the becoming conscious of an "unconscious content" which is the structure of temporality implied throughout Freud's texts (*Speech and Phenomena*, p. 63/Fr. p. 70f).

---

[67] "Aber eben diese beständige Möglichkeit, meine gegenwärtige Interessenkraft in die vergegenwärtigte Vergangenheit hineinspielen zu lassen und vom Jetzt aus nicht nur, sie, wie sie konkret war, sondern was in ihr 'liegt' zu Worte zu bringen, jetzt, nachträglich, ist doch wichtig auch in konstitutiver Hinsicht" (D 14/21 [1931-32]).

A fairly common strategy amongst commentators that have been unwilling to acknowledge the rigour of Derrida's argumentation (which will be examined closer shortly), has been to look to a well-known appendix in Hua X for quick support.[68] There, Husserl (contrary to what Freud and Derrida suggest) seems to deny the possibility of any kind of "unconscious contents" becoming conscious only subsequently. That is to say, it seems to be the impossibility of *Nachträglichkeit* as such that is at stake, and by implication, we seem to have a Husserlian argument stating the impossibility of the Freudian unconscious ever becoming conscious, which is to say its death certificate – at least, that is how the text has often been treated. A more careful analysis however shows that such a conclusion is not warranted, as Husserl is clearly discussing a different topic. Since this passage is the source of some confusion, it will be necessary to deal with it at length:

> What about the beginning phase of an experience that is in the process of becoming constituted? Does it also come to be given only on the basis of retention, and would it be "unconscious" if no retention were to follow it? We must say in response to this question: The beginning phase can become an object only after it has elapsed in the indicated way, by means of retention and reflection (or reproduction). But if it were intended only by retention, then what confers on it the label "now" would remain incomprehensible. At most, it could be distinguished negatively from its modifications as that one phase that does not make us retentionally conscious of any preceding phase; but the beginning-phase is by all means characterized in consciousness in quite positive fashion. It is just nonsense to talk about an "unconscious" content that would only subsequently become conscious [*Es ist eben ein Unding, von einem "unbewussten" Inhalt zu sprechen, der erst nachträglich bewusst würde*]. Consciousness is necessarily consciousness in each of its phases. Just as the retentional phase is conscious of the preceding phase without making it into an object, so too the primal datum is already intended – specifically, in the original form of the "now" – without its being something objective (Hua X, Beilage IX p. 119/CW 4, p. 123).[69]

[68] See for instance Zahavi, *Self-Awareness and Alterity* p. 86f. According to Zahavi, Husserl in the appendix that I quote and comment upon here, "anticipated Derrida's line of thought, and although he occasionally seriously considered it, he ultimately and quite explicitly rejected it" (p. 86). This interpretation stems from a misunderstanding of the problem that Husserl is discussing in this text.

[69] According to Boehm this appendix stems from 1910-17 (see Hua X, p. 99), whereas Bernet leaves it undated in his edition (Meiner, 1985). The original

What Husserl is doing here is first to introduce two hypotheses that are immediately seen to be absurd and that are therefore discarded, which strengthens the view of the extended now as necessitating both *Urimpression* and retention (the role of protention is not discussed here). Following this *reductio ad absurdum* Husserl then comes to the major point, which is to disclose inner time-consciousness as providing us with a preobjective self-manifestation. First hypothesis: if no retention were to follow upon an experience not yet fully constituted, then this experience could not be constituted at all. Second hypothesis: if, however, this experience-on-its-way were to be intended only by retention, then it could not become a part of a "now", in which case again it would not be constituted at all. That is to say, for an experience to become constituted, it must be intended both as originary "now" and as retention: the subsequent reflection or reproduction would only confirm this.[70]

The "conclusion" is reached when Husserl, now dismissing these two counterfactual and invalid hypotheses, states that the experience-on-its-way after all really is given in consciousness as a positive phenomenon: "sie ist ja bewusstseinsmässig durchaus positiv charakterisiert". Thereby the final point of this passage has been reached, according to which the workings of inner time-consciousness is said to always also bring about a preobjective self-manifestation.

Thus, the pivotal phrase is not our usual suspect ("It is just nonsense …" etc.); for there Husserl only states that retention without impression – and vice versa – is unthinkable: when we perceive the world there is no experiential delay caused by retention. It is in this sense that it is, as Husserl puts it, *ein Unding, von einem "unbewussten" Inhalt zu sprechen, der erst nachträglich bewusst würde*. In perception, what we perceive is what we get (although with it there also comes a non-

---

manuscript has not been located.

[70] Needless to say, the full picture also calls for the *protentional* intentionality to be included – which Husserl often disregards in his analyses at this time; this passage examines only a special case: the relation between the *Urimpression* and the retention. In later texts, beginning with the Bernau-texts, the role of protention is given a much more prominent role in the analysis of time-consciousness (see Hua XXXIII, Texts Nr. 1 & 2 p. 3-49). And once the genetic perspective is more firmly in place, the protentional direction of intentionality is further strengthened through the discovery of the intentionality of the drives, which will occupy us later on.

objectified awareness of ourselves, plus that which is co-intended (*mitgemeint*), such as the underside of the table) – there is no remainder that subsequently becomes conscious. The point that Husserl is making here is that even an experience-on-its-way to be constituted is given in a non-objectified way to consciousness, something that can always be confirmed through reflection. Again, it is the intentional implication between the retention-originary impression and objectifying consciousness, that binds the whole structure together, thus making consciousness "necessarily consciousness in each of its phases".

The emphasis on the becoming-conscious of an experience-on-its-way, indicates that Husserl is here beginning to explore a theme that was to become his central concern soon after, with genetic phenomenology. And as should be clear by now, any discussion of the issue of the unconscious in phenomenology and psychoanalysis must take its starting point in Husserl's fully developed genetic phenomenology. To claim that this text warrants the general denial by transcendental phenomenology of the possibility of the Freudian concept of the unconscious should thus simply be ruled out.[71]

But even though I have followed Derrida's argumentation concerning temporality and the other[72] (the two major fields where Husserl is said to "break" with the metaphysics of presence that phenomenology otherwise is an expression of), I nevertheless see my own investigation as questioning a certain dominating movement in Derrida's interpretation. In *La voix et le phénomène*, Derrida uses the analysis of the sign in order "to indicate the principle of a general interpretation of Husserl's

---

[71] Zahavi in *Self-Awareness and Alterity* refers to this text in the common (but as I have argued mistaken) way, thereby also inadvertently ruling out at least a standard possibility of accounting for the psychoanalytical unconscious (p. 85f): there can be no contents that become conscious *nachträglich*. In the "Appendix on the unconscious" (p. 203ff) he then criticizes Freud in a somewhat superficial way. Although Zahavi doesn't connect the critique of Freud with the interpretation of Beilage IX, it is difficult not to see their inner relation.

[72] See "'Genesis and structure' and phenomenology": "The constitution of the other and of time refer phenomenology to a zone in which its 'principle of all principles' (as we see it, its *metaphysical* principle: the original *self-evidence* and *presence* of the thing itself in person) is radically put into question" (*Writing and Difference*, p. 164). This is often repeated.

thought", and when he states that the privilege of consciousness as pure self-presence is only possible via the phenomenological voice of soliloquy, where the ideal *Lebendigkeit* of transcendental life is upheld without interruption (since soliloquy does not admit the exteriority of the sign but is pure interiority), this is true of the Cartesian way to the reduction, but not of the others, which are of equal importance for Husserl.[73]

This neglect on Derrida's part has its immediate counterpart in Heidegger's reading, which also overplays the Cartesian tendencies of Husserl's thought. At the same time that Derrida has raised the level of the debate between phenomenology and psychoanalysis significantly by bringing for instance Freudian *Nachträglichkeit* into the phenomenological analysis of inner time-consciousness, his particular strategy to employ the former as a lever for criticizing retention has now perhaps served its purpose.[74] For there are significant similarities between Freud's concept of *Nachträglichkeit* and Husserl's analysis of retention that Derrida has overlooked.

Or has come to overlook: the theme of "originary delay" (*retard originaire*), first "imposed" itself on him while working with Husserl's

---

[73] *La Voix*, p. 1n2, 14ff, 85ff. In interviews, Derrida often admits that his approach towards Husserl was ambivalent from the outset: in part directed at obtaining the truth, in part subjected to the wish to revolt. Although the critical instruments were given to him by Husserl, he still represented "school-philosophy", one of the great H's (together with Hegel and Heidegger) that it was necessary to revolt against (as he explains in many interviews). This ambivalence is clearly visible in all of his works on Husserl I think, starting with the attempt to overcome methodological shortcomings by means of an "originary dialectics" in the wake of Tran-Duc-Thao and Cavaillès in *Le Problème de la Génèse*, traces of which are still clearly visible in *La Voix, De la grammatologie* and even *Glas*.

[74] The main point that Derrida advances against Husserl is succinctly captured in the following phrase, which focuses on the position that the retention occupies in the midst of the extended now: "As soon as we admit this continuity of the now and the not-now, of perception and nonperception in the zone of primordiality common to primordial impression and retention, we admit the other into the self-identity of the *Augenblick*: nonpresence and nonevidence are admitted into the instantaneous blink of the eye. There is a duration to the blink, and it closes the eye" (*Speech and Phenomena* p. 65/Fr. p. 73; cf. *De la grammatologie* p. 97f). This, as has been pointed out often, seems to threaten Husserl's endeavour right at the heart, but many of the temporal arguments deny this, since there is strictly speaking no "instant" that retention could dislodge: the "now" is a concrete unit which can be abstractively divided into impression, protention and retention, but the one is never given without the others. Retentional consciousness already presupposes impressional consciousness, and therefore cannot be that which grounds it.

late text on geometry, and in 1962 he actually considered phenomenology as the sole possibility for philosophy to think and to express such a notion.[75] The phenomenological reduction, he goes on to say, is nothing other than the thought of this delay: "In the lackluster guise of a technique, the Reduction is only pure thought as that delay, pure thought investigating the sense of itself as delay within philosophy".[76] But by 1967 Derrida no longer saw these possibilities in Husserl's thought, and from thereon instead affirmed that it is a philosophy of presence to which one must oppose a "thought of non-presence".[77]

As Derrida often admits, he became highly influenced by Levinas (and vice versa), in particular by his theories of time and intersubjectivity, which instead of the unity of transcendental consciousness emphasize the diachrony of time as founded by the infinity of the other, by her radical alterity.[78] In the following Chapters of this investigation, I intend to show that this Derridean-Levinasian critique of Husserlian phenomenology is precipitate and does not, at least not on these grounds, warrant the necessity of a step beyond Husserl.

In conclusion, it has become clear that although the unearthing of this prereflective self-awareness requires an archaeological effort, for which Husserl himself employs expressions such as the unconscious and *Nachträglichkeit*, it is now becoming possible to begin to see more clearly both the differences and the similarities between Husserl and Freud. Both of them, along different paths, investigated the deferral of objectivated manifestation (that we only "know" what previously occurred by ontifying it after the event), and also attempted to clarify what it is that connects the two events. But while Husserl, at least in so

---

[75] See *L'ecriture et la différence*, p. 302/Engl. p. 203, 329n5; and *L'origine de la géométrie* (p. 170/Engl. p. 152): "that delay is the destiny of Thought itself as Discourse – only a phenomenology can *say* this and make philosophy equal to it.".

[76] *L'origine de la géométrie*, p. 170/Engl. p. 153.

[77] *La voix et le phénomène*, p. 70. Françoise Dastur, in one of the best articles I've read on Derrida, reasonably suggests that it is the impact of Levinasian heterology and Heideggerian destruction of ontotheology that lies behind this shift on Derrida's part (see her "Derrida and the question of presence", 2006, p. 52f).

[78] See *Le temps et l'autre* (2004), p. 10; "Intentionality and sensation", in *Discovering Existence with Husserl* (1988) p, 143, 148. On this, see R. Bernet, "Levinas's Critique of Husserl" (2004), p. 82-99.

far as we have seen here, restricted his analyses to the no doubt essential and foundational level of inner time-consciousness in relation to the perceptual field, Freud, by admitting also the free play of imagination was able to go yet further.

Freud could do this since he based his investigations of deferred understanding more firmly on feelings and sexuality and the links they uphold with imagination. At the same time, however, it has become clear that Freud's analyses are from a philosophical point of view severely lacking in terms of an explanation of how the unconscious is connected to consciousness, particularly as concerns the dimension of time, which is something that all of his analyses simply presupposes. Although it may still be an open question whether the phenomenon of *Nachträglichkeit* is really best explained in terms of sexual deferral as Freud would have it, I have argued that it is philosophically more plausible to say that it is a part of the structure of subjective life itself.

Chapter Five

"FREE ASSOCIATION" – FREUD'S *GRUNDREGEL* CLARIFIED BY MEANS OF THE "UNIVERSAL PRINCIPLE OF PASSIVE CONSTITUTION"

Psychoanalytic research [...] seeks merely to uncover connections by tracing that which is manifest back to that which is hidden (Freud)

Psychology is constantly involved in this great process of development, involved, as we have seen, in different ways; indeed, psychology is the truly decisive field. It is this precisely because, though it has a different attitude and is under the guidance of a different task, its subject matter is universal subjectivity, which in its actualities and possibilities is one (Husserl)

1. Introduction.

This chapter investigates Freud's concept of "free association" from the perspective of Husserl's analysis of association as it was developed in his transcendental genetic phenomenology. Husserl's account of association undergoes considerable change from the early conception to his mature position where it becomes the most basic process in the phenomenology of passivity (as will be shown in the next section), a change that is intimately connected with the expansion from static to genetic phenomenology. The analysis of temporality provides the phenomenology of the extended concept of consciousness with its "general form", but it also becomes clear that this only represents a first, non-independent part.[1] The full constitution of time requires a phenomenology of originary association to bring impressional-kinaesthetic consciousness in contact with inner time-consciousness, as Husserl

[1] *Erfahrung und Urteil*, p. 75f/Engl. p. 73.

repeatedly emphasizes in the 1920's.[2] As Holenstein puts it, the investigation of inner time-consciousness comes to its "consummation only within a phenomenology of association".[3]

By founding association in inner time-consciousness and sensuous affectivity, it becomes possible to sketch out a plausible philosophical connection between the 'shallowness' of free association and the 'depth' of the repressed unconscious. This is something that Freud's account of free association presupposes but cannot explain, since there is no clear account of the relation between the unconscious (which is the repressed "source" of the associations) and consciousness where the associations manifest themselves. The role of free association as indicating the unconscious depths means that the investigation here encounters a decisive question: either it accepts the common interpretation of the psychoanalytical unconscious as "radical alterity", or it argues that Husserl's extended concept of consciousness can actually accommodate and ultimately clarify the basic processes of the Freudian unconscious.

The examination of association in this chapter therefore plays a pivotal part in a twofold sense. On the one hand, it argues that the phenomenological analysis of association in the ordinary sense – which is founded upon the doctrine of intentional implication – is able to explain how Freudian free association as the method which unravels the relation between the unconscious and consciousness is possible. And on the other hand since it shows how originary association functions at the most fundamental level of genesis, thereby throwing further light on the constitution of the living present (which was examined in a preliminary sense in Chapter Three).

---

[2] See the lectures on passive synthesis, Hua XI § 27, "The Presuppositions of Associative Synthesis. The Syntheses of Original Time-Consciousness" (and Beilage XII), and *Erfahrung und Urteil*, § 16 "The field of passive pregivennesses and its associative structure". But as Landgrebe has pointed out, Husserl's earlier analysis of time-consciousness in the 1905 lectures was not integrated with the impressional-kinaesthetic syntheses: "Die passiven Synthesen des Zeitbewußtseins sind dort [Hua X] noch nicht mit den kinästhetischen Synthesen zusammengebracht. Versucht man dies aber, so ergibt sich: ohne Impressionen gibt es keine zeitkonstituierenden Leistungen und ohne Kinästhesen gibt es keine Impressionen" (Landgrebe, *Faktizität und Individuation*, p. 81). See also Claesges's discussion of this in "Zeit und kinästhetisches Bewusstsein. Bemerkungen zu einer These Ludwig Landgrebes" (1983).

[3] Holenstein, *Husserls Phänomenologie der Assoziation*, p. 64.

In the second section (§ 2) I will present a brief outline of Husserl's theory of association, before moving on to Freud's account of "free association" with a particular interest in its mediating function between consciousness and the unconscious. I will discuss the position of Holenstein's *Husserls Phänomenologie der Assoziation*, which is still the main work that engages psychoanalysis and phenomenology in a confrontation from the point of view of association.

In the next section (§ 3), I will briefly trace the background of Husserl's phenomenology of association, before approaching the main theme, which concerns the reinterpretation of association as a properly transcendental phenomenon. Here it is the relation between association and the phenomenological reduction that is at stake, since it must be shown that we can gain access to association in its relation to the fundamental investigation of inner time-consciousness from within a methodologically clarified position. This theme will therefore connect with discussions in previous chapters of the living present.

The following section (§ 4) will examine a problem that surfaced in Freud's theory concerning the relation between free associations occurring in the present and an unconscious order which determines them. What is the intentional relation between on the one hand present-day associative chains where "one calls attention to the other", as Husserl describes it in *Erfahrung und Urteil*, and on the other hand the presence of a hidden nucleus which this chain circles around? This problem will be approached by means of Husserl's theory of sedimentation, which shows how a past lived experience that is now "dead", "unconscious" and no longer exerts an affective force, can still be awakened by means of association.

In the final two sections, the direct approach is taken up once more. In § 5, this second attempt at direct clarification of repression focuses on texts where Husserl analyzes the phenomenological possibility of sedimented concrete complexes (lived experiences, feelings, thoughts and kinaesthesia etc.) whose affective force does not diminish with time: contrary to normal retentional procedure, these complexes live on, actively engaging other sedimented events and attracting attention from presentifying consciousness; this strange living on Husserl calls "perseverance" (*Perseveranz*). This would correspond to the mode of being of the repressed according to Freud's theory. In connection with this there is also an analysis of how repressed memories can "break through" to intuition, and this would correspond to the "return of the repressed" in Freud's theory. The third direct approach (§ 6) investigates Husserl's analysis of memories that interpenetrate one another so as to form an "illusion" (*Scheinbild*) of a past that has never occurred. Furthermore, it sets out to give an account of what is argued to be one of Freud's most important concepts – *psychische Realität* – in terms of intentional analysis.

2. Association in Husserl and Freud

Beginning with Husserl, one may start by asking where association in the most fundamental sense takes place: is it at the higher level which we most commonly think of, such as the bringing back of a previous event, or is it in the first gathering of the affective-hyletic material into the sense fields, which then taken together make up the "perceptual field" (*Wahrnehmungsfeld*)? Or does the genuine associability of the psyche lie at an even more remote level of consciousness? There are two major but fundamentally different processes in conscious life that Husserl distinguishes here: first we have associations in the ordinary sense, that is to say reproductive and inductive association that lead to the awakening of memories and to expectations in the future (association here occurs between two or more already constituted objects).

But Husserl also operates with another concept of association, the so called "originary association" (*Urassoziation*), which accounts for the most basic organization of the impressional sphere within the living present.[4] An important aspect of this is the fusing (*Verschmelzung*) of affective and preaffective unities within the living present, and originary association thus brings about a unification of sensuous affective life. In

[4] Thus Holenstein for instance already in his introduction to *Husserls Phänomenologie der Assoziation* notes that Husserl differentiates between "two large groups of associations" (p. 32) and devotes two sections to them in Part I, Ch. 2: § 7 "Assoziationen im gewöhnlichen Sinn", and § 8 "Urassoziationen". For references to the latter, see XI, p. 151, 180, 273, 286. See also HuMat 8, p. 53, 122, 437; XV, p. 74. In D 14/52, Husserl distinguishes "Fernassoziation" from "der kontinuierlichen Assoziation, die ursprünglich Einheit macht"; cf. also E III 9/23b.

§ 38 of the lectures on transcendental logic, Husserl describes the process of "transition" of the awakened empty presentations which turns them into rememberings, and there presents the first level of this transition as that of the *Urassoziation.* Originary association, it is said there, is ...

> ... that systematizing affective awakening that makes possible the objectlike structure of the living present, all kinds of original syntheses proper to the formation of unity of manifolds (XI, § 38 p. 180).

If taken by itself, outside of its insoluble connection with originary association, originary affection would be a "pure chaos", a "maelstrom of data".[5] Originary association is thus something that is presupposed by all kinds of constitution of objects, and it can only be separated from originary affection by means of abstraction. Association for Husserl thus gradually gains a novel meaning and finally becomes a name for the "universal principle" which guides passive consciousness as such.[6] This means that it comes to stand in an "immediate connection with the teaching of original time-consciousness", and association can therefore be seen as that which at the lowermost level of genetic constitution "gives unity to our lives".[7] Due to this extension of the concept of association whereby "originary association" has come to cover the most

---

[5] *Erfahrung und Urteil*, § 16, p. 75/Engl. p. 72: "*Chaos, ein blosses 'Gewühl' von 'Daten'*". Since Kant, the thought of sensuality as a pure chaos that must be schematized by means of the concepts of reason, has threatened the philosophical world like an attack by aliens from Mars: "so würde es möglich sein, daß ein Gewühle von Erscheinungen unsere Seele anfüllte, ohne daß doch daraus jemals Erfahrung werden könnte [...] mithin würde sie zwar gedankenlose Anschauung, aber niemals Erkenntnis, also für uns soviel als gar nichts sein" (KrV, A 111).

[6] I, CM, § 39.

[7] See *Erfahrung und Urteil*, § 16 where the link between inner time-consciousness as the formal framework and passive association as that which provides this structure with sensuous material is clearly established. For the first quotation, see Husserl's letter to Mahnke from 1926 in *Briefwechsel* Bd. III, p. 453f; and for the second quotation see the manuscript D 14/12b: "Die ganze Einheit des Lebens ist Einheit aus universaler Verschmelzung, also aus Assoziation". The latter point is also developed in several of the C-manuscripts, see for instance HuMat 8, Nr. 13 p. 42: "das Leben ist umspannt von einer universalen Wesensgesetzmässigkeit der Passivität: der Synthesis der Assoziation"; cf. also XI, p. 405 "Synthesis in ihren verschiedenen Gestalten als universale Einigung des Lebens eines Ich = Assoziation im weitesten Sinn".

important aspect of the phenomenon, Husserl often refers to this without the prefix "Ur-".[8]

Both of these paths will be employed in order to try to clarify Freud's account of free association. Husserl's transcendental account of association in the ordinary sense is able to do so by virtue of its being based on a thorough examination of the relations that hold between inner time-consciousness and sensuous affectivity. Thereby it makes it clear how that which Freud calls the surface-phenomenon of free association can be founded in an extended concept of consciousness, instead of bypassing the latter in favour of jumping directly from a "skimming of the surface" of consciousness to the deepest, most inaccessible repressed unconscious. For Freud's "free association" always presupposes precisely such an account of the relation between various levels of consciousness (or between consciousness and the unconscious). Here the investigation of Husserl's extended concept of consciousness will be put to the test, since his analysis of association does not acknowledge anything unconscious in the strong sense that many align with Freud.

A proper understanding of association may therefore come to occupy a pivotal position in the overall argument, since it may turn out that Freud's basic methodological rule for making the unconscious speak actually plays a part in the denial of the thesis of the unconscious as "radical alterity". But Husserl's analysis of "originary association" will also be examined, since it shows how association in an extended sense also functions at the most fundamental level of conscious life. Thereby the phenomenological analysis of consciousness throws light on processes and structures that precede and make possible that which stands in focus for Freud, for whom free association is tantamount to "skim off the surface of consciousness".[9]

The analysis of originary associations is approached in the lectures on passive synthesis (in Hua XI), where they account for the unification

[8] Whether it is association in the ordinary sense or "originary association" that is referred to is almost always immediately discernible from the context. In general, from 1917 onwards roughly, reference to association is in fact often to (what was later to be called) originary association; an early reference to the term *Urassoziation* is in the lectures on passive synthesis (see XI, §§ 33, 38), and then in manuscripts from the 1930's it is frequent; see for instance HuMat 8 Nr. 13, 17, 21, 29, 33, 57, 66, 79, 96, 97.

[9] See Freud's "Short Account of Psychoanalysis", PFL 15, p. 166.

of the temporal sequence, thereby making possible "the object like structure of the living present".[10] In other texts, such as ms. A VII 13 (written in October 1921, shortly after Husserl had first presented the lectures on passive synthesis), there is an attempt to begin to account for this genetically deeper level of passive constitution by means of an analysis of association as an "intentionality of drives":

> The association as association of drives. We not only have to do with a mere association of "ideas", but with an association of acquired drives and processes of drives that have a direction, of passive processes of striving and their immanent effects. It is not the mere "idea" of such a process that is awakened, but the I as a subject of drives and its drive itself is awakened (A VII 13/20a [1921]).[11]

But it is above all in later texts, notably in the C-manuscripts, that a more precise account of this process is given as it occurs at the level of "temporisation" (*Zeitigung*, *Urzeitigung*).[12] This theme will therefore recur in the final Chapter Six, in connection with the final analysis of the structure of the living present.

It was only gradually that Freud came to see that free association was more than one way amongst others for the disclosure of the unconscious.[13] But by and large, Freud came to regard it as the "fundamental rule" (*Grundregel*) of the psychoanalytical praxis.[14] This method attempts a step beyond the associationist psychology of Wundt's school, in that Freud does not regard it as sufficient to account for the stream of associations merely by recourse to the concepts of contiguity and similarity, understood in a narrow sense.[15] For these theories do not take

---

[10] XI, § 38 p. 180.

[11] "Die Assoziation als Assoziation von Trieben. Wir haben es nicht mit einer blossen Assoziation von 'Ideen' zu tun, sondern mit einer Assoziation erworbener Triebe und gerichteter Triebverläufe, von passiven Strebensverläufen und ihren immanenten Auswirkungen. Nicht die blosse 'Idee' eines solchen Verlaufs wird geweckt, sondern das Ich als Subjekt des Triebes und sein Trieb selbst wird geweckt" (A VII 13/20a [St. Märgen, Oktober 1921]; cf. 24a).

[12] See for instance HuMat 8, Nr. 13, 29, 66, 79, 96.

[13] In a text from 1910 ("Five Lectures On Psychoanalysis", § 3), Freud presents three ways of reaching the unconscious that are regarded as being of equal rank: free association, the interpretation of dreams and of parapraxes (SE 11).

[14] See "Two Encyclopaedia Articles", PFL 15, p. 134f.

[15] Freud discusses and criticizes Wundt's theory of association repeatedly; see for

into account the givenness of resistance between different agencies in the psyche, which has its source in processes that are beyond the reach of the conscious I.[16] Specific attention is given by the analyst to precisely those associations which awaken resistance in the analysand:

> We may assume that whatever associations, thoughts and memories the patient is unable to communicate to us without internal struggles are in some way connected with the repressed material or are its derivatives. ("The Question of Lay Analysis" [1927] PFL 15, p. 305).

Here Freud on the one hand establishes the highly important connection between the free associations occurring in the present, and that which is repressed, i.e. the personal history of the subject; while at the same time noting that what indicates the presence of such a connection is the resistance to the analysis.

Several things must be taken into account when it comes to "free association" in psychoanalysis, and particularly two common and related misunderstandings must be discarded. First it should be noted that free association is by no means a magical carpet flying us directly into the promised land of the Unconscious. As Freud clearly states, when the subject initiates the process of free association by modifying her ordinary self-perception and thus turning herself into "an attentive and dispassionate self-observer", what she is asked to do is "merely to read off all the time the surface of her consciousness".[17] From the material thus provided the analyst will then begin to find the path leading to what had been forgotten or avoided, since "everything that occurred to a patient setting out from a particular starting point must also stand in an internal connection with that starting-point".[18]

---

instance *The Interpretation of Dreams*, Ch. 1 and *The Psychopathology of Everyday Life*, Ch. 5.

[16] Thus he states in *The Interpretation of Dreams*: "Whenever one psychical element is linked with another by an objectionable or superficial association, there is also a legitimate and deeper link between them which is subjected to the resistance of the censorship" (PFL 4, p. 677).

[17] "Two Encyclopaedia Articles", PFL 15, p. 134. See also "Short Account of Psychoanalysis" PFL 15, p. 166, where Freud says that he would ask his patients "to refrain from any conscious reflection and to abandon themselves, in a state of quiet concentration, to follow the ideas which occurred to them spontaneously (involuntarily) – "to skim off the surface of their consciousness"."

[18] "Two Encyclopaedia Articles", PFL 15, p. 134f.

This discovery is by and large what puts genetic phenomenology in a position where it can be called upon for clarification, for it is clear that Freud's theory of free association corresponds to Husserl's theory of intentional implications, in that it allows the analyst to trace the meaning-connections that hold between various lived experiences and representations backwards as it were.

Second point: it is not the case that Freud regarded the free associations as being "free" in the strong sense of being beyond the influence of the conscious I – that is to say, as something given "straight" from its unconscious source (whatever that could mean). Instead, Freud stresses that the "free" association is upon closer examination actually unfree and that that which restrains it is precisely the "unconscious" material which – in ways to be determined – helps to organize the paths that the associations will follow.[19] So the "inner connections" between a lived experience (what Freud called the "starting point" above) and the associations that arise, are also bound to yet another starting point, more distant, that will gradually begin to disclose itself as the hidden, unconscious centre of associations, dreams etc. Thus Freud said that he was led to the expectation that...

> ... the so-called "free" association would prove in fact to be unfree, since, when all conscious intellectual purposes had been suppressed, the representations that emerged would be seen to be determined by the unconscious material. This expectation was justified by experience ("Short Account of Psychoanalysis", PFL 15, p. 166; tr. mod.).

It is thus not the practical impossibility of giving a full report of the ongoings in the mind that places restrictions on the "freedom" of associations. It is the philosophically more important fact that with the "increased attention" and the "elimination of criticism" (that make up parts of what I have called the psychoanalytical epoché), the representations that emerge are in fact shown to be determined by an unconscious order.[20] This point was suggested as one of the two "basic pillars" of the psychoanalytical technique in *The Interpretation of Dreams*:

---

[19] "Short Account of Psychoanalysis", PFL 15, p. 166; see already *The Interpretation of Dreams*, PFL 4, p. 675, 679.

[20] See already *The Interpretation of Dreams*, PFL 4 p. 675, 679.

> In the psychoanalysis of neuroses the fullest use is made of these two propositions [*Sätze*] [21] – that, when conscious purposive representations are abandoned, concealed purposive representations assume control of the sequence of representations, and that superficial associations are only substitutes by displacement for suppressed deeper ones. Indeed, these propositions have become basic pillars of psychoanalytic technique (PFL 4, p. 679; tr. mod.).

This implies that the method of free association is in a fundamental way correlated to the unconscious, such that by repeatedly following an indefinite series of such associations, we gradually acquire the material necessary for the analyst to construct interpretations for the analysand to either reject or take up as part of a growing acquisition of her unknown life. There is accordingly a basic scheme which underlies the whole psychoanalytical investigation, but which is never really outspoken in Freud's writings: free association is an inverted mirroring of an unconscious order. By following this inverted mirroring it becomes clear that the involuntary representations that occur in free association are determined by a hidden *telos*, rather than representing the sheer immanence of surface phenomena:

> For it is demonstrably untrue that we are being carried along a purposeless stream of representations [*ziellosen Vorstellungsablauf*] when, in the process of interpreting a dream, we abandon reflection and allow involuntary representations to emerge. It can be shown that all that we can ever get rid of are purposive representations [*Zielvorstellungen*] that are known to us; as soon as we have done this, unknown – or, as we inaccurately say, "unconscious" – purposive representations take charge and thereafter determine the course of the involuntary representations (*The Interpretation of Dreams*, PFL 4, p. 675; tr. mod.).

But this talk of free association as being a kind of reflection of unconscious processes is a simplification which covers the more radical hermeneutical principle at work, for it suggests that the hidden representations are there in a sufficiently clear and distinct manner already prior to the association being outspoken. Before this articulation, they may have existed in a more oblique manner, as a non-objectified mood,

---

[21] And not "theorems" as PFL suggest for *Sätze* (in mathematical and logical contexts, a theorem is a *Satz*, a proposition which follows from the axioms whereas for Freud here *Satz* is used as a presupposition in a more lax sense).

a complex of feelings, phantasies or bodily comportments etc., which means that the manifestation in free association is often not a reflection of a previously existing representation, but (on the way to) its very first discursive articulation.[22]

It is this "purposiveness" which is unknown to us, this hidden teleology, that the further analysis will try to disclose for as long as it proceeds. In this sense, the method of free association has as its main goal to gradually disclose the rationality of the seemingly "irrational", the bringing to light of the hidden order that determines the unconscious. Following up on Husserl's suggestion of a division of labour, we see that the Freudian method picks up just where Husserl's investigation came to a halt, namely in the further specification of motives characteristic of "irrational" acts that are infused with sensibility, "the driven in the sphere of passivity".[23] The investigation of rationality may indeed proceed to shed light also on these obscure preliminary stages of rational thought and action, as the motives that have their source there indeed also comply to rationality – they belong (as we saw previously) to what Husserl calls a "stratum of hidden reason".[24]

But it is not only the connection with what is unconscious that is important, for the analysis of free association must also show that it is

[22] This hermeneutical principle is the basis of the whole analysis of dreams, in that Freud explicitly states that the memory of the dream necessarily brings about a distortion (*Entstellung*) of the dream as dreamt: the transformation which occurs when the latent content of the dream is interpreted as a manifest content is what makes up the essence of the dreamwork. See "Remarks on the Theory and Practice of Dream-Interpretation", SE 19; see also *The Interpretation of Dreams*, PFL 4, p. 650n [1925 addition]. And Freud also emphasizes that this is essentially a matter of selfinterpretation, although mediated by transference: "The technique which I describe in the pages that follow differs in one essential respect from the ancient method: *it imposes the task of interpretation upon the dreamer himself*" (PFL 4, p. 171fn2; my italics).

[23] *Ideen II*, § 56b p. 222f.

[24] *Ideen II*, § 61 p. 276. This connects with the issue of prepropositional states in accounting for irrational phenomena and the unconscious; see Sebastian Gardner, *Irrationality and the Philosophy of Psychoanalysis* (1993), p. 104f, 116, 154ff, 189ff. Although wary of conceiving of the unconscious in terms of "prepropositional content", Lear admits that it could nevertheless be seen as "the stuff from which a reason might develop", which brings his analysis close to Husserl's transcendental logic too; see his *Freud* (2005) p. 38 and "The Heterogeneity of the Mental" (1995) p. 869f.

connected with thoughts occurring in normal, awakened conscious life. When recounting a dream and making each of its separate images into a starting point for free associations, these function as a kind of communicative bridge between the borders of rational, discursive thought and "irrational" dream life, or between secondary and primary processes:

> By pursuing these associations further we obtain knowledge of thoughts which coincide entirely with the dream but which can be recognized – up to a certain point – as genuine and completely intelligible portions of waking mental activity ("Two Encyclopaedia Articles", PFL 15, p. 137f).[25]

There is yet another factor in this intriguing unfreedom of the free association to take into account, in that each association occurring in the analysis will also be motivated by the relation of transference to the analyst.[26] Although this latter factor is in some sense "external", the method, which proffers neutrality on the part of the analyst, brings with it that the focus will be shifted to "inner" factors, that is to say to the intentional world of the analysand. In the case of the influence exerted upon the free associations that stem from the relation to the analyst, i.e. transference, this shift would be one from genuine, real life facts about the personality etc. of the analyst (which the analysand would know nothing or very little about), to the inner expectations, prejudices etc. of the analysand.

Eventually, and during the course of a psychoanalytical process, this may not only reveal expectations concerning a person in singular: a whole, preformed set of personae that so to speak inhabit the inner stage of the analysand may become visible that correspond to the most important characters with whom one peoples one's inner life. The analyst may come to represent one or several of these "inner" characters during the analysis, and by coming to realize the difference between these pre-formed "personae" and people in real life, outside of the

---

[25] See also *An Autobiographical Study*, PFL 15, p. 227.

[26] "We shall be justified in assuming that nothing will occur to him that has not some reference to that situation [of transference]" (*An Autobiographical Study*, PFL 15, p. 224).

analysis, the analysand will have achieved a greater freedom which may in turn enable a more genuine experience of the world.[27]

However, when one takes a closer look at the philosophical foundation of these "basic pillars" or "basic rule" of the psychoanalytical technique, in particular as concerns how this correlation between present, conscious free associations and an order that is unknown ("unconscious") but which yet determines them is possible, then one has to conclude that Freud has very little to say. If the free associations are that which connects the irrational with the rational, then by means of what processes in consciousness (taken in an extended sense) is this made possible? How must subjectivity be structured in order for the free associations to be connected to that which was repressed a long time ago? What are the operations in the mind that bring about this "deeper link" between repressed occurrences and the present representations? In short, what is the relation between the unconscious and consciousness? To all these questions, which are ultimately of a philosophical character, Freud has no response.

It is not the first time that association has been singled out as a point of connection between psychoanalysis and transcendental phenomenology.[28] In fact, already Holenstein wanted to respond to the provocation that came from the French-speaking phenomenologists, who had "unlocked" the psychoanalytical findings and had begun to speak of a "dépossesion de la conscience immédiate", "désaississement du moi" etc.[29] So in order to arrive at a fuller picture not only of Husserl's phenomenology of association, but also of its capacity to respond to the Freudian challenge, we must take into account the material that was left

---

[27] In this sense, psychoanalysis is a truly critical discipline in that it enables one to draw boundaries between the self and the other, between the self and the world, that were previously muddled: it is a critique of the self (from the Greek *krisis*, boundary, taken up by Kant in his three *Critiques*). This differentiation is also the foundation for the ethical aspect of psychoanalysis.

[28] See for instance Ricœur, *De l'interprétation*, p. 371f/Engl. p. 381f; Hart (2004), p. 145ff.

[29] Holenstein (1972), p. 2. Despite this praiseworthy interdisciplinary initiative, the discussion of psychoanalysis is then postponed all the way until the final chapter. But Holenstein comes to the conclusion that there are greater similarities between *Gestalt*-psychology and Husserl, thus the critical confrontation between phenomenology and psychoanalysis concerning association is never really performed.

out by Holenstein. If it can be shown that the genetic perspective that Husserl develops in texts from the 1930's concerning the drives and originary association is indeed part of a systematic *Neuorientierung*, then Holenstein's conclusion on the relevance of these texts must be revised.

3. The transcendental reinterpretation of association in genetic phenomenology

In Husserl's early works the phenomenon of association was primarily seen as a psychological concept.[30] Thus in the analysis of the sign in the first *Logische Untersuchungen*, genuine indication (as for instance in the phenomenon of empirically "pointing to" something) was said to have its origin in association. Association was therefore tied to the facticity of the here and now, and accordingly something that had to be excluded from the field of phenomenological investigations.[31] But despite this, the actual analysis of association in *Logische Untersuchungen* is remarkably acute. Husserl says that the "continuous result of the associative function" is to fashion that which is merely together in an unconnected way into "intentional unities that appear as belonging-together".[32] And when Husserl in *Ideen II* began to analyze associations in relation to motivation as the "fundamental lawfulness" (*Grundgesetzlichkeit*) of all spiritual life, he already from the outset did so by insisting on its temporal horizon.[33] For associations always occur as "relations between earlier and later consciousness", but within the "stream of actual time-consciousness".[34]

---

[30] See *Philosophie der Arithmetik*, Hua XII, p. 199ff, 211f, 252f. This holds also for *Logische Untersuchungen* and the 1905 lectures on inner time-consciousness. A more promising position is taken in the 1907 lectures on *Ding und Raum* (Hua XVI) since association there is seen not as a "genetic-psychological fact" but instead, and perhaps for the first time, as a "phenomenological fact" expressing a law of the formation of succession; but that is still some way from acquiring a transcendentally-constitutive power though (XVI, § 51 p. 177f).

[31] XIX/1, § 4 p. 33ff.

[32] XIX/1, § 4 p. 36.

[33] *Ideen II*, § 56 "Motivation as the fundamental lawfulness of spiritual life". The whole idea to treat association as a form of motivation was not self-evident; as late as in 1916 Husserl asked himself whether it was legitimate to "speak of association as motivation at all" (A VI 25/11; quoted in HuDo 1 p. 204.

[34] *Ideen II*, § 56 p. 222. In the 1905 lectures on inner time-consciousness, the

Now, in order for association to really leave its empiricist background behind and to step forth as a truly transcendental, that is to say constitutive concept it must first of all find its place within a systematically undertaken theory of the phenomenological reduction. For thereby the associative bond between intentional objects – and thus no longer real, natural objects or "ideas" of them – can be investigated as it manifests itself immanently, without risk of being regarded as a mechanist-causal bond as it is in the empiricist philosophies of Locke and Hume.[35] Further, association can only come forth in its own right once static phenomenology has been supplemented with a systematic investigation of its temporal substructure, which genetic phenomenology provides. For association, as the intentional awakening of one content by means of another, carries within it a temporal order of the genesis of sense, and this static phenomenology cannot thematize.[36] But this "change of sense" that is implied here never the less leaves the phenomenon itself unaltered, which means that that which was excluded in the early works, is at a later stage not only incorporated into the sphere of phenomenological investigations, but furthermore given a foundational position in the phenomenology of passivity:

---

phenomenon of association is conspicuously absent (also from the Beilagen in Hua X); when it occurs it is almost without exception treated in a negative manner, as in the critique of Brentano in §§ 3ff (which was taken up again in Hua XI, p. 77); cf. however X p. 106, 167, 304. In *Ideen I* association is actually conceptually absent, although the discussion of "noematical intentionality" in §§ 101 and 104 is clearly related to it. In *Ideen III* Husserl, on the way towards the discovery of a passive association, said that not everything pertaining to the soul has to be related to the I, since associations are formed "whether the I participates or not" (V, § 3 p. 19 [1912]).

[35] On this, see Husserl's analysis in *Erste Philosophie*, VII, p. 170ff. The relation between Husserl and Hume is the subject of Richard T. Murphy's book, *Hume and Husserl. Towards radical subjectivism* (1983), although I think that Murphy exaggerates the influence that Hume had on Husserl's genetic turn.

[36] This transcendental reformulation of the concept of association is clearly brought out in a passage from *Erfahrung und Urteil*, § 16 p. 77/Engl. p. 74: "What in a purely static description appears to be likeness or similarity must therefore be considered in itself as being already the product of the one or the other kind of synthesis of coincidence, which we denote by the traditional term association, but with a change of sense [*aber unter Verwandlung seines Sinnes*]. It is the phenomenon of associatve genesis which dominates this sphere of passive pregivenness, established on the basis of syntheses of internal time-consciousness."

> That association can become a general theme of phenomenological description and not merely one of objective psychology is due to the fact that the phenomenon of indication [*Anzeige*] is something which can be exhibited from the point of view of phenomenology. (This insight, worked out as early as the *Logical Investigations*, already constitutes there the nucleus of genetic phenomenology.) Every interpretation of association and its laws which makes of it a kind of psychophysical natural law, attained by objective induction, must therefore be excluded here. Association comes into question in this context exclusively as the purely immanent connection of "this recalls that", "one calls attention to the other". [...] And this relationship is itself capable of being shown phenomenologically. It presents itself in itself as a genesis; one of the elements is characterized relative to consciousness as that which awakens, the other as that which is awakened (*Erfahrung und Urteil*, § 16 p. 78/Engl. p. 74f).

What lies behind this reinterpretation of association? This will be investigated in the remainder of this section. Let us first see whether the connection between inner time-consciousness and sensuousness can be given a more precise determination which could serve as a starting point. Husserl's whole phenomenology of passivity is in fact founded upon the analysis of inner time-consciousness as it cooperates with impressional-kinaesthetic consciousness, although in the early texts this cooperation is not yet clearly present. One text in particular in Hua X suggests itself in this context, since it contains a tentative appeal to the experience of association as that which brings about the *Zusammenhang* of the past:

> We can say; the present is always born from the past, a determinate present from a determinate past, of course. Or better: A determinate flow runs its course again and again; the actually present now sinks away and passes over into a new now, and so on. Even if there may be a necessity of an apriori kind involved here, an "association" nevertheless conditions it; that is, the nexus of the past is determined by experience, and it is further determined by experience "that something or other will come" (X, Beilage III, p. 106/CW 4, p. 111 [1909-10]; cf. XXIII, p. 258).

This is one of few instances where Husserl speaks of association in relation to inner time in Hua X (apart from his critique of Brentano). In this text a genetic approach starts to announce itself in the midst of a purely static conception of time: the present is not a staccato-like sequence of nows, instead it is "born" from the past, it is a "flow" that "runs its course", thereby opening the possibility to see the constitution of meaning in *statu nascendi*. There are other passages from the early texts on time-consciousness where Husserl emphasizes this connection, passages that were first made famous by Merleau-Ponty, Derrida and Levinas (after whom a whole suite of interpreters notably amongst the French phenomenologists has followed such as Michel Henry, Marc Richir and others).[37] These texts suggest a slightly different, more concrete approach in comparison to the abstract-formal unity of *Urimpression*-retention-protention that is the theoretical foundation of the 1905-lectures:

> We regard sensing as the original consciousness of time [*Das Empfinden sehen wir an als das ursprüngliche Zeitbewusstsein*] [...]. Sensation is presentifying time-consciousness [*Empfindung ist gegenwärtigendes Zeitbewusstsein*]. Representification is also sensing, in the sense that it is present and becomes constituted as a unity in the presentifying time-consciousness (X, Beilage III p. 107/CW 4, p. 112; tr. mod.).

This determination of inner time as *Empfinden* is wider and in a sense more fruitful in that it leads directly to the temporality of Husserl's "transcendental aesthetics", as this theme is developed notably in the lectures on passive syntheses and *Erfahrung und Urteil*.[38] With this connection between time and sensibility in mind, the analyses of "sensibility as the psychic basis of the spirit [*seelischen Untergrund des Geistes*]" from *Ideen II* take on a deeper significance that will gain in clarity in the many later texts that continue the discussion of primary passivity first opened up there.[39] For this "psychic basis" that is dis-

[37] It is notably two texts in Hua X, Beilage I and III, that are relevant here; see also Hua XXIII, Nr. 7 p. 251. See for instance Henry, *Phénoménologie matérielle*: "La phénoménologie du temps est une phénoménologie de l'impression [...]" (p. 43).

[38] A problem for the general interpretation of this whole area is that Husserl never succeeded in presenting a systematic overview of a phenomenological transcendental aesthetics, one that spans over both static and genetic analyses and that connects the passive syntheses of inner time-consciousness with those of bodily-kinaesthetic syntheses and the constitution of space. On this, see Vincenzo Costa, "Transcendental Aesthetic and the Problem of Transcendentality" (1998), pp. 9-28.

[39] IV, Beilage XII, Part I, § 2 p. 334/CW 3, p. 346. Holenstein unrightly dismisses the whole analysis of association from *Ideen II* on the grounds that it is "ein wenig einheitlich und straff geglückter Versuch" that hardly transgresses the status of "Hinweisen, Aperçus und Exkursen", and leaves it out of his account (see *Husserls*

cussed in *Ideen II* is nothing other than inner time-consciousness considered in conjunction with impressional consciousness:

> Primal sensibility [*Ursinnlichkeit*] is composed of the sensuous data [...]. Likewise, the sensuous feelings are founded in these sensuous data, and so are the sensuous drivedata [*sinnlichen Triebdaten*], the drives not as something supposedly transcendent to consciousness but as primal lived experiences [*Urerlebnisse*], always belonging to the content of the psychic basis. That is a primal content of sensibility [*ein Urbestand an Sinnlichkeit*] (IV, Beilage XII, p. 334/CW 3, p. 346 [1917]; tr. mod.).

It is on the basis of the intentionality that is discovered in these originary processes which proceed passively, without the participation of the I, that the new concept of association takes form. However, it must be kept in mind that Husserl at first regarded the intentionality that is operative in the passive sphere as an "improper" intentionality, in for instance the important appendix XII to *Ideen II*.[40] This hesitancy concerning whether to ascribe intentionality to the originary processes in passivity is consistent with a static perspective on constitution, but with genetic phenomenology even the simple syntheses of perception in the field of the living present show that the basic forms of objectivation occurs passively.[41] Intentionality can therefore no longer be restricted to the awakened I, but must be extended to the passive I. The characterization of "primal sensibility" that stems from the texts just prior to the genetic breakthrough in 1917-18, is relevant for coming to understand "originary association" in that Husserl includes not only sense data, feelings and drives within it, but also primary modes of pre-predicative relations. Amongst these we find the temporal binding of one phase with the next, and also the pre-perceptive syntheses of noematical contents within these; both of which are early forms of genetic constitution.

Phänomenologie der Assoziation, p. 10).

[40] IV, p. 335. See also HuMat 8, Nr. 24 p. 112f, where Husserl talks of the originary temporising consciousness as "uneigentlich" and says that it is not intentional; but this is only true from a static point of view. On this, see Montavont *De la passivité dans la phénoménologie de Husserl*, p. 86 and Bégout *La généalogie de la logique*, p. 31.

[41] "They are not syntheses that the ego has actively instituted; rather they are syntheses that are produced in pure passivity" (XI, p. 76/CW 9, p. 118).

In the Bernau-texts from 1917-18, Husserl developed this temporal articulation of association further, but in direct relation to a necessary modification or deepening of the reduction. Continuing the phenomenological deepening of the reduction that was so successfully attempted in the 1910-11 lectures (*Grundprobleme*), where the double reduction led us to intersubjectivity, Husserl here following a less extensive path distinguishes between two levels within the first, ordinary epoché that had not previously been kept apart. So that after having performed the first epoché (the bracketing of the world) whereby I reach my stream of lived experience, or more exactly, "a "living" and in this livingness necessarily movable "present"", Husserl in one important text attempts a step further in the practice of the reductions, in order to reach the sphere of "originary sensuality".[42]

If we compare the presentation of the phenomenological reduction in *Grundprobleme* with this Bernau-text, we can see two different, though not in any way contradictory lines of research that were to be developed into major themes in Husserl's later thinking: a reduction to intersubjectivity versus a reduction to the primordial-sphere of the singular I.[43] In the Bernau-text, Husserl after having calibrated his methodological optics, notes that we can move on to a further step so that we do not stop the reduction prematurely already at the first level of immanent time, where we encounter sense data and sensuous feelings (warmth, cold, hunger, sex etc.). This is the sphere of the drives that affect us in the direction of the I, that is to say that affect the pre-egological I that was later on simply called the *Vor-Ich*.

These affections and proto-actions are passive in that they occur without being initiated from the I (which, as Husserl later on saw more

---

[42] XXXIII, Nr. 14 "Mein Erlebnisstrom und Ich" p. 274 [1917-18]: "Wenn ich in phänomenologischer Reduktion auf den Bewusstseinsstrom all das Meine, alles im weitesten Sinn mir reell Gegebene betrachte (ein Mich-Selbst will ich jetzt vergessen), so finde ich meinen 'Erlebnisstrom'. Genauer gesprochen, ich finde eine 'lebendige', in dieser Lebendigkeit notwendig bewegliche 'Gegenwart', d.h. meine subjektive Gegenwart vor, mit ihrer Struktur Urpäsenz und 'Horizont' der Eben-Gewesenheit und einer Zukunft".

[43] The most coherent public presentation of these two "endpoints" of the reduction (cf. I, p. 15), is in *Cartesianische Meditationen* (§§ 44 ff); and the seemingly antinomic character of these two directions has been the source of severe criticism in the past.

clearly, does not mean that they fully lack relation to the I: on the contrary, they call upon the I to engage with these drive-actions, either by going along or by denying them). But this whole sphere must also be bracketed if we wish to reach that which is even more distant from the I in the sphere of sensuality, for underneath we find a domain of sensuous tendencies of association and reproduction. This important abstraction from the I and all that pertains to the I as active, will disclose an apriori necessary "structure" of originary, passive sensuality at the deepest level of pre-egological functioning time-consciousness.[44]

This passive, hyletic-temporal structure has also surfaced at several places in *Ideen II* (as we saw in Ch. 3, § 7), and it will be investigated in great detail in several manuscripts from the 1930's.[45] Let us take a look at the text:

> Now we fully consciously want to perform a sort of reduction that we have already performed until now, but without clearly designating it: the reduction to the "originary sensuality". Namely, when we reach the realm of pure subjectivity by means of the phenomenological reduction, it turns out that two things must be distinguished. The reduction that we mean and that yields an apriori necessary structure, is the abstraction from an I and of all things belonging to the I – a mere abstraction to be sure, but an important one. Then we have sensory data and sensuous feelings in the first immanent temporal order. Sensuous drives are affections directed towards the I; and the passive directedness of the I, even the "sensuous" realizations, the "drive-actions" are passive reactions, but passive, nothing there stems from the I, flowing out of it as actus. That is the sphere of "stimulus" and reactions upon stimuli: irritability. But now we would like to exclude also this sphere, since it brings the I into play. From this domain therefore we distinguish that of

---

[44] In texts no. 14 & 15 of the Bernau-texts, the I (which had until then not been an important theme) begins to assume the centre role, notably the genetic conception of the I. The closeness between this text and the C-manuscripts is also emphasized by Kortooms in *Phenomenology of time*, p. 210f: the "ego cannot be conceived of as a formal pole of identity. The ego too has a genesis: every ego has a history that makes it into a personal ego. Husserl anticipates this aspect of genetic phenomenology in the two texts in Hua XXXIII in which he pays attention to the ego. Furthermore, many of the reflections in these texts foreshadow the manner in which he analyzes time-consciousness in the C-manuscripts. [...] The distinction between the domain of sensuality and the domain of the ego causes several new issues to emerge in Husserl's analysis of time-consciousness".

[45] We find references to this originary structure of the living present notably in Hua XV, Nr. 22 and related texts from the A-, B-, D- and E-manuscripts, which must all be interpreted in the light of certain C-manuscripts where its temporal basis is most clearly presented.

> the “completely I-less” sensuous tendencies: sensuous tendencies of association and reproduction, and the horizonal formations that are determined from these. The question is how things stand already at the level of originary time-consciousness. Passive intentionality. Here the I is thought of as being put out of play also as pole of affections and reactions, or rather it is abstracted from. Thus we have a first, “abstract” structure that is to be elevated, that of the passivity of originary sensuality (XXXIII, Nr. 14 p. 275f).

In this remarkable text, even though it is merely a first draft of ideas that are developed in the years to come, the return to originary sensuousness at the deepest level of inner time-consciousness gives a primary role to association in the “living present”.[46] In later texts (as we will see), the distribution of phenomena at the lowermost level of inner time-consciousness will be somewhat different, just as the distinction between what pertains to the I and what is (in a relative sense) *ichlos* will be presented in a slightly different way, although the basic idea will remain.[47]

The sketch above of the gradual development of a genetic approach to association, is what lies behind the phenomenological interpretation of Hume’s principles of association. This interpretation does not start out from an immediate adherence to the traditional “laws” (resemblance, contrast and contiguity as they were first suggested by Aristotle), in order then to analyze the structural relations etc. between them.[48] Instead, Husserl wants to bring out the inner unity that lies behind these somewhat incoherent “laws” by disclosing its constitutive force. In the lectures on passive synthesis Husserl had come to see that the living present must be intimately connected to association as a decisive

[46] Holenstein also notes that Husserl from around 1917/18 gives increasing attention to the concept of association, and assumes that this is a consequence of the thematization of phenomenology as genetic intentional-analysis (*Phänomenologie der Assoziation*, p. 12).

[47] This “transcendental aesthetics” which is a part of the temporal foundation for the genetic analyses, is an important theme for the investigations of phenomena that Husserl gathered in the D-group of manuscripts under the title of “Primordiale Konstitution – Urkonstitution”.

[48] See Aristotle, *On Memory and Recollection*, 451 b.

principle of passive synthesis, i.e. as the "source" of all awakenings and memory.[49]

It is this early analysis of the structure of the living present that enables the reinterpretation of the traditional laws of association, which prior to that appeared to be a mere arbitrary coalition of empirical-psychological generalities. This undoubtedly richer analysis of presence – which no longer conceals its intimate engagement with factical, associative life – however essentially remains within the boundaries of the extended now as analyzed in the 1905 lectures. For that which enables Husserl to make sense of the laws of reproductive association is precisely the fact that there is a connection between the now, the past and the future which makes it possible to intuitively see whether a particular phenomenon is associated as being "similar" to, "contiguous" to or as standing in "contrast" to a given datum.[50]

The heart of this transcendental reinterpretation is accordingly the analysis of the living present, since Husserl here tries to show how these laws stem from the bond that is upheld therein between what is present and what has passed out of this field of presencing.[51] For it has to be shown that the effectivity of the laws of association does not depend on the previous givenness of elements that are already constituted, but that these latter are only possible through the functioning of these very same laws, and there is therefore no attempt to present a systematic enumeration of the laws of association in the lectures on transcendental logic. This is why the *Urassoziation* as the originary connection between likewise originary elements given through affection must be able to account for the very genesis of meaning in the impressional field.

Association is thus shown to be in the aesthetic-sensible sphere what the Kantian categories are for logical consciousness. As Bégout says with great insight, association thereby becomes "the mark of a transcendental legality".[52] But as his later investigations were to show, these

[49] XI § 38, p. 181.

[50] XI, §§ 37f, p. 180f; cf. XI, p. 480. See also Hart (2004), p. 145.

[51] See Hart (2004), p. 145.

[52] "Après avoir ainsi fourni à la forme catégoriale une matière intuitive (l'intuition catégorial de la VIème des *Recherches Logiques*), Husserl, comme par un mouvment de balancier, accorde à présent à la matière intuitive, sensible, des formes quasi catégoriales: les lois *apriori* de l'association qui, sur bien des points, constitueront le fondement opératoire des fonctions catégoriales elles-mêmes (*La généalogie de la*

insights into the relations that connect affective-associative consciousness with inner time-consciousness were nevertheless held back in an important respect. For the reduction in the lectures on passive synthesis leads only to a noetic-noematic stream of experiences, whereas the "radicalized reduction" (as we have seen) that leads to the "streaming-living present", shows us that the representation of consciousness as such a stream of experiences is merely a necessary yet naïve pre-stage.

The genetic analysis of association brings a kind of intentionality into view that leads to a deeper understanding of the noesis-noema correlation that is basic to static phenomenology, and which indicates a path out of this seemingly self-enclosed correlation. By being able to recuperate the various intentional relations that are excessive in relation to the constitution of a mere noematic correlate, association gains access to a whole new field of phenomenological exploration. Through its capacity to gather the multiple meaning-overflowing that occurs in passivity and to connect these ideally without restriction across the borders of the past and the future, the frozen moment of the act-object correlation (which makes static phenomenology forever an abstraction) is superseded.

Husserl from the outset calls upon the higher order reproductive associations for their ability to give an account of a certain creative aspect of consciousness, its spontaneous ability to bring us into contact with that which is not meant by us, with matters that we are bound to without knowing it beforehand, i.e. to account for our ability to step into new worlds as it were.[53] This is what enables him to speak of association as "the apriori of passive subjectivity" as "the constantly hidden life, towards which the I is not directed".[54] Although at first absent, the coming into presence of that which is given by means of association is made possible by its being located within my field of horizontal intentionality: that which awakens and that which is awakened stand in a relation of intentional implication. In *Cartesianische Meditationen*,

---

logique, p. 138).

[53] This "genetic" function of association was underlined by Husserl in the 6th of the *Logische Untersuchungen* (§ 15), in connection with both ordinary "wordless recognition" of objects (such as when we see a specific kind of drill whose name we have forgotten), and in scientific thinking.

[54] IX, p. 504.

Husserl admits that it was only at a very late stage that phenomenology gained access to the proper exploration of the phenomenon of association. Although association was shortly after the *Logische Untersuchungen* discovered to be a "constantly co-functioning lawlikeness in genetic processes", the insight of the transcendental, i.e. the universally constitutive meaning of association was, as *Cartesianische Meditationen* claim, a much later insight.[55]

4. Sedimentation and the universality of association

If the psychoanalytical work consists in a "tracing back" of what is manifest towards its hidden sources, then this implies that the opposite path where the covering over or "repression" of the trauma takes place, must first have been trodden.[56] Therefore the progression by means of free associations towards the resistance and thus towards the repressed centre of ill-being, must in a sense be the opposite of a work that has already been performed, along analogous paths.[57] In this section we will examine this hypothesis, which basically argues that there are hidden intentional relations that govern Freud's notion of free association. It will be shown that there is a dual movement operative in Freud's account, in that there is both freedom and unfreedom in the associative method, and that it is actually the latter that poses the real problem. For it is the restraints upon the associative process which indicate the unconscious resistance, and in order to frame a phenomenological

[55] I, CM § 39, p. 113f/Engl. p. 80: "The universal principle of passive genesis, for the constitution of all objectivities given completely prior to the products of activity, bears the title association. Association, it should be clearly noted, is a matter of intentionality, descriptively demonstrable as that [...]. Association is a fundamental concept belonging to transcendental phenomenology [*ein transzendental-phänomenologischer Grundbegriff*] (and, in the psychological parallel, a fundamental concept belonging to a purely intentional psychology)." See ms. A VII 13/187 [1918]: "Die Art, wie Assoziation universale konstitutive Bedeutung hat, habe ich sehr spät durchschaut, obschon ich sie schon in der ersten Göttingen Jahren als einen Titel für eine universale und immer mitfungierende Gesetzlichkeit der Genesis erkannte."

[56] "... psychoanalytic research [...] seeks merely to uncover connections by tracing that which is manifest back to that which is hidden [*nichts anders als Zusammenhänge aufdecken, indem sie Offenkundiges auf Verborgenes zurückführt*] ("On the Universal Tendency to Debasement in the Sphere of Love (Contributions to the Psychology of Love II)", PFL 7, p. 256/SA 5, p. 206).

[57] This point is also discussed by Holenstein (1972), p. 333.

response to this issue Husserl's theory of sedimentation will be employed. According to this theory, everything that is sedimented remains alive. When combined with Husserl's late insight into the universality of association, it can be shown that also that which is in the deepest sense unconscious (Freud) must be inscribed within this potential horizon of possible retrieval.

The most prominent feature of association, essential for the purpose of clarifying the Freudian basic rule, concerns the question of freedom of association: how can a Husserlian analysis account for that? The operative force of association, according to Husserl, lies in its capacity for (ideally) unrestrained binding, and its being completely indifferent as to the nature of what it combines. It can bring anything into connection with anything, and this is the reason why Husserl calls it the most universal type of synthesis. Since association is essentially an expression of the fundamental openness of consciousness for the ever new coming, for the arrival of an event that it cannot foresee (which however always has to encounter consciousness's own sedimented life-history), it may justly be called synthesis in general. Thus Husserl says that ...

> ... nothing can fall like rain into my life [...], nothing can arrive that does not subject itself to the unity of connection (XI, p. 408; cf. p. 391).

However, there is another noteworthy feature of association in Freud's analysis, namely the "unfreedom" which means that the so-called "free associations" are actually bound to an unknown source, which they encircle like blind moths around a night lamp. This unfreedom of the associative chain which imposes a restriction in the associative process, poses considerable difficulties for any philosophy of mind. It can be seen as a first, albeit negative, adumbration of that particular "resistance" which has led some higher agency in the subject to push this unknown source away from consciousness.[58] The free association thus gradually brings about the coming to presence of the repressed, at

[58] "The unconscious – i.e the 'repressed' – offers no resistance whatever to the efforts of the treatment. [...] Resistance during treatment arises from the same higher strata and systems of the mind which originally carried out repression" (*Beyond the Pleasure Principle*, PFL 11, p. 289).

first in the mode of an absence, which thereafter gains in contours as it moves from pre-predication to discursivity.

One way to begin to respond to the problems that the unfreedom of free association poses is by means of Husserl's theory of sedimentation of past lived experiences. Every thought, phantasy or lived experience that occurs in the present is always in part determined by our previous thoughts etc., since everything that has been present, whether as actuality or as inactuality, whether as primary target of attention or in the unnoticed background-horizon, becomes sedimented in the I. And as the retentional intentionality that structures our past also allows for associative-intentional relations between its elements, the way is open for what is ideally an unlimited possibility of connections between the contents of consciousness. Phenomenology could here show that "free association" is a part of a scientifically understood transcendental aesthetics, by inscribing it in a larger and more coherent framework. Such a framework would consist of originary association at the lowermost level of constitution which accounts for the ever new structuration of the living present. This would also interact with what becomes sedimented, and given that the psychoanalytical "repressed" could be interpreted as something that lives on in sedimentation, it would also be a part of unconscious motivations that associatively communicate with the living present.

If we picture the constitutive process as a living being, then at the head we have the temporalizing flow where the ceaseless renewal of the "world" takes place, while everything that has been pre-constituted sinks down towards the feet, where it settles down into secondary passivity:

> [...] every accomplishment of the living present, that is, every accomplishment of sense or of the object becomes sedimented in the realm of the dead, or rather, dormant horizonal sphere, precisely in the manner of a fixed order of sedimentation: while at the head the living process receives new, original life, at the feet everything that is as it were in the final acquisition of the retentional synthesis, becomes steadily sedimented (XI, § 37 p. 178/CW 9, p. 227).

According to Husserl's dynamic conception of the psyche which holds that it is in a constant state of change – *das Seelenleben ist nach*

Wesensnotwendigkeit ein Fluss – all previous lived experiences have an afterlife in that they partake in the continuous "new formation or re-formation of dispositions" in the form of habits, memory, and the orientation of convictions, feelings and will; all at the ready disposal of association.[59] All experiences are thus sedimented into practical possibilities, potentialities for further action, so that each action is always in part the result of our previous actions.[60] There can therefore never be a purely spontaneous action, it is always already a response from our own sedimented history just as it is a response to the passive pregivenness of the world. All these processes of sedimentation are only possible if association is constantly at work:

> Constitution in all its forms is association in a sense which continuously expands itself. All association presupposes the originary association in the sphere of originary temporisation. Wherever this association does not do its work, there nothing can become sedimented, and when acts pertaining to the I and the I do not appear in this sphere of originary temporisation, then they cannot enter any associations (HuMat 8, Nr. 79 p. 345 [C 16/1931]).

What is the relation between association at this level of passivity and the I? The "originary association" is clearly not related to the active, awakened I of normally functioning consciousness, and Husserl therefore speaks of the *Vor-Ich* or the "antechamber of the I" here.[61] After the event what has been present becomes a part of the living history of the I as habituality and practical possibility; though this is not in some "afterchamber" of the I, but precisely something that becomes a part of the pure I, as a motivational tendency.

Association as the condition of possibility of sedimentation is accordingly nothing without an established relation to the I as a centre of affection, to which both parts of an association in the ordinary sense

[59] IV, § 32, p. 132, 135f.

[60] "Die praktische Intention ist verwirklichung einer bleibenden praktischen 'Überzeugung'" (A VII 13/18 [1921]; quoted in Lee (1993), p. 90. Cf. *Erfahrung und Urteil*, § 19.

[61] Lee has a good discussion about the status of the "I" at this level of originary association, and argues against the often voiced requirement that there be a fully active and awakened I ready at hand already at this level of genesis; see *Husserls Phänomenologie der Instinkte*, p. 165.

relate, and as a unifying "pole of originary instincts" when it comes to the *Vor-Ich* as the genetic forerunner to the pure I.[62] The mode of being of an object that has passed into retentional sedimentation is that of a "has-been-conscious", and this does not change with the gradual loss of affective force.[63] So even when the constituted object reaches its limit of affective zero, and thus is no longer "alive", its meaning is still implicitly there in the shape of the "dead": it is only lacking in flowing life. It is important here to note that Husserl regards the whole problematic of how this "dead" but not meaningless object can come alive again, as pertaining to association.[64] This is how the associative awakening is described:

> A remote past suddenly dawns on me, the thought that just came to me comes into relief from the so-called unconscious in which the object given to consciousness, in the specific sense of a special prominence, is merely an island. Every present flows once more into this undifferentiated subsoil of the distant retention. The subsoil itself is without any prominence – though once in a while something does come into relief. It comes into relief: That is, a completely non-intuitive affection is there in entirely the same way that a chord that has just faded away emerges in a non-intuitive manner, possibly drawing my attention to it – albeit a chord that I (perhaps entirely in vain) want to make intuitive again (XI, Beilage X p. 385/CW 9, p. 476f [1920]).

Everything that is sedimented is therefore "still "alive"", as it is expressed in a later text.[65]

In what way can this presentation of central aspects of Husserl's theory of association help us with the main question concerning the clarification of the *Grundregel* by means of genetic phenomenology? First of all by showing the scope of Husserl's reflections: when originary association is taken into account, association becomes the general principle that accounts for the passivity of consciousness as that which precedes all conscious activity.[66] If the main hypothesis that is investigated here is

---

[62] E III 9/18 [1931]: "Der Ichpol [als] Pol von ursprünglichen Instinkten"; see also HuMat 8, Nr. 57 p. 252f.

[63] XI, § 37 p. 177.

[64] "How it can become efficacious and even constitutively efficacious in a new shape is the problem of association" (XI, § 37 p. 177).

[65] XXXIV, Nr. 35 p. 472 [1934]: "Alles Sedimentierte ist noch 'lebendig'".

[66] CM, § 38 p. 112/Engl. p. 78 (tr. mod.): "every construction on the part of ac-

correct, then this means that all of Freud's investigations of the unconscious and a large segment of the processes that he locates in the preconscious would be inscribed within the processes that Husserl ascribes to association. Would such a position not immediately entail a reduction of Freud's investigations, making (parts of) the unconscious into consciousness in one stroke?

That can only depend on whether there are processes presented by Freud that indeed fall out of the picture once they are subsumed under the transcendental-phenomenological concept of association. But since the widened concept of consciousness that followed from the genetic discovery of passive processes, led Husserl to locate association as the most foundational type of movement within the psyche, it is this whole analysis which must be taken into account in answering this question. The discovery that association has a "universally constitutive meaning" thus brought with it that not only the impressional sphere gained its inner unity by means of association; everything that pertains to the life of transcendental consciousness becomes united through association:

> Life is encompassed by a universally essential lawlikeness of passivity: that of the syntheses of association (HuMat 8, Nr. 13 p. 42 [C 3/1931]).[67]

That association in the ordinary sense is a universal process in so far as nothing is alien to it, also means that it completely disregards any differences concerning the ontological status of what it combines. What is there in association is there as a given for consciousness, with its particular meaning-compound, totally indifferent to whether it crosses regions of being or time and thus essentially unfaithful to any schematizations of the world. Association is thus something of a ruthless, uninhibited procurer that will couple any given object with anything, and at a non-stop rate.

---

tivity necessarily presupposes, at the lowest level, a passivity that recieves the object as pregiven, and, when we trace anything built actively, we run into constitution by passive genesis".

[67] Cf. A VI 34/36 [1931]: "Nicht nur hyletische Daten konstituieren sich als Einheiten, auch das konstituierende Leben, auch die Kinästhese, die Akte des Ich, kurz alles und jedes, was zum Bewusstseinsleben gehört, konstituiert sich vermöge der immerfort wirkenden Assoziationen als Einheit" (quoted in Lee 1993, p. 178).

But this is also what accounts for its creative aspect, which constantly reopens our own past and brings back elements that would otherwise have remained sedimented. This also opens the future for us into something that can be lived, since we have already projected ourselves into it beforehand in phantasmatic "as if"-life; the anticipatory or "inductive" associations are intentions directed towards the future that fill out the empty horizon more or less concretely.[68] The constitution of meaning here takes on the form of mimetic projection of the past into the future by means of previous similar lived experiences, of course always checked and modified against what is encountered.[69]

5. Direct approach b) Perseverance of affective force: memories that will not come to rest

The second attempt at a direct clarification focuses on the problem of how to account for affection stemming from unconscious sources, which is a central issue in Freud's theory of repression, and the discussion in the present section will begin with a brief discussion of this. As a next step, an important feature of Husserl's analysis of passive motivation from *Ideen II* will be presented, where a division of labour is suggested between transcendental phenomenology and psychoanalysis. The investigation proper of the problem of unconscious affection then focuses on texts (notably from D 14) where Husserl analyzes the possibility of sedimented concrete complexes (lived experiences, feelings, thoughts and kinaesthesia etc.), whose affective force does not diminish with time. Contrary to normal retentional procedure these complexes live on, actively engaging other sedimented events and attracting attention also from presentifying consciousness; this strange

[68] XI, p. 119f, 184-191, 243ff.

[69] This prepredicative experience is then analyzed as the preliminary stage to the logical theory of induction; see *Erfahrung und Urteil*, § 8. Holenstein (1972, p. 35) quotes a clarifying passage from ms. A VII 11/107 [1932]: "Induktion ist in erster Ursprünglichkeit nicht ein logisch schliessender Prozess, also der Sphäre prädikativen Urteils zugehörig und korrelativ der Titel für eine Art von Beweisen [...], sondern ein zum Bereich der Erfahrung selbst und der aus Erfahrung erworbenen Seinsgewissheit gehöriger Prozess der 'Vorzeichnung', bzw. 'Verweisung', eben Induktion".

living on Husserl calls "perseverance" (*Perseveranz*).[70] Let us first turn to Freud's theory of repression.

We know from Freud's analysis of the drives that the "object" of the drive, which enables the latter to reach its goal, is what is most variable of all the central aspects of the drive. The object is not originarily tied to the drive, and is often replaced by another object.[71] This motility of the object in relation to the originary drives and the feelings that are associated with it, is made use of by Freud in his later account of trauma. There it enables him to separate the "affective cathexis", i.e. the sphere of *Gemüt* (which is called *Affektbetrag*, quota of affect) from the event that is too painful to keep in consciousness and that must accordingly be repressed.[72] The feelings that are separated from the event become repressed, whereas the now "colourless mnemic content" can be left in the conscious sphere, since it by itself poses no threat:

> Repression [here] makes use of another, and in reality a simpler, mechanism. The trauma, instead of being forgotten is deprived of its affective cathexis; so that what remains in consciousness is nothing but its ideational content [*Vorstellungsinhalt*], which is perfectly colourless and is judged to be unimportant (*A Case of Obsessional Neurosis*, PFL 9, p. 76).

Thus Freud is fully in his right when he adds in a footnote that the subject both knows his traumas and does not know them:

> [...] there are two kinds of knowledge, and it is just as reasonable to hold that the patient "knows" his traumas as that he does not "know" them. For he knows them in that he has not forgotten them, and he does not know them in that he is unaware of their significance. It is often the same in ordinary life (*A Case of Obsessional Neurosis*, PFL 9, p. 77).[73]

---

[70] On the notion of "perseverance", see IV, § 61 p. 276f; IX, Beilage XIX p. 415f; XXIX, Nr. 15 p. 195ff; D 14/53f.

[71] "Instincts and their Vicissitudes", PFL 11, p. 119.

[72] "For this other element of the *psychischen Repräsentanz* the term *affect-charge* [Affektbetrag] has been adopted. It corresponds to the drive in so far as the latter has become detached from the *Vorstellung* and finds expression, proportionate to its quantity, in processes which are sensed as affects. From this point on, in describing a case of repression, we shall have to follow up separately what, as the result of repression, becomes of the *Vorstellung*, and what becomes of the energy of the drive which is linked to it." ("Repression", PFL 11, p. 152/SA 3, p. 113; tr. mod.)

[73] In a similar key, Freud speaks of things "that have always been known, only

That which has been repressed is due to this separation between the affect and the conscious *Vorstellung* able to persist in the unconscious, where it loses none of its (passive) activity in the sense of attracting other contents by means of associative bonds, and thus constituting new meaning as a part of what is pre-given, as part of the *Vor-habe* of the subject.[74] But what is it that makes this twofold knowledge possible? What goes on at the level of the repressed (which in the example above contained the feeling-component as separated from its representation, but which in other cases is reversed so that it is the representation that is repressed and the quota of affect that remains conscious)? Let us look at one further complication in Freud's theory, which will then serve as the starting point of the discussion in this section. One of the most obscure aspects of Freud's theory of repression concerns the activity that he claims goes on in the unconscious, whereby new associative connections are formed:

> ... we are inclined to forget too easily that repression does not hinder the *Triebrepräsentanz* from continuing to exist in the unconscious, from organizing itself further, forming derivatives [*Abkömmlingen*] and establishing connections. Repression in fact interferes only with the relation of the *Triebrepräsentanz* to one psychic system, that of the conscious one ("Repression", PFL 11, p. 148/SA 3, p. 109f; tr. mod.).

Before the investigation proceeds with the discussion of this issue, one of the rare points of connection between phenomenology and psychoanalysis in Husserl's published works – a connection that has been guiding the whole analysis so far but without yet surfacing – must be presented. In *Ideen II*, where Husserl discusses "motivation as the basic law of the spiritual world", he argues that motivation is operative

---

never thought about" or the possibility "to unite a conscious knowing with a not-knowing", or again of neurosis as a "not knowing about psychical processes that one ought to know of"; see "Erinnerung, Wiederholung, Durcharbeiten" (SA *Erg. Band* p. 208), and "Zur Einleitung der Behandlung" (SA *Erg. Band* p. 201); and *Introductory Lectures* PFL 1, p. 321/SA 1, p. 279 (tr. mod.) respectively. Cf. what Merleau-Ponty says in *Phénoménologie de la perception*, p. 189: "dans l'hystérie et dans le refoulement, nous pouvons ignorer quelque chose tout en le sachant". This theme is also discussed by for instance C. Bollas who interprets the unconscious in terms of the "unthought known" in *The Shadow of the Object* (1995).

[74] Freud speaks of this attraction (*Anziehung*) in for instance "Repression", PFL 11, p. 148.

not only in higher-level rational thought but also in the lower sphere of sensuous reason, which includes "the entire realm of associations and habits", i.e. "passive motivation".[75] This led Husserl to suggest (what will here be called) a *division of labour* between the phenomenologist and the psychoanalyst. Speaking of this passive motivation, Husserl in this crucial passage says that:

> What is specific therein is motivated in the obscure background and has its "psychic grounds", about which it can be asked: how did I get there, what brought me to it? That questions like these can be raised characterizes all motivation in general. The "motives" are often deeply buried but can be brought to light by "psychoanalysis". A thought "reminds" me of other thoughts and calls back into memory a past lived experience, etc. In some cases it can be perceived. In most cases, however, the motivation is indeed actually present in consciousness, but it does not stand out; it is unnoticed or unnoticeable ("unconscious") (IV, § 56 p. 222f/CW 3, p. 234).

First of all this suggests that the subject investigated by the two disciplines is on Husserl's view one and the same, albeit from two different perspectives. What the "division of labour" further suggests is that the job of tracking down the hidden, motivating lived experience is not the phenomenologist's, but that of the psychoanalyst.[76] This obviously requires more material in terms of associations, personal history, present concerns and future projects etc. The full investigation of this, although approaching the phenomenological analysis, can only be the proper theme for that specific kind of in-depth project that psychoanalysis is.[77] The phenomenologist, on the other hand, is interested in

---

[75] IV, pp. 211, 222f.

[76] There is a link here between *Ideen II* and Husserl's later investigations of passive motivation (in the Freiburg lectures on ethics for instance; see XXXVII, Beilage XII p. 339ff). This so to speak genetic trail stands in some contrast with Husserl's static analysis in the early lectures on ethics (Hua XXVIII), in that values and feelings (as an essential aspect of passive motivation) in the latter are encountered as a separate layer that is attached to the thing, whereas in the former the thing is always alreday imbued with emotion. On this, see Melle "The development of Husserl's ethics" (1991); see also "Husserl's personalist ethics" (2007), p. 4ff.

[77] This is not only a quantitative issue, but also something related to psychoanalytical methodology and in particular the intersubjective dimension developed in the relation of transference and countertransference. Although the foundations of this are investigated in the present work (in terms of Husserl's analysis of intersubjectivity), a more specific analysis of transference cannot be undertaken here.

discovering the general structure that is disclosed by the type of motivation that for instance free association makes up; by the very fact that in life we do undergo these lived experiences that are motivated by "that which imposes itself" from out of an obscure background, itself being "unnoticed or unnoticeable" in that background, but "indeed actually present in consciousness [*im Bewusstsein wirklich vorhanden*]".[78]

Husserl's investigations into passive motivations in *Ideen II* furthermore led him to the discovery of sensibility as a stratum of "hidden reason" (*eine Schicht verborgener Vernunft*), operating according to its own "rules of understanding" underneath higher level processes of reason. It is in the explication of this hidden reason that we first come across the idea of perseverance:

> In the sphere of the senses, in the sphere of the basis, grasped as extensively as possible [*in der Sphäre des weitest zu fassenden Untergrundes*], we have associations, perseverances, determining tendencies [*Assoziationen, Perseverationen, determinierende Tendenzen*], etc. These "make" the constitution of nature, but they even extend further, since this constitution is also there for spirits: all life of the spirit is permeated by the "blind" operation of associations, drives, feelings which are stimuli for drives and determining grounds for drives, tendencies which emerge in obscurity, etc., all of which determine the subsequent course of consciousness according to "blind" rules [*durch alles Leben des Geistes hindurch geht die "blinde" Wirksamkeit von Assoziationen, Trieben, Gefühlen als Reizen und Bestimmungsgründen der Triebe, im Dunkeln auftauchenden Tendenzen etc., die den weiteren Lauf des Bewusstseins nach "blinden" Regeln bestimmen*] (IV, § 61 p. 276f/CW 3, p. 289).

According to Lotz, Husserl's analysis of affection can only discover the theoretical conditions for the turning-towards of the I, but never answer the more fundamental question of why the I turns towards this rather than to that.[79] The solution says Lotz, is to be found in those budding analyses by Husserl where he emphasizes the inseparability of affectivity and value: every affection is connected with a feeling. This line of thinking is also explored here in connection with motivation and the passivity of reason, but the aim is set higher since Freud's analysis

---

[78] IV, § 56 p. 222f/CW 3, p. 234.

[79] Christian Lotz, "Husserls Genuss. Über den Zusammenhang von Leib, Affektion, Fühlen und Werthaftigkeit" (2002), p. 25.

of repression has shown even more complex patterns to be operative than the phenomenology of concrete subjectivity was able to disclose on its own.

Let us now move on to the main theme of this section, concerning a genetic clarification of unconscious affection. As we have seen from Husserl's analyses of passive syntheses, there is a constant repression going on already at the level of the hyletic data, such that the pre-constituted object which exerts the most affective force upon us at a given time will simultaneously repress the other pre-constituted objects of less affective force, when our attention is directed towards it.[80] This structure, where that which has become conscious exerts a suppressive force upon the rivalling moments, is also to be found at the higher level of practical beliefs, in for instance the phenomenon of convictions. As Husserl states in the lectures on passive synthesis, when I carry out the unbroken thesis "it is so", in a mode where certainty is upheld, there may well be cases where I so to speak actively disregard other or even better options. In this case, I am conscious only of one possibility, and this is only made possible by my rejection (*Verwerfen*) of the other possibilities, i.e. by inhibiting the other ones to come forth:

> Different witnesses speak and present their testimonies, having different weight. I weigh them and decide for the one witness and his testimony. I reject the other testimonies. Here the weight of the other testimonies can even become null and void. [...] And yet it must also be the case that they do retain a weight [...]. But this one testimony in particular has such an "overpowering weight" that I decide for it and do not "accept" the other, do not "take them up", and in this sense reject them (XI, § 9 p. 45/CW 9, p. 85).

My taking a position in this case is built on the active rejection of the alternatives, and Husserl adds to this passage a note in the margin:

> What does "being conscious" of mean here? Being in relief. I am "unconscious" of the other possibilities or entirely indeterminate other

[80] Preconstitution is discussed in for instance XXXI, p. 3f, 15, 40f, 51ff; and in related passages in XI, Ch. 2 on the phenomenon of affection; see also *Erfahrung und Urteil*, § 23a.

> possibilities; they are not awakened, but inhibition is still there (XI, § 9 p. 45/CW 9, p. 85).

Being "unconscious" here means little more than being simply unaware, although there is one essential feature that points forward to a possible opening towards more complex determinations: I am conscious of x due to the prior inhibition of y. But what of repression at genetically earlier levels than perceptual affection and practical belief? More importantly, can we find any evidence there of meaning-structures that affect us even though they are inhibited from becoming conscious? If such a possibility could be shown it would be an important step in the overall argumentation. In a text called "Zur Phänomenologie der Assoziation" from 1926, Husserl enriches his earlier analysis by investigating whether there may not also be repression operative at such a level of unconscious affection:

> There is still the question concerning how affections relate to one another, apart from or in addition to propagation (i.e. as awakening salience or awakening from the unconscious). Affections can play to each other's advantage here, but they can also disturb one another. An affection, like that of extreme contrast ("unbearable pain"), can suppress all other affections [...] – this can mean to reduce to zero – but is there not also a suppression of the affection in which the affection is repressed or covered over, but is still present, and is that not constantly in question here? (XI, Beilage XIX p. 415/CW 9, p. 518; tr. mod.)

In response to this question, Husserl goes on to affirm the possibility of there being unconscious affection from that which is repressed but which retains its affective force, such as when there is a conflict of affections. This is particularly relevant when it comes to affection that excites the I:

> In particular: affection of the modus excitandi of the ego, being irritated, conflict of affections. The one winning out does not annihilate the other ones, but suppresses them. (In the sphere of feelings or drives: feelings, strivings, valuations, that come to naught due to certain motivations, just as the absence of value becomes evident through clarification, and the affection of value comes to naught through an appropriation coming from the inside. On the other hand, feelings, valuations that are overcome, suppressed from the outside, suppressed in conflict, while the conflict does not lead to any settlement, to any actual "peace".) Perseverance. There can accordingly be affections progressing from the "unconscious", but suppressed. (XI, p. 415f/CW 9, p. 518f; tr. mod.).

Repressed feelings and drives can according to this analysis "persevere" in the unconscious and still exercise an affective calling upon the I, which means that a dynamic relation between consciousness and the unconscious has been indicated also from the point of view of feelings and drives (and not only perception).[81] The direction of this analysis is confirmed by several of Husserl's late manuscripts, where the intentionality of the drive is analyzed in relation to the sphere of the *Gemüt* and the unconscious.[82]

In the manuscript D 14 Husserl examines various aspects of the unconscious that take us closer still to the fundamentals of repression as Freud presents it.[83] The realm of the forgotten springs forth from the originary association and fusion of succession, but this unity of the "unconscious" stream of memories, of the sedimented in continuous overlapping, is not eternal frozen immobility: "it does not remain at rest".[84] Instead a passive movement takes place, a silent "living on" through which

[81] Yamaguchi for instance regards this text as a link between on the one hand the genealogy of logic that forms the horizon of these lectures and also *Erfahrung und Urteil*, and on the other hand the originary intentionality of the drives from the 1930's: "Durch diese Fragestellung ist ein dynamisches Gesamtverhältnis zwischen Bewusstsein und Unbewusstsein im Streit der affektiven Kräfte in 'der Sphäre der Gefühle und Triebe' hervorgehoben" (*Passive Synthesis und Intersubjektivität bei Edmund Husserl*, p. 35).

[82] See for instance the following three texts from the same highly productive period in June, 1934 in Kappel that together make up the peak of Husserl's reflections on the drives from a psychoanalytical point of view: Hua XXXIV, No. 35 "Trieb – Trieb-Instinktleben. Aktleben – Askese, Epoché" [B II 3/2a-13b]; the (yet unpublished) continuation of this manuscript B II 3/14-19; and (the likewise unpublished) E III 10/3 "Eingeklammerte Affekte – Askese" that was analyzed above in Ch. 4, § 2. These texts are closely related, and from a psychoanalytical point of view they contribute greatly to the understanding of Husserl's reflections on the drives. See also E III 9/1-15 "Zur Lehre von den Instinkten" (1931-33). In published texts this issue is approached in a more inarticulate form in for instance Hua IV, p. 332ff; Hua XIV, p. 34ff, 50ff; Hua IX, p. 478ff, 486ff; Hua XV, p. 597ff, p. 608ff; and *Krisis*, § 69.

[83] Of particular interest here is a part of the manuscript (D 14/52-55, dated "before 1930"), which has the title "Zur Theorie der Assoziation, Veschmelzung unter Verdeckung, und zur Klärung der Reproduktion auf Grund der Assoziation und insbesondere zum Problem der falschen Wiedererinnerung durch Überschiebung".

[84] D 14/53: "Aus der ursprünglichen Assoziation und Verschmelzung der Sukzession entspringt das Reich der Vergessenheit – die Einheit des 'unbewussten' Erinnerungsstroms, der sedimentierte in kontinuierlicher Verdeckung sukzessive Zusammenhang. Aber der bleibt nicht in Ruhe."

remote connections are established by association, a *Paarung* between the new present and something long forgotten, which furnishes the character of familiarity upon everything new, everything that is brought together in synthesis.[85]

In this unconscious passivity such faraway-associations must occur all the time, according to Husserl, but why – and here a crucial question is posed – does one sedimented content gain the "force" necessary to pass over from the pre-constituted of the "not yet actually as being" in order to connect with something going on in the present?[86] And what is that force that he talks of? What Husserl is after here, as I will try to show, is the co-functioning role of feelings, of the sphere of the heart (*Gemüt*), but since this whole layer is not integrated with the analysis he cannot come up with a satisfactory answer to the question of what it is that governs the move from *Vor-habe* or pre-constitution to conscious attention.

Previously in D 14 Husserl repeatedly stresses that the bracketing of feelings, moods and drives is "a lack" and that this whole sphere is only taken *ad notam*.[87] Let us therefore follow this question and see how Husserl deals with the role of feelings in the context of awakenings, turning-towards, shifts of interest etc. in some other texts, before we come back to D 14.

Although Husserl analyzed the function of *das Gemüt* repeatedly in central works of static phenomenology (such as *Ideen I* and *II*), it was never investigated for the role it plays in affection and consciousness' attentive turning-towards something (*Zuwendung*), although it obvi-

---

[85] D 14/53: "Es bilden sich Fernpaarungen (Fernassoziationen) die Fernzusammenhänge herstellen, die schon jedem Neuen, das mit Altem sich paart, den Paarungscharakter (Relationscharakter) die Bekanntheit verleihen."

[86] D 14/53: "Verschmelzung, in der 'eines' sich 'konstituiert', aber noch nicht wirklich als seiend – in der Passivität müsste es ins Endlose Fernassoziation geben; aber warum gewinnt eine Kraft?"

[87] D 14/16: "Ein Manko bei allen diesen und zunächst auch den weiteren Betrachtungen liegt natürlich darin, dass keine Frage nach der ev. Verschiedenartigkeit der Interessen aufgeworfen ist. [...] Das Wort Gefühl verweist uns auf die 'Gemütssphäre' und den Zusammenhang von Interesse als Streben und Gemüt. Also diesen Fragenkomplex nehmen wir jetzt nur *ad notam*." Later on he comes back to this once more: "[...] das verweist uns zugleich wieder auf das Manko aller dieser Ausführungen: dass wir das Problem der Verschiedenartigkeit der Interessen nicht in Rechnung gezogen haben, die Fragen des Gemütes und die Fragen der doppelten Habitualität – der erworbenen und der der ursprünglichen Instinkte" (D 14/23a-b).

ously plays an important part there.[88] In genetic phenomenology this lack is partly overcome, in that Husserl often acknowledges that emotions, strivings and drives (i.e. *Gemüt*) play an important part in this process:

> Mere sensation-data, and at a higher level sensory objects as things, that are there for the subject but there as "value-free", are abstractions. There is nothing that does not affect the emotions [...] (A VI 26/42a).[89]

But beyond the important but fairly general recognition that "everything that exists touches our feelings; every existant is apperceived in a value-apperception and thereby awakens desirous attitudes", there seems to be little in terms of actually carried out phenomenological investigations in the public discourse (books and lectures): most often this task is referred to as something that would need to be done, only elsewhere.[90]

In the lectures on passive synthesis Husserl however takes a step towards an understanding of the role of feelings in the context of perceptual *Zuwendungen* and shifts of interest. Even though no full analysis takes place there, it is clear that Husserl has worked through the issues elsewhere and has reached a much clearer understanding of the role of emotions also in passivity.[91] At this point it must be made clear that it is not the analysis of higher order emotive acts that were investigated in *Logische Untersuchungen* and *Ideen I* that is at stake. The genetic analysis here focuses on the living present which is at the source of, and therefore enables the disclosure of "the sense and accomplishment of that life of consciousness that is completely hidden

[88] For central analyses of *das Gemüt* in static phenomenology, see III/1 §§ 28, 95, 117, 121, 127; IV, §§ 4-7. See also XXXI, §§ 2f/CW 9, Part 3 §§ 50ff.

[89] "Bloße Empfindungsdaten und in höherer Stufe sinnliche Gegenstände, wie Dinge, die für das Subjekt da sind, aber wertfrei da sind, sind Abstraktionen. Es kann nichts geben, was nicht das Gemüt berührt" (A VI 26/42a [1921-31]). Cf. also XXXIX, Nr. 26 p. 269, Nr. 43 p. 476.

[90] Typical in this respect is XI, § 32 p. 150f. The quotation is from XV, Beilage XXIII p. 404f: "Alles, was ist berührt das Gefühl, alles Seiende wird in Wertapperzeptionen apperzipiert und weckt damit begehrende Stellungnahmen [...]". See also E III 9/23.

[91] See also *Erfahrung und Urteil*, § 15 p. 73f/Engl. p. 71: "Therefore, there is an original passivity not only of sensous givens, of "sense data", but also of feeling [...]".

from us *because* it is our living life [*das uns völlig verborgen ist,* weil *es unser lebendiges Leben ist*]".[92] In its most concrete make up this living present is rich not only with the openness of primal impression-retention-protention, but is further thickened out with the sedimented habitualities, acquired evaluations, emotions and interests which make up the theme of originary affection, and it is this thickened structure of the living present that makes up "the heart" (*das Gemüt*):

> Thus we consider functions of affectivity that are founded purely in the impressional sphere. Accordingly, we may only take from the sphere of the heart [*der Gemütssphäre*] some feelings that are co-original with the sensible data, and say: on the one hand, the emergent affection is functionally co-dependent upon the relative size of the contrast, on the other hand, also upon privileged sensible feelings like a passionate desire founded by a prominence in its unity. We may even allow originally instinctive, drive related preferences [*Auch ursprünglich instinktive, triebmässige Bevorzugungen dürfen wir zulassen*] (XI, § 32 p. 150f/CW 9, p. 198).

What is decisive in these analyses from the 1920's is that Husserl here raises the question of awakening and turning-towards as a problem that also involves the sphere of the heart. What is the associative bond that forms between one content of consciousness and another, what is the motivating source of the awakening? From where does it gain its direction, picking out that experience rather than this? For even though resemblance, contrast or contiguity – the classical laws of association – may be present here, there is a great number of possible candidates for the present noematic content to "choose" from. What more than say resemblance between two contents can Husserl appeal to in order to explain this quite central feature of association? These questions could find no satisfactory answer on the previous static analysis, but the unconscious weight accorded to the one that rises to prominence is in part due to *das Gemüt*, according to Husserl's analysis of affection in *Erfahrung und Urteil* and the lectures on passive synthesis:

> The motives [for the awakening association] must lie in the living present, where perhaps the most efficacious of such motives (which we were not in a position to take into consideration) are "interests" in the broad, customary sense, original or already acquired valuations of the

[92] XI, Beilage VII, p. 365/CW 9, p. 450.

> heart [*Gemüt*], instinctive or even higher drives, etc. (XI, § 37 p. 178/CW 9, p. 227).[93]

Coming back to the argument in D 14 after this digression on the role of feelings in the phenomenon of turning-towards, Husserl after having raised (and abandoned) the question of why one passive association rather than another wins out, goes on to distinguish between different kinds of awakening of sedimented experiences. Besides awakening brought about by an association from the present to the distant past Husserl also, and more interestingly, speaks of a passive-tendential bringing-forth (*passiv Tendenziöses Hervortreten*). This affects me even when the I does not turn towards it, and is therefore a process which brings about a passive awakening, by directly affecting the sedimented sphere without the participation of the I.[94] This passive awakening, Husserl notes, can occur in the form of unconscious perseverance (where it is strictly speaking not awakened but rather remains active):

> Something sedimented can remain in "interest" although it is not in the mode of attention proper. This being interested can obtain its form of inactivity, of "unconscious" remaining-in-grasp and from there on its still being "affective" (tendency of perseverance), from the form of attentive undertaking pertaining to awakenness. [...] That is accordingly not awakening but remaining in force (D 14/53f).[95]

Furthermore, there is the associative awakening that goes out from one memory to a similar one but which was not intended to be brought back.[96] Once the associative awakening backward into memory has begun, it can start to lead a life of its own; and interest is transferred

[93] Cf. *Erfahrung und Urteil*, § 11 p. 49, § 14 p. 68f.

[94] D 14/53: "Hier tritt neu ein eben die eigentliche Reproduktion, die besondere 'Weckung', die nicht nur Fernassoziation ist [...] sondern die ein passiv Tendenziöses Hervortreten, Affizieren ist und auch ohne Zuwendung ein Sich-passiv-auswirken, ev. als wiedererinnernde Wiederverwirklichung (obschon nicht eigentlich aktive Reaktivierung)."

[95] D 14/53f: "[...] eine Versunkenes kann auch ohne Aufmerksamkeit im 'Interesse' bleiben. Das Interessiertsein kann aus der Form der aufmerksamen Beschäftigung der Wachheit die Form der Inaktivität, des 'unbewussten' In-Griff-behaltens und davon fort 'affiziert' werdens erhalten (Perseverationstendenz). [...] Das ist also nicht Weckung sondern in Kraft Bleiben."

[96] D 14/54: "Es kann auch ein Gewecktes ein Anderes assoziativ wecken, Interesse für Ähnliches weckt Interesse für Ähnliches, das früher da war (und damals vielleicht unbeachtet, uninteressant war)."

from similar to similar along paths that are beyond the reach of the active I. In previous chapters it has been shown how the ordinary intentional modification of retentional consciousness starts out from the now, thus enabling that which is present to become modified into sedimentation. Both the general temporal and affective-impressional aspects of this process have been dealt with at length. What is new in this manuscript, is that Husserl here also describes the opposite intentional movement, i.e. the modification that stems from the sedimented unconscious. This modification starts out from the sedimented past, may then go on to awaken other sedimented contents, before it eventually is met with the turning-towards of the active I:

> The "unconscious", that which is sedimented in a unified form from out of the I and its interests, can take on different tendentious modes. In the effective development of these tendencies, it can enter into intentional modifications in the type of reproductive realization. That is the reversed genetic mode of the first intentional modification – (yes, but the double, the inactive and the "remaining" in the active sense!) – the retentional, the sedimenting stands over against the reproductive, the recollecting, "re"-actualizing modification (D 14/54).[97]

The sedimented "unconscious" can thus also function as the initiator of new processes of awakening. With the givenness of this reversed, genetic mode of ordinary intentional modification, we accordingly have movements of intentional modification being initiated from both directions, i.e. going out from the present towards that which is past, but also from the past to the present. The relevance of this analysis is that it throws new light on two central and closely related aspects of Freud's theory of repression: the living on in a peculiar form of active passivity of the repressed (i.e. a kind of *Abschattung* of the proper life of the unconscious), and the possibility of the return of the repressed. I will end this section by taking a look at these two issues, one after the other.

[97] D 14/54: "Das 'Unbewusste', das einheitliche Sedimentierte von dem Ich und seinen Interessen her, kann verschiedentliche tendenziöse Modi annehmen. Es kann in Auswirkung dieser Tendenzen in intentionale Modifikationen der Art der reproduktiven Verwirklichung eintreten. Das ist der umgekehrte genetische Modus der ersten intentionalen Modifikation – (Ja, aber der doppelten, der inaktiven und der 'behaltenden' im aktiven Sinne!) – der retentionalen, der sedimentierenden steht gegenüber die reproduktive, die erinnernde, 'wieder'-verwirklichende."

Freud is led to the existence of affection stemming from repressed, unconscious complexes by evidence obtained from his case studies: they are hypotheses that gain whatever evidential status they have to the clarifying power they show in retrospect. Although Freud is in the clear about the reconstructed nature of such a process, i.e. that it is a reconstruction of something assumed to have taken place but whose nature is such that it is essentially withdrawn from direct confirmation, he doesn't really attempt to clarify this reconstruction. This is something that Husserl does (as we have seen in Chapter Three), and the analysis of unconscious perseverance addresses precisely the formal possibility of how contents of consciousness can retain their affective force and form ceaseless associations, all while remaining unconscious. This analysis remains formal as long as it is abstractively dissociated from the co-functioning of feelings and the sphere of *Gemüt*, but once the analysis of perseverance is supplemented in that direction (which has been indicated here), I can no longer see any major difference between Husserl's and Freud's analysis on this point.

Secondly, the return of the repressed – which does not encounter the same inherent difficulties of manifestation as the perseverance or living on of the repressed – can be seen to be a kind of awakening that relies on the possibility of affection going out from the unconscious towards presentifying consciousness. So once the general possibility of such processes has been established as transcendental occurrences, it seems that yet another step has been taken against the thesis of a radical separation between the two disciplines and that the closer confirmation and differentiation between the two models instead announces possibilities for promising future analyses.

6. Direct approach c) The manifestation of the repressed in "psychic reality"

In this section (the third and final direct approach) Freud's concept of "psychic reality" (*psychische Realität*) will be presented as central to metapsychology and to the psychoanalytical conception of a concrete subjectivity. It is argued that psychic reality in Freud's work is so to speak the psychoanalytical version of the phenomenological "intentional field", wherein the repressed comes to manifestation and grafts itself onto the normal, objective apperception of the world. Then an intentional analysis of this concept will be attempted that centres on central passive syntheses that are argued to lie behind its constitution. The focus will here be on Husserl's analysis of the phenomenon of "interpenetration" (*Durchdringung*) between different experiences, such as one memory fusing with another into a "memory" of something that has never occurred. This analysis will serve as an example of the malleability of the conscious experience of the world, and brief outlooks towards other essential issues for the clarification of psychic reality – such as phantasy and temporality – will be given.[98] If psychic reality is the everyday manifestation of the repressed, our interface with the world so to speak, then it could only have come about as a fusion between perceptual normality and phantasy having its source in the repressed unconscious.

Freud first introduced the notion of psychic reality in order to designate the novelty of the psychoanalytical approach to the unconscious against contemporary philosopher-psychologists (such as Lipps, von Hartmann and others).[99] It was already from the start an attempt to outline the essential novelty that psychoanalysis brought forth in comparison with what he called "material reality" and the psychological reality of conscious and preconscious phantasy: a dimension of the in-between, something new. This concept, which occurs throughout Freud's work in various forms, primarily designates reality as understood from the point of view of the unconscious.[100]

---

[98] Obviously it is only a sketch of certain relevant issues that is attempted, not a fuller explanation of psychic reality.

[99] See *The Interpretation of Dreams* where already the text of the first edition speaks of the unconscious as "das eigentlich reale Psychische" (SA 2, p. 581/PFL 4, p. 773).

[100] For central references to psychic reality, see for instance *Aus den Anfängen der Psychoanalyse*, 1950, p. 452; *Studies on Hysteria*, PFL 3, p. 107, 126fn; *The Interpretation of Dreams*, PFL 4, p. 782; "Formulations on the Two Principles of Mental Functioning" PFL 11, p. 42f; *Totem and Taboo*, PFL 13, p. 131, 144f, 222f; "The Claims of Psycho-Analysis to Scientific Interest" PFL 15, p. 38; "On the History of the Psychoanalytic Movement" PFL 15, p. 75; *Introductory Lectures* PFL 1, p. 414f; "The Uncanny" PFL 10, p. 367, 370ff; "The Loss of Reality in Neurosis and Psychosis" PFL 10, p. 223ff; *Moses and Monotheism* PFL 13, p. 319; *An Outline of Psychoanalysis* PFL 15, p. 405f.

In a preliminary form, the criteria that must be met with for a lived experience to be a part of psychic reality is that it is determined by repressed phantasies, emotions and wishes etc. that taken together have the force and internal coherence to modulate our conception of reality. In psychic reality, as in perception, the objects are posed as real and they have sufficient force to constitute a reality of its own. Freud therefore stresses the inability (on the part of the neurotic subject) to distinguish psychic reality from what he calls "material", i.e. intersubjective reality: it becomes a "state within the state".[101] This means that it is a concept that can only be gained from within the partial epoché of psychoanalysis, and not from the perspective of everyday life, psychology or philosophy.

The phenomenological givenness of psychic reality is not one of conflict (*Widerstreit*) with the normal world, instead it is grafted on to this world and is thereby characterized precisely by its ability to fuse with it in order to constitute a subjective, "primordial" transcendence which has validity for me but not for the other: it is therefore not an "objective" transcendence.

Although Freud never presents a systematic definition due to the tentative character of his approach (which as he repeatedly stresses is always open for revision with the advent of new evidence), it seems likely that psychic reality as conceived above has implications of a more general nature concerning the psychoanalytical conception of subjectivity.[102] Freud's discussions of psychic reality generally occur in relation to neurosis (and psychosis), but in his first theoretical discussion of it in *The Interpretation of Dreams* he is engaged in the larger project of redefining the "essential nature of consciousness" in accord-

[101] "They [neurotic phenomena] are, one might say, a State within a State, an inacessible party, with which co-operation is impossible, but which may succeed in overcoming what is known as the normal party and forcing it into its service: If this happens, it implies a domination by an internal psychical reality over the reality of the external world and the path to a psychosis lies open" (*Moses and Monotheism*, PFL 13, p. 319).

[102] On the preliminary nature of the psychoanalytical theory, see *The Interpretation of Dreams* PFL 4, p. 770; "On narcissism", PFL 11, p. 69ff; *Beyond the Pleasure Principle*, PFL 11, p. 338; *An Autobiographical Study*, PFL 15, p. 216.

ance with the discovery of the unconscious, thus extending its validity beyond the particular case of neurotics.[103]

The philosophical question that this poses is how we are to understand this modulation of reality: how is it possible that the unconscious can affect us so that we come to disregard objective reality and instead, and without noticing it, give ourselves over to a conception of reality that is informed by unconscious phantasy and repressed desire? How is this malleability between our subjective phantasies, emotions and wishes on the one hand and our conception of reality on the other hand to be understood? How can we account philosophically for this fusion between objective reality and phantasy, this interpenetration of phantasy with our conception of reality? It is in bringing this type of question to the fore of the debate in psychology and philosophy of mind that Freud's greatness resides.[104] Let us begin by taking a preliminary look at how Freud conceives of psychic reality in the decisive Chapter Seven of *Traumdeutung*:

> Whether we are to attribute reality [*Realität*] to unconscious wishes, I cannot say. It must be denied, of course, to any transitional or intermediate thoughts. If one looks at the unconscious wishes, brought to their ultimate and most truthful expression, then one shall have to conclude that psychic reality [*psychische Realität*] is a particular form of existence [*eine besondere Existenzform*] not to be confused with material reality [*materiellen Realität*] (PFL 4, p. 782/SA 2, p. 587; tr. mod.).[105]

[103] See PFL 4, p. 226; see also p. 685f, 771 and the "systematization" of consciousness into the conscious, preconscious and unconscious systems. This movement away from the particulars of psychopathology to a general theory of consciousness is also clear from many passages in Freud's metapsychological works.

[104] Laplanche & Pontalis define psychic reality as a "heterogenous core" within the psychological field (*Fantasme originaire*, p. 23f). But if psychic reality is a heterogenous core within the psychological field, which is a correct description to a certain degree, then this heterogeneity must be related to psychic reality as also *homogenous* to the psychological field of normal perception of material reality: it cannot be distinguished from it as long as the neurosis maintains its grip. For the analyst, and for the other persons in the subjects surrounding world, this distinction will often be immediately clear; afterwards, it may be so also for the person who was subjected to the neurosis.

[105] This crucial passage is a genuine palimpsest: the first two sentences of the quote stem from 1900, the final sentence stems from 1919. In the 1914-edition, it read: "[one shall have to conclude] that *psychic reality* [psychische *Realität*] is a particular form of existence not to be confused with *factual* reality [faktischer

Commenting in a later text on the fact which at first puzzled Freud greatly, that childhood experiences brought to light in the analysis could at times be shown to be true, at other times false, but were in fact most often a "compound of truth and falsity", he says that he later came to realize that it was "the low valuation of reality *[die Geringschätzung der Realität*]" that had perplexed him so in his patients' narratives, the "neglect of the distinction between reality and phantasy":

> We are tempted to feel offended at the patients having taken up our time with invented stories [*erfundenen Geschichten*]. Actual reality [*die Wirklichkeit*] seems to us something worlds apart from invention [*Erfindung*], and we set a very different value on it. Moreover the patient, too, looks at things in this light in his normal thinking [*in seinem normalen Denken*]. [...] He too wants to experience actual realities [*Wirklichkeiten*] and despises everything that is merely "imaginary" [*"Einbildungen"*] (*Introductory Lectures*, PFL 1, p. 414f/ SA 1, p. 358f; tr. mod.).

What Freud gradually came to realize when confronted with this compound of truth and falsity, was that the most fruitful way to deal with it is not to demand an immediate retreat from invention and imagination to the safe shores of a supposed objective "reality", but instead to go along with it and instead turn it into a methodological requirement:

> It will be a long time before he can take in our proposal that we should equate phantasy and actual reality [*Phantasie und Wirklichkeit gleichzustellen*] and not bother to begin with whether the childhood experiences under examination are the one or the other. Yet this is clearly the only correct attitude to adopt towards these productions of the soul. They too possess a reality of a sort [*eine Art von Realität*]. It remains a fact that the patient has created these phantasies for himself, and this fact is of scarcely less importance for his neurosis than if he had actually experienced [*wirklich erlebt*] what the phantasies contain. The phantasies possess psychical as contrasted with material reality [*psychische Realität im Gegensatz zur materiellen*], and we gradually learn to understand that in the world of neuroses it is psychic reality

---

Realität]". And in the 1909-edition it read: "If we look at unconscious wishes reduced to their most fundamental and truest shape, we shall have to remember, no doubt, that psychical reality too has more than one form of existence" (SE 4, p. 620n). There is no German text for this in GW.

which is the decisive kind (*Introductory Lectures*, PFL 1, p. 414f/SA 1, p. 358f; tr. mod.).

This implies that psychic reality cannot be identified with phantasy pure and simple. The reason for not doing so is that all phantasies do not meet the criteria of psychic reality outlined above: in normal phantasy, the phantasized world is merely posited as quasi-existing, i.e. in a mode of "as if...".[106] That is to say, normal phantasies are never understood as being a "reality" for the subject. Psychic reality according to Freud therefore always in part has a character of phantasy, but one which is in particularly close connection with the unconscious, for we know that it is precisely one of the most distinct features of the unconscious that it disregards the distinction between phantasy and reality, and treats of phantasies as being of equal importance as real events.[107] Psychic reality can therefore be seen as the manifestation of unconscious processes in a phantasy which cannot be distinguished from normal reality, i.e. the intersubjectively available objective world. Thus, that these phantasies are "unconscious" should be understood to mean only that the source from which they spring (in the most fundamental sense: a set of drives centred around the Oedipus-complex) is unconscious, for the phantasies themselves are anything but unconscious: it is precisely the fact of their being at first inseparable from ordinary consciousness of the surrounding world that characterizes them. The decisive criterion is accordingly that the phantasy takes on the form

[106] This has been clearly outlined by Husserl; cf. Hua XXIII, p. 54ff, 313ff, 320f, 341ff. Husserl distinguishes between illusions, hallucinations and dreams on the one hand, and phantasy on the other, since the former all stand in a relation to perception which the latter does not: in dreams, perceptual illusions and hallucinations we believe that what we percieve is real, it is only in retrospect that we can come to know that our beliefs were mistaken. In phantasy proper (imaginative acts), the images hover before our inner eye, but the real world is not fully abandoned, as in the former cases; see p. 6ff, 41ff. Freud's concept of psychic reality would share the central characteristic of the first group (the force of conviction), but it also shares a characteristic of the imaginative acts, in that the perceptual world is not *ausgeschaltet*, and retains its validity (this latter characteristic does not hold for psychosis.)

[107] Laplanche argues that psychic reality is to be conceived of as a "third domain of reality", neither material nor subjective (see p. 169; cf. p. 90ff, 152f, 168ff, 196). But without a clear philosophical conception of consciousness such a move can only lead to ontological confusion and to a psychologizing of the subjective, which both Husserl and Heidegger have argued vehemently against from the outset.

of reality for the subject to such an extent that she cannot distinguish it from material reality.

The degree to which psychic reality interferes with the perception of material reality of normal, awakened consciousness, can be seen as a measure of the distance that has been established between "normality" and "abnormality", between "sanity" and "insanity". Broadly speaking, if this contamination of phantasy and reality occurs only in our sleep, and without interfering with our awakened abilities and habitualities, then we are dealing with normal dreams, which Freud correctly calls "a psychosis of short duration".[108] If, however, it interferes with our awakened, normal life in the sense that material reality is partly ignored and psychic reality to a corresponding extent is over-valued, then we are dealing with neurosis.[109] But if, finally, the interference with normal life is such that material reality is not only ignored, but is denied (*Verleugnung*) and psychic reality replaces it, then we have psychosis.[110]

In neurosis therefore, the inability to uphold the distinction between phantasy and reality is not extended to cover the whole domain of consciousness (understood in an extended sense), but is only a local phenomenon. So long as psychic reality is restricted to a relatively small part of our conscious life, in the rest of which the distinction between phantasy and reality is upheld, our relation to the common world may be disturbed but it is not destroyed. But as soon as the subject no longer has the ability of keeping the domains separate, as soon as psychic reality has taken the upper hand, the common world is disintegrated and lost. The concept of psychic reality represents an attempt on Freud's part to designate the measure to which unconscious phantasies influence our conscious, normal life.[111] The general thesis for what psychic reality

---

108 *An Outline of Psychoanalysis*, PFL 15, p. 405f.

109 "Formulation on the Two Principles of Mental Functioning", PFL 11, p. 42f; *Totem and Taboo*, PFL 13, p. 131, 144f, 222f; *An Autobiographical Study*, PFL 15, p. 218; *Moses and Monotheism*, PFL 13, p. 319.

110 "The Loss of Reality in Neurosis and Psychosis", PFL 10, p. 223f.

111 If Freud had been able to define more sharply the contours of psychic reality, to formulate the relation in which it stands to notably the unconscious and to phantasy more clearly, and then to relate these determinations to a concept of consciousness with sufficient potential of expansion and plasticity, then I believe that the concept of psychic reality could well have served to denominate the central field to which psychoanalytical investigations is correlated.

is in psychoanalysis would therefore be: it is the unconscious in so far as it manifests itself within and for a consciousness.

The basic idea behind the phenomenological clarification of psychic reality is the hypothesis that is merely Freud's psychoanalytical twist on the general phenomenological idea of intentionality, of the individualized field of intentional objects, with its projects, reminiscences etc., as informed by the unconscious.[112] The focus on the intentional relation as a relation of meaning (and not a real-causal relation) which the phenomenological reduction establishes, means that, strictly speaking, all kinds of intentional objects exercise stimuli upon the subject, and thus "motivate" it to engage with them, disregarding whether they are real, remembered or merely dreamt objects.[113] Therefore Husserl famously separates the intentional from the real relation:

> This relation is not immediately a real relation but an intentional relation to something real. [...] The real relation collapses if the thing does not exist; the intentional relation, however, remains (IV, § 55 p. 215).

The correlates of the intending acts may eventually come to be characterized as real, actual objects, depending on the outcome of further investigations, but this does not alter anything concerning their first phenomenological givenness precisely as given for an intending consciousness.[114] This suggests that intentionality is well suited to account for that which Freud outlined as "psychic reality", an expression that seems quite apt, phenomenologically speaking, in that it speaks of what is experienced as having the validity of reality in a subjective sense while still clearly emphasizing that it is not a question of objective reality. Proceeding further on the basis of this characteriza-

[112] This is where Brentano's influence is perhaps strongest on Freud: psychoanalysis operates in the vicinity of an intentional analysis, and a clear expression of this is to be found in the concept of psychic reality. The strong impact that Brentano had upon the young Freud is reflected in the letters to Silberstein; see Sigmund Freud, *Jugendbriefe an Eduard Silberstein 1871-1881* (1989).

[113] IV, p. 189; cf. 232. This was already clear from the analysis of the intentional object in the 5th of the *Logische Untersuchungen*.

[114] "Precisely for that reason it makes no essential difference whether or not the correlates correspond to actualities, whether or not they have in general the 'sense' of actualities [*den 'Sinn' von Wirklichkeiten*]. I am afraid of the ghost, perhaps it makes me quiver, although I know that what is seen is nothing actual" (IV, § 56 p. 232/CW 3, p. 244).

tion of intentionality, the analysis now moves on to the genetic intentional analysis in this attempted direct clarification of the return of the repressed in psychic reality.

There are three possibilities discussed by Husserl here concerning a "repressed" memory that "breaks through" to intuition.[115] As we saw in the previous section, "repressed" is understood by Husserl not only in the more shallow sense (a sudden loud sound represses the conversation) but in certain texts as stemming from an unconscious affection that motivates the *Zuwendung*. Although this dimension often remains in the background, it is useful to keep it in mind here. Either the memory that is associatively awakened gradually spreads out so that it finally completely overtakes the intuitive sphere, whereby the originary situation from which the awakening departed becomes correspondingly submerged (repressed).[116] Secondly, it may instead be the case that due to their own affective forces, both the awakening and the awakened lived experience "stand their ground", that they both "triumph", but without fusing or connecting. The field of intuition is then, Husserl says, "spottily filled out" (*sheckig ausgefüllt*).[117]

But it is the third option that is really of interest here, since it is phenomena of fusion (*Verschmelzung*) and interpenetration (*Durchdringung*) that are most promising for the clarification of psychic reality, given its nature as a fusion between reality and unconscious phantasy. Let us say that I remember a certain event. Upon reflection however I may come to realize that this event shares characteristics of two or more separate events, the reality of which I am more certain of, and thus I discover the phenomenon of ...

> ... the splitting of rememberings into rememberings, that have, as we say, been pushed through one another such that the memorial images of separate pasts have blended to form a unity of an illusory image (XI, § 26, p. 119/CW 9, p. 164; tr. mod.).[118]

[115] XI, § 43 "The possibilities of a repressed memory breaking through to intuition".

[116] XI, § 43 p. 198.

[117] XI, § 43, p. 198/CW 9, p. 249f.

[118] The problem of fusion of memories that is opened in XI, § 26 is then taken up again in §§ 42f. On the phenomenon of *Durchdringung*, see further XIX/1, p. 458f;

When the phenomenon of interpenetration is analyzed in relation to the field of memory it can thus account for one recollected event becoming associated with another event from the past, to the point of fusing into an illusion of a past that has never occurred:

> rememberings can link up to form a connected remembering that has joined the elements of different memories into an intuitively concordant image. What makes the fusion into an illusory image is the force of apperception (XI, § 43 p. 199/CW 9, p. 250).

How can this process be understood? In terms of an intentional analysis what happens is that intentional bonds form associatively between the memories, such that certain parts of the one remain in conscious relief whereas other parts from the same memory are pushed away. The salient parts meet the salient parts of the second memory (which also has parts that have been pushed away), in such a way that they are together able to create a non-actual image of an event that never occurred. The ontic-visual example of two photographs torn into halves suggests itself, where the gaps of the one fits into the peaks of the other. Husserl here speaks of the protests coming from the parts that are about to be repressed as being "too weak":

> That is to say, to put it at first in a suggestively rough and provisional manner: the components a and b are, now as before, elements of intentional wholes, they have repressed supplementary elements that protest from the subsoil against the demands directed in the illusory image from a to b and vice versa, and they protest above all against their reciprocal fulfilments, although the protests are too weak, not loud enough to lead to a clear doubt and to a negation (XI, § 43, p. 199/CW 9, p. 250).

This analysis shows with an example from the perceptual sphere how we can constitute something that is at the limit untrue, while still holding it to be true: it is the constitution of self-deception, i.e. a kind of "psychic reality" that covers the real events.[119] It is important to note

---

Erfahrung und Urteil, § 42 p. 209; HuMat 8, Nr. 33 p. 133, Nr. 64 p. 276fn; XXIX, Nr. 15 p. 196.

[119] Scheler, who was one of the first philosophers to engage seriously with Freud's work, investigates the theme of self-deception (*Selbsttäuschung*) as it occurs in Freudian psychoanalysis in *Die Idole der Selbsterkenntnis* from 1911, where an early but inadequate phenomenological reinterpretation of the psychoanalytical unconscious occurs; see *Vom Umsturz der Werte* (1955), Engl. tr. in *Selected Philosophical*

that all these processes take place in the domain of passivity without any participation by the I: the awakening radiates from what is presently perceived whether we want it or not, even active remembering "is possible only on the basis of the associative awakening which has already taken place".[120] This might at first seem odd, but shows just how far Husserl is willing to take his analysis of passivity: even when I desire to recall a previous event, the most that the active I can do is to tentatively actualize the stretches of memory that are not forgotten, and thus help the awakening ray on its way to what is submerged in the unconscious. The possibility of awakening therefore rests upon a previously performed passive association, so that a sensuous unity is pre-constituted between the present event and an event that may be, at the limit, completely out of reach for the I.[121]

The same analysis is used when Husserl accounts for recollections of our childhood from the perspective of adulthood as occurring in factical life. Here also we encounter the mixture of what is true and false in memory:

> Going back into my childhood to the extent that I have reasonably clear memories, I accomplish not only memory but also a retrospective interpretation and correction, admittedly this is mostly an unconscious falsification of memories [*eine unbewusste Erinnerungsfälschung*] by means of an apperceptive reinterpretation and reconfiguration of earlier experience, a retrospective apperception from the present (XV, Nr. 10 p. 141 [1930]).

The phenomena that Husserl investigates here as interpenetration of memories can be seen as a sort of phenomenological prolegomenon to Freud's analysis of "screen memories" (*Deckerinnerungen*), where an

Essays (1973). Edith Stein then responded to his discussion in *On the Problem of Empathy*, p. 72ff/Germ. p. 82ff. Sartre, pursuing Scheler's analysis, also regarded the theme of self-deception and *mauvaise foi* as central to Freudian psychoanalysis in *Being and Nothingness*, but he argued that Freud had "cut the psychic whole into two" with the distinction between the ego and the id, thereby adopting the radical alterity thesis concerning the unconscious; see (2005) p. 50ff. See also Gardner (1993), p. 40ff for a critique of Sartre's views.

[120] *Erfahrung und Urteil*, § 42, p. 209ff/Engl. p. 179.

[121] *Erfahrung und Urteil*, § 42, p. 209ff/Engl. p. 179. Regrettably Husserl ends this promising investigation by stating that "the analysis of all this is the theme of a phenomenology of presentifying consciousness [*einer Phänomenologie des Vergegenwärtigungsbewusstseins*], which cannot here be further carried out."

early event is "screened" by a later memory so that access to the former is denied due to repression.[122] But more importantly, using this analysis as a platform one can also extend it to give an account of "psychic reality" as a more complex form of fusing memories, phantasies and so forth with perceptual life. On the basis of the suggestion that Freud's concept really denotes an intentional structure (that has incorporated unconscious phantasy and desire etc.), "psychic reality" can be said to correspond directly to what Natanson has called the "intentional field".[123] Husserl's analysis of interpenetration will here function as presenting the more general structure which Freud, as it were, provides a psychoanalytical interpretation of by investigating the same phenomenon from the point of view of the repressed unconscious.

[122] We find this in a first outline in Freud's early text "Screen memories" [*Über Deckerinnerungen*] (1899), in SE 3, p. 301-322/GW 1, p. 331-354; but the more developed analysis is in *Psychopathology of everyday life* (1901), Ch. 4 "Childhood memories and screen memories" (PFL 5, p. 83-93). See also "Erinnerung, Wiederholung, Durcharbeiten" (1914), *SA Ergänzungsband* p. 208; "Über *fausse reconnaissance*" (1914), *SA Ergänzungsband* p. 236f.

[123] See Maurice Natanson, "Being-In-Reality" (1959), p. 234.

Chapter Six

INDIRECT CLARIFICATION OF REPRESSION BY MEANS OF THE INTENTIONALITY OF THE DRIVES

... philosophers have formed their judgement on the unconscious without being acquainted with the phenomena of unconscious mental activity, and therefore without any suspicion of how far unconscious phenomena resemble conscious ones or of the respects in whith they differ from them (Freud)

Alltagsinterpretationen und von aussen her mit Alltagspsychologie (oder auch "moderner" Psychologie) operериende geben kein wissenschaftliches Verstehen, keine Rekonstruktion des anomal Seelischen, keine Möglichkeit einer Innenpsychologie der Anomalität. Dazu bedarf es einer schon sehr weit fortgeschrittene Phänomenologie. (Husserl)

1. Introduction

In this final chapter, the function of the drives will be examined in relation to both Husserl's genetic phenomenology and Freud's metapsychology. The analysis of the "drives" (*Triebe*) or "instincts" (*Instinkte*) in transcendental phenomenology (the terminology will be discussed below) brings the investigation to an end in an important sense: the genetic attempt to disclose the structure of the living present as the source point of intentional life discovers drives as one of its most basic and primitive constituents. Similarly, the analysis of the drives in psychoanalysis also brings the investigation to an end in the sense that it is ultimately the demands made upon the I by the drives (or their representatives) that bring about repression. Repression is the primary defence-mechanism employed by the I in order to ward off the demands that the drives make. This means that the two major paths that we have followed here – the genetic investigation of the structure of the living present as the mode of access to the proper philosophical understanding of Freudian repression (its "clarification") – converge with the analysis of the drive. Needless to say, there are many more themes to investigate and other ways to proceed, but given the approach chosen for this investigation the clarification of repression is finished with the analysis of the drives.

The indirect clarification of repression that is attempted here sets out to show that we find repression in the phenomenological sense (first shown to be operative at the reduced perceptual level in the lectures on passive synthesis), also at this deepest genetic level of investigation. There are constant processes of "covering", "inhibition" and "repression" going on in the living present, and thus also amongst the drives. Simply put, the drives or instincts for Husserl are integrated moments of the living present that make up the genetic preliminary stage of all kinds of intentionality (bodily, temporal, "rational" and "irrational" etc.) partaking in the constitution of the world.[1] The drives are not to be regarded as isolated parts of originary life: just as the thematizing of a single "intentional act" in static phenomenology remains an abstraction whose fuller aspect includes not only the object but also the feeling, the attitude taken towards the object etc., so the drive is a mere skeleton in itself. The drive as a preintentional directionality of originary life is always intertwined with for instance kinaesthesia as practical possibilities of fulfilment of the lived flesh, feelings and moods that determine the affectional colour with which the fulfilling aim is eventually apprehended. Taken together, these structural aspects thicken the living present into a concrete configuration of subjective life.

All of these various aspects may undergo repression at one stage or other of this preconstitution, and according to Husserl's model of consciousness with its marked emphasis on passivity, this is also the actual fate of nearly all of these aspects. Association plays a key role here since it, as the guiding principle of passive genesis, can be shown

[1] XV, Nr. 11 p. 148 "Das Ich als spezifisches Subjekt der instinktiven Triebe (als Triebhabitualitäten), der durch alle lebendige Gegenwart hindurchgehenden Triebintentionalitäten; dabei als Subjekt der in wachen Affektionen und Akten sich auslebenden und sich mit ihnen neu stiftenden Akthabitualitäten." See also XV, Nr. 22 p. 385; and E III 10/7b: "Zu jeder konkreten Gegenwart gehört eine Strukturtypik instinktiver Triebe, bzw. zum Ich gehört jederzeit seine Triebintentionalität".

to govern all the processes pertaining to preconstitution, also at the deepest level of originary temporization and spatialization. Wherever association is at work, establishing a ceaseless wealth of connections along every conceivable axis, there is also a corresponding process of hindrance, keeping nearly all of these connections at bay and refraining them from reaching the level of conscious apprehension.

The first section (§ 2) gives a preliminary account of Husserl's theory of drives based on the concept of "originary instinct" as primary world-disclosing process. The interpretation is here more insecure than in previous chapters since virtually all of Husserl's analyses of drives are in manuscripts. It is argued that the drives, which are disclosed by reconstructive phenomenology, are the genetic continuation of static intentionality. Even though Husserl at times refers to "inborn instincts", these are understood from a phenomenological point of view, which is to say as fused with habituality, thereby bringing the historicity of subjective and intersubjective sedimented life into play. The focal point for the analysis of the drives is the originary meaning-structure of the streaming living present that the genetic *Rückfrage*, guided by the radicalized reduction, leads to.

In the next section (§ 3), Husserl's account of the lifedrives and the intersubjective drives are discussed. Some texts suggest that these are situated at a genetically higher level than the "originary drive", which is an undetermined, intentional preliminary stage with as yet no objects. The analogy between my past and the other is examined from the perspective of the radicalized reduction, showing that Husserl's account in *Krisis* can be better understood with support from manuscripts. This brings out the role of the sexual drives as a concrete expression of a pre-empathic intersubjectivity. It is shown that Husserl here develops a view of the drive-intentionality which is not restricted to the intentional directedness of a singular I, but where the reciprocal aspect is emphasized: the drive is first and foremost a *Wechseltrieb*. This is clearly a bodily type of protointentionality (or one pertaining to the flesh), but Husserl also makes clear that it is likewise a temporal kind of protointentionality where originary hyle cooperates with the originary flesh in the process of originary temporization (*Urzeitigung*), which is the genetically deepest layer for all constitution.[2] The level of originary temporization is reached by the radicalized reduction and here we find the process of originary streaming, which is also called the *Ur-Ich* (see Chapter Three, §§ 4-6). It is suggested that this pre-egoic or even non-egoic (*ichlose*) streaming must be closely correlated with the level of originary drives. According to this hypothesis, Husserl reached the level of non-egoic originary streaming from two kinds of reductive praxis: the radicalized reduction disclosing the *Ur-Ich* but also the analysis of the drives (following a more general genetic *Rückfrage*). At this level, the concept of originary association gains its full understanding: all processes in the streaming living present are held together by means of association.

In the following two sections, some fundamental aspects of Freud's theory of the drives will be presented. In the fourth section (§ 4) it is explained what it is that makes the "drive" into the basic concept of psychoanalysis. Further, the role that the drives play in the constitution of both the object and the subject is investigated, and in particular the function of narcissism for the constitution of the I is examined. These two are not presupposed as given, basic constituents by Freud but are the result of complex and fragile drive-processes. This account is intended to add more detail to the account of repression that was presented earlier on (Chapter One, § 2), by showing the importance of personal genesis in Freudian theory. As the famous case-histories show (Emma, Anna O, the Rat-man, the Wolf-man etc.), repression and childhood or adolescence make up a fertile ground for the anomalous constitution of self and world.[3] It will also be shown that Freud does not presuppose a closed dualism (infant-mother) in the personal genesis of the I, but extends this to a larger intersubjective social context and at the limit to a generative context.

Thereafter, the deathdrive is presented in its relation to the sexual drives (§ 5), starting with Freud's account of the "negative therapeutical

[2] All talk of "layers", "levels" etc. here should not be taken in a literal sense: "Alle diese Ausdrücke, die die Worte Zeitigung, Zeit, Welt, damit auch Gegenstand, enthalten, sind, wo sie nicht mundan verwendet werden, von einem Sinne, der erst aus der in notwendiger Konsequenz geübten transzendentalreduktiven Methode sich herausstellt, also der natürlichen Sprache völlig fremd ist" (HuMat 8, Nr. 2 p. 4).

[3] To examine this closer has not been possible given the limitations of this work.

reaction". The reason why this is of such importance is that this reaction according to Freud has "deeper roots":

> Here we are dealing with the ultimate things which psychological research can learn about: the behaviour of the two primal drives, their distribution, mingling and defusion – things which we cannot think of as being confined to a single province of the mental apparatus, the id, the ego or the super-ego (*Analysis Terminable and Interminable*, SE 23, p. 242; tr. mod.).

It is shown that the sexual drive or Eros has the primary function of keeping the deathdrive in check, but that it cannot do so fully. This so to speak "failure" accounts for various manifestations of behaviour that was inexplicable according to the pleasure principle, such as the negative reaction but also the will to destroy oneself or other living beings and the world. There is a particular problem with the deathdrives on Freud's view which will be examined, namely their inability to manifest themselves intuitively. It is suggested that they depend on the interaction with the sexual drives in order for manifestation to be possible. Finally the question of the relation between the two basic drives in metapsychology is discussed and it is argued that the deathdrives should not be regarded as founding the sexual drives but that they should be seen as equiprimordial.

In the final section (§ 6) we come back to Husserl and the discussion of genetic phenomenology as "archaeology" that was discussed at the beginning of Part II and the indirect clarification of repression (Chapter Three, § 2). This time however, the *archai* are investigated in relation to the reconstruction of early childhood and infancy. It will be explained that "transcendental genesis" and the *Rückfrage* that accompanies it can be interpreted in the two senses as both leading back to constitutive layers of sedimented meaning, and to childhood. Like Freud, Husserl also devoted much thought to the fragility of personal genesis and its importance for adult life. As will be shown, Husserl attempts a reconstruction of intrauterine being for the infant and discusses pre-empathic intersubjectivity also here.[4] The communication between adults presupposes the development of a reciprocal, instinctive communication

[4] XV, Beilage XLV p. 605 [1935].

between the mother and child. This is a retrogression to the originary streaming *Ur-Ich* in which the being of both my own I and that of the other is predelineated.[5] With the analysis of the early communication between the mother and her newborn, Husserl gives a second concrete example (besides sexual enjoyment in § 3 below) of the flowing intersubjective intentionality whose abstract, theoretical structure was presented with the radicalized reduction (see Chapter Three, § 4). In these analyses, Husserl employs the psychological way to the reduction to its maximum degree, stretching egology not only in the direction of a primary twofoldness (which as soon reveals itself to be that of open intersubjectivity), but also into the personal being that in infancy precedes the constitution of the I. That being said, Husserl is careful to maintain the methodological primacy of egology also here, since it is always from the point of view of the mature I looking back and reconstructing that the investigations proceed.

At this point, the relation between egology and intersubjectivity is expanded in the direction of generative phenomenology, and it is shown that on Husserl's views also the empty and formal structure of the I is inherited as well as dispositions, in the form of act-habitualities.[6] This is not blind, mechanical repetition but an intentional unification of inherited meaning, so that we also become other through the others. This transference of "the personal" from the generative tradition takes place by means of a transformative concealment (*Wandlung durch Verdeckung*): we take up what is personal from our tradition into ourselves and thereby cover what was already there, or we cover what stems from the others by means of what remains in place within ourselves. The analysis thus shows that both repression and alterity are central for generative phenomenology. Obviously, here egology is stretched even further but as soon as one admits of an originary transference of meaning going on between mother and infant, then it seems hard to deny that also the transference from say mother and her primary caretakers, and so forth, effect our present life. This was also, in a sense, Freud's position.[7]

---

[5] XV, Nr. 33 p. 582 [1933].

[6] HuMat 8, Nr. 96 p. 436. See also D 14/23b.

[7] See "The Unconscious", PFL 11, p. 199f; *Beyond the Pleasure Principle*, PFL 11, p. 310; *The Ego and the Id*, PFL 11, p. 378, 397.

2. Husserl on drives and instincts: preliminary notes

What is the drive or instinct according to Husserl? First let me say that if intentionality is indeed the first word of transcendental phenomenology (in the sense of being a living problem), then it should come as no surprise that the "preliminary form" of intentionality in passivity surfaces as a major concept in genetic phenomenology.[8] Speaking of the worldly life of the monad, Husserl says that the inborn instincts we find there should be seen as "an intentionality that belongs to the originary essential structure of psychic being".[9] It is well known that Husserl criticized first Lipp's theory of instincts, and then Scheler for relying on similar "inborn 'representations'" that are merely posited as foundational but with no evidence to show it.[10] As we will see, Husserl not only accepts inborn instincts as a worldly phenomenon, but also argues that there are instincts on a transcendental level. How is this done?

James Hart has argued that the theory of drives falls prey to the same argument that Husserl himself had used at an earlier stage against Lipps and Scheler.[11] But what Hart fails to acknowledge is that Cartesian evidence is the basis also for Husserl's reconstructive phenomenology, and therefore the drives can never become a part of what Hart calls "the

---

[8] On instincts as "preliminary forms", see XV, Beilage XXX p. 511: "Aber vor dem Willen und seinen Willenszielen liegen Vorformen des Ichstrebens, des affiziert Hingezogenwerdens, des Sich-entscheidens, die wir instinktiv nennen.". Cf. HuMat 8, Nr. 71 p. 326: "Der instinktive Trieb ist also die Vorform der Vorhabe, so wie die Trieberfüllung die Vorform des eigentlichen Aktes". Cf. B II 3/16a-b [1934]: "... obschon wir hier zuerst in einer *Vorintentionalität* stehen, die in aller expliziten Intentionalität ihre Rolle spielt".

[9] HuMat 8, Nr. 46 p. 169f "Die angeborenen Instinkte als eine Intentionalität, die zur ursprünglichen Wesensstruktur des seelischen Seins gehört."

[10] Husserl's early critique of Lipps' theory of empathy is in XIII, Nr. 2 [1909]. The critique of Scheler is in XIV, Nr 16 p. 335 [1924].

[11] See James Hart *The person and the common world* (1992), p. 180ff. Hart argues that the concepts of "drive" and "instinct" must be abandoned if phenomenology is to remain transcendental, since they rely on "reconstruction" for their manifestation. According to Hart, once the instincts (and reconstructive phenomenology in general) is accepted, we have "methodological dualism" (p. 185f) and thus the breakdown of transcendental phenomenology; see also Hart (1998).

most fundamental reflection on primal presencing".[12] The evidence that the analysis of drives provides is only a supplement, due to the interplay between the different ways to the reduction (Ch. 2, § 3).

Prior to the effectuation of the radicalized reduction to the level of the *Ur-Ich*, where the drives are shown to be an integrated part of the structure of the streaming living present, the dependency of their worldly appearance cannot be fully overcome. So in a certain sense, all of Husserl's previous analyses of the drives and instincts at the deepest, non-manifest level remained worldly and were not touched by the epoché. The vague references to a level of "originary existence" that still governed the analysis in the late 1920's is clearly insufficient to really establish that the drives "can", as Husserl put it, "be explored in the phenomenological reduction".[13] This also means that any critical objection that focuses on the specific problem of the givenness of the drives, has to come up with arguments not only against this as a regional problem but against the very idea of a genetic deepening of the reduction. If reconstructive phenomenology is to be used then one cannot merely pick out one part (the drives) and say that it is unphenomenological. By that argument, it is the whole consisting of the originary structure of the living present that should be abandoned, and that does not leave genetic phenomenology with much.

Considering the sheer multitude of references in Husserl's texts – for the concepts of drive and instinct abound in manuscripts, notably from the 1920's and 1930's but apparently starting already with the *Studien zur Struktur des Bewusstseins* (1909-1914) – then one assumes that he must indeed have struck upon a satisfactory answer to the question of the givenness of the drives.[14] But this question is only rarely broached.[15] We obviously know of drives and instincts as immediate psychological datums, and as such they are also available for transcendental reflection

[12] Hart, *The Person and the Common World*, p. 185.

[13] XIV, Nr. 21 p. 405.

[14] If we look at the main work in this area, Nam-In Lee's *Edmund Husserls Phänomenologie der Instinkte* (1993), the question of the givenness of the drives is not taken up as major point for discussion. Probably this is because Lee sees no decisive problem in regarding the drives as biologically inborn rather than as say a question of phenomenological self-transcendence. Bernet discusses Husserl's early theory of drives in (2006).

[15] See however XIV, p. 333, 405ff (= Hua IX, p. 514ff); IX, p. 486; XV, p. 152.

by means of the psychological way. But it is a wholly different question when it comes to the sphere of the drives as preliminary forms to all intentional activity: these are clearly not given in the same way. Here we need a philosophical method for their disclosure. Husserl therefore distinguishes between the concealed originary drives as preliminary forms of intentionality and the higher-order manifest drives (hunger, sexuality, self-preservation etc.).[16] In so far as the manifest drives are concerned, it seems that their immanent givenness cannot be doubted; but the drives as preliminary forms of intentionality have to be "reconstructed" on the basis of a genetical *Rückfrage*, a regressive *Abschichtung* etc.

When it comes to a drive that begins as concealed "originary drive" and then progresses towards becoming conscious, Husserl suggests that in this passage from anonymity to manifestation we have to do with one and the same drive, in various modes of disclosure. We here see quite clearly Husserl's ambition to give an account of the *whole* consisting of both the anonymously functioning I and the conscious manifestation of the drive. This is obviously a more tempting position than that of Freud, who encounters severe difficulties with his assumption of forever unconscious drives that necessitate the notion of *Triebrepräsentanz* in order to become manifest.[17] However, the question is whether this is really more than a mere terminological issue.

Expressed in a negative fashion, one could say that neither of them succeeds in giving an account of the drives in their originary, funtioning mode. The only difference being that whereas Freud accepts this, Husserl insists that the methodology of the reductions does manage to display the continuity between functioning anonymity and conscious awareness. And in fact, this can be turned into a positive statement concerning the givenness of our deepest functioning life: the "processes", "operations" going on there (that can only be named by means of ontic, and to some extent falsifying terms such as "processes" etc.) are only given by means of reconstructive dismantling. In this sense,

[16] For instance in E III 9/6b [1931-33] Husserl distinguishes between "die Urtriebe und die neu durchgebrochenen Triebe höherer Stufe".

[17] HuMat 8, Nr. 60 p. 258 [C 13/1934]: "Jeder Instinkt ist unsterblich, nur ist er in verschiedenen Modis der Verwirklichung". Cf. XV, Nr. 11 p. 148 [C 11/1930-31].

phenomenology fills in the gaps left behind by the psychoanalytical appeal to unconscious drives, and in this sense "clarifies" or contributes to the clarification of its basic concepts.

What I take Husserl to mean here is that by positing the drive as identical through a genetic process, one moves all the way from the most originary source of intentional life to its radiant presencing in awakened consciousness. In its first phase, which we can only access by reconstruction in relation to *Rückfrage*, the drive is in close connection with the functioning I, it is indeed a part of the originary structure of the streaming living present as one of its aspects. Once the drive has moved away from this source into the state of awakened consciousness, which presupposes a certain affective force on the part of the drive, it has thereby also become available as a fact for reflection.

Let us now see how Husserl differentiates the transcendental from the psychological concept of instinct:

> Transcendental instincts. Naturally this psychological concept of instincts (the originary drives and the drives at a higher level that have just broken through), which are to be inborn in the individual soul and in the community of souls, is a constituted image and belongs to the constituted world. Against this, the transcendental research leads to the problem of a transcendental genesis as the basic concept of transcendental teleology, to which the transcendental instincts belong (E III 9/6b [1931-33]).[18]

Inborn instincts are constituted, whereas genetic phenomenology shows that there are instincts as preliminary forms of intentionality that are operative at the heart of the living present. The disclosure of the transcendental instincts thus shows that they are not posited randomly but as the result of meticulous methodological processes. In the same text from 1924, Husserl opens the reflection on how the instincts are phenomenologically given, a reflection which was continued in the

[18] "Transzendentale Instinkte. Natürlich ist dieser psychologische Begriff des Instinktes (die Urtriebe und die neu durchgebrochenen Triebe höherer Stufe), der eingeboren sein soll der einzelnen Seele und der seelischen Verbundenheit – ein konstituiertes Gebilde und gehört zur konstituierten Welt. Demgegenüber führt die transzendentale Forschung auf die Problem einer transzendentalen Genesis, zu der die transzendentalen Instinkte gehören, als Grundbegriff der transzendentalen Teleologie." (E III 9/6b [1931-33])

methodological investigations on the reduction in the 1930's.[19] The outcome of these, as we have seen, was to show that instincts are integrated moments of a whole that also comprises feelings, hyle, moods and kinaesthesia joined together in the living present. On the basis of this, Husserl can say that the general aim of the theory of instincts is to show the way "from the lower instinctual life up towards the life of willing and finally to a life in 'humanity'".[20]

Before the investigation proceeds to examine this general description, a terminological issue must first be solved. It cannot be simply assumed that what Husserl and Freud respectively mean by "Trieb" or "Instinkt" is the same. Although Husserl seems to use the two concepts interchangeably, Freud (as will be shown below) makes a distinction between them and reserves "Trieb" for psychoanalytical theory. But what Freud discards from psychoanalysis – mainly inherited animal behaviour – is included in Husserl's discussions of drive and instinct. This is in accordance with the most general aim of transcendental phenomenology: to account for the full concreteness of the I in the constitution of the world. Husserl's notions of drive or instinct and Freud's notion of drive however share the most essential determinations such as having its source within the lived body, and being paradigmatically related to the bodily needs of hunger, thirst and sexuality.[21] Thus in a fundamental sense, phenomenological analyses of instincts and drives are *Abschattungen* of the same subjective structure as the psychoanalytical interpretation of drives.

In his mature theory of drives, Husserl posits an "originary" drive or instinct which accounts for the general tendency in subjective life to proceed from intention to fulfilment, not merely in the one case but as a

---

[19] XIV, Nr. 16 p. 333; cf. Nr. 21 p. 407.

[20] XV, Beilage XLIII p. 599 [E III 9/1933].

[21] For recent articles that investigate the relation between Husserl and Freud from the vantage point of the drives, see Nathalie Depraz "Pulsion, instinct, désir: que signifie *Trieb* chez Husserl à l'épreuve des perspectives de Freud, Merleau-Ponty, Jonas, Scheler" (2001); Jagna Brudzinska, "Die phänomenologische Erfahrung und die Frage nach dem Unbewussten: Überlegungen im Anschluss an Husserl und Freud", (2006); and Rudolf Bernet "Zur Phänomenologie von Trieb und Lust bei Husserl" (2006).

"whole process".[22] This originary instinct is also called "curiosity", and first and foremost relates to the experiential givenness of the world.[23] To this originary drive always corresponds a given amount of lust (*Lust*), which translates the Aristotelian idea that everybody by nature takes pleasure in *aisthesis*.[24] Besides this, Husserl also speculates on whether to posit "a second originary instinct", namely the "instinct to objectivation".[25] Curiosity as primary drive would have as its "correlate" the drive to objectivation of that which becomes manifest.[26]

The tentative character of Husserl's analysis comes forth in for instance the discussion of whether it is instead "hunger" (and not objectivation) that should be posited as the "second originary instinct" besides that of curiosity.[27] The conclusion in this text however is that both hunger and curiosity are present together: "Beides ist ineins da". Regardless of whether they should both be called "originary drives" or not, these two (or three) drives obviously go together. The notion of *Urinstinkt* represents Husserl's effort to differentiate in the sphere of instincts and to posit a ground of sorts, upon which the other instincts can be based.[28] Besides "Urinstinkt" and "Urtrieb", Husserl often

[22] HuMat 8, Nr. 71 p. 328. Husserl speaks of "Urtrieb" already in ms. A VII 13/23 (1921), which carries the title: "Grundlegende Untersuchungen über Vorgegebenheit [...]. Entwürfe zu einer neuen Grundlegung. Genesis der Konstitution der Dinglichkeit (ursprüngliche Konstitution). Triebsystem der Dingkonstitution"; cf. HuDo 1, p. 255. See also XV, Beilage X p. 184f ; Beilage XLVII p. 611; HuMat 8, Nr. 96 p. 434; E III 9/2-4; B II 3/14a; B III 9/67.

[23] HuMat 8, Nr. 70 p. 325: "Das unterste, allfundierende Interesse ist also das der ursprünglichen und immer weiter fungierenden Neugier, oder wir sagen besser, das erfahrende und, in der Tat zuunterst genommen, das sinnliche erfahrende Interesse." Cf. Held, *Lebendige Gegenwart* p. 41ff.

[24] HuMat 8, Nr. 69 p. 321; cf. Nr. 71. On "Lust" in perceptual fulfilment, see also XXVIII, p. 424; E III 10/6b; B III 9/67; A VI 26/42b.

[25] HuMat 8, Nr. 60 p. 257f.

[26] HuMat 8, Nr. 69 p. 321.

[27] E III 9/28 [1932]: "Aber welche Interessen sind als ursprüngliche Instinkte mit dem der auf Naturkonstitution und so auf Objektivation gerichteten von vornhereien verflochten und sind in der konstitutiven Ordnung in schon konstituierter Objektivität (primordialer) zu Natur, zu Wertobjekten, zu praktischen Zweckobjekten führend? Aber zu dieser Abstraktion würde nur der Nahrungsinstinkt gehören als zweiter Urinstinkt (gegenüber dem der 'Neugier'). Aber das kann keine Ordnung sein. Beides ist ineins da, und eigentlich ist Hunger das erste."

[28] See further A V 20/2: "Hier haben wir verborgene 'Vernunft' als Trieb, der ständig lebendig ist und dem Menschen als solcher, als Streben in einen Horizont bewusst ist. [...] Aber das sind als Erstes Einzelheiten – der Trieb ist universaler Trieb mit universalem Triebhorizont, der Sondertrieb ist auf etwas 'gerichtet', etwas

speaks of "Urinstinkte" or "Urtriebe" in plural, in a more inclusive sense.[29] In a similar fashion, there are also references from early on to "ursprüngliche Instinkte" denoting mainly hunger, thirst and sexuality.[30] The notion of "intersubjective drives", which include the sexual drives, will be examined in the following section (§ 3).

Concerning the order of the instincts and their inner relation, I take Husserl's references to the single, originary instinct to relate to the primal manifestation of the world, the subjective process in passivity whereby something like the givenness of the world as such comes about. But as always, such characterizations remain abstract skeletons so long as the full account of the subjective (or proto-subjective) processes in the living present are left out.[31] And in certain texts Husserl insists on the "constant being-together" of the most basic drives, thereby making the analysis more concrete.[32]

An important question concerns the connection between "originary instincts" and the acquired habitualities: is there any communication between these two fundamental structures in passive life, or do they operate in isolation from one another? Freud, as we will see, argues that there is unlimited variability amongst the objects that can become attached to the drives, so that a particular object may for individual reasons be connected to for instance the sexual drive (as in shoe-

---

im Horizont. Der Mensch ist schon im menschlichen Trieb, er ist als relativ Erwachsener im Willen auf dies und jenes gerichtet, der aktuelle Wille im Willenshorizont, d.h. in der Mannifgaltigkeit und Einheit vorgewordener und geltender, fortgeltender Interessen – darüber hinaus ein dunkler Horizont von möglichen neuen Interessen, von Sondertrieben und Sonderinteressen, die sich melden und ausbilden werden."

[29] See XV, Nr. 22 p. 385; XV, Beilage XLVII p. 611; E III 4/16; E III 9/4, 6b; or the ",blinden' Urinstinkten, Urtrieben" as in E III 10/7b. On the cover of the manuscripts that are now published as texts Nr. 69–75 (C 16), Husserl has noted "Urinstinkte"; see HuMat 8 p. 318n1.

[30] IV, § 59 p. 255 (cf. p. 276); XIV, Nr. 16 p. 333. See also XXXIX, Nr. 51 p. 583n1; E III 9/28.

[31] See A VII 13/23 [1921]: "Das Allgemeinste des Triebes und zunächst des Urtriebes ist die Form eines unwillkürlichen Triebverlaufes, der aber konkret nur ist mit einem Inhalt, dem in Steigerung oder Minderung erfüllenden (enttäuschenden)." Cf. HuMat 8, Nr. 57 p. 252f.

[32] B II 3/17a [1934]: "Die Triebe (Nahrungstrieb, Geschlechtstrieb etc.) sind im Miteinander ständig da, aber in verschiedenen Modis". (This text is the continuation of XXXIV, Nr. 35.)

fetishism). On Husserl's view, the originary instincts are "constantly intermingled" with the acquired habitualities, so that in principle a connection between sexuality and any given habitual tendency can be established.[33] Or as it is expressed in another text, the general pursuit of genetic questioning means that one sooner or later is bound to come across the instincts, and these Husserl says, are "reshaped" in the course of life.[34] This opens for richly diversified investigations where inborn elements fuse with cultural aspects, and this compound, Husserl says, also extends to the individual aspects of instinctual subjective life.[35] Husserl's theory of instincts would accordingly admit that for instance "desire" in the psychoanalytical sense (of a Lacan, a Zizek or a Butler etc.) – that is to say, not natural instinct but something culturally informed according to the different norms and values of popular culture, fashion, erotica etc. – can be grafted upon the instincts.

More precisely, the genetic *Rückfrage* finally leads back to the "originary structure" of the living present, where hyletic material is constantly interacting with kinaesthesia, moods, feelings and drives all together. This "originary material" proceeds in an essential and unified form *prior* to the constitution of the world according to an apriori teleology:

> Now I reflect upon the fact that the *Rückfrage* finally results in the originary structure in its transformation of the originary hyle etc with

---

[33] B II 3/22a: "Die untere Stufe, das natürliche, das Habituelle der Instinkte, und erworbenen Gewohnheiten meldet sich immer wieder und Leben in der Durchstreichung der natürlichen Affektionen." See also HuMat 8, Nr. 57 p. 254; XV, Nr. 11 p. 148; Beilage XLVII p. 611; E III 10/7b: "Die Genesis im Triebleben, bzw. in der Triebstruktur des Ich, der Habitualität des Ich in der konstitutiven Fortbildung der Bedürfnisse und der Ausbildung von Willensrichtungen mit fernen Zielen, schliesslich mit Lebenszielen. Ziele als Zwecke und Mittel für den Zweck. Diese Habitualität als Entwicklungshabitualität, Wesensform des sich von den 'blinden' Urinstinkten, Urtrieben, bzw. Urhabitualitäten (verborgenen) aus entwickelnden Ich."

[34] XXXIX, Nr. 43 p. 476 [1931]: "Ich stelle, strömende Genesis erkennend, allgemeine genetische Fragen und stosse da auch auf die *Instinkte* neben den erworbenen Habitualitäten, finde zwar auch Umbildung der Instinkte im Laufe des Lebens, von innen her betrachtet, aber immer doch Instinkte."

[35] HuMat 8, Nr. 46 p. 169: "Jede Tierspezies hat die ihren [angeborene Instinkte]; aber nicht nur nach Spezies unterschieden in der instinktiven Ausstattung, sondern Instinkte sind auch individuell differenziert, sind in der Erfüllung, z.B. in der geschlechtlichen Liebe, als gerade auf dieses Individuum einzig bezogene charakterisiert."

> the originary kinaesthesia, originary feelings, originary instincts. According to this it resides in the fact that the originary material proceeds precisely in a form of unity that is an essential form prior to the worldliness. Thereby the constitution of the whole world seems to be predelineated for me already "instinctively", such that the functions that make this possible themselves have their essential-ABC, their grammar of essence in advance. That is to say that it lies within the fact that a teleology occurs in advance (XV, Nr. 22 p. 385 [1931/E III 9]).

To every concrete living present there accordingly belongs a "structural typicality of instinctive drives" such that there to every I belongs an "intentionality of drives".[36] By methodologically situating the phenomenological givenness of the drives at this radically reduced level, Husserl's previous investigations, that are often far-ranging but precocious and thus in a sense homeless, can be seen in a new light. But in a certain sense, Husserl had it all worked out already in 1921:

> The constitutive process of genesis springs forth from out of an originary drivelike inclination in which a kinaesthetically subjective movement proceeds in factical guidance from "sensory images"; that is to say from out of an intentionality of consciousness that originarily has no goals (A VII 13/23a).[37]

> The system of drive-intentionality is a system of associatively connected drives, a system of drive-associations that modify themselves by associations into developed capabilities. This does not come about mechanically, instead the drives necessarily develop themselves into such forms according to the lawlikeness of the drive-passivity [...] which pertains to the constantly affected I that gives in to these affections. This takes place on the condition that there is a lawbound allocation of perceptual images and kinaesthetic processes (A VII 13/24a).[38]

---

[36] E III 10/7b: "Zu jeder konkreten Gegenwart gehört eine Strukturtypik instinktiver Triebe, bzw. zum Ich gehört jederzeit seine Triebintentionalität".

[37] A VII 13/23a [1921]: "Der konstitutive Prozess der Genesis erwächst aus einer ursprünglichen Triebhaftigkeit, in der kinästhetisch subjektive Bewegungen in faktischer Begleitung von 'Empfindungsbildern' verlaufen; also aus einer ursprünglich ziellosen Bewegungsintentionalität [...]".

[38] A VII 13/24a [1921]: "Das System der Triebintentionalität ist ein System von assoziativ verflochtenen Trieben, ein System von Triebassoziationen durch Assoziationen sich modifizierend zu ausgebildeten Vermögen, die nicht mechanisch aber in der Gesetzmässigkeit der Triebpassivität [...] des stetig affizierten und den Affektionen nachgebenden Ich sich notwendig in solchen Formen ausbilden: vorausgesetzt dass eine gesetzliche Zuordnung von Empfindnisbildern und kinästhetischen

As we have seen in the previous chapter, Husserl already in the lectures on passive synthesis was convinced that the enigmas of association and the unconscious belonged together and could only be solved by means of what he there called a "radical theory" of the living present.[39] We further noted that when association is considered genetically, it becomes an "association of drives". Now we see that in the core-structure of the living present we find an "associative originary lawlikeness" which functions as a passive predelineation of the next temporal phase, of the future, which stems from what is retended but also from a larger horizon of habitualities and drives.[40] The associative process at work in the unconscious is thus presupposed both by the activity and the passivity pertaining to the I.[41]

3. The lifedrives, originary empathy and intersubjective drives.

The previous analysis of genetic phenomenology has provided the necessary background in order to understand the presence and function of the drives in the originary structure of the living streaming present, as this was presented in the previous section. Besides the "originary drives" one can distinguish two other main directions for Husserl's analysis of the drives: drives whose aim is the living-on of the I (lifedrives, self-preservation) and drives by means of which the I directs itself to the other (intersubjective drives). In this section, we will highlight the intersubjective drives, in contrast with the ego- or lifedrives (which we will first discuss).[42] There is an abundance of manuscripts from the 1930's mainly, that sketch out relatively consis-

Verläufen besteht."

[39] XI, § 34 p. 165; cf. § 37 p. 180.

[40] HuMat 8, Nr. 21 p. 95. On this lawlikeness, see also Nr. 49 p. 190.

[41] HuMat 8, Nr. 13 p. 53.

[42] As Housset has pointed out in *Personne et sujet selon Husserl*, p. 143, Husserl's theory as presented in certain texts bears a striking resemblance to Freud's first duality of drives: "Husserl précise sa théorie des pulsions en distinguant deux types de pulsions (E III 4): les pulsions de conservation et les pulsions par lesquelles le sujet s'oriente vers l'autre." In a footnote he adds: "Cette distinction est assez proche de celle faite par Freud, dans sa première théorie des pulsions, entre pulsion du moi et pulsion sexuelle. De plus, dans le deuxième dualisme, Freud assimile la pulsion sexuelle à la pulsion de vie, c'est-à-dire à une force que tend à la liaison."

tent views (although there is no single, unified theory) on temporalization and pre-empathic life in terms of the intentionality of drives.

Husserl speaks of "the universal lifedrive" as a constant drive that runs through all of life, awake and sleeping.[43] This is a way to characterize the whole of intentional life, the backbone, so to speak, that runs through both activity *and* passivity. The self-preservative aspect of life has its genetic source in the instinctive needs and in the instinctive striving for their satisfaction.[44] This is how Husserl expresses it at one place:

> Here the word "instinct" is used in an unusually broad sense, first of all for that drive-intention which originally is not yet disclosed in its sense. Instincts in the usual sense relate to remote, originally hidden goals in a chain of partial drives aiming at them and serving the preservation of the species, or else, the self-preservation of the individual of the species (E III 10/6a [1930]).[45]

The drive can be unconscious for me, or it can proceed from the I as its centre demanding attention. These two modes are "modal transformations" of the lifedrive which gains its unification through the "drive-temporality".[46] The partial drives relate to the total-drive as parts of a whole: "Ein Partialtrieb – im Totaltrieb", as it is expressed at one place.[47] Instinct is a "general expression for different particular instincts", which each has its own direction, its specific character of enjoyment, acquired habit and saturation.[48] In a general sense then,

---

[43] B II 3/5b [1934]: "[…] dem ständigen Trieb, der auch im Schlaf universaler Lebenstrieb ist". This text is the unpublished continuation of Hua XXXIV, No. 35.

[44] A V 24/17a [1927-33]: "Ernstes Leben ist das Leben der Selbsterhaltung, das seine genetisch ursprünglichste Sphäre hat in der instinktiven Bedürftigkeit und im instinktiven Streben nach ihrer Befriedigung."

[45] E III 10/6a: "Hier ist das Wort Instinkt in ungewöhnlich weitem Sinne gebraucht, zunächst nur für jede Triebintention, die ursprünglich noch nicht enthüllt ist in ihrem Sinn. Die Instinkte im gewöhnlichen Sinn beziehen sich auf ferne, ursprünglich verborgene Ziele, in Verkettung von Partialtrieben auf sie hintreibend und denen der Arterhaltung, bzw. der Selbsterhaltung des Individuums der Art."

[46] B II 3/16a-b [1934]: "Modi […] der Trieb im Modus des Unbewusst-Seins, des mir unbewusst-Seins, gegenüber dem Trieb in dem Modus der vom Ich-Zentrum ausgehenden begehrenden Zuwendung. Der Lebenstrieb in seinen modalen Verwandlungen einheitlich in seiner einheitlichen Trieb-Zeitlichkeit".

[47] B II 3/14b [1931].

[48] HuMat8, Nr. 60 p. 257.

instinct "is one" and yet it is a "multitude of particular instincts" that can compete with one another: an instinct may become temporarily put out of play, but not permanently.[49]

Moving on now to the intersubjective drives, we saw in § 2 above that there is a proto-empathy in transcendental genesis prior to the explicit empathic acts according to Husserl. In texts from the 1920's he argues that we must first show that the empathic act has its motivation in something that does not itself presuppose empathy, something that is situated at a concrete psychic level where "everything is originary existence" and which can be experienced in originary egological experience.[50] What kind of experience is that? In a text from the same period, Husserl notes that the connection of my I to a plurality of souls (*Gemeingeist*) does not arise solely from social acts, and he proceeds further by investigating the "obscure, blind passivity" which precedes this social activity:

> But already passivity, the instinctive life of the drives can bring forth intersubjective connection. In this way a sexual community is already brought forth at its lowermost level by means of the sexual instinctual life, even though it may be that its essential intersubjectivity is only revealed in its fulfilment. Here it is to be noted that also this passivity belongs within the framework of pure subjectivity and as such can be explored in the phenomenological reduction (XIV, Nr. 21, p. 405).[51]

Husserl is in this text wrestling with the issue of how to understand the fact that the constitution of the world seems to require that all subjects participate, while it is at the same time a practical impossibility that all subjects actually be empathically connected. A seeming way out of this dilemma suggests itself by the appeal to instincts, and Husserl thus concludes by stating that "the instinctive connections nevertheless remain".[52] As the context suggests, if we are to have any kind of substantive knowledge of the drives as our own drives, then this must

---

[49] HuMat 8, Nr. 57 p. 253.

[50] See for instance XIV, Beilage LXIII [1927], p. 479.

[51] XIV, Nr. 21 p. 405 [1927] (= Hua IX, p. 514). From the same period, see also IX, p. 486 [1928]: "Gegenüber der durch spezifische Aktivität gestifteten Sozialität stehen die intersubjektiven rein geistigen Verbindungen aus dunklen und erst in der Enthüllung der Befriedigung ihren Sinn zeigenden intersubjektiven Instinkte."

[52] XIV, Nr. 21 p. 407. See also XI, p. 150: "Auch ursprünglich instinktive, triebmässige Bevorzugungen dürfen wir zulassen".

be something which mainly occurs in relation to the lived body. It is the body, my lived body, which is my primary source of knowledge of the drives. But my body is also related intimately to other bodies, both in a cognitive mode (I know of the other as a person, i.e. as something more and other than a three-dimensional object, primarily via the pairing synthesis of our bodies), and a more direct, pre-cognitive mode (in my originary drives towards the body of the other, I am always already connected to her). Similarly, I also "know" of the drives stemming from the other that are directed towards me.

Pursuing the analogy between recollection and empathy also at the level of the radicalized reduction, Husserl is able to probe deeper into this complex issue. As we saw previously, Husserl in *Krisis* (§ 54b) explained that the two aspects of "self"-constitution by means of a primary "self"-alteration (my temporal differentiation from myself as *Ent-Gegenwärtigung* and my empathic-bodily differentiation from the other as *Ent-Fremdung*) function together. Husserl's analysis here complies with the most general methodological requirements of transcendental phenomenology, its egological "Cartesianism", even though admittedly there is not much of an "ego" to be found at this point. In this passage of *Krisis*, Husserl brings the investigations of originary constitution that were developed in for instance the C-ms and Hua XV into play. But instead of reiterating the laborious methodological paths that lie behind these texts (the various late reductions and their relations to the different ways to the reduction), Husserl in *Krisis* goes straight to the *Ur-Ich*. As we know however, focus on the *Ur-Ich* remains an abstraction so long as it disregards the concrete whole that is made up of the streaming living present in its originary structure.[53] Let us see how Husserl discusses this analogy (recollection/empathy) in one of the C-manuscripts.

Whenever recollection sets in, the continuity of my past from out of my constant self-coinciding based on retention, is always already there,

[53] See HuMat 8, Nr. 2 p. 4, which shows that the *Ur-Ich* is located at the level of the "Urströmen der lebendigen Gegenwart". See further XXXIV, Nr. 20 p. 300f, which shows that it is the radicalized reduction that is at work in disclosing the *Ur-Ich*. See also XV, Nr. 33 and Beilage XLI for vintage statements on the *Ur-Ich* that expand and clarify the exposition in *Krisis*.

as a presupposed foundation. In a similar fashion, Husserl had started to realize that as soon as empathy sets in, intersubjectivity is already present prior to the empathic act which thus only discloses what is in a sense already there.

> When empathy enters, is it then the case that the community is already there, that intersubjectivity is already there and that empathy is thus merely a disclosing achievement? That all the I's coincide together, infinitely? (HuMat 8, Nr. 96 p. 436 [C 17/1931]).[54]

Many other texts, as we will see, suggest that such a community prior to the empathic act is actually given with the sexual drives, which suggests a quite broad conception of sexuality on Husserl's part. Not broad in Freud's sense (polymorphic perversion, infantile sexuality etc.), but clearly probing deeper than reproductive sexuality into the foundations of social communalization. Every streaming present in its functioning constantly brings about its own continuation and self-consistency by means of a proto-retentional process (*Urkontinuierung*), and to this there always belongs "originary empathy". But as empathy only makes explicit what is already there, Husserl suggests that we speak of a mediated "originary intentionality that announces a continuity with the others".[55] The radicalized reduction shows that the alterity of the other which is situated at the heart of the living streaming present of the *Ur-Ich* (which is not "mine" just as it is not "your", "our" or "their"), is that of an open intersubjectivity.[56]

At this point, it becomes clear that the analysis of drives in relation to intersubjectivity, far from representing spurious explorations into unphenomenological territories, is in part an answer to the vexing problem that was first raised in the 1910/11 lectures: how to understand the co-givenness of two streams of consciousness. By reconstructing a sphere of originary, passive being-together which as intersubjective

---

[54] This idea is frequently discussed elsewhere; see for instance XIV, Beilage XXXI, p. 275f; Beilage XLV p. 373f; IX, Amsterdamer Vorträge § 15, p. 345; I, Pariser Vorträge, p. 12, 34ff; I, CM p. 166f, 181; HuMat 8, Nr. 89 p. 389; Nr 94 p. 425ff.

[55] HuMat 8 Nr. 96, p. 437.

[56] On this, see Franck, *Chair et corps* (1981) p. 136ff; and further "La chair et la constitution temporelle" (1984) p. 153ff.

drives precede active empathy, and by reconstructing the genesis of the monad in order to show how it proceeds from the passive sphere of the drives that stem from an immemorial past, Husserl is also trying to give a richer account of the idea of intersubjective time.[57] There is no "channel" leading from my temporality to that of the other, as Husserl claimed not without a certain frustration in *Grundprobleme*, yet the connection is somehow already there.[58] This temporal perspective that was so important in the beginning of Husserl's phenomenology of intersubjectivity, is not abandoned with the focus on drives but undergoes a change of meaning. The line of thought that will be examined here is that the sexual drives represent a new perspective on the deepest intentionality presented in static phenomenology, one that couldn't be thematized properly prior to a more radical engagement with the reduction.[59]

There is a wealth of analyses spanning over nearly two decades that engage with sexuality from an intentional perspective.[60] Here, we will at

---

[57] Lanei Rodemeyer in her book *Intersubjective temporality. It's about time* (Dordrecht: Springer, 2006), argues that we should introduce the figure of "intersubjective temporality" as a notion that expresses our individual temporalizing structure in its immediate connection with intersubjectivity which underpins it. "Intersubjective temporality", as she puts it, "is the aspect of temporalizing consciousness that, structurally, reaches out for and maintains a connection between consciousness and other consciousness, and, with regard to content, indicates intersubjectivity both through retained experiences of intersubjective horizons and through affectivity. [...] Thus we find the link between the temporalizing subject and intersubjectivity through recognizing the intersubjective links and indications within the phenomenological subject itself. Further, because intersubjective temporality reveals the bridge between my consciousness and that of the other, it also reveals our interdependence: The consciousness of the other must also reach out to me" (p. 191). Though she doesn't mention "instincts" nor for instance the "radicalized reduction", I would suggest that her analysis is played out at this level and in close connection to these themes.

[58] XIII, Nr. 6 § 39, p. 189; cf. Beilage XXVIII, p. 227.

[59] See the presentation of inner time-consciousness and the "transcendental 'absolute'" in *Ideen I*, § 81; and the discovery of absolute consciousness in Hua X, Nr. 39-47 [1906-09]. As Depraz has argued, these analyses anticipate the flowing intersubjectivity disclosed by the radicalized reduction; see *Transcendance et incarnation*, p. 252f.

[60] For analyses of sexuality, see for instance: Hua XIV, Nr. 9 [1921], Nr. 21; HuMat 8, Nr. 46, Nr 60; Hua XV Beilagen X, XXX, Nr. 34, Beilage XLIII; Hua VI, § 55; Hua XXIX, Nr. 27 [1936], 32 [1936-37]; see also E III 9/5aff; E III 10/3aff; B II 3/17a.

first take a brief look at one of the most interesting texts. The drive, Husserl says in this text, can be in a mode of undetermined hunger when the direction to its object is not yet carried within it, but it can also be determined so that the direction to its affecting object becomes one with the drive.[61] Continuing this line of thought, Husserl says that the sexual drive can be determined so that its goal is the other person, and here the fulfilment is preliminarily determined as sexual intercourse. In the drive itself lies the direction towards the other, just as the "correlative drive of the other" carries within it the direction towards me, a "reciprocal drive" (*Wechseltrieb*).[62] Both my drive and that of the other can be in a mode of abstention and antipathy, but in its originary mode it is "'uninhibited', unmodalized drive".[63] A closer look at fulfilment here however shows that it is not an isolated experience, and that in simple unmodalized fulfilment there are not two separate fulfilments in each primordiality, but instead there is a unity of both primordialities which is produced through one fulfilment within the other:

> In the originary mode it is however unmodalized drive "without inhibition", which always reaches into the other and whose intentionality of drives has always reached through to the other through her correlative intentionality of drives. In the simple, originary mode of fulfilment we do not have two separate fulfilments each in the one and the other primordiality, but a unity of both primordialities that is brought about by means of the fulfilment of one-within-the-other (XV, Nr. 34 p. 593f).

When I interpret this from the point of view of my worldly being, I can only do so as a sexual being, from one human related to another by means of actual empathy.[64] Now, is this "intersubjective drive" which

[61] XV, Nr. 34 "Universale Teleologie. Der intersubjektive, alle und jede Subjekte umspannende Trieb transzendental gesehen. Sein der monadischen Totalität" p. 593 [1933/E III 5].

[62] XV, Nr. 34 p. 594: "Im Trieb selbst liegt die Bezogenheit auf den Anderen als Anderen und auf seinen korrelativen Trieb."

[63] XV, Nr. 34 p. 594.

[64] XV, Nr. 34 p. 594: "Wenn ich in meiner Weltlichkeit das in grösster Ursprünglichkeit auslege, so kann ich es nur als geschlechtlicher Mensch und damit von Mensch zu Menschen in aktueller Einfühlung, von Mann zu Weib (das, so allgemein gesprochen, natürlich schon mittelbar)." Husserl's careful phrasing suggests that the interpretation of the originary sexual drives as they manifest themselves at the worldly level is primarily to be understood from the point of view of myself as a sexual being to other human beings, and secondarily as the relation between man and

according to the title "covers all subjects" to be identified with the sexual drive? Most likely not, for Husserl suggests that there is a stage of instinctual life prior to this which is not yet determined in terms of object and aim (the other and copulation): the intentionality of drives has "a preliminary stage" which precedes the developed constitution of the world.[65] The sexual drive would accordingly already be the determination of something more primary, such as the originary drive that was discussed in the previous section. Anne Montavont, in connection with this, has suggested that this originary drive is an indeterminate intentionality whose movement of transcendence inaugurates the constitution of the world.[66]

This analysis is bound to have consequences for Husserl's conception of primordiality, and following Kern's suggestions primordiality after late 1929 no longer means "sphere of ownness" as it still does in *Cartesianische Meditationen*.[67] "Das Eigene" as what is reached by so to speak switching off all intentionality related to the other, is the result of a static analysis whereas the primordial is reached by a genetic analysis, and includes the other as my intentional positing.[68] This is how Husserl expresses it:

> Primordiality is a system of drives. When we understand it as originary standing streaming we also find therein this drive which strives into other streams and possibly also into other ego-subjects [*Wenn wir sie verstehen als urtümlich stehendes Strömen, so liegt darin auch jeder in andere Ströme, und mit evtl. anderen Ichsubjekten, hineinstrebende Trieb*]. This intentionality has its transcendent "aim", transcendent as something foreign that has been introduced, although in primordiality as its own aim, which is to say that in its core it is constantly originary modal intention which becomes salient and fulfills itself (XV, Nr. 34 p. 594).

---

woman.

[65] XV, Nr. 34 p. 594. See also B II 3/16b.

[66] Montavont, *De la passivité dans la phénoménologie de Husserl*, p. 267.

[67] Kern, XV, p. XVIIIff, XXXIII

[68] See CM § 44 in relation to XV, Beilage I; for the genetic account of primordiality, see HuMat 8, Nr. 94; XV, Nr. 36; VI, § 72 p. 261f. Cf. Depraz, *Transcendance et incarnation*, p. 105ff; and Zahavi, *Husserl und die transzendentale Intersubjektivität*, p. 23ff.

There is an important reductive step at work here, before we can come to see the reciprocal transcendence of the drives that make up the hidden foundation of our communal being-together. As Husserl states elsewhere, the reduction to the living present discloses the other as always already intentionally implicated in my intentionality, and here we come to see that this primordiality is a system of drives.[69] That is to say, whereas Husserl in *Krisis* stops short of introducing the drives, this passage shows clearly that a continued genetic analysis reveals an intentionality of the drives in the most originary meaning-structure of the living present.

As Strasser suggested already in 1975, Husserl's analyses of sexuality may bring about a change in the foundations of Husserl's philosophy, or what he (following Theunissen) calls his "social ontology".[70] This change would be one from a "primordial nature" of an isolated subject to the "becoming unified" and "personal fusion" that occurs in sexual enjoyment.[71] The two persons (it is assumed they are not more) are not bound together by means of an external third element such as sexual enjoyment; instead they find enjoyment together and through one another such that they produce a "unity of enjoying community".[72] The other is not merely the means for sexual enjoyment: it is the fact *that* she partakes, *that* a unity of willing which encompasses both and that leads to a unity of twofold activity occurs, which is the object of enjoyment.[73] What is enjoyable is for each *that* the other enjoys. According to Strasser, this leads to *eine entscheidende Wendung* in that it is no longer separated streams of consciousness but two and by implication a plurality of such streams that make up the foundation.[74]

[69] VI, § 71 p. 260/Engl. p. 257: "Alle Seele bilden eine einzige durch die Phänomenologie systematisch zu entfaltende Einheit der Intentionalität in wechselseitiger Implikation der Lebensströme der einzelnen Subjekte; was in der naiven Positivität oder Objektivität ein Aussereinander ist, ist von Innen gesehen ein intentionales Ineinander." Cf. VI, § 72 p. 262.

[70] Strasser, "Grundgedanken der Sozialontologie Edmund Husserls" (1975), p. 15ff. Strasser has been criticized by Yamaguchi (1982) and Zahavi (1996) for assuming that Husserl's final position is that egology is secondary and intersubjectivity primary.

[71] Strasser (1975) p. 16f.

[72] XIV, Nr 9 p. 177 [1921]; Strasser is commenting this text amongst others.

[73] XIV, Nr 9 p. 177 [1921].

[74] Strasser (1975) p. 15ff. However, he suggests further on that the analysis must be continued beyond this to the level of the *Ur-Ich* which precedes the differentiation

But Husserl's analysis of sexuality does not stop with this presentation of sexual fusion and *jouissance*, and the question is what happens to the "foundation" once these further steps are taken into account. In the same text from 1921 Husserl goes on to examine rape, sexual violence and the masochistic pleasure that can be obtained from being forced.[75] And in a text written some ten years later, it is said that just as there can be understanding and concordance in communication, so there is hatred and a will to annihilation of the other, both on a personal level and on the level of communities of a higher order.[76] Strasser does not discuss these ideas, but they do announce that there is something problematic with a conception of sexuality in a worldly form which only acknowledges reciprocal confirmation of will, and that bypasses the *Negativum* where one will overrides another. We will come back to this.

So far we have emphasized the relation between the drives and the body without paying closer attention to the interaction of bodily-sensuous affection (lived flesh) and temporality, but this is a simplification. The genetic analysis shows that the basic constituents of static phenomenology (such as the duality of hyle and morphe) are actually the result of already highly complex processes of constitution. In the 1920's Husserl ascribed the character of being "alien to the I" (*Ichfremd*) to the hyle, and around 1930 he introduced the notion of "originary hyle" (*Urhyle*) to designate the properly genetic conception of the hyle.[77] Here origi-

between my stream and yours; cf. p. 19f.

[75] XIV, Nr 9 p. 177f [1921]: "Es kann aber auch sein, dass auf die fremde Subjektivität keine Rücksicht genommen, dass der Genuss gegen ihren Willen erzwungen, ihr damit Leid aufgezwungen, ja dass sie vernichtet wird. Dann fällt die höhere Freuden- und Wertschicht nicht nur weg, sondern es tritt an ihre Stelle ein Negativum, von dem zu fragen ist, ob es nicht einen Wertwiderstreit herbeiführt, der nicht nur den Wert mindert, sondern aufhebt. Es kommt dann in Frage: der Zwang, zu Willen zu sein (also Willensunterwerfung des Anderen), und das den Genuss Erzwingen unter Gegenwillen des Anderen, ohne dass dabei auch nur erzwungene Einwilligung, Willensunterwerfung statthat. Es kann sein, dass auf der gezwungene Seite zwar kein Wunsch bestand, aber in der Unterwerfung Lust erwächst und Wunsch geweckt wird und danach Befriedigung."

[76] HuMat 8, Nr. 73 p. 334. Husserl here adds: "In diesem Durcheinander muss Klarheit geschaffen werden!!" See also XV, Beilage XLVII p. 611.

[77] See XIV, p. 379. On the *Urhyle*, see HuMat 8 Nr. 17, 23, 79; XV Nr. 22. For

nary spacing joins hands with originary temporizing since *Urhyle* and *Urzeitigung* denote two closely connected aspects of the meaning-structure of the streaming living present.[78] These two always function in close cooperation, so that the originary hyle as the *ichfremde Kern* can be said to have its own temporization in the concrete living present.[79] As a consequence of the intentionality of drives, the lived body is always given in the temporal flow: we have a constant, primordial 'perception' of our own bodies which traverses immanent time in the temporization.[80] How is this perception to be understood? Franck suggests that it is a primary sort of *con-tact* of my flesh to itself, a touching which is at the same time a touching and being touched by the other.[81]

The intentionality of drives that stands at the centre of these discussions is the genetic account of the very same intentionality that was analyzed in the early lectures on inner time-consciousness. The main difference is that Husserl in the earlier text did not regard this intentionality as one pertaining to the I: instead, the intentional opening of the world was there represented by the transcendence of the now in its necessary intertwinement with protention and retention.[82] Although the

---

thorough discussions of this, see Franck, *Chair et corps* p. 182ff; Lee, *Husserls Phänomenologie der Instinkte* p. 115ff; Depraz, *Transcendance et incarnation* p. 253ff; Montavont, *De la passivité dans la phénoménologie de Husserl* p. 248ff.

[78] HuMat 8 Nr. 23 p. 110: "Diese urimpressionale strömende Gegenwart der konkreten Urpräsenz hat dann folgende allgemeinste Struktur: a) das phänomenologische Residuum der eigentlich wahrnehmbaren Seiten von mundanen Realitäten etc., nämlich die Empfindungshyle, die Urhyle in ihrer eigenen Zeitigung; b) das 'Ich' mit allen offenen und verborgenen ichlichen Beständen, dahin gehörig".

[79] HuMat 8 Nr. 23 p. 110: "Die Urhyle in ihrer eigenen Zeitigung ist der sozusagen ichfremde Kern in der konkreten Gegenwart."

[80] HuMat 8 Nr. 23 p. 112: "In der strömenden Urpräsenz haben wir unabänderlich immer schon Leibwahrnehmung, und so in der Zeitigung der immanenten Zeit geht durch diese ganze Zeit kontinuierlich hindurch mein Leibwahrnehmen, synthetisch identisch denselben Leib allzeitlich konstituierend."

[81] Franck, *Chair et corps* p. 190f. See also Derrida's discussion of Franck on this in *Le toucher, Jean-Luc Nancy* (2000), § 10.

[82] Discussing the intentionality pertaining to sexual drives and intercourse, Husserl in a text from 1933 goes to say: "In my old doctrine of inner time-consciousness, I treated the intentionality that has been demonstrated here precisely as intentionality – aimed forwards through the protention and modifying itself through retention, although preserving the unity – but I did not there speak of the I, did not characterize it as pertaining to the I (in the widest sense of an intentionality of willing). Later on I introduced this egoic intentionality of willing as one founded in non-egoic intentionality ('passivity')" (XV, Nr. 34 p. 594f [1933]).

early account may appear somewhat restricted by comparison, it is the same basic idea that is presented in both cases.[83] Thus the lifedrive, which undergoes modal transformations when it is split up into various particular drives, remains in unity but precisely by being in a constant state of becoming and self-transformation, since it is always unified by means of its own "drive-temporality".[84] Association plays a decisive role here, since the radicalized reduction shows that association is the fundamental process which connects the various aspects of the streaming living present into a concrete whole. Once the function of originary association is discovered also at this genetic level it gains its maximum of activity, but at the same time it disappears from intuition and can only be grasped by way of reconstruction.[85] Discussing association in this context also means that we can bring the previous analyses (Chapter Five and Chapter Six, § 2) to an end.

If association is the universal principle of passive genesis, then the particular intentionality that it consists in has its source in the temporization that takes place together with primary hyle, kinaesthesia, feelings etc. in the streaming living present. But association is not something that is external to this meaning-structure, since the living present is itself a "unity of an associative fusion".[86] Ordinary association proceeds from what is already given, but always on the basis of an already performed, passive "preassociation" and this originary association is a "'passive' temporization".[87] To this extent, one can say that association

---

[83] This has also been suggested by Rudolf Bernet (2002), p. 335: "If one calls this self-affection of subjective life 'drive' or 'instinctual drive' (*Trieb*) then this inner time-consciousness clearly merits the name which Husserl actually uses: 'drive-intentionality' or 'intentionality of instinctual drive' (*Triebintentionalität*). As an inner experience of intentional life this is both instinctual drive and representation (*Repräsentation*) of drive in one".

[84] B II 3/16b [1934]: "Der Lebenstrieb in seinen modalen Verwandlungen einheitlich in seiner einheitlichen Trieb-Zeitlichkeit in einem ständigen Werden, Sich-Verwandeln in Verwandlung der Sondertriebe, die also einzeln, im Miteinander in einer ständigen Genesis stehen, in einer 'intentionalen' Genesis, obschon wir hier zuerst in einer *Vorintentionalität* stehen, die in aller expliziten Intentionalität ihre Rolle spielt."

[85] HuMat 8, Nr. 96 p. 437: "Alle Urassoziation, Urintentionalität wird erst durch Abbau und Rekonstruktion ausgelegt".

[86] HuMat 8, Nr 66 p. 296.

[87] HuMat 8, Nr 49, p. 190; Nr 67 p. 309.

is what brings unity also to the deepest genetic level of the pre-I, just as it is the drive-intentionality that propels the associative nexus forward, making all content into "content of drive-fulfilment".[88] "Association" here runs through the whole of intentional life, both patent and latent, and it takes on an "extraordinarily broad" sense.[89]

Let us conclude this discussion with a view to our theme. What is of decisive importance for our present purposes is that this whole analysis suggests that inhibition and also repression is a necessary, structural aspect of the living present even at the deepest genetical level of analysis. Let us see what that can mean.

1) The first and most general point is that due to the nature and the central role of association also at this level of genetic investigation, we are able to deduce the necessary givenness also of processes of "covering" (*Verdeckung*), "inhibition" (*Hemmung*) and "repression" (*Verdrängung*) in the streaming living present.[90] Without going into the details, it can still be said that everywhere that association is at work it is accompanied by one of these processes: in order for an associative connection to be established in pre-consciousness, i.e. prior to the turning-towards of the I and the becoming conscious, there are always an at least potential manifold of competing alternatives that "flourish" briefly before settling down into the sedimented sphere. The nature of association, here as well as on higher levels of genesis (as in the lectures on passive synthesis), is such that in general there is a multitude of connections in the making between drives, kinaesthesia, feelings, moods etc. in all kinds of combinations. This passive life is by its nature such that it constantly inhibits, covers and represses that which for various reasons never breaks through to conscious or pre-conscious manifestation.

2) The movement of the drive in its "originary mode" is, as we saw, that of an "uninhibited drive" which proceeds from its first manifestation as a coming into salience onto fulfilment. In this "unmodalized" progression, my drive reaches into the other where it joins her recipro-

---

[88] XV, Nr. 34 p. 595.

[89] HuMat 8, Nr 97 p. 446.

[90] On *Verdeckung*, see HuMat 8, Nr. 18, 20, 33, 64; on *Hemmung*, see XI, §§ 42f; EU § 21; HuMat 8 Nr. 49, 52; and B II 3/14-19.

cal drive aimed at me. But of course, this progression of the drive may at all times encounter various kinds of obstruction, in the shape of other competing forces (other drives, the impact of new sensuous affection, the encounter with different volitions etc.), whereby it may become inhibited and finally repressed. The drives, Husserl says, can be in the "mode of satisfaction" as well as "in the mode of inhibition".[91]

One kind of inhibition that the drives may encounter is the competition between different drives (such as when sleepiness is overcome by a sexual impulse), another kind is the encounter with a resistance (as when a sexual impulse is restrained by cultural praxis).[92] Further, the reawakening of a drive can lead to kinaesthetic disappointment when something new suddenly appears and takes over our interest. Or else, the kinaesthesia may have initiated its typical progression towards fulfilment when suddenly paralysis occurs, which is beyond willpower (as in the case of sexual impotence or a hysterical symptom).[93] Even what we from the point of view of the active I consider to be a fully uninhibited action, is based on inhibited desires and different strivings in struggle with each other.[94] When a drive is fully inhibited it can yet remain within the subject ("persevere") in every living present as a constant search for fulfilment.[95] At the limit, Husserl says, the analysis

---

[91] B II 3 /14a [1934]: "Trieb – Instinkt, die ursprünglichen Triebe, Triebarten, in ihrer allgemeinen Typik, Trieb, Bedürfnis, im Modus der Befriedigung, Trieb im Modus der Hemmung." See also p. 15a: "Trieb im Modus der Sättigung in der Positivität der Erfüllung, das ist das Gegenstück der vollen Hemmung."

[92] B II 3/17a [1934]: "Aber ist die Konkurrenz verschiedener Triebe Hemmung in demselben Sinn, wie die Auswirkung eines Triebes auf Widerstand stösst; und das hat wohl selbst wieder verschiedene Bedeutung, verschiedene Weisen."

[93] B II 3/17a "Z.B. Trieb in 'Wiederholung', wiedergeweckt, Auslösung der kin.<ästhetische> Enttäuschung, 'Es kommt anderes', schliesslich Erfüllung, Hemmung in der Enttäuschung und 'Überwindung' in der schliesslichen Erfüllung. Oder ganz anders: die Kin.<ästhese> bringt mit den Erfüllungsgang, aber plötzliche 'Lähmung' oder sonstige Widerstandshemmung, durch 'Kraftanspannung', eine Strecke überwunden und dann stehen bleiben, Kraftanspannung hilft nicht etc. Die Triebe (Nahrungstrieb, Geschlechtstrieb etc.) sind im Miteinander ständig da, aber in verschiedenen Modis, aber im Sich-Auswirken können sie sich hemmen, diejenige des einen die des anderen ausschalten [...]." See already IV, § 59 p. 253f: "I can also have a nervous disorder and lose the mastery of my limbs."

[94] D 14/58b: "Das ungehemmte Tun ist gehemmtes, erfülltes Begehren verschiedener Strebungen im Kampf – Affektion und Aktion Strebensmodi."

[95] B II 13/15-16 [1934]: "Aber ganz anders geht Sättigung ins Leben ein, als 'Erledigung', mit der ein Element des Wohlgefühls in der Verwandlung des

has to account for the possibility that a drive fulfils itself unconsciously, without the participation of the I.[96]

3) On the basis of this sketch of the drives we have found an intentionality of drives that precedes both intersubjectivity and the constitution of the world, and that functions as originary transcendence in the sense of an open interest or hunger that as yet has no aim or object. There is an analogy here with Freud's account which (as we will see shortly) emphasizes that the object of the drive is what is most variable, and which leads to the rich investigations of the various *Triebschicksale*. But whereas Freud starts out from the duality of the ego- or lifedrives and the sexual drives in the first theory of drives (which is replaced by the duality of eros and the deathdrives in the second theory), Husserl locates a stage prior to such dualities.

This suggests a deeper and more thorough conceptualization – at least in terms of genesis. What the outcome of such a comparison will be once we have also taken Freud's fuller position into account must await the investigations of the following sections. We have further seen that there is inhibition and repression going on also at this level of genetic primordiality, as a necessary part of the meaning-structure of the living present. This analysis connects with Husserl's general account of repression in the perceptual field (as discussed above in Chapter One, § 3) and thereby it strengthens the overall coherence of Husserl's philosophy of passivity. Furthermore, this analysis of sexuality in transcendental phenomenology permits us to confirm our previous interpretation of *Nachträglichkeit* (Chapter Four, § 5) which was lacking in precisely this aspect.

Behaltens (das hier eine Passivität besagt, also der 'Sedimentierung'), im Lebensuntergrund fortfungiert, während das ganze unerfüllt-bleiben eines Triebs als absolut gehemmt sein fortdauernd in der Subjektivität, in jeder lebendigen Gegenwart treibende Aktualität ist, sozusagen ständig nach Erledigung schreit."

[96] B II 3 /14a: "Muss aber nicht auch auf die Möglichkeit hingewiesen werden, dass ein Trieb 'unbewusst', ohne Ichbeteiligung, sich erfüllt (Selbstentladung, Entspannung); liegt nicht im Unwohl-Sein des Kranken ein Trieb, der sich im Wandel des Befindens entspannt, in einem einsteigend wohltätigen Besser-Werden, ohne dass das Ich beteiligt zu sein braucht?"

4. The drives as basic concepts of psychoanalysis

The general importance of drive-like notions in accounting for the passive layers of subjective life is clearly visible from early on in Freud's writings, albeit initially under a different name.[97] It is only with *Three Essays on the Theory of Sexuality* from 1905 that the terminology is settled so that the drives (*Triebe*) as impulses stemming from the body, can be separated from the *Reize* and *Instinkte* as impulses from the outside world.[98] Besides the difference in source, what further distinguishes drive from stimulus and instinct is the temporality of its effect upon the mind, for whereas stimuli operate with a single impact [*einmaliger Stoss*] so that they can be disposed of by escape, the drive never operates as a momentary force of impact but always as a *constant* force.[99]

The characterization of the drive that Freud gives suggests that he considers it to be a fundamental and daemonic force in our lives: the drive "attacks" from the inside of our lived bodies, and therefore there is no escape from it by means of evasion.[100] "Instinct" (unlike drive) for Freud generally has the meaning of animal, self-preservative behaviour and denotes "inherited mental formations".[101] Typical examples of such behaviour are the sudden, "instinctive [*instinktiv*] recognition of dangers" which many animals show but which is lacking for instance in children.[102] In contrast, the concept of "drive" serves to differentiate the body from the soul, it is a *Grenzbegriff*.[103] Furthermore, the drive is an

---

[97] In the 1890's, Freud instead speaks of endogenous excitations (*endogener Erregungen, Reizen*); see for instance part one of the 1895 *Entwurf* (§§ 2a, 10-11).

[98] As has often been noted, Freud distinguishes the concept of drive from that of instinct (*Instinkt*) which is rarely used: see *Hemmung, Symptom und Angst* SA 6, p. 305/PFL 10, p. 328; "Das Unbewusste" SA 3, p. 154/PFL 11, p. 200; *Aus der Geschichte einer infantilen Neurose*, SA 8, p. 230/PFL 9, p. 364. This difference is obliterated in all the English translations where "instinct" is used to cover both the German *Trieb* and *Instinkt*.

[99] "Instincts and their Vicissitudes", PFL 11, p. 115/SA 3, p. 82.

[100] "Instincts and their Vicissitudes", PFL 11, p. 114f/SA 3, p. 82.

[101] "The Unconscious", PFL 11, p. 199f.

[102] *Inhibitions, Symptoms and Anxiety* , PFL 10, p. 328; cf. From the history of an infantile neurosis, PFL 9, p. 364.

[103] See *Three essays on sexuality*, 1915-addition, PFL 7, p. 82f/SA 5, p. 76f; "Instincts and their Vicissitudes" PFL 11, p. 118/SA 3, p. 85; and *Notes on autobiographical account case of paranoia* (Schreber), PFL 9, p. 213/SA 7, p. 196.

"endosomatic, continuously flowing source of stimulation" unlike the instinct, which stems from the outside world and is of a more momentary character. It is the concept of *Trieb* (and not that of *Instinkt*) which poses a central problem to the psychoanalytical conceptualization of subjectivity: "The theory of drives [*Trieblehre*] is the most important, but at the same time the least complete part of psychoanalytic theory".[104] Furthermore, it is from the psychoanalytical investigations of the mentally ill that Freud expects any progression concerning the theory of drives.[105]

In the 1915 paper on "Triebe und Triebschicksale", Freud introduced important phenomenological distinctions that have played a fundamental role in later psychoanalytical thinking, by distinguishing between the pressure [*Drang*], the aim [*Ziel*], the object [*Objekt*] and the source [*Quelle*] of the drive.[106] The excited body is the "source" of the drive, and it is by means of the "object" chosen that the drive is able to reach its "aim" which is the removal of that excitation.[107] It is on the way between source and aim that the drive becomes "psychically operative", and this is experienced as a "pressure" that corresponds to the "demand made upon the mind for work".[108] Thus Freud employs the concept of drive to denote the demands that the body poses and more importantly the psychic work that this calls for:

---

[104] *Three Essays*, 1924-addition, PFL 7, p. 83n1; tr. mod. See also "On narcissism", PFL 11, p. 70; *Notes on Autobiographical Account Case of Paranoia* (Schreber), PFL 9, p. 213; *Beyond the Pleasure Principle*, PFL 11, p. 306. A similar point is made in the *Autobiographical Study*: "There is no more urgent need in psychology than for a securely founded theory of the drives on which it might then be possible to build further. Nothing of the sort exists, however, and psychoanalysis is driven to making tentative efforts towards some such theory" (PFL 15, p. 241; tr. mod.).

[105] *Notes on Autobiographical Account Case of Paranoia* (Schreber), PFL 9, p. 213.

[106] "Instincts and their Vicissitudes", PFL 11, p. 118/SA 3, p. 85. This text is translated as "Instincts and their Vicissitudes", but since I employ the expression "drive" throughout this work for Freud's *Trieb*, I will often refer to this text under its German name, so as to avoid confusion. In fact, if *Instinkt* denotes an innate, biologically determined mode of behaviour with predetermined objects (drinking – water), then the very thought of instincts as undergoing vicissitudes is actually inconceivable; cf. Lear, *Love and its place in nature*, p. 124.

[107] "Instincts and their Vicissitudes", PFL 11, p. 118; see also *New Introductory Lectures on Psycho-analysis*, PFL 2, p. 128f.

[108] *New Introductory Lectures on Psycho-Analysis*, PFL 2, p. 128f; Three Essays, 1915-addition, PFL 7, p. 82f.

> We give these bodily needs, in so far as they represent an instigation to mental activity, the name of "*Triebe*" a word for which we are envied by many modern languages ("The Question of Lay Analysis", PFL 15, p. 300).

The most fruitful and intriguing aspect of Freud's concept is precisely this: the drive is a "measure of the demand of work" imposed upon the psyche by the lived body.[109] Every drive is accordingly a "piece of activity" which brings about a negotiation between the drive, the world and the self.[110] This demand of psychic work in conjunction with the almost complete variability of the "object" of the drive, is what opens up the whole field of subjective life to psychoanalytic research. But for our present concerns, it must first be noted that here the drive is explicitly and for the first time posited as a "basic concept" (*Grundbegriff*) of psychoanalysis:

> A conventional basic concept of this kind, which at the moment is still somewhat obscure [*vorläufig noch ziemlich dunkler Grundbegriff*] but which is indispensable to us in psychology, is that of the drive ("Instincts and their vicissitudes"; PFL 11, p. 114, tr. mod. /SA 3, p. 81f).

In order to establish the drive as a basic concept for psychic life (*das Seelenleben*), Freud must first turn away from the perspectives of physiology and biology – and with them the focus on physiological stimuli, the reflex arc, the nervous system etc. – where the drive was first thematized.[111]

---

[109] "Instincts and their Vicissitudes", PFL 11, p. 118; cf. *Three Essays*, PFL 7, p. 82f.

[110] "Instincts and their Vicissitudes", PFL 11, p. 118/ SA 3, p. 85.

[111] This important shift in perspective is eradicated in the English translation of "Triebe und Triebschicksale" which in fact states quite the opposite: "If now we apply ourselves to considering mental life from a *biological* point of view, an 'instinct' appears to us as a concept on the frontier between the mental and the somatic..." (emphasis added by Strachey; PFL 11, p. 118). The German text however is clear: "Wenden wir uns nun von der biologischen Seite her der Betrachtung des Seelenlebens zu, so erscheint uns der 'Trieb' als ein Grenzbegriff ...." (SA 3, p. 85). The German expression here is equivalent to the phrase: "das Gluck wendete sich von ihm", where good fortune is indeed lost, not won. The French translation is in agreement with this reading: "Si nous abandonnons le côté biologique...", in *Métapsychologie* (1952).

On Freud's view, the drive never manifests itself in person: it is only the *Vorstellung* which represents the drive that can become an object for consciousness.[112] If the drive did not attach itself to a representation or else make itself manifest as an affective state (anxiety, happiness etc.), then there would be no way of knowing about the drive. This means that the distinction between "conscious" and "unconscious" is of no use in relation to the drives: the drive itself is neither conscious nor repressed into the dynamic unconscious, but is an unknowable entity postulated by Freud.[113] The representation of a drive can be repressed into the unconscious, but never the drive itself.

It is only because of the multitude of representations attaching themselves to the basic drives – and in such various ways – that the concept of drive can become the *Grundbegriff* of psychoanalysis. The various representations of the drives make up an interconnected network of acts and protoacts to such an extent that it determines our inner, psychic life. Emphasizing the subjective response to the manifestation of the world, Freud (in the energetic phrasing characteristic of the economical conception of the unconscious) says that "almost all the energy with which the apparatus is filled arises from its innate drive-impulses".[114]

Freud's analysis shows that the two poles of the I and the object (and by extension the world as a world of objects) are not to be regarded as given ready-mades but that both are instead constituted by processes of the drives. Thus Freud is here examining the processes which precede the formation of the I and the object, that is, what Husserl calls passive syntheses. The object that becomes associated with the drive may be changed indefinitely during the course of time, according to how the aim of satisfaction is to be most suitably accomplished. This means that the object of the drive is not something that is given in advance, as a pole of reference towards which an intact cogito directs itself: it is constituted by the drives. The connection between drive and object (the

[112] "The Unconscious", PFL 11, p. 179.

[113] "The Unconscious", PFL 11, p. 179. To give an example from everyday life: what is often referred to as "selfpreservation" is generally not taken to manifest itself in the flesh, only the spontaneous reactions that it is supposed to give rise to (instant withdrawal of the hand from excessive heat, etc.).

[114] *Beyond the Pleasure Principle*, PFL 11, p. 279; tr. mod.; cf. p. 306.

"object-pole" in Husserl's terminology) is thus above all a functional relation according to Freud:

> The object [*Objekt*] of a drive is the thing in regard to which or through which the drive is able to achieve its aim. It is what is most variable about a drive and is not originally connected with it, but becomes assigned to it only in consequence of being peculiarly fitted to make satisfaction possible ("Instincts and their Vicissitudes", PFL 11, p. 119; tr. mod.).

Likewise, the analysis of the I shows that it cannot be taken as an unproblematic given but is also the result of processes of the drives, most notably those involved in narcissism.[115] For, as Freud says,

> ... we are bound to suppose that a unity comparable to the I cannot exist in the individual from the start [*eine dem Ich vergleichbare Einheit nicht von Anfang an im Individuum vorhanden ist*]; the I has to be developed [*das Ich muss entwickelt werden*]. The auto-erotic drives, however, are there from the very first [*uranfänglich*] ("On narcissism", PFL 11, p. 69/ SA 3, p. 44; tr. mod.).

Amongst the various sources that led Freud to adopt the hypothesis of narcissism, the strongest is said to be those cases where a disturbance of the libidinal development has occurred (perversion), i.e. where the choice of love-objects is "the own person [*ihrer eigenen Person*]".[116] Thus narcissism is an instance of that particular destiny of the drive named a "turning towards the own person".[117] The narcissistic object-choice represents the sole alternative to the anaclitic object-choice, where the primary caretaker (often the mother) serves as the *Vorbild*:

> We say that the human being has two original sexual objects: herself and the woman who nurses her, and thereby we presuppose a primary

[115] The three most important texts here are "Formulations on the Two Principles of Mental Functioning" (1911), "Instincts and their Vicissitudes" (1915) and "Negation" (1925) where he says: "The opposition between that which is subjective and that which is objective does not exist from the beginning" (PFL 11, p. 440; tr. mod.).

[116] "On narcissism", PFL 11, p. 81/SA 3, p. 54.

[117] "Instincts and their Vicissitudes", PFL 11 p. 124f : "They are plainly seeking themselves as a love-object".

> narcissism in every human being [*wir setzen dabei den primären Narzissmus jedes menschen voraus*].[118]

It is when a part of this proto-I takes another part of itself as its sexual object, that the constitution of the I is propelled.[119] Already at the level of the proto-I, there are drives that both emanate from this and that are directed to it (this is the meaning of the *uranfängliche* auto-erotism); while there at the same time are drives directed outwards, to the world (the self-preservative drives). Thus narcissism proper presupposes the prior formation of the I in order for the love of self to be able to come about; whereas auto-erotism in the form of the auto-erotic drives is a pre-form directed towards an I that has not yet come about. What is required here is "a new psychical action" which leads to a more developed and stable form of the proto-I that eventually becomes the "I".[120] The Freudian I is therefore not a substance since it is characterized by mobility and development.

In the constitution of the I, the role of what he calls the ideal I (*Idealich*) is of central importance, and Freud insists on the role of the primary caretaker (often the mother) in this process. In order for the I to come into being, it must project before itself this *Idealich*, which is the introjected ideal of the mother, thus alterity is involved from the start in the becoming of the subject.[121] In accordance with this, Freud says that the formation of the *Ichideal* "arose from the critical influence of his parents (conveyed to him by the medium of the voice)".[122] The I is thus so to speak whispered into the ear of the infant, arising from the breath of the other. The full scope of this intersubjective context, however extends well beyond any supposedly self-enclosed dualism of the infant

---

[118] "On narcissism", PFL 11, p. 81f/ SA 3, p. 54 (tr. mod.); cf. p. 84/57.

[119] Cf. Lear: "It is only when Freud realizes that an I can be the object of its own sexual investment that the concept of an I becomes a focus of psychoanalytic attention" (*Love and its Place in Nature*, p. 137). See also Ricœur, *De l'interprétation*, p. 129ff.

[120] "On narcissism", PFL 11, p. 69.

[121] "On narcissism", PFL 11, p. 88. As clinical psychoanalytical investigations of infants have shown, the infant tends to die without this caretaking; cf. already the classical studies by R. Spitz (1945, 1946). See also the more recent investigations (based on the works of Dolto) by C. Eliacheff, *À Corps et à Cris. Être Psychoanalyste avec les Tout-Petits* (1993).

[122] "On narcissism", PFL 11, p. 90. For an alternative view, see Laplanche & Pontalis, *The Language of Psychoanalysis*, p. 144f.

and the mother, as Freud is well aware of. For included in this process, are all those engaged in her education, as well as the "innumerable and indefinable" host of people from her surrounding world, her fellow men and public opinion (*Die Mitmenschen, die öffentliche Meinung*).[123] With the second topic (the division of the psychic apparatus into the I, the Id and the *Über-Ich*), the ideal-I (and the related phenomena of guilt, conscience etc.) is transposed into the *Über-Ich*. Later on, Freud connects this open intersubjectivity with the notions of generativity, tradition and inherited endowment:

> ... the installation of the *Über-Ich* can be described as a succesful instance of identification with the parental agency. [...] Thus a child's *Über-Ich* is in fact constructed on the model not of its parents but of its parents *Über-Ich*; the contents which fill it are the same and it becomes the vehicle of tradition and of all the time-resisting judgements of value which have propagated themselves in this manner from generation to generation (*New Introductory Lectures on Psychoanalysis*, PFL 2, p. 95, 99).

Freud's focus on the intersubjective and communicative context into which the subject is born thus extends beyond the dual infant-mother relation to open intersubjectivity in a generative sense.

5. Repetition, masochism and the deathdrive

In this final section on Freud, the analysis approaches phenomena such as originary masochism and the deathdrive, as this manifests itself in the compulsion to repeat. Although Freud had come to regard the specific type of neurosis that manifests itself only in relation to the analyst in the clinical situation, i.e. the transference neurosis, as a manifestation of what he already in 1914 called the compulsion to repeat (*Wiederholungszwang*), he at the time could not fully understand why such a phenomenon arose in the psychoanalytic meeting.[124] Freud had long ago come to realize that in order for the analysis to be effective, it was not sufficient that the analysand be *told* what it is that makes her suffer: it is

[123] "On narcissism", PFL 11, p. 90. Freud stresses the medium of the voice in this process.

[124] See "Remembering, Repeating and Working-Through", SE 12 p. 150ff.

decisive that the subject lives through the experience (*Erlebnis*) and thus not only intellectually comes to accept a given interpretation.

This calls for an extensive amount of psychic work on the side of the analysand that Freud with a happy choice of words calls working through (*Durcharbeiten*). This process is however hindered by several kinds of (repressed) resistances that arise along the way, the most threatening and powerful of which is what Freud calls the "negative therapeutic reaction", where every expected advance is met with a worsening of the condition of the analysand, as though she wishes to suffer instead of being cured.[125] But also in less dramatic forms of resistance, the same factor that underlies the negative reaction is operative, which indicates that we are at the root of that in the subject which opposes her well-being in the world.[126]

The question of the relation between the compulsion to repeat and the pleasure principle stands at the centre of *Beyond the Pleasure Principle*. Freud now emphasizes the danger that is involved when the neurotic behaviour is so to speak invited to the new arena that the psychoanalytic situation represents. The "transference neurosis" is therefore to be kept within the narrowest limits, and as much as possible

[125] The "deterioriation" that may occur in analysis was discussed in the "Remembering, Repeating and Working-Through"; but it was only in *The Ego and the Id* that this was more fully treated; PFL 11, p. 390ff. Here Freud launches a whole series of negative reactions, correlated with different types of neurosis, and they are all centered around a somewhat vaguely outlined moral sense of "guilt", which finds satisfaction by way of illness: "But as far as the patient is concerned this sense of guilt is dumb; it does not tell him he is guilty; he does not feel guilty, he feels ill. This sense of guilt expresses itself only as a resistance to recovery which it is extremely difficult to overcome" (PFL 11, p. 391). The much discussed topic of "unconscious feelings" is actually rejected on phenomenological grounds by Freud in "The Unconscious", whereas he in *The Ego and the Id* (§ 5) and "The Economic Problem of Masochism" tries to evade this problem by replacing the talk of "unconscious sense of guilt" with that of a "need for punishment" (cf. PFL 11, pp. 179ff; and 421). However, if one takes the change of attitude involved in psychoanalysis into account, this confusion diminshes quite substantially: within the psychoanalytical setting, the analyst is free to suggest as a reconstructive interpretation that a certain comportment on the part of the analysand is actually the roundabout expression of feelings of which she is not aware. Outside of the psychoanalytical situation, such claims hardly have any meaning.

[126] See *The Ego and the Id*: "The description we have given applies to the most extreme instances of this state of affairs, but in a lesser measure this factor has to be reckoned with in very many cases, perhaps in all comparatively severe cases of neurosis" (PFL 11, p. 392).

is to be forced into the channels of memory so that only a minor part is left to emerge as repetition.[127] For if the latter takes the upper hand the analysand may no longer be able to recognize "that what appears to be reality is in fact only a reflection [*Spiegelung*] of a forgotten past".[128] The compulsion to repeat, as manifested by the negative therapeutic reaction in the transference neurosis, is the ontic guide which leads Freud to announce the hypothesis of a deathdrive in *Beyond the Pleasure Principle*, which hereafter is regarded as equiprimordial with the lifedrive:

> If we are to take it as a truth that knows no exception that everything living dies for *internal* reasons, and returns [*zurückkehrt*] to the inorganic, then we shall be compelled to say that *the aim of all life is death* (PFL 11, p. 311/ SA 3, p. 248; tr. mod.)

In the decisive article on the "Economic problem of masochism" (1924), the first task of the lifedrive (or the sexual drive, Eros) is to keep the deathdrive under control, to make it harmless, a task which it accomplishes by *diverting it outwards*, towards objects in the external world: then it is called destructive drive, the drive for mastery, or will to power (*Destruktionstrieb, Bemächtigungstrieb, Wille zur Macht*).[129] As this already indicates, the lifedrive and the deathdrive never appear isolated from each other, but always in fusions (*Triebmischung*) of various degrees: in fact, unless it is tinged with sexuality, the deathdrive could never manifest itself.[130] This sexually infused deathdrive, which is diverted from its originary direction inwards, is sadism proper when directed towards other people, just as it, when directed towards the world, is bent on destruction and will to power.[131] But the sexual drive

[127] *Beyond the Pleasure Principle*, PFL 11, p. 289.
[128] *Beyond the Pleasure Principle*, PFL 11, p. 289.
[129] "Economic problem of masochism", PFL 11, p. 418.
[130] See *Civilization and its Discontents*, PFL 12, p. 312f. Henry's criticism of Freud for falling into "enormous contradictions" concerning the relation between the deathdrive and Eros in *Beyond*, is unfounded if we take into account the development that was reached already in the article on masochism; see *La Généalogie de la psychanalyse*, p. 382f.
[131] This sadistic drive, can in a later movement be turned back onto the self, as in the case of melancholia, in which case it gives rise to a secondary form of masochism: "That which now dominates the *Über-Ich*, is like a pure culture of the deathdrives [*wie eine Reinkultur des Todestriebes*], and often enough it actually

is not able to reroute and thus ward off the deathdrive in its entirety, and this failure on the part of the libido is what enables that most enigmatic aspect of the *Triebleben* to make its appearance:

> Another part of the drive does not partake in this transposition outwards [*Verlegung nach aussen*], it remains within the organism, and with the help of the accompanying sexual excitation [...], becomes libidinally bound there. It is in this part that we must recognize the originary, erogenous masochism" ("The Economic Problem of Masochism", PFL 11, p. 418/ SA 3, p. 347; tr. mod.).

This is the *triebmässige* foundation of the negative therapeutic reaction, which is the greatest danger to a successful analysis, although the eroticized, originary masochistic drive in such cases has been desexualized into that which Freud calls "moral masochism". The existence of masochism in the *Triebleben* of the subject poses considerable problems for Freud's previous classification of the drives, while at the same time providing him with a decisive clue to the whole analysis of the drives, whereby the configuration of human life as such gains considerably in focus. For if human life in general is believed to be directed towards pleasure, or at least the avoidance of pain and displeasure, i.e. if it is wholly based on the pleasure principle (which Freud had assumed up until *Beyond...*), then masochism is truly incomprehensible.

When the subject posits pain and unpleasure as the aims of life, then the pleasure principle is paralysed, the guardian of our psychic life, as Freud says, "has become narcotized".[132] The desire to inflict pain upon the self is on Freud's analysis not restricted to the specific sexual and strongly symbolical act between the sadist and the masochist, but is seen in the light of a much more general theory, of which the eroticized masochism is only the most striking manifestation.

Here the main thing is the suffering *itself*, rather than the condition that this be caused by another person which is central in sexual masochism. In such clinical cases of the compulsion to repeat as the negative reaction to therapy, the gain that the illness brings with it is the satisfaction of an unconscious sense of guilt, or as Freud shortly thereafter prefers to put it, a need for punishment:

---

succeeds in driving the I into death" (*The Ego and the Id*, PFL 11, p. 394/SA 3, p. 319f; tr. mod.).

[132] "The Economic Problem of Masochism" (1924), PFL 11, p. 413; tr. mod.

> The satisfaction of this unconscious sense of guilt is perhaps the most powerful bastion in the subject's (usually composite) gain from illness – in the sum of forces which struggle against his recovery and refuse to surrender his state of illness. The suffering that the neuroses brings with it, is precisely that part which makes them valuable to the masochistic tendency ("The Economic Problem of Masochism", PFL 11, p. 421).

If we go back to the unsolved problem of *Beyond the Pleasure Principle*, we now see that the relation between actions based on the deathdrive and the pleasure principle can be given a more satisfactory answer. The enigma of experiences that are repeated by the subject although they each time cause unpleasure – the compulsion to repeat – is made less enigmatic once we come to see that such experiences satisfy the demands of the *Über-Ich*. Thus they do not "override the pleasure principle", but give rise to a pleasure that is, paradoxically, experienced as unpleasure – the pleasure of the masochist. That which is pleasure for one system (the *Über-Ich*), can be unpleasure for another (the I). This means that the dominance (*Herrschaft*) of the pleasure principle is maintained, and there is strictly speaking no "beyond".[133]

As Freud notes, the primary difference in their respective modes of givenness is that whereas the lifedrives (covering the self-preservative as well as the sexual drives) are easily recognized due to the role they play in our pre-reflexive self-awareness, the deathdrives operate in profound silence.[134] The deathdrives, unlike the lifedrives, cannot be

---

[133] Both Derrida and Nicolas Abraham have argued that the phenomenological concept of experience is incapable of grasping these metapsychological implications (where pain is experienced as pleasure); see Derrida, "To speculate – on "Freud"" in *Freud and the Post Card* (1987), p. 288ff; and Abraham, *L'écorce et le noyau* (1987) p. 208f. According to Derrida, it is precisely the phenomenon of repression that makes this experience possible, and neither the "classical logos of philosophy" nor phenomenology is able to account for this. Abraham argues that the metapsychological concepts and thus psychoanalytical experience cannot be subjected to the reduction, since phenomenology is restricted to the intentionality of acts; this is the same critique that Merleau-Ponty presented in for instance *Le visible et l'invisible*.

[134] See *Beyond the Pleasure Principle*: "Another striking fact is that the lifedrives have so much more contact with our internal perception – emerging as breakers of the peace and constantly producing tensions whose release is felt as pleasure – while the deathdrives seem to do their work unobtrusively" (PFL 11, p. 337f). See also *The Ego and the Id*: "... we are driven to conclude that the deathdrives are by their nature mute and that the clamour of life proceeds for the most part from Eros" (PFL 11, p.

anchored in concrete experience in any direct way when approached in isolation, but are posited on the basis of a theoretical reconstruction of what must be there, in order to make the most daemonic aspects of subjective life comprehensible.[135]

Although both the deathdrive and the lifedrives are said to be present and operative from the very beginning of life, this difference between them also leads to the situation that whereas the further destinies of the lifedrives are comparatively more easy to follow, those of the deathdrive are often very hard to trace. However, with the establishment of the *Über-Ich*, the destructive drives directed towards the self become fixated within the I, and there constitute one of the greatest threats to the future health and sanity of the subject. Hence it is by tracing the severe dictates from an inner, self-critical agency that the *Schicksale* of the deathdrives can be disclosed.[136]

It is essential to note that this "silence" of the deathdrive does not rule out the phenomenological demand of self-givenness. A major point in the present discussion of Freud has been to show that it is only in so far as something presents itself that cannot be accounted for by other means, that he speaks of the unconscious. This also holds for the deathdrives which becomes clear as soon they are regarded not in isolated abstraction, but in concrete life where they always appear in connection with the lifedrives. That is to say, even the deathdrive is essentially tied to manifestation, whether in the form of a constant readiness for aggression or an unwillingness to work one's way out of a depression (a clinging to despair). Obviously, this also holds outside of the analytical session, in so far as we encounter phenomena that correspond to those that Freud outlined clinically also in everyday life.

---

387); and finally *An Outline of Psychoanalysis*: "So long as the deathdrive operates internally, as a death drive, it remains silent; it only comes to our notice when it is diverted outwards as a drive of destruction" (PFL 15, p. 381; tr. mod.).

[135] In *The Interpersonal World of the Infant*, Stern uses results stemming from observation in order to attack the duality of Eros and the deathdrive, in a quite naïve way (p. 239). But this seems bound to fail, considering the fact that Freud clearly stated that the deathdrive does not manifest itself as such: the "silence of the deathdrives" thus implies that the direct observation of infants can neither be taken to confirm nor disqualify the givenness of the deathdrive.

[136] See *The Ego and the Id*, PFL 11, p. 387, 397; "The Economic Problem of Masochism", PFL 11, p. 418f; and *An Outline to Psychoanalysis*, PFL 15, p. 381.

Even if one holds on to the model of conflict as the most basic in Freud's thought, this model will begin to erode of its own accord, as soon as one of the poles of the conflict is seen to be that of strife and dissolution. For the deathdrive, which has no psychical energy of its own at its disposal but has to make use of the libido, would constantly tend to dissolve that which *Eros* gathers and attempts to unite. The most that *Eros* can hope for, is to assure that the deathdrive will be kept in check so as to avoid that the death which inevitably results, will be an "improper" death (premature, for instance).

The role of the self-preservative drives (as a part of the lifedrives) was already in *Beyond the Pleasure Principle* said to be to "assure that the organism shall follow its own path to death, and to ward off any possible ways of returning to inorganic existence other than those which are immanent in the organism itself".[137] As a consequence, there would strictly speaking only be the one drive of the libido, which however is first set in dynamic motion by the equiprimordially operating strive for fragmentation (of unity), dissolution (of synthesis) etc., all in the name of a prolonged and deferred regression. Such an interpretation of the relation between the deathdrive and the libidinal forces of life have led both philosophers and psychoanalysts to regard the former as something resembling a transcendental principle, which serves to ground and make possible that confused assembly of repetitions that make up life.[138]

---

[137] PFL 11, p. 311.

[138] See Gilles Deleuze, *Différence & répétition:* "Il [l'instinct de mort] joue le rôle d'un principe transcendantal, tandis que le principe de plaisir est seulement psychologique. [...] Érôs et Thanatos se distinguent en ceci que Érôs doit être répété, ne peut être vécu que dans la répétition, mais que Thanatos (comme principe transcendantal) est *ce qui donne* la répétition à Éros, ce qui soumet Éros à la répétition. Seul un tel point de vue est capable de nous faire avancer dans les problèmes obscurs de l'origine du refoulement, de sa nature, de ses causes et des termes exacts sur lesquels il porte" (p. 27, 29; my italics; cf. p. 128-153). See also his *Présentation de Sacher-Masoch*, p. 98-105; and (together with Félix Guattari) *L'anti-œdipe*, p. 396ff. Cf. Hans-Dieter Gondek for an analysis of Deleuze's interpretation in *Angst - Einbildungskraft - Sprache. Ein verbindender Aufriss zwischen Freud, Kant und Lacan* (1990), p. 205ff. See also Laplanche & Pontalis, in a similar vein: "What is designated here [the deathdrive] is more than any particular type of instinct – it is rather that factor which determines the actual principle of all instincts" (*The Language of Psychoanalysis*, p. 102). According to Laplanche's analysis in *Life and Death in Psychoanalysis*, "the deathdrive is the very soul, the constitutive principle of libidinal

According to this interpretation the *Gegeneinanderwirken* of Freud's two *Urtriebe* in fact consists in that the deathdrive to a certain extent commands eros, dictates its possibilities and circumscribes its operational area.[139] Thus the model of conflict and the dualism that is inherent in it, is actually jeopardized from the outset by the deathdrive. For if the deathdrive is the basic principle of the metapsychology, then it actually has no foundation, but only the repetitive ongoings of dissolution and destruction of the material provided by the co-originary lifedrives. But this interpretation can be questioned, since it overemphasizes the role of the deathdrive to the detriment of *Eros*. Although hesitant about the precise, inner delimitation of the two major drives even at the end (and for good reasons), Freud's final position seems to be that of an equiprimordiality of *Eros* and the deathdrive such that they always manifest themselves in the mode of originary intertwinement:

> That is to say, as well as *Eros* there was a deathdrive; the phenomenon of life is to be explained through the cooperation and opposition of these two drives. [...] It might be assumed that the deathdrive operated silently within the organism towards its dissolution [...] A more fruitful idea was that a portion of the deathdrive is diverted towards the external world and comes to light as a drive of aggressiveness and destructiveness [*Trieb zur Aggression und Destruktion*]. In this way, the drive itself could be pressed into the service of *Eros*, in that the organism was destroying some other thing, whether animate or inanimate, instead of destroying its own self. Conversely, any restriction of this aggressiveness directed outwards would be bound to increase the self-destruction, which is in any case proceeding. At the same time, one can expect from this example that the two kinds of drives seldom – perhaps never – appear in isolation from each other, but are alloyed with each other in varying and very different proportions and so become unrecognizable to our judgment (*Civilization and its Discontents*, PFL 12, p. 309f /SA 9, p. 246f).

With the gradual unravelling of the deathdrive as a will to destruction both of the self, others and the world Freud is clearly stating something fundamental in psychic life that must be accounted for in any theory of subjectivity, and that has been overlooked by most since Schelling.[140]

---

circulation", p. 124. See also J. Lacan, *Écrits* p. 848.

[139] "Die endliche und die unendliche Analyse", SA *Ergänzungsband,* p. 382f.

[140] In the brief text entitled "Zeitgemässes über Krieg und Tod", written some six months after the outbreak of the first World War, Freud says: "In reality, there is no such thing as 'eradicating' evil. [...] psychoanalytical investigation shows instead

6. Touching foundations: Husserl's genetic phenomenology of childhood

Die Konkretion ist aber immer nur Aufgabe, immerzu in Relativität, immerzu in Horizonten und Auslegung der Horizonte (Husserl, [August, 1936]).

Let us finally turn to Husserl's investigations of genesis in the direction of personal development, starting from the newborn infant and her early interaction with the surrounding world and her primary caretakers.[141] This will allow us to reconnect with the analysis of phenomenological archaeology from earlier on, that served as an introduction to the indirect clarification of repression (Chapter Three, § 2). The question discussed there was how to conceive of the *archai* that make up the "konstitutiven Bauten" of intentional life, and this meant inquiring into the sphere of latent being. The question now is whether this archaeology, as that which reconstructive phenomenology leads to, should also be construed of as childhood and notably the analysis of "transcendental childhood".

The reason why this ambiguity between latency and childhood arises is because "reconstruction" can either follow the transcendental trail and focus on the constitutive layers that make up a sedimented, meaningful lived experience, or else it can follow the natural attitude and instead reconstruct the beginnings of perceptual, predicative etc life which leads to infancy. "Transcendental childhood" is (in at least some texts) construed simply as the person's childhood as a reduced given, following the psychological way.[142]

---

that the deepest essence of human nature [*das tiefste Wesen des Menschen*] consists of *Triebregungen* which are of an elementary nature, which are similar in all men and which aim at the satisfaction of certain primal needs." (PFL 12, p. 68/SA 9, p. 41)

[141] For Husserl's analysis of the role and function of childhood in transcendental philosophy, see for instance XIV Nr. 3, 6, 16 (and the related Beilagen etc.); XXXIV Nr. 1; I, CM §§ 36, 38, 50, 61; HuMat 8 Nr. 17, 46, 55, 95-97; XV Nr. 1, 10f, 14, 22, 33ff; XXIX Nr. 28; VI § 55. See further Cairns, *Conversations with Husserl and Fink*, pp. 12f, 52, 64.

[142] See for instance HuMat 8, p. 435; see further I, CM § 36 p. 108. This phenomenology of the family is a difficult area to interpret since Husserl discusses the "child" and "birth" in many different ways, not always easy to distinguish. Thus "transcendental child/childhood" is also analyzed outside of this transformation of the natural attitude (HuMat 8, p. 431), and what does it signify then? Is transcenden-

Early childhood represents a special case here, since it occurs prior to our having "knowledge" of the world, of physical objects and so forth that could be explicated as world, object etc. in an objective sense.[143] But we can nevertheless follow the intentional references that lead from the present back to our own history and the coming-into-being of experiential life as such.[144] This is again a sphere of being that has to be reconstructed according to Husserl, it is something that must-have-happened-to-me but of which I have no memory.[145] This reconstructive-phenomenological process encounters a limit at conception, after which a growing stock of proto-experiences accumulate (intrauterine life, birth etc.).[146]

Here Husserl even sketches a reconstruction of intrauterine being for the infant and argues that the child in the womb "already has kinaesthesia and by means of this kinaesthetic mobility it has its 'things'".[147] In the same manuscript he goes on to say that the child at birth is thus "already an experiencing I on a higher level, it has already acquired experiences from its existence in the womb, it has its perceptions with its perceptual horizons already".[148] My childhood is obviously "there" and in that sense ready and waiting, but its meaning, its content is not a

---

tal childhood the same as the problem of the "beginning of constitutive genesis" (HuMat 8 p. 279)? Is "my transcendental birth" (E III 9/4a) something different than my worldly birth, considered in transcendental reflection? How does that relate to the "first" and "second" birth as discussed in connection with the bodily apperception of me and the other (XIV, Nr. 1 p. 6)? What is "first" childhood and what is "second" (XXXIX, p. 467f; HuMat 8, p. 74f)? What is the *Urkind* (XV, p. 184, 604)? How does this relate to the *Weltkind* (XXXIV, p. 8f)? The *Gotteskindern* (XXXIX, p. 27f) etc? I know of no study that has investigated this fully, although many of the works discussed here make partial contributions; in particular Yamaguchi (1982) and Depraz (1995).

[143] See I, CM § 38 p. 111f; § 50 p. 141; HuMat 8, Nr 97 p. 443f.

[144] I, CM § 38 p. 112f; § 50 p. 141.

[145] XXIX, Nr. 28. "Die anthropologische Welt" p. 333 [1936]: "Ich weiss auch von meiner Kindheit, und das ich als Kind solche Erkenntnis nicht haben konnte; ich kann aber <meine> Kindheitswelt transzendental rekonstruieren von meiner reifen Wachheit aus. Und so kann ich vielleicht Wege finden, in die wirkliche Kindperiode einzudringen und sie <zu> rekonstruieren in ihrer Weise der Lebenstranszendentalität." Similar analyses abound; see for instance XXXIX, Nr. 43 p. 466f, Nr. 51 p. 582ff; XV, Beilage XLVI p. 608f.

[146] HuMat 8, Nr 97 p. 443f.

[147] XV, Beilage XLV <Das Kind. Die erste Einfühlung> p. 604f [1935].

[148] XV, p. 605.

ready-made that can be transferred intact through time. It clearly manifests itself differently:

> Going back into my childhood, in so far as I have a clear memory to some extent, I not only recollect but also perform a regressive interpretation and correction, and in most cases admittedly also an unconscious falsification of memory by means of apperceptive reinterpretation and reconfiguration of previous experience, a regressive apperception that starts out from what is present now (XV, Nr. 10 p. 141).

Clearly this line of investigation is not a random exploration brought on by the nostalgia of childhood that comes with old age, it is something that is called for by the very method of genetic phenomenology. Husserl even came to suggest that to make the inner-life of the infant understandable by means of a "psychology of infancy" is a "task" that is set before the phenomenologist.[149] From a phenomenological point of view we here approach a genuine limit of the first person perspective, since I can never know about such early experiences as the beginning of life (which admittedly is something that cannot be called an "originary instauration" proper). In order to have an account of my own birth, I cannot simply reach back into my own memory but must instead rely on *hypomnemata*, accounts from other persons and so on. Even so, such accounts would still have to match "experiences" or pre-forms of experiences that are unassailably mine: for my birth is fundamentally my own even though may I have no memories of it.

Stretching this further yet, Husserl also began to explore the idea of a generative phenomenology which deals with the transcendentally constitutive contribution of generations that extend beyond my intragenerational community.[150] This analysis also has consequences for that of the concrete I and intersubjectivity, in so far as it now becomes

[149] XV, Nr. 35 p. 620. Cf. XIV, Nr. 16 p. 335 for an important methodological statement concerning a phenomenology of childhood.

[150] This is the theme of Steinbock's work *Home and Beyond. Generative Phenomenology after Husserl*. As Hopkins (2001) and Bruzina (2001) have pointed out, the transcendental status of phenomenology becomes highly problematic once generative phenomena are taken into account. Although Steinbock's aim is not merely to offer an interpretation of Husserl, the methodological question of evidence and the relation between egology and generativity from within a Husserlian perspective nevertheless becomes a pressing issue that is not solved.

clear that the most basic structural properties of each I are inherited from one's parents, in the continuous inheritance that runs through the "chain of generations".[151] Similarly, empathy as that which merely discloses something that was already there prior to the thematic act, is now also shown to rest in part on archaic "memories" of the tradition that we are born into. This represents complex patterns of pregivenness that are relatively stable but yet undergo constant transformation, as specific cultural patterns arise, are transformed and finally perish. But the appropriation of this "heritage" (*Erbschaft*) is not blind, mechanical repetition but is something that must be unified into an intentional heritage, and thus become if not manifest than at least ideally retrievable for me:

> [...] association or coinciding is transference of meaning, heritage of meaning only in so far as it is transference, heritage of habitualities of acts, so that what is personal is finally inherited on to other persons from the mode of being of the I, from the person. Heritage is not repetition however, but intentional unification, transformation, a covering over and even transformation by means of this covering over. We stand in the tradition, and through the others we become others, by taking up what is personal in them into ourselves, and so necessarily transforming it within us. Generatively: what is inherited is not merely the empty, formal monadic-egoic structure but the inherited properties of character (HuMat 8, Nr. 96 p. 436 [C 17/1931]).

The I is here disclosed as a pre-egoic centering which occurs by means of a passive association that picks up what is handed over from the other. Even the most formal skeleton that the monadic-egoic structure represents is a meaning-structure that is inherited, in the first instance from one's parents but ultimately from a whole chain of generations.[152] This pre-egoic structure, as we have seen, is not mere

[151] See IX, p. 500; XXXIV, p. 287; E III 10/10b-11a [1931]: "Die Rückbezogenheit jedes Wesen auf seine Geburt besagt zunächst: jedes einzelne Wesen hat einen Anfang und von da Einheit seiner Entwicklung in steter Verwirklichung seiner möglichen Selbsterhaltung. Sie besagt weiter: die Entwicklung reicht weiter zurück auf die sich entwickelnden Eltern und Voreltern – durch all diese generative Vergangenheit, von innen her gesehen, geht eine Einheit der Entwicklung hindurch, in der wundersamen Form der Kette der Erzeugungen, die jede einen Anfang durch eine geistige Erbschaft schafft, die in ihrer konkreten Bestimmtheit durch die ganze Kette vorausbestimt ist in ihren Typus, aber individuell bestimmt ist durch die Eltern 'von innen her gesehen'."

[152] HuMat 8, Nr. 96 p. 437.

form but also has concrete contents in the shape of drives, hyle, moods, feelings and kinaesthesia, and also these are in part inherited. The infant receives that which is most proper from its parents and overtakes this in a drive-like manner. The intersubjective dimension of the drive thus assures the givenness of an originary community prior to empathy which is genetically speaking a later phenomenon: it occurs in close connection with the givenness of the world, of lived bodies in the world that are given to me perceptually, or rather that ensure that I can experience myself fully as both body and lived body in the very same process whereby the other is constituted in pairing.

Husserl's late accounts of these processes are in a certain sense developments of insights reached much earlier.[153] In an anticipatory gesture (that reveals a startling affinity with Freud's analysis in "On narcissism" and also with Lacan's *objet a*), Husserl suggested that the voice and the kinaesthetic experience of the movement of the vocal chord, play a fundamental role in the mutual process of self-objectivation and the constitution of the other that takes place in the infant.[154] The voice of the infant calls forth both itself and the other from out of a hidden, common source, and it is this originary community that exists before the intersubjective constitution of the world that is investigated in the later texts. What Husserl finds at this source is – at least at this point – the ceaseless movement of tradition and inheritance of meaning, in its most concrete form as the transposition of drive-like habitualities.[155] At the limit, Husserl's analysis leads to the suggestion that even the most originary drive is already inheritance, a habituality that as Anne Montavont suggestively puts it "has no mem-

[153] See for instance XIV, Beilage XXVIII p. 222f.

[154] "Zur Abhebung von Gespenst und realer Verleiblichung einer Subjektivität mit ihrem Ich ist die Rückbeziehung auf Phantome nicht ganz korrekt. Und nicht Rücksicht genommen ist auf die grundwesentliche Rolle der Verlautbarung in der eigenen selbsterzeugten, zu den eigenen, ursprünglich gegebenen Kinästhesen der Stimmuskeln gehörigen Stimme. Es fehlt das auch in der ursprünglich entworfenen Lehre von der Einfühlung, die zuerst ausgeführt werden müßte. Es scheint, nach meiner Beobachtung, im Kinde die selbsterzeugte und dann analogisch gehörte Stimme zuerst die Brücke für die Ichobjektivierung, bzw. die Bildung des 'alter' abzugeben, bevor das Kind schon eine sinnliche Analogie seines visuellen Leibes mit dem des 'Anderen' hat und haben kann, und erst recht: dem Anderen einen taktuellen Leib und einen Willensleib zuordnen kann." (IV, § 21 p. 95n)

[155] See XV, Beilage XLVI p. 609.

ory" and that is already a response to a more originary calling.[156] Generative phenomenology thus teaches that what is supposedly the most archaic, most originary part of our inner life is partly already the product of a superindividual, generative genesis which becomes sedimented within us: it is something foreign.[157] This position is similar to that reached by Freud, who also speaks of how lived experiences in the individual can, under certain circumstances, become sedimented and so be transformed from secondary to originary passivity.[158]

Freud's account of destructive and self-destructive behaviour has, as we saw, its basis in the deathdrives. These can play a considerable part in personal life when they – as repressed – are repeated again and again, but this return of the repressed can be arrested, understood and made visible by means of psychoanalysis. What can finally be said from the point of view of phenomenology concerning this?

We have seen that Husserl does not postulate a separate kind of drive to account for aggression and destructivity (which would counter his more monist approach of the drives which has its epistemic basis in the clearly monist theory of intentionality). There is, as far as I can see, no aggression-drive that parallels the sexual drives or the curiosity-drive in Husserl's theory of instincts. He does however speak of aggression, animosity as a potential habituality of the I, hatred (on both an individual and a communal level), power, violence and even sexual violence where the will of the other person is "annihilated" etc.[159] In the latter case, which opens with an analysis of the "instinctual I", the higher

---

[156] Montavont, *De la passivité dans la phénoménologie de Husserl*, p. 262.

[157] Here the distinction between originary and secondary passivity becomes less rigid, and Husserl actually speaks of it as the question of a double habituality: "die Fragen der doppelten Habitualität – der erworbenen und der der ursprünglichen Instinkte" (D 14/23b).

[158] "The experiences of the I seem at first to be lost for inheritance; but when they have been repeated often enough and with sufficient strength in many individuals in successive generations, they transform themselves, so to say, into experiences of the *Es*, the impressions of which are preserved by heredity. Thus in the *Es*, which is capable of being inherited, are harboured residues of countless I-existences, and when the I forms its *Über-Ich* out of the *Es*, it perhaps only brings older I-formations back into appearance" (*Das Ich und das Es*, PFL 11, p. 378; tr. mod.).

[159] See XIV, Nr. 9 p. 176ff; XXXIV, Nr. 2 p. 42f; IV, § 29 p. 113f; HuMat 8, Nr. 73 p. 334; XV, Beilage XLIII, Beilage XLVII; E III 10/3-4.

levels of joy and value not only disappear Husserl says, but in their place enters a negativity [*ein Negativum*] which annuls the value.[160]

Apart from this account of aggression in a wide sense, we have also seen that repression is an integrated aspect of perceptual life and also of the living present, and that there is repression amongst the drives. This means that although there is no immediate convergence here between Husserl and Freud, and that this enigmatic yet so important deathdrive in its most specific sense eludes Husserl's structural account of consciousness, the central component parts involved are all there. To show that repression of aggressive instinctual life can also be accounted for in principle by means of genetic phenomenology is an outcome of the indirect attempt at clarification of repression. The difficulties envisaged already at the outset of this project concerning this part of Freudian theory was also one of the factors behind the decision to opt for an indirect rather than a direct approach.

Let me conclude by suggesting a continuation of this path. What happens at this junction where negativity usurps the values and joys of the "instinctual subject" and also of communal life? If we take a step back from the restricted sphere of analysis of individual and communal subjectivity and instead turn our attention towards Husserl's analysis of culture and society, there are more prosperous vistas. For can it not be said that the whole analysis of the crisis of the European sciences is also an analysis of our scientific culture as a culture that in part seeks destruction, even promotes death? Although our late modern scientific culture also enables life and technological solutions that radically improve conditions of living on a planetary scale, it is the same rationality which produces high-tech solutions for the annihilation of life. "The spiritual need of our time has, in fact, become unbearable", Husserl announced already in 1911, and he added that it is a need that leaves no point of our lives untouched.[161]

On Husserl's view, the crisis of the sciences is above all a crisis of psychology.[162] The crisis of psychology is much more serious and

[160] XIV, Nr. 9 p. 177; see p. 164f for the analysis of the *triebhafte Subjekt*.
[161] XXV, *Philosophie als strenge Wissenschaft* p. 56.
[162] On this, see IX, §§ 5f; VI, §

complex than the crises in the other sciences, such as that in mathematics (concerning for instance the foundations of Hilbert's program in the light of Gödel's theorem), since it has to do with what we are ourselves and who we are. There is, Husserl says in the introduction to the lectures on passive synthesis, a "deeper and more consequential tragedy of modern scientific culture that what one is in the habit of lamenting in scientific circles".[163] The leading back of all the sciences to phenomenology as a transcendental logic is Husserl's well-known reply, whereby it would become possible not only to calculate the world but to understand it:

> To be sure, only transcendental logic allows one to understand completely that the positive sciences can only bring about a relative, one-sided rationality, a rationality that leaves in its wake a complete irrationality as its necessary counterpart. But only a comprehensive rational science is science <in> the highest sense, like ancient philosophy originally wanted to be (XVII, p. 355f/CW 9, p. 7).

In the development and conceptualization of this more encompassing view of rationality that includes the "irrational", Husserl and Freud are fighting the same battle and on the same side. And one of the most important motives behind Freud's postulation of the deathdrive came from precisely this scientific culture of the deathdrive: the repetition of bad dreams amongst shell-shocked war veterans. Freud in his seminal but today little read texts on war suggests both that the lust to aggression and destruction is an ineradicable part of subjective life, and that psychoanalysis holds important keys in how to avoid the fulfilment of these drives.[164] In a philosophy to come, which would be as much a psychoanalysis to come, the new conceptualization of reason that this points to should play an important part.

---

[163] XVII, Ergänzende Text IV p. 353/ CW IX, p. 4 [1921].

[164] See "Zeitgemässes über Krieg und Tod" from 1915, and above all "Warum Krieg?" from 1932; both in SA 9.

CONCLUSION

The central argument that has been developed throughout the book is that the structure of the *lebendige Gegenwart* as the core of Husserl's theory of passivity, consists of preliminary forms of bodily kinaesthesia, feelings and drives in a constantly ongoing process, where repression occurs as a necessary part of all constitution. The clarification of Freudian repression thus consists in two steps: first by showing that it presupposes a broad conception of consciousness such as that presented by Husserl's genetic phenomenology, and secondly by presenting a plausible interpretation of the relevant aspects of the latter centered around the living present.

It has been argued that in order to begin to evaluate the philosophical relevance of Freud's theory of the unconscious and in particular repression from the point of view of phenomenology, it is not enough to limit oneself to the works published by Husserl with the often predominantly static conception of phenomenology one finds therein. The importance and depth of Freud's analyses have forced us to explore all the resources of transcendental phenomenology, which has meant drawing to a large extent on material from Husserl's *Nachlass*, and has from there led us to a careful reflection on its methodological assets. A systematic presentation of genetic phenomenology that shows how the "I" is constituted in the living present in a necessary and constant cooperation with that which is foreign to the I, has also made it possible to display the function of repression in phenomenology.

The direct and the indirect approaches that have structured this investigation have both advantages and weaknesses. The main advantage of the direct approach is that it presents examples of Husserl's thought that come closer to psychoanalytical thought than is perhaps generally assumed, although this closeness was ultimately deemed to be insufficient by itself. The advantage of the indirect approach on the other hand is that it is totally integrated with transcendental phenomenology, indeed what is presented under the "indirect" approach is simply an interpretation of the deepest structure of the living present that genetic phenomenology has reached. It is therefore not tailored to meet the specific interest that guides this investigation, nor is it adapted for a psychoanalytically coloured exposition of phenomenology.

The value of the indirect approach for the specific question concerning a phenomenological clarification of psychoanalytical repression instead comes from the configuration of the living present, which makes up the "the concrete originary reality of phenomenology, to which all transcendental self-understanding has to come back in all its infinitely progressing work of interpretation".[1] The basic structure of the living present is presented as a self-transcending proto-unity which is centred around drives, feelings and kinaesthesia and whose main task it is to account for the constitution of the world, the other and the self in its constant negotiation with the many forms of otherness that it encounters. This wider framework of concrete subjectivity connects with Freud's analysis of repression, which is presented precisely as something foreign within us that lives on despite its being kept away from consciousness. It is therefore only by means of a certain overlapping between the direct and the indirect approaches that a clarification of repression can finally be reached.

The aim of this book has been to investigate the possibilities of a phenomenological clarification of Freudian repression, as a central aspect of what constitutes the dynamic unconscious. It has been argued (in Chapter One) that repression consists in the process of keeping contents within the psyche away from consciousness, and that this holds for both phenomenology and psychoanalysis. The phenomenological analysis of repression started out with examples from the perceptual

[1] In B III 9/10 [1931] Husserl speaks of the *lebendige Gegenwart* as an "originary phenomenon" (*Urphänomen*) and determines this as "die konkrete Urwirklichkeit der Phänomenologie, auf die alle transzendentale Selbstverständigung in ihrer unendlich aufsteigenden Auslegungsarbeit zurückgehen muss".

sphere, not because Husserl wished to restrict his fuller analysis of consciousness to a limited sphere of neatly isolated experiences, but because he was convinced that this was the only way to get a hold of the more complex issues he knew any serious philosophical investigation of conscious life is up against.

Unlike Heidegger, Husserl was not a prodigious reader, but in 1913 he acquired Jung's recently published book *Versuch einer Darstellung der psychoanalytischen Theorie* (which is based on the lectures held in New York in 1912).[2] Unlike the few works he had by Freud, this book shows clear signs of being read, and certain passages are heavily marked. In particular, Husserl has underlined and marked with double lines in the margin some passages where Jung speaks of association as a privileged means to disclose what is repressed.[3] Holenstein, after having presented an overview of Husserl's theory of association, comes to the conclusion that the influence of psychoanalytical thought on transcendental phenomenology is zero.[4] In a similar vein, Cairns and Fink objected strongly to Husserl in a conversation from 1932 when he presented the idea – well known from the lectures on passive synthesis, and taken up again by Landgrebe in his editorial work that resulted in the book *Erfahrung und Urteil* – that representifying consciousness (such as involuntary memories) can repress the "original impressional contents".[5] But as we have seen, this idea of repression at the perceptual level is actually a central part of Husserl's mature theory of perception, and furthermore (as Bernet has shown), it is stretched out to the analyses of the relation between presentifying and representifying consciousness which is fundamental to the genetic investigations.[6]

---

[2] See HuDo I, p. 183. Jung's book is in Husserl's private library at the Husserl-archives in Leuven. It is to be noted that Jung at this time had not yet deviated far from Freudian psychoanalysis (which he subsequently did), even though these nine lectures are considered to initiate the break.

[3] These passages are on p. 2-8, 114-124 in Jung (1913). It is unclear when Husserl read this work.

[4] Holenstein (1972), p. 321f.

[5] See Cairns, *Conversations with Husserl and Fink*, p. 91f: "This extraordinary account awoke lively objections from both Fink and me." See also Klaus Conrad, "Das Unbewusste als phänomenologisches Problem" [1957], p. 193f.

[6] See Bernet (2002), p. 330ff, 340ff.

In order to explain how this occurs, it was deemed necessary to situate Husserl's genetic analyses in the context of the development of his theory of reductions in Chapter Two. The starting point here was to be found in Freud's characterization of the repressed as a foreign body within me, operating without the participation of the I. Picking up the idea first presented by Levinas and later on developed by Franck and Depraz, according to which Husserlian phenomenology is an exemplary interpretation of alterity, it was argued that the theme of otherness (in its rich and varied modes) is a suitable starting point from which to analyze repression. The proper investigation of this hypothesis called for a differentiation of the most central ways to the reduction, where the psychological way was found to represent a privileged point of entry to a transcendental account of the lived experiences at stake. It was further argued that the psychological way relies on and presupposes the validity of the Cartesian way, but that the latter also called for a necessary supplementation in order to avoid transcendental phenomenology becoming a sterile project. This supplement comes from two directions: the ontology of the life-world and the psychological experiences of everyday life.

A particular problem that Freud's analyses clearly pointed to, was that what is repressed remains active even though it is kept away from consciousness. This poses a distinct question to any philosophy of consciousness: how is it possible to give an explanation of this "activity" (which is genuinely passive, in the sense that it occurs without the participation of the I), without betraying its character of being unconscious? This question, addressed already in the Introduction and Chapter One, is the main question that the preceding chapters have tried to give an answer to. When speaking of explanation here, it is important to note that Husserl attempts to go beyond the position which ties scientific explanation primarily to the possibility of prediction. As explained in *Krisis*, the main issue is not to secure objectivity but to come to understand it:

> One must finally achieve the insight that no objective science, no matter how exact, explains or ever can explain anything in a serious sense. To deduce is not to explain. To predict, or to recognize the objective forms of the composition of physical or chemical bodies and to predict

> accordingly – all this explains nothing but is in need of explanation. The only true way to explain is to make transcendentally understandable (VI, § 55 p. 193/Engl. tr. p. 189).

The transcendental explanation of repression that was attempted in a first step in Chapter Three, focussed on the analyses of inner time-consciousness and in particular on the structure of the living present as the core of Husserl's theory of passivity. The starting point was the archaeology of subjectivity that came to the fore in early genetic-phenomenological investigations, which suggested the need for a new methodology and also a new conceptuality. Dismantling lived experience by means of a questioning backwards of the process of constitution, led to the need to reconstruct those constitutive layers that were beyond the reach of the I. A decisive step was taken when it could be shown that the living present was the source of the unconscious, and that the disclosure of this structure could not be reached by means of the reduction as portrayed in static phenomenology. Husserl here introduced what he called the radicalized reduction, which sought to methodologically secure the access to these levels of originary constitution. In a next step, it was shown how there was, beyond the pre-egoic level that was attained in the public discourse (the lectures on passive synthesis), an even more originary proto-I operative that no longer merited the name of "I", properly speaking. The originary I (*Ur-Ich*) is called "I" only by equivocation, since the ordering of the personal pronouns (I, you, we, they etc.) is no longer (or rather, not yet) applicable here.

At this level of constitutive analysis, Husserl points to two integrated aspects that were deemed essential for the coming-to-be and the maintenance of this originary "I": de-presentification and self-alienation. This double process is constantly operative in the anonymity of the I, and it is responsible for the constitution of the I as the manifest being I can find in, for instance, self-reflection. Husserl is here giving a deconstructive analysis of subjectivity, by pointing out that the differentiation of the ego – alter ego structure that we find in the natural attitude (and also in static phenomenology), has its source in both a temporal movement away from presence (the past and the future) and a movement away from what is not yet a proto-I, guided by a kind of pre-empathic flight into the other person.

This analysis poses succinct problems for the phenomenology of higher order accounts of subjectivity and intersubjectivity, and therefore it was necessary to provide an analysis of individuation in terms of Husserl's theory of monadology. Also here it was shown that new aspects of the theory of reduction had been worked out by Husserl, and this was approached at first as the intersubjective reduction which set out to show that if the reduction was carried through in a sufficiently radical way, then the reduction led not only to the I but also to the other person whom I am empathically tied to, and vice versa. As a companion to this reduction, the universal reduction showed that in a further step it is not only the restricted duality of ego – alter ego that can be reached, but a multi-headed subjectivity. This is the most expansive part of Husserl's late theory of reductions, in that when combined with the radicalized reduction, it leads to originarily streaming intersubjectivity which is the expression of an intentionality that is implicated in all egoic intentional life. Husserl calls this "communalization" and it corresponds to the potentiality of a consciousness of the world. This is the source of genuine objectivity, and the disclosure of this complex is a good example of a transcendental explanation.

In Part II the attempted clarification of repression was mainly based on the methodological insights that were developed in Part I, as a necessary framework to address the main question. On the basis of this framework, three thematic encounters between psychoanalysis and phenomenology occurred that dealt with temporality, association and the drives, which were discussed in the final three chapters. In Chapter Four, the central theme was the temporality of the unconscious, and it started by presenting the two texts by Husserl where he mentions Freud by name. The outcome of this discussion was to show that there is a real point of connection between Husserl and Freud on the theme of the repressed unconscious, which could be strengthened by taking into account those texts where Husserl refers to psychoanalytical themes in a laxer sense (the direct and the indirect approaches). It became clear that the philosophical problem that repression poses – being operative while being kept away from consciousness – was left as an open question by Husserl in these texts. The most fundamental question here concerns the connection between consciousness and the unconscious, and this must be sought in the passive syntheses of inner time-consciousness. Genetic phenomenology could nevertheless be seen as a preliminary interpretation of psychoanalysis, according to Husserl. Seen from the perspective of these two texts, the whole endeavour in this book has been to explain what such an interpretation might consist of.

Thereafter, Husserl's analysis of consciousness of conflict was presented with the aim of showing that even when there are gaps in consciousness, the syntheses of inner time-consciousness are operative. Freud often discusses the unconscious in terms of "gaps" in consciousness and the hypothesis was that also these must be understood as ultimately being connected by means of passive syntheses. This suggestion was important to have in mind before facing Freud's idea that the unconscious is actually timeless. It was shown that there are strong philosophical arguments against the timelessness of the unconscious, and also that Freud's clinical analyses provide good counter-examples. To find the genuine discussion of the temporality of the unconscious, we turned towards Freud's concept of *Nachträglichkeit*. This notion poses a great challenge to any phenomenological account of consciousness, and the attempt was made to show that an interpretation of horizonal consciousness would be able to locate central aspects of *Nachträglichkeit* as an integrated feature of subjective life.

In Chapter Five, the problem of association stood at the centre, and taking our cue from the basic rule of clinical psychoanalysis – free association – it was argued that the analysis of passive constitution in genetic phenomenology can show how free association functions. This chapter supplements the previous discussions of notably temporality by showing the necessary co-functioning of time and affection in Husserl's theory, and thus gives a more coherent account of passive synthesis. It was argued that free association is a decisive methodological tool for the interpretation of the repressed unconscious for Freud. Care was taken to show that association is indeed a transcendental concept for Husserl, and particular emphasis was given to the analysis of sedimentation. At the end of that chapter, the direct approach was taken up again, now in connection with the central notions of perseverance and of psychic reality. Husserl's analysis of perseverance of the sedimented experiences was shown to be decisive for clarifying the main question concerning repression. The final theme in this chapter concerned the possibility to come to understand what Freud means by psychic reality in terms of Husserl's theory of intentionality.

The final Chapter Six examined drives and instincts in both Freud and Husserl. The previous investigation has followed a double trajectory – an analysis of the structure of the living present as the source point of intentionality, and an analysis of the repressed unconscious – and both of these are brought to an end with the investigation of the drives. It was argued that the deepest genetic accounts of the living present show repression to be operative also here. Although this could have been presented at an earlier stage of the investigation, it was deemed appropriate to await the fuller presentation of the structure of the living present as including also the drives before doing so. The drives or instincts are by Husserl regarded as fully integrated aspects of the living present and there are constant processes of repression, inhibition and covering going on there. This analysis continues the previous investigations of temporality and association, and it was argued that association as the universal principle of passive constitution plays a pivotal role in all pre-constitution. Conceptual clarifications concerning the various kinds of drives and instincts that Husserl and Freud employ were presented. It was argued that the drives are the basic concepts of Freudian metapsychology, and their dual role as Eros and deathdrive was examined. Towards the end, Husserl's archaeology of subjectivity was approached once more, now in terms of childhood. The psychological way to the reduction opened for a discussion of the centrality and importance of childhood in order to understand adult life and, by extension, rationality. It was argued that repression and alterity is central also for generative phenomenology.

BIBLIOGRAPHY

Works by Husserl

1. Works published in the *Husserliana* edition:

a) *Gesammelte Werke*

I *Cartesianische Meditationen und Pariser Vorträge*, Hrsg. S. Strasser (Den Haag: Nijhoff, 1963)

II *Die Idee der Phänomenologie. Fünf Vorlesungen*, Hrsg. W. Biemel (Den Haag: Nijhoff, 1973)

III/1 *Ideen zu einer reinen Phänomenologie und phänomenologischen Philosophie. Erstes Buch: Allgemeine Einführung in die Phänomenologie*, Hrsg. K. Schuhmann, (Den Haag: Nijhoff, 1976)

III/2 *Ideen zu einer reinen Phänomenologie und phänomenologischen Philosophie. Erstes Buch: Allgemeine Einführung in die Phänomenologie. Ergänzende Texte (1912-1929)*, Hrsg. K. Schuhmann, (Den Haag: Nijhoff, 1976)

IV *Ideen zu einer reinen Phänomenologie und phänomenologischen Philosophie. Zweites Buch: Phänomenologische Untersuchungen zur Konstitution*, Hrsg. M. Biemel (Den Haag: Nijhoff, 1952)

V *Ideen zur einer reinen Phänomenologie und phänomenologischen Philosophie. Drittes Buch: Die Phänomenologie und die Fundamente der Wissenschaften*, Hrsg. M Biemel (Den Haag: Nijhoff, 1971)

VI *Die Krisis der europäischen Wissenschaften und die transzendentale Phänomenologie. Eine Einleitung in die phänom-*

enologische Philosophie, Hrsg. W. Biemel, (Den Haag: Nijhoff, 1976)

VII *Erste Philosophie (1923/4). Erster Teil: Kritische Ideengeschichte* Hrsg. R. Boehm (Den Haag: Nijhoff, 1956)

VII *Erste Philosophie (1923/4). Zweiter Teil: Theorie der phänomenologischen Reduktion*, Hrsg. R. Boehm (Den Haag: Nijhoff, 1959)

IX *Phänomenologische Psychologie. Vorlesungen Sommersemester 1925*, Hrsg. W. Biemel (Den Haag: Nijhoff, 1968)

X *Zur Phänomenologie des inneren Zeitbewusstseins (1893-1917)*, Hrsg. W. Biemel (Den Haag: Nijhoff, 1969)

XI *Analysen zur passiven Synthesis. Aus Vorlesungs- und Forschungsmanuskripten (1918-1926)*, Hrsg. M. Fleischer (Den Haag: Nijhoff, 1966)

XII *Philosophie der Arithmetik. Mit ergänzenden Texte (1890-1901)*, Hrsg. L. Eley (Den Haag: Nijhoff, 1970)

XIII *Zur Phänomenologie der Intersubjektivität. Texte aus dem Nachlass. Erster Teil: 1905-1920*, Hrsg. I. Kern (Den Haag: Nijhoff, 1973)

XIV *Zur Phänomenologie der Intersubjektivität. Texte aus dem Nachlass. Zweiter Teil: 1921-1928*, Hrsg. I. Kern (Den Haag: Nijhoff, 1973)

XV *Zur Phänomenologie der Intersubjektivität. Texte aus dem Nachlass. Dritter Teil: 1929-1935*, Hrsg. I. Kern (Den Haag: Nijhoff, 1973)

XVI *Ding und Raum. Vorlesungen 1907*, Hrsg. U. Claesges (Den Haag: Nijhoff, 1973)

XVII *Formale und transzendentale Logik. Versuch einer Kritik der logischen Vernunft*, Hrsg. P. Janssen (Den Haag: Nijhoff, 1974)

XVIII *Logische Untersuchungen. Erster Band: Prolegomena zur reinen Logik*, Hrsg. E. Holenstein (Den Haag: Nijhoff, 1975)

XIX/2 *Logische Untersuchungen. Zweiter Band: Untersuchungen zur Phänomenologie und Theorie der Erkenntnis*, ed. U. Panzer, Haag: Nijhoff, 1984,

XXIII *Phantasie, Bildbewusstsein, Erinnerung. Zur Phänomenologie der anschaulichen Vergegenwärtigungen. Texte aus dem Nachlass (1898-1925)*, Hrsg. E. Marbach (Den Haag: Nijhoff, 1980)

XXIV *Einleitung in die Logik und Erkenntnistheorie. Vorlesungen 1906/07*, Hrsg. U. Melle (Den Haag: Nijhoff, 1984)

XXV *Aufsätze und Vorträge (1911-1921)*, Hrsg. T. Nenon & H. R. Sepp (Den Haag: Nijhoff, 1986)

XXVII *Aufsätze und Vorträge (1922-1937)*, Hrsg. T. Nenon & H. R. Sepp (Den Haag: Kluwer Academic Publishers, 1989)

XXVIII *Vorlesungen über Ethik und Wertlehre (1908-1914)*, Hrsg. von U. Melle, (Den Haag: Kluwer Academic Publishers, 1988)

XXIX *Die Krisis der europäischen Wissenschaften und die transzendentale Phänomenologie. Ergänzungsband: Texte aus dem Nachlass 1934-1937*, Hrsg. R. N. Smid (Dordrecht: Kluwer Academic Publishers, 1993)

XXXI *Aktive Synthesis, aus der Vorlesung "Transzendentale Logik" 1920/1921. ergänzungsband zu "Analysen zur passiven Synthesis"*, Hrsg. R. Breeur (Dordrecht: Kluwer, 2000)

XXXIII *Die Bernauer Manuskripte über das Zeitbewußtsein (1917/1918)*, Hrsg. R. Bernet & D. Lohmar (Dordrecht: Kluwer, 2001)

XXXIV *Zur phänomenologischen Reduktion. Texte aus dem Nachlass (1926-1935)*, Hrsg. S. Luft (Dordrecht: Kluwer Academic Publishers, 2002)

XXXV *Einleitung in die Philosophie. Vorlesungen 1922/1923*, Hrsg. B. Goossens, (Dordrecht: Kluwer, 2002)

XXXVII *Einleitung in die Ethik. Vorlesungen Sommersemester 1920 und 1924*, Hrsg. H. Peucker (Dordrecht: Springer, 2004)

XXXIX *Die Lebenswelt. Auslegungen der vorgegebenen Welt und ihrer Konstitution. Texte aus dem Nachlass (1916-1937)*, Hrsg. R. Sowa (Dordrecht: Springer, 2008)

b) *Materialen*

Husserliana Materialen 8. *Späte Texte über Zeitkonstitution (1929-1934): Die C-Manuskripte*, Hrsg. D. Lohmar (Dordrecht: Springer, 2006)

c) *Dokumente*

Husserliana Dokumente 1. *Husserl-Chronik. Denk- und Lebensweg Edmund Husserls*, Hrsg. K. Schuhmann (Den Haag: Nijhoff, 1977)

Husserliana Dokumente 2/2. Eugen Fink, *VI. Cartesianische Meditation. Teil 2: Ergänzungsband*, Hrsg. G. van Kerckhoven (Dordrecht: Kluwer Academic Publishers, 1988)

Husserliana Dokumente 3. *Briefwechsel, Vol. I-X*, Hrsg. E. Schuhmann & K. Schuhmann (Dordrecht: Kluwer Academic Publishers, 1994)

2. Other works by Husserl

Erfahrung und Urteil: Untersuchungen zur Genealogie der Logik, Hrsg. L. Landgrebe (Hamburg: Meiner, 1985)

Briefe an Roman Ingarden: mit Erläuterungen und Erinnerungen an Husserl, Hrsg. R. Ingarden (Den Haag: Nijhoff, 1968)

"Grundlegende Untersuchungen zum phänomenologischen Ursprung der Räumlichkeit der Natur" (Ms. D 17 [7-9 Mai, 1934]), in Marvin Farber (ed.) *Philosophical Essays in Memory of Edmund Husserl* (New York: Greenwood Press, 1975) pp. 307-325

3. Unpublished manuscripts

A I 36
A V 20
A VI 26
A VI 34
A VII 11
A VII 13
B II 3
B III 3
B III 9
D 14
E III 4
E III 9
E III 10

4. English translations

a) *Collected Works*

1 *Ideas Pertaining to a Pure Phenomenology and to a Phenomenological Philosophy, Third Book: Phenomenology and the Foundations of the Sciences*; tr. T. E. Klein and W. E. Pohl (The Hague: Nijhoff, 1980)

2 *Ideas Pertaining to a Pure Phenomenology and to a Phenomenological Philosophy, First Book: General Introduction to a Pure Phenomenology*; tr. F. Kersten (The Hague: Kluwer Academic Publishers, 1982)

3 *Ideas Pertaining to a Pure Phenomenology and to a Phenomenological Philosophy, Second Book: Studies in the Phenomenology of Constitution*; tr. R. Rojcewicz and A. Schuwer, (The Hague: Kluwer Academic Publishers, 1989)

4 *On the Phenomenology of the Consciousness of Internal Time (1893 – 1917)*; tr. J. B. Brough (The Hague: Kluwer Academic Publishers, 1991)

6 *Psychological and Transcendental Phenomenology and the Confrontation with Heidegger*; ed. & tr. T. Sheehan & R. Palmer (Dordrecht: Kluwer Academic Publishers, 1997)

9 *Analysis Concerning Passive and Active Syntheses. Lectures on transcendental logic*, ed. & tr. A. Steinbock (Dordrecht: Kluwer Academic Publishers, 2001)

10 *Philosophy of Arithmetic. Psychological and Logical Investigations - with supplementary texts from 1887-1901*; tr. D. Willard (Dordrecht: Kluwer Academic Publishers, 2003)

11 *Phantasy, Image Consciousness, and Memory (1898-1925)*; tr. J. B. Brough (Dordrecht: Springer, 2005)

12 *The Basic Problems of Phenomenology. From the Lectures, Winter Semester, 1910-1911*; tr. I. Farin & J. G. Hart (Dordrecht: Springer, 2006)

b) *Other translations*

Formal and Transcendental Logic, tr. D. Cairns (The Hague: Nijhoff, 1969)

Cartesian Meditations. An Introduction to Phenomenology, tr. D. Cairns (The Hague: Nijhoff, 1969)

Experience and Judgment. Investigations in a Genealogy of Logic, tr. K. Ameriks & J. Churchill (Evanston: Northwestern University Press, 1973)

Husserl. Shorter Works, ed. P. McCormick & F. Elliston, (Notre Dame, Indiana: University of Notre Dame Press and Brighton, Sussex: The Harvester Press, 1981)

Logical Investigations, 2 vol.; tr. Findlay, ed. D. Moran (Routledge: London & New York, 2001)

"Philosophy as rigorous science", in Q. Lauer (ed.) *Phenomenology and the Crisis of Philosophy* (New York: Harper & Row, 1965)

The Crisis of European Sciences and Transcendental Phenomenology; tr. D. Carr (Evanston: Nortwestern University Press, 1970)

Works by Freud

a) *Studienausgabe*

Works published in the *Studienausgabe*, 11 volumes, edited by Alexander Mitscherlich, Angela Richards and James Strachey (Frankfurt am Main: Fischer, 1969-1975)

Band 1. *Vorlesungen zur Einführung in die Psychoanalyse / Neue Folge der Vorlesungen zur Einführung in die Psychoanalyse*

Band 2. *Die Traumdeutung*

Band 3. *Psychologie des Unbewussten*

Band 4. *Psychologische Schriften*

Band 5. *Sexualleben*

Band 6. *Hysterie und Angst*

Band 7. *Zwang, Paranoia und Perversion*

Band 8. *Zwei Kinderneurosen*

Band 9. *Fragen der Gesellschaft / Ursprünge der Religion*

Band 10. *Bildende Kunst und Literatur*

Ergänzungsband. *Schriften zur Behandlungstechnik*

b) *Gesammelte Werke*

Works published in *Gesammelte Werke*, 19 volumes (Frankfurt am Main: Fischer, 1991ff)

GW 1. *Werke aus den Jahren 1892-1899*

c) *Engish translations*

Works published in the *Penguin Freud Library*, 15 volumes, translated under the general editorship of James Strachey, edited by Angela Richards and Albert Dickson (Hammondsworth: Penguin Books, 1973-1986).

PFL 1. *Introductory Lectures on Psychoanalysis*

PFL 2. *New Introductory Lectures on Psychoanalysis*

PFL 3. Josef Breuer & Sigmund Freud, *Studies on Hysteria*

PFL 4. *The Interpretation of Dreams*

PFL 5. *The Psychopathology of Everyday Life*

PFL 7. *On Sexuality*

PFL 8. *Case Histories I*

PFL 9. *Case Histories II*

PFL 10. *Psychopathology*

PFL 11. *Metapsychology*

PFL 12. *Civilization, Society and Religion*

PFL 13. *The Origins of Religion*

PFL 14. *Art and Literature*

PFL 15. *Psychoanalysis: its History and Development*

d) *Standard Edition*

Works published in the *Standard edition of the complete psychological works of Sigmund Freud*, 24 volumes, translated under the general editorship of James Strachey in collaboration with Anna Freud, assisted by Alix Strachey and Alan Tyson (London: The Hogarth Press and the Institute of Psychoanalysis, 1953-1974).

SE 3. (1893-1899): *Early Psycho-Analytic Publications*

SE 4. (1900): *The Interpretation of Dreams (First Part)*

SE 11. (1910): *Five Lectures on Psycho-Analysis, Leonardo da Vinci and Other Works*

SE 12. (1911-1913): *The Case of Schreber, Papers on Technique and Other Works*

SE 17. (1917-1919): *An Infantile Neurosis and Other Works*

SE 19. (1923-1925): *The Ego and the Id and Other Works*

e) *Other works by Freud*

Jugendbriefe an Eduard Silberstein 1871-1881 (Frankfurt am Main: Fischer, 1989)

Aus den Anfängen der Psychoanalyse. Briefe an Wilhelm Fliess, Abhandlungen und Notizen aus den Jahren 1887-1902 (London: Imago, 1950)

Briefe an Wilhelm Fliess 1887-1904, Hrsg. J.M. Masson (Frankfurt am Main: Fischer, 1986)

The Complete Letters of Sigmund Freud to Wilhelm Fliess 1887-1904, ed. J. Masson (Cambridge, Massachusetts: Harvard University Press, 1985)

Sigmund Freud – Oskar Pfister. Briefe 1909-1939 (Frankfurt am Main: Fischer, 1963)

Métapsychologie (Paris: Gallimard, 1952)

Works by other authors

Nicolas Abraham, *L'écorce et le noyau* (Paris: Flammarion, 1987)

Paul-Laurent Assoun, *Freud, la philosophie et les philosophes* (Paris: P.U.F., 1976)

BIBLIOGRAPHY

Bégout, Depraz, Mavridis & Nagaï, "Passivité et phénoménologie génétique", in *Alter* 3 (1995), pp. 409-502

Bruce Bégout, *La généalogie de la logique. Husserl, l'antéprédicatif et le catégorial* (Paris: Vrin, 2000)

Frederick Beiser, *The Fate of Reason. German philosophy from Kant to Fichte* (Cambridge, Massachusetts: Harvard University Press, 1993)

Jocelyn Benoist, *Autour de Husserl* (Paris: Vrin, 1994)

Werner Bergmann & Gisbert Hoffmann, "Habitualität als Potentialität: Zur Konkretisierung des Ich bei Husserl", in *Husserl Studies* (1984), pp. 281-305

Rudolf Bernet, "Zur Teleologie der Erkenntnis: Eine Antwort an Rudolf Boehm", in *Tijdschrift voor Philosophie* (1978), pp. 662-668

— "Perception as a Teleological Process of Cognition", in *Analecta Husserliana* vol. 9 (1979), pp. 119-132

— "Bedeutung und intentionales Bewußtsein. Husserls Begriff des Bedeutungsphänomen", in *Studien zur Sprachphänomenologie. Phänomenologische Forschungen 8* (München: Karl Alber, 1979), pp. 31-64

— "Is the Present ever Present? Phenomenology and the Metaphysics of Presence", in *Research in Phenomenology* vol. 12 (1982), pp. 85-112

— "Die ungegenwärtige Gegenwart. Anwesenheit und Abwesenheit in Husserls Analyse des Zeitbewusstseins", in *Zeit und Zeitlichkeit bei Husserl und Heidegger. Phänomenologische Forschungen 14* (München: Karl Alber, 1983), pp. 16-57

— "Einleitung", in E. Husserl, *Texte zur Phänomenologie des inneren Zeitbewusstseins (1893-1917)*, Hrsg. R. Bernet (Hamburg: Meiner, 1985), pp. XI-LXVII

—— "Husserl's Theory of Signs Revisited", in *E. Husserl and the Phenomenological Tradition*, ed. R. Sokolowski (Washington DC: The Catholic University of America Press, 1989), pp. 1-24

—— "Husserl's Concept of the World", in *Crises in Continental Philosophy*, ed. Dallery & Scott (Albany: State University of New York Press, 1990), pp. 3- 21

—— "Délire et réalité dans la psychose", in *Études Phénoménologiques* 15 (1992), pp. 25-54

—— *La vie du sujet. Recherches sur l'interprétation de Husserl dans la phénoménologie* (Paris: PUF, 1994) [1994a]

——"An Intentionality Without Subject or Object?", in *Man and World* 27 (1994), p. 231-255 [1994b]

—— "Inconscient et conscience: sur la nature de la pulsion, du désir, de la représentation et de l'affect", in *Création et événement. Autour de Jean Ladrière*, éd. par J. Greisch et G. Florival (Louvain/Paris: Peeters, 1995)

—— "L'analyse husserlienne de l'imagination comme fondement du concept freudien de l'inconscient", in *Alter* 4 (1996), pp. 43-67 [1996a]

— "The Unconscious between Representation and Drive: Freud, Husserl and Schopenhauer", in *The Truthful and the Good. Essays in Honour of Robert Sokolowski*, ed. J. Drummond & J. Hart (Dordrecht: Kluwer, 1996), pp. 81-95 [1996b]

—— "Husserls Begriff des Phantasiebewußtseins als Fundierung von Freuds Begriff des Unbewußten", in *Grundlinien der Vernunftkritik*, Hrsg. C. Jamme (Frankfurt am Main: Suhrkamp, 1997), pp. 277-306

— "Derrida-Husserl-Freud: the Trace of Transference", in *Alter* 8 (2000), pp. 13-31 [2000a]

— "The Traumatized Subject", in *Research in Phenomenology* Vol. 30 (2000), pp. 160-179 [2000b]

— "Pulsion, plaisir et déplaisir. Essai d'une fondation philosophique des concepts psychanalytiques", in *Philosophie* 71 (2001), pp. 30-47 [2001a]

—— "Désirer connaître par intuition", in *Revue philosophique de Louvain*, tome 99, No. 4 (2001), pp. 613-629 [2001b]

— "Unconscious Consciousness in Husserl and Freud", in *Phenomenology and the Cognitive Sciences* (2002), pp. 327–351

— *Conscience et existence. Perspectives phénoménologiques* (Paris: PUF, 2004)

— "Levinas's critique of Husserl", in *The Cambridge Companion to Levinas*, ed. Critchley & Bernasconi (Cambridge: Cambridge UP, 2004), pp. 82-99

— "Zur Phänomenologie von Trieb und Lust bei Husserl", in *Interdisziplinäre Perspektiven der Phänomenologie. Neue Felder der Kooperation: Cognitive Science, Neurowissenschaften, Psychologie, Soziologie, Politikwissenschaft und Religionswissenschaft*, Hrsg. D. Lohmar & D. Fonfara (Dordrecht: Springer, 2006), pp. 38-53

Rudolf Bernet, Iso Kern and Eduard Marbach, *Edmund Husserl. Darstellung seines Denkens* (Hamburg: Meiner, 1989)

Ludwing Binswanger, *Analyse existentielle et psychanalyse Freudienne* (Paris: Gallimard, 1970)

— *Schizophrenie* (Pfullingen: Neske, 1957).

— *Melancholie und Manie. Phänomenologische Studien* (Pfullingen: Neske, 1960)

— *Wahn* (Pfullingen: Neske, 1965)

Wilfred R. Bion, *Second Thoughts* (London: Heinemann, 1967)

Daniel Birnbaum, *The Hospitality of Presence: Problems of Otherness in Husserl's Phenomenology* (Stockholm: Almqvist & Wicksell International, 1998)

Wolfgang Blankenburg, *Der Verlust der natürlichen Selbstverständlichkeit* (Stuttgart: Enke, 1969)

— "Phänomenologische Epoché und Psychopathologie", in *Alfred Schütz und die Idee des Alltags in den Sozialwissenschaften*, Hrsg. W. M. Sprondel & R. Grathoff (Stuttgart: Enke, 1979), pp. 125-139

Cristopher Bollas *The Shadow of the Object: Psychoanalysis of the Unthought Known* (New York: Columbia University Press, 1989)

Richard Boothby, *Freud as philosopher. Metapsychology after Lacan* (London: Routledge, 2001)

Gerd Brand [1955], *Welt, Ich und Zeit. Nach unveröffentlichten Manuskripten Edmund Husserls* (Den Haag: Nijhoff, 1969)

Jagna Brudzinska, "Die phänomenologische Erfahrung und die Frage nach dem Unbewussten. Überlegungen im Anschluss an Husserl und Freud", in *Interdisziplinäre Perspektiven der Phänomenologie. Neue Felder der Kooperation: Cognitive Science, Neurowissenschaften, Psychologie, Soziologie, Politikwissenschaft und Religionswissenschaft*, Hrsg. D. Lohmar & D. Fonfara (Dordrecht: Springer, 2006), pp. 54-71

— *Assoziation, Imaginäres, Trieb. Phänomenologische Untersuchungen zur Subjektivitätsgenesis bei Husserl und Freud* (diss., 2005) http://deposit.ddb.de/cgi-bin/dokserv?idn=1001710487&dok_var=d1&dok_ext=pdf&filename=1001710487.pdf

Ronald Bruzina, "The Transcendental Theory of Method in Phenomenology; the Meontic and Deconstruction", in *Husserl Studies* 14 (1997), pp. 75–94

— "Limitations: on Steinbock's 'Generative Phenomenology'", in *The new yearbook for pheonmenology and phenomenological philosophy* 1 (2001), pp. 369-376

—— *Edmund Husserl and Eugen Fink: Beginnings and Ends in Phenomenology 1928-1938* (New Haven & London: Yale University Press, 2004)

Dorion Cairns, *Conversations with Husserl and Fink* (Den Haag: Nijhoff, 1976)

Piera Castoriadis-Aulagnier, *La violence de l'interprétation. Du pictogramme à l'énonçé* (Paris: PUF, 1975)

Marcia Cavell, *Becoming a Subject. Reflections in Philosophy and Psychoanalysis* (Oxford: Clarendon Press, 2006)

Ulrich Claesges, *Husserls Theorie der Raumkonstitution* (Den Haag: Nijhoff, 1964)

— "Zeit und kinästhetisches Bewusstsein. Bemerkungen zu einer These Ludwig Landgrebes", in *Philosophische Forschungen* 14 (München: Karl Alber, 1983), pp. 138-151

Klaus Conrad, "Das Unbewusste als phänomenologisches Problem" [1957], in *Beiträge zur Psychologie der Persönlichkeit*, Hrsg. N. Petrilowitsch (Darmstadt: Wissenschaftliche Buchgesellschaft, 1967)

Vincenzo Costa, "Transcendental Aesthetic and the Problem of Transcendentality", in *Alterity and Facticity*, N. Depraz & D. Zahavi ed. (Dordrecht: Kluwer, 1998), pp. 9-28

Françoise Dastur, "Réduction et intersubjectivité ", in *Husserl*, éd. par É. Escoubas et M. Richir (Millon: Grenoble, 1989), pp. 43-64

— "Phenomenology of the Event: Waiting and Surprise", in *Hypatia: A Journal of Feminist Philosophy* Vol. 15, no. 4 (2000), pp. 178-189

— "Derrida and the Question of Presence", in *Research in Pheno-menology* (2006), pp. 45-62

Gilles Deleuze, *Présentation de Sacher-Masoch* (Paris: Minuit, 1967)

— *Différence & répétition* (Paris: PUF, 1969)

Gilles Deleuze & Félix Guattari, *Capitalisme et schizophrénie. L'anti-œdipe* (Paris: Minuit, 1972)

Natalie Depraz, "Temporalité et affection dans les manuscrits tardifs sur la temporalité (1929-1935) de Husserl", in *Alter* 2 (1994) pp. 63-86

— *Transcendance et incarnation. Le statut de l'intersubjectivité comme altérité à soi chez Husserl* (Paris: Vrin, 1995)

— "Pulsion, instinct, désir. Que signifie Trieb chez Husserl? À l'épreuve des perspectives de Freud, Merleau-Ponty, Jonas et Scheler", in *Alter* 9 (2001), pp. 113-125

Natalie Depraz & Dan Zahavi (ed.) *Alterity and Facticity* (Dordrecht: Kluwer Academic Publishers, 1998)

Jacques Derrida, *Le problème de la génèse* [1956] (Paris: PUF, 1990)

— *L'origine de la géométrie* (Paris: PUF, 1962)

— *Edmund Husserl's Origin of Geometry, an Introduction*, tr. J.P. Leavey (Lincoln: University of Nebraska Press, 1989)

— "La phénoménologie et la clôture de la métaphysique" [1966], in *Alter* 8 (2000), pp. 69-84

— *De la grammatologie* (Paris: Minuit, 1967)

— *Of Grammatology*, tr. G. C. Spivak (Baltimore and London: Johns Hopkins University Press, 1976)

— *L'écriture et la différence* (Paris: Seuil, 1967)

— *Writing and Difference*, tr. A. Bass (London: Routledge, 1997)

— *La voix et le phénomène* (Paris: PUF, 1967)

— *Speech and Phenomena*, tr. D. B. Allison & N. Garver (Evanston: Northwestern University Press, 1973)

——*Marges de la philosophie* (Paris: Minuit, 1972)

—— *Margins of Philosophy*, tr. A. Bass
(Brighton, Sussex: The Harvester Press, 1982)

—— *Positions. Entretiens avec Henri Ronse, Julia Kristeva, Jean-Louis Houdebine, Guy Scarpetta* (Paris: Minuit, 1972)

—— *Positions*, tr. A. Bass
(Chichago: University of Chicago Press: 1981)

—— *Glas* (Paris: Galilée, 1974)

—— *Glas*, tr. JP Leavey (Lincoln: University of Nebraska Press, 1990)

—— *La carte postale. De Socrate à Freud et au-delà*
(Paris: Flammarion, 1980)

—— *The Post Card. From Socrates to Freud and Beyond*, tr. A. Bass
(Chicago and London: University of Chicago Press, 1987)

—— *Mal d'archive. Une impression freudienne* (Paris: Galilée, 1995)

—— *Resistances – de la psychanalyse* (Paris: Galilée, 1996)

—— "Let Us Not Forget – Psychoanalysis",
in *The Oxford Literary Review* 12 (1990) pp. 3-7

—— *États d'âme de la psychanalyse* (Paris: Galilée, 2000)

—— *Le toucher, Jean-Luc Nancy* (Paris: Galilée, 2000)

—— *Apprendre à vivre enfin. Entretien avec Jean Birnbaum*
(Paris: Galilée, 2005)

Alwin Diemer, "La phénoménologie de Husserl comme métaphysique",
in *Les Études Philosophiques* 9 (1954), pp. 21-49

—— *Edmund Husserl. Versuch einer systematischen Darstellung seiner Phänomenologie* (Meisenheim am Glan: Anton Hain K.G., 1956)

BIBLIOGRAPHY

James Dodd, *Crisis and Reflection. An Essay on Husserl's* Crisis of the European Sciences (Dordrecht: Kluwer Academic Publishers, 2004)

John Drummond, "Husserl on the Ways to the Performance of the Reduction", in *Man and World* (1975), pp. 47-69

Knut Ebeling & Stefan Altekamp (Hrsg.), *Die Aktualität des Archäologischen. Wissenschaft, Medien, Künste* (Frankfurt am Main: Fischer, 2004)

Caroline Eliacheff, *À corps et à cris. Être psychanalyste avec les tout-petits* (Paris: Éditions Odile Jacobs, 1993)

Eugen Fink, *VI. Cartesianische Meditation: Teil I: Die Idee einer transzendentalen Methodenlehre.* Texte aus dem Nachlass Eugen Finks (1932) mit Anmerkungen und Beilagen aus dem Nachlass Edmund Husserls (1933/34). Husserliana Dokumente II/1; Hrsg. H. Ebeling, J. Holl and G. van Kerckhoven (Dordrecht: Kluwer Academic Publishers, 1988)

— *VI. Cartesianische Meditation: Teil II: Ergänzungsband.* Texte aus dem Nachlass Eugen Finks (1932) mit Anmerkungen und Beilagen aus dem Nachlass Edmund Husserls (1933/34). Husserliana Dokumente II/2; Hrsg. G. van Kerckhoven (Dordrecht: Kluwer Academic Publishers, 1988)

— "Das Problem der Phänomenologie Edmund Husserls" [1939], in *Studien zur Phänomenologie. 1930–1939* (Den Haag: Nijhoff, 1966), pp. 179–223

Didier Franck, *Chair et corps. Sur la phénoménologie de Husserl* (Paris: Minuit, 1981)

— "La chair et la constitution temporelle", in *Phénoménologie et métaphysique*, éd. par J.-L. Marion & G. Planty-Bonjour (Paris: PUF, 1984), pp. 125-156.

Birgit Frostholm, *Leib und Unbewußtes. Freuds Begriff des Unbewußten interpretiert durch den Leib-Begriff Merleau-Pontys* (Bonn: Bouvier, 1978)

BIBLIOGRAPHY

Hans-Georg Gadamer, *Wahrheit und Methode. Grundzüge einer philosophischen Hermeneutik.* Gesammelte Werke Bd. 1 (Tübingen: Mohr, 1990)

Moritz Geiger, "Fragment über den Begriff des Unbewußten und die psychische Realität" in *Jahrbuch für Philosophie und phänomenologische Forschung* 4 (1921), pp. 1-137

Daniel Giovannangeli, *Le retard de la conscience. Husserl, Sartre, Derrida* (Bruxelles: Ousia, 2001)

Hans-Dieter Gondek, *Angst - Einbildungskraft - Sprache. Ein verbindender Aufriss zwischen Freud, Kant und Lacan* (Klaus Boer Verlag: München, 1990; in PDF-Ausgabe: München, 2002)

André Green, *The Fabric of Affect in the Psychoanalytic Discourse* (London: Routledge, 1999)

Adolf Grünbaum, *The Foundations of Psychoanalysis: a Philosophical Critique* (Berkeley: University of California Press, 1984)

— *Validation in the Clinical Theory of Psychoanalysis* (Madison Connecticut: International University Press, 1993)

Stephan Günzel, "Zick-Zack. Edmund Husserls phänomenologische Archäologie" in Ebeling & Altekamp, 2004, pp. 98-117

James G. Hart, "A Précis of an Husserlian Philosophical Theology", in S. Laycock & J. Hart (ed.), *Essays in Phenomenological Theology* (Albany: State University of New York Press, 1986), pp. 89-168

— *The Person and the Common Life. Studies in a Husserlian Social Ethics* (Dordrecht: Kluwer Academic Publishers, 1992)

— "Genesis, Instinct, and Reconstruction: Nam-In Lee's *Edmund Husserl's Phänomenologie der Instinkte*", in *Husserl Studies* 15 (1998), pp. 101–123

— "A Phenomenological Theory and Critique of Culture: a Reading of Michel Henry's *La Barbarie*", in *Continental Philosphical Review* 32 (1999), pp. 255-270

— "Review Essay of Husserl, *Collected Works vol. 9 (Analyses Concerning Passive and Active Synthesis. Lectures on Transcendental Logic*)", in *Husserl Studies* 20 (2004), pp. 135–159

George Heffernan, *Bedeutung und Evidenz bei Edmund Husserl* (Wien: Bouvier Verlag, 1983)

Martin Heidegger, "Religionspsychologie und Unterbewußtsein", in Gesamtausgabe Bd. 16, *Reden und andere Zeugnisse eines Lebensweges (1910-1976)*, Hrsg. H. Heidegger (Frankfurt am Main: Klostermann, 2000), pp. 18-27

— *Prolegomena zur Geschichte des Zeitbegriffs*, Gesamtausgabe Bd. 20, Hrsg. P. Jaeger, (Frankfurt am Main: Klostermann, 1988)

— *Einleitung in die Philosophie (Wintersemester 1928/29)*, Gesamtausgabe Bd. 27, Hrsg. O. Saame & I. Saame-Speidel (Frankfurt am Main: Klostermann, 1996)

— *Sein und Zeit* (Tübingen: Niemeyer, 1986)

— *Der Satz vom Grund* (Pfullingen: Neske Verlag, 1978)

— *Vier Seminare (Le Thor 1966, 1968, 1969 - Zähringen 1973)*, in *Seminare (1951-1973)*, Gesamtausgabe Bd. 15, Hrsg. C. Ochwadt (Frankfurt am Main: Klostermann, 1986)

— *Zollikoner Seminare*, Hrsg. M. Boss (Frankfurt am Main: Klostermann, 1994)

— *Martin Heidegger/Heinrich Rickert – Briefe 1912-1933*, Hrsg. A. Denker (Frankfurt am Main: Klostermann, 2002)

Sara Heinämaa, *Toward a Phenomenology of Sexual Difference: Husserl, Merleau-Ponty and Beauvoir* (Lanham: Rowman & Littlefield, 2003)

Klaus Held, *Lebendige Gegenwart. Die Frage nach der Seinsweise des transzendentalen Ich bei Edmund Husserl, entwickelt am Leitfaden der Zeitproblematik* (Den Haag: Nijhoff, 1966)

Michel Henry, *Généalogie de la psychanalyse. Le commencement perdu* (Paris: PUF, 1985)

—— *Phénoménologie matérielle* (Paris: PUF, 1990)

Elmar Holenstein, *Phänomenologie der Assoziation. Zu Struktur und Funktion eines Grundprinzips der passiven Genesis bei Edmund Husserl* (Den Haag: Nijhoff, 1972)

Burt Hopkins, "The Transcendental Problematic of Generativity and the Problem of Historicism: Remarks on Steinbock's *Home and beyond*", in *The New Yearbook for Phenomenology and Phenomenological Philosophy* 1 (2001), pp. 377-390

Emmanuel Housset, *Personne et sujet selon Husserl* (Paris: PUF, 1997)

—— *Husserl et l'énigme du monde* (Paris: Seuil, 2000)

David Hyder, "Foucault, Cavaillès, and Husserl on the Historical Epistemology of the Sciences", in *Perspectives on Science* vol. 11, no. 1 (2003), pp. 107-129

Carl Jung, *Versuch einer Darstellung der psychoanalytischen Theorie* (Leipzig: Deuticke, 1913)

Ulrich Kaiser, *Das Motiv der Hemmung in Husserls Phänomenologie* (München: Wilhelm Fink Verlag, 1997)

Gunnar Karlsson, *Psychoanalysis in a New Light* (Cambridge: Cambridge University Press, 2010)

Iso Kern, "Die drei Wege zur transzendental-phänomenologischen Reduktion in der Philosophie Edmund Husserls", in *Tijdschrift voor Philosophie* (1962), pp. 303-349

—— "The Three Ways to the Transcendental Phenomenlogical Reduction", in *Husserl. Expositions and Appraisals*, ed. F. Elliston & P. McCormick (Notre Dame: Notre Dame University Press, 1977), pp. 126-149

— *Husserl und Kant. Eine Untersuchung über Husserls Verhältnis zu Kant und zum Neukantianismus* (Den Haag: Nijhoff, 1964)

— *Idee und Methode der Philosophie. Leitgedanken für eine Theorie der Vernunft* (Berlin & New York: Walter de Gruyter, 1975)

— review of Husserliana XXXII, *Natur und Geist, Vorlesungen Sommersemester 1927*, in *Husserl Studies* 19 (2003), pp. 167–177

Toine Kortooms, *Phenomenology of Time. Edmund Husserl's Analysis of Time-Consciousness* (Dordrecht: Kluwer, 2002)

Julia Kristeva, *La révolte intime. Pouvoirs et limites de la psychanalyse 2* (Paris: Le livre de poche, 2000)

Friederike Kuster, *Wege der Verantwortung. Husserls Phänomenologie als Gang durch die Faktizität* (Dordrecht: Kluwer, 1996)

Jacques Lacan, *Le séminaire I (1953-54). Les écrits techniques de Freud* (Paris: Seuil, 1975)

— *Écrits* (Paris: Seuil, 1966)

Ludwig Landgrebe, "Husserls Abschied vom Cartesianismus", in *Der Weg der Phänomenologie* (Gütersloh: Gerd Mohn, 1978)

— "Das Problem der passiven Konstitution", in *Faktizität und Individuation. Studien zu den Grundfragen der Phänomenologie* (1982), pp. 71-87

——"The Problem of Passive Constitution", in *Phenomenology. Critical Concepts in Philosophy. Vol. 1 Phenomenology: Central Tendencies and Concepts*, ed. D. Moran & L. Embree (London: Taylor & Francis/Routledge, 2004), pp. 265-278

— *Faktizität und Individuation. Studien zu den Grundfragen der Phänomenologie* (Hamburg: Meiner, 1982)

Jean Laplanche, *Life and Death in Psychoanalysis* (Baltimore: Johns Hopkins Uniersity Press, 1976),

— *Essays on Otherness* (London: Routledge, 1997)

BIBLIOGRAPHY

Jean Laplanche & Jean-Bertrand Pontalis, *Fantasme originaire, fantasmes des origines, origines du fantasme* (Paris: Hachette, 1985)

—— *The Language of Psychoanalysis* (London: Karnac Books, 1988)

Leonard Lawlor, *Derrida and Husserl. The Basic Problem of Phenomenology* (Bloomington: Indiana University Press, 2002)

Jonathan Lear, "The Heterogeneity of the Mental" in *Mind* vol. 104 (1995), pp. 863-879

—— *Love and its Place in Nature. A Philosophical Interpretation of Freud's Psychoanalysis* (New Haven and London: Yale University Press, 1998)

—— *Freud* (London: Routledge, 2005)

Nam-In Lee, *Edmund Husserls Phänomenologie der Instinkte* (Dordrecht: Kluwer Academic Publishers, 1993)

Leibniz, *Nouveaux essais sur l'entendement humain* (Paris: Flammarion, 1990)

Karl-Heinz Lembeck, "'Faktum Geschichte' und die Grenzen phänomenologischer Geschichtsphilosophie", in *Husserl Studies* 4 (1987), pp. 209-224

—— *Gegenstand Geschichte: Geschichtswissenschaftstheorie in Husserls Phänomenologie* (Dordrecht: Kluwer, 1988)

Emmanuel Levinas, *Le temps et l'autre* (Paris: PUF, 2004)

—— *En découvrant l'éxistence avec Husserl et Heidegger* (Paris: Vrin, 1988)

—— *Discovering Existence with Husserl and Heidegger*, tr. R. Cohen (Bloomington: Indiana University Press, 1988)

—— *Totalité et infini. Essai sur l'extériorité* (Paris: Le livre de poche, 1990)

—— *Autrement qu'être ou au-delà de l'essence* (Paris: Le livre de poche, 2004)

Ni Liangkang, "Urbewusstsein und Reflexion bei Husserl", in *Husserl Studies* 15 (1998), pp. 77-99

Christian Lotz, "Husserls Genuss. Über den Zusammenhang von Leib, Affektion, Fühlen und Werthaftigkeit", in *Husserl Studies* 18 (2002), pp. 19–39

—— "Das Ereignis des Unverständlichen. Husserls Hermeneutik und der Ursprung der genetischen Phänomenologie", in *Ereignis auf Französisch. Von Bergson bis Deleuze*; Hrsg. Marc Rölli (München: Fink, 2004), pp. 63-71

Sebastian Luft, *"Phänomenologie der Phänomenologie". Systematik und Methodologie der Phänomenologie in der Auseinandersetzung zwischen Husserl und Fink* (Dordrecht: Kluwer Academic Publishers, 2002)

—— "Die Archivierung des husserlschen Nachlasses 1933-1935", in *Husserl Studies* (2004), pp. 1-25

—— "Husserl's Theory of the Phenomenological Reduction: Between Life-World and Cartesianism", in *Research in Phenomenology* 34 (2004), pp. 198-234

—— "Faktizität und Geschichtlichkeit als Konstituentien der Lebenswelt in Husserls Spätphilosophie, in *Phänomenologische Forschungen* 10 (2005), pp. 13-40

Alasdair MacIntyre, *The Unconscious. A Conceptual Analysis* (Bristol: Thoemmes Press, 1997)

Peter Madison, *Freud's Concept of Repression and Defence, its Theoretical and Observational Language* (Minneapolis: University of Minnesota Press, 1961)

Edouard Marbach, *Das Problem des Ich in der Phänomenologie Husserls* (Den Haag: Nijhoff, 1974)

BIBLIOGRAPHY

Konrad Marc-Wogau, *Freuds psykoanalys - presentation och kritik* (Stockholm: Bonniers, 1967)

Jean-Luc Marion, *Réduction et donation* (Paris: PUF, 1989)

Ulrich Melle, "The Development of Husserl's Ethics", in *Études Phénoménologiques* 13/14 (1991), pp. 115–135

—— "Husserl's personalist ethics", in *Husserl Studies* 23 (2007), pp. 1–15

Maurice Merleau-Ponty, *Phénomènologie de la perception* (Paris: Gallimard, 1996)

—— "L'œuvre et l'esprit de Freud. Préface à l'ouvrage de Angelo Hesnard", in *Parcours deux, 1951-1961* (Lagrasse: Éditions Verdier, 2000), pp. 276-284

—— *Le visible et l'invisible, suivi de notes de travail,* ed. Claude Lefort (Paris: Gallimard, 1999)

—— *The Visible and the Invisible*, tr. A. Lingis (Evanston: Northwestern University Press, 1968)

Aaron L. Mishara, *Phenomenology and the Unconscious. The Problem of the Unconscious in the Phenomenological and Existential Traditions: E. Husserl, V. von Weizsaecker and L. Binswanger*; dissertation, Pennsylvania State University, 1989

—— "Husserl and Freud: Time, Memory and the Unconscious", in *Husserl Studies* 7 (1990), pp. 29-58

Anne Montavont, *De la passivité dans la phénoménologie de Husserl* (Paris: PUF, 1999)

Richard T. Murphy, *Hume and Husserl. Towards Radical Subjectivism* (Den Haag: Nijhoff, 1983)

Maurice Natanson, "Being-In-Reality" in *Philosophy and Phenomenological Research* Vol. 20 (1959), pp. 231-237

Paolo Ravalli, *Husserls Phänomenologie der Intersubjektivität in den Göttinger Jahren. Eine kritisch-historische Darstellung* (Utrecht: Edition Zeno, 2003)

Paul Ricœur, *Le volontaire et l'involontaire* (Paris: Aubier, 1988)

— *De l'interprétation. Essai sur Freud* (Seuil: Paris, 1965)

— *Freud and Philosophy. An Essay on Interpretation*, tr. D. Savage (New Haven and London: Yale University Press, 1970)

— *À l'école de la phénoménologie* (Paris: Vrin, 2004)

Lanei Rodemeyer, *Intersubjective Temporality. It's About Time* (Dordrecht: Springer, 2006)

Jacob Rogozinski, "The Chiasm and the Remainder", in *Rethinking Facticity*, ed. Raffoul & Nelson (Albany: SUNY Press, 2008), pp. 229-252

Georg Römpp, *Husserls Phänomenologie der Intersubjektivität und ihre Bedeutung für eine Theorie intersubjektiver Objektivität und die Konzeption einer phänomenologischer Philosophie* (Dordrecht: Kluwer Academic Press, 1992)

Tetsuya Sakakibara, "Das Problem des Ich und der Ursprung der genetischen Phänomenologie bei Husserl", in *Husserl Studies* 14 (1997), pp. 21-39

Bob Sandmeyer, *Husserl's Constitutive Phenomenology. Its Problem and Promise* (London: Routledge, 2009)

Maria Manuela Saraiva, *L'imagination selon Husserl* (Den Haag: Nijhoff, 1970)

Jean-Paul Sartre, *L'imaginaire. Psychologie phénoménologique de l'imagination* (Paris: Gallimard, 1940)

— *The Imaginary. A Phenomenological Psychology of the Imagination*, tr. J. M. Webber (London: Routledge, 2006)

— *L'être et le néant* (Paris: Gallimard TEL, 1996)

—— *Being and Nothingness. An Essay on Phenomenological Ontology* tr. H. E. Barnes [1958] (London: Routledge, 2005)

Max Scheler, "Die Idole der Selbsterkenntnis", in *Vom Umsturz der Werte* (Bern: Francke, 1955), pp. 213-292

—— "The Idols of Self-knowledge", in *Selected Philosophical Essays*, tr. D. Lachterman (Evanston: Northwestern U.P., 1973)

Alexander Schnell, "Das Problem der Zeit bei Husserl. Eine Untersuchung über die husserlschen Zeitdiagramme", in *Husserl Studies* 18 (2002), pp. 89–122

Karl Schuhmann, *Index Nominum*; unpublished, Husserl-archives Leuven 1975

Alfred Schütz, "The Problem of Transcendental Intersubjectivity in Husserl", in *Collected Papers III: Studies in Phenomenological Philosophy* (Den Haag: Nijhoff, 1970), pp. 51-84

John R. Searle *The Rediscovery of the Mind* (Massachusetts: MIT Press, 1992)

Hans Rainer Sepp, *Praxis und Theoria. Husserls transzendental-phänomenologische Rekonstruktion des Lebens* (München: Alber, 1997)

David Livingstone Smith, *Freud's Philosophy of the Unconscious* (Dordrecht: Kluwer, 1999)

Nicholas Smith, "Är Husserls meningsteori platonistisk? En analys av *Logische Untersuchungen*", in *Fenomenologiska perspektiv. Studier i Husserls och Heideggers filosofi*; ed. H. Ruin & A. Orlowski (Stockholm: Thales, 1996), pp. 65-94 [Translation of title: "Is Husserl's theory of meaning Platonistic? An analysis of *Logische Untersuchungen*"]

— "Kropp och kött. Psykoanalysens plats i Merleau-Pontys sena tänkande", in *Divan. Tidskrift för psykoanalys och kultur* nr. 1-2 (2001), pp. 56-70 [Translation of title: "Body and flesh. The position of psychoanalysis in Merleau-Ponty's later thinking"]

—— "Freuds tre begrepp om det omedvetna", in *Divan. Tidskrift för psykoanalys och kultur* nr. 1-2 (2003), pp. 19-31 [Translation of title: "Freud's three concepts of the unconscious"]

—— "The role of psychoanalysis in Derrida's thought" (unpublished conference paper; deliverd at the 2nd Swedish-Finnish phenomenological workshop, *Derrida and phenomenology*, October 7–9, 2005 at Södertörn University, Stockholm.)

Herbert Spiegelberg, *The Phenomenological Movement. A Historical Introduction* (The Hague: Nijhoff, 1982)

René Spitz, "Hospitalism—an inquiry into the genesis of psychiatric conditions in early childhood", in *Psychoanalytic Study of the Child* vol. I (1945), pp. 53-74

— "Hospitalism: a follow up report", *Psychoanalytic Study of the Child* vol. II (1946), pp. 113-117

Edith Stein, *Zum Problem der Einfühlung*, (Halle: Buchdruckerei des Waisenhauses, 1917)

—— *On the Problem of Empathy*. The Collected Works of Edith Stein, vol. 3; 3rd revised ed., tr. Waltraut Stein (Washington DC: Institute of Carmelite Studies Publications, 1989)

Anthony Steinbock, *Home and Beyond. Generative Phenomenology after Husserl* (Evanston: Nortwestern University Press, 1995)

Daniel Stern, *The Interpersonal World of the Infant. A View from Psychoanalysis and Developmental Psychology* (New York: Basic Books, 2000)

Stephan Strasser, "Grundgedanken der Sozialontologie Edmund Husserls", in *Zeitschrift für philosophische Forschung* 29 (1975), pp. 3-33

Shigeru Taguchi, *Das Problem des "Ur-Ich" bei Edmund Husserl. Die Frage nach der selbstverständlichen "Nähe" des Selbst* (Dordrecht: Springer, 2006)

Michael Theunissen, *Der Andere. Studien zur Sozialontologie der Gegenwart* (Berlin & New York: De Gruyter, 1977)

Helmut Thomä and Neil Cheshire, "Freud's *Nachträglichkeit* and Strachey's "Deferred Action": Trauma, Construction and the Direction of Causality", in *International Review of Psychoanalysis* 18 (1991), pp. 407-427

Michael Titze, "Epoché und Reduktion in der Psychotherapie", in R. Kühn & M. Staudigl (Hrsg.): *Epoché und Reduktion* (Würzburg: Königshausen & Neumann, 2003), pp. 229-239

John Tryssesoone, "Les chemins de l'intersubjectivité dans la philosophie de Husserl", in *Bulletin d'analyse phénoménologique*, II/5, octobre 2006, pp. 3-76 [http://www.bap.ulg.ac.be/index.htm]

Paolo Volonté, *Edmund Husserls Phänomenologie der Imagination. Zur Funktion der Phantasie bei der Konstitution von Erkenntnis* (Freiburg/München: Karl Alber, 1997)

Thomas Vongehr, "Husserl über Gemüt und Gefühl in den 'Studien zur Struktur des Bewusstseins'", in *Fenomenologia della ragion pratica. L'etica di Edmund Husserl*, Beatrice Centi and Gianna Gigliotti (ed.) (Napoli: Bibliopolis: 2004), pp. 227-254.

Karl Weigelt, *The Signified World. The Problem of Occasionality in Husserl's Phenomenology of Meaning* (Stockholm: Acta Universitatis Stockholmiensis, 2008)

Talia Welsh, "The Retentional and the Repressed: does Freud's Concept of the Unconscious Threaten Husserlian Phenomenology?", in *Human Studies* 25 (2002), pp. 165–183

Donn Welton, *The Other Husserl. The Horizons of Transcendental Phenomenology* (Bloomington: Indiana University Press, 2000)

Ichiguro Yamaguchi, *Passive Synthesis und Intersubjektivität bei Edmund Husserl* (Den Haag: Nijhoff, 1982)

— "Gewalt vom Aspekt der Affektion bei Husserl", in

Phänomenologie und Gewalt, Hrsg. Maye & Sepp (Würzburg: Königshausen & Neumann, 2005), pp. 100-112

Dan Zahavi, *Husserl und die transzendentale Intersubjektivität. Eine Antwort auf die sprachpragmatische Kritik* (Dordrecht: Kluwer, 1996)

— *Self-awareness and Alterity. A Phenomenological Investigation* (Evanston: Nortwestern University Press, 1999)

— "Time and consciousness in the Bernau manuscripts", in *Husserl Studies* 20 (2004), pp. 99–118

Stockholm Studies in Philosophy
Published by Stockholm University
Editors: Gunnar Svensson and Torbjörn Tännsjö

1. Stig Kanger. *Provability in Logic*. Stockholm 1957. 47 pp.

2. Jan Berg. *Bolzano's Logic*. Stockholm 1962. 214 pp.

3. Dag Prawitz. *Natural Deduction. A Proof-Theoretical Study*. Stockholm 1965. 113 pp.

4. Lars Bergström. *The Alternatives and Consequences of Actions. An essay on some fundamental notions in teleological ethics*. Stockholm 1966. 141 pp.

5. Torbjörn Tännsjö. *The Relevance of Metaethics to Ethics*. Stockholm 1976. 226 pp.

6. Lars O. Ericsson. *Justice in the Distribution of Economic Resources. A critical and normative study*. Stockholm 1976. 150 pp.

7. Per-Erik Malmnäs. *From Qualitative to Quantitative Probability*. Stockholm 1981. 73 pp.

8. Gunnar Svensson. *On Doubting the Reality of Reality. Moore and Wittgenstein on sceptical doubts*. Stockholm 1981. 120 pp.

9. Torkel Franzén. *Provability and Truth*. Stockholm 1987. 81 pp.

10. Fredrik Stjernberg. *The Public Nature of Meaning*. Stockholm 1991. 173 pp.

11. Lars-Göran Johansson. *Understanding Quantum Mechanics. A realist interpretation without hidden variables*. Stockholm 1992. 177 pp.

12. Claudio Marcello Tamburrini. *Crime and Punishment?* Stockholm 1992. 293 pp.

13. Markku Leppäkoski. *The Transcendental How. Kant's transcendental deduction of objective cognition*. Stockholm 1993. 280 pp.

14. Folke Tersman. *Reflective Equilibrium. An Essay in Moral Epistemology*. Stockholm 1993. 144 pp.

15. Hans Ruin. *Enigmatic Origins. Tracing the Theme of Historicity through Heidegger's Works*. 1994. 304 pp.

16. Björn Eriksson. *Heavy Duty. On the Demands of Consequentialism*. Stockholm 1994. 210 pp.

17. Cesare Cozzo. *Meaning and Argument. A theory of meaning centred on immediate argumental role*. Stockholm 1994. 216 pp.

18. Sören Häggqvist. *Thought Experiments in Philosophy*. Stockholm 1996. 206 pp.

19. Henrik Bohlin. *Groundless Knowledge. A Humean Solution to the Problem of Skepticism*. Stockholm 1997. 231 pp.

20. Daniel Birnbaum. *The Hospitality of Presence. Problems of Otherness in Husserl's Phenomenology*. Stockholm 1998. 200 pp.

21. Henrik Hållsten. *Explanation and Deduction. A Defence of Deductive Chauvinism*. Stockholm 2001. 165 pp.

22. Filip Widebäck. *Identity of Proofs*. Stockholm 2001. 85 pp.

23. Ulrik Kihlbom. *Ethical Particularism. An Essay on Moral Reasons*. Stockholm 2002. 159 pp.

24. Charlotta Weigelt. *The Logic of Life. Heidegger's Retrieval of Aristotle's Concept of Logos*. Stockholm 2002. 236 pp.

25. Håkan Salwén. *Hume's Law. An Essay on Moral Reasoning*. Stockholm 2003. 154 pp.

26. Marcel Quarfood. *Transcendental Idealism and the Organism. Essays on Kant*. Stockholm 2004. 221 pp.

27. Jens Johansson. *Mortal Beings. On the Metaphysics and Value of Death*. Stockholm 2005. 180 pp.

28. Robert Callergård. *An Essay on Thomas Reid's Philosophy of Science*. Stockholm 2006. 164 pp.

29. Arvid Båve. *Deflationism: A Use-Theoretic Analysis of the Truth-Predicate*. Stockholm 2006. 207 pp.

30. Anna-Karin Andersson. *Libertarianism and Potential Agents. A Libertarian View of the Moral Rights of Foetuses and Children*. Stockholm 2007. 122 pp.

31. Karl Weigelt. *The Signified World. The Problem of Occasionality in Husserl's Phenomenology of Meaning*. Stockholm 2008. 343 pp.

32. Karl Karlander. *The Normativity of Thought and Meaning*. Stockholm 2008. 131 pp.

33. B. Ingemar B. Lindahl. *On Causal Attribution*. Stockholm 2009. 369 pp.

34. Nicholas Smith. *Towards a Phenomenology of Repression – a Husserlian Reply to the Freudian Challenge*. Stockholm 2010. 336 pp.

Subscriptions to the series and orders for single volumes should be addressed to any international bookseller or directly to the distributor:
eddy.se ab, P.O. Box 1310, SE-621 24 Visby, Sweden.
Phone: +46 498 253900
Fax: +46 498 249789
E-mail: order@bokorder.se
http://acta.bokorder.se

ACTA UNIVERSITATIS STOCKHOLMIENSIS

Corpus Troporum
Romanica Stockholmiensia
Stockholm Cinema Studies
Stockholm Economic Studies. Pamphlet Series
Stockholm Oriental Studies
Stockholm Slavic Studies
Stockholm Studies in Baltic Languages
Stockholm Studies in Classical Archaeology
Stockholm Studies in Comparative Religion
Stockholm Studies in Economic History
Stockholm Studies in Educational Psychology
Stockholm Studies in English
Stockholm Studies in Ethnology
Stockholm Studies in Film History
Stockholm Studies in History
Stockholm Studies in History of Art
Stockholm Studies in History of Ideas
Stockholm Studies in History of Literature
Stockholm Studies in Human Geography
Stockholm Studies in Linguistics
Stockholm Studies in Modern Philology. N.S.
Stockholm Studies in Musicology
Stockholm Studies in Philosophy
Stockholm Studies in Psychology
Stockholm Studies in Russian Literature
Stockholm Studies in Scandinavian Philology. N.S.
Stockholm Studies in Social Anthropology. N.S.
Stockholm Studies in Sociology. N.S.
Stockholm Studies in Statistics
Stockholm Theatre Studies
Stockholmer Germanistische Forschungen
Studia Fennica Stockholmiensia
Studia Graeca Stockholmiensia. Series Graeca
Studia Graeca Stockholmiensia. Series Neohellenica
Studia Juridica Stockholmiensia
Studia Latina Stockholmiensia
Studies in North-European Archaeology

US-AB
universitetsservice
digitaltryck
Printed in Sweden 2010, www.us-ab.com